Other books by Jonathan Gathorne-Hardy

Fiction
One Foot in the Clouds
Chameleon
The Office
The Centre of the Universe is 18 Baedekerstrasse (short stories)
The City Beneath the Skin
Particle Theory – A Novel
The Voice of God & Other Disasters (short stories)
(As Sylvia Thornton) The Man from the Sea

For Children
Jane's Adventures In and Out of the Book
Jane's Adventures on the Island of Peeg
Jane's Adventures in a Balloon
The Terrible Kidnapping of Cyril Bonhamy
Cyril Bonhamy *v.* Madam Big
Cyril Bonhamy and the Great Drain Robbery
Cyril Bonhamy and Operation Ping
Cyril of the Apes
The Munros' New House
The Tunnel Party
The Twin Detectives

Non-fiction
The Rise and Fall of the British Nanny
The Public School Phenomenon
Love, Sex, Marriage and Divorce
Doctors
The Interior Castle – A Life of Gerald Brenan
Alfred C. Kinsey: A Biography – Sex the Measure of All Things

Half an Arch

A Memoir by

Jonathan Gathorne-Hardy

TIMEWELL
PRESS

First published in Great Britain in 2004 by
Timewell Press Limited
63 Kensington Gardens Square, London W2 4DG

ISBN 1 85725 201 2

Typeset by Antony Gray
Printed and bound in Great Britain by
Biddles Ltd, King's Lynn

For Nicky

There is a mind common to all individual men. Of the universal mind each individual is one more incarnation. All its properties consist in him.

RALPH WALDO EMERSON

I have been giving the History of my own mind.

SAMUEL TAYLOR COLERIDGE,
The Friend, Volume I

'Goodbye,' says the dying man to the mirror they hold before him. 'We won't be seeing each other any more.'

PAUL VALÉRY

Acknowledgements

The author gratefully acknowledges permission to reproduce photographs as follows:

© *Harriet Frazer* and *Anne Hill*, for numbers: 5, 13, 15, 17, 27, 29, 30, 32, 33, 36, 45, 46.

© *Fidelity Cranbrook*, for number: 12.

© *Basil Johnston* and *Oliver Riviere*, for number: 19.

© *Nell Dunn*, for number: 20.

© *Janetta Parlade*, for numbers: 20, 23, 24, 35.

© *Sammy Gathorne-Hardy*, for numbers: 6, 40.

© *Rose Battye*, for number: 42.

Comparative values of the pound

In nearly all biographies and autobiographies the figures of money earned, inherited, spent or lost are, usually, almost meaningless. That is because no account has been taken of inflation. Sometimes, an 'at today's value' figure is put in a bracket, but no indication given as to how the figure was arrived at.

These figures have been compiled for me by Dolf Mootham from statistics provided by the Central Statistical Office. Although they must be regarded as impressionistic, they do nevertheless give some idea of changing money values during my lifetime and that of my immediate close relatives. The base is June 2004. In other words, a pound in 1900 was worth £73 at June 2004 prices.

1900	£73	1940	£41	1980	£3
1905	£71	1945	£27	1985	£2
1910	£66	1950	£20	1990	£1.50
1915	£52	1955	£16	1995	£1.25
1920	£26	1960	£14	2000	£1.10
1925	£36	1965	£12	2001	£1.08
1930	£40	1970	£10	2002	£1.05
1935	£47	1975	£6	2003	£1.03
				2004	£1.00

Introduction

The Spider's Palace by Richard Hughes, one of the best children's books ever written in my view, has a story called 'The Glass Ball Country'. An old charcoal burner, his wife and little girl live in a cottage they've built inside a ruined castle on top of a high rock to keep them safe from all the warring armies there are around. One day they shelter an old pedlar who, when he leaves, gives them a glass ball as big as a football. It contains a tiny country. A little later, they see some soldiers approaching from one of the warring armies. The charcoal burner and his wife are terrified but the little girl says, why don't we all hide in the country inside the glass ball? So they make themselves absolutely tiny and do this.

Unfortunately, the soldiers, fooling about, throw the glass ball off the high rock. It hurtles down into the field below, smashes to pieces and the little country falls out. But now a strange thing happens. The little country, a few inches across, begins to grow, and the three people with it. By the afternoon, it is three feet across. By next morning, it covers the field. And they now discover a second odd thing about it. No one fighting, none of the warring armies, can enter it. In the end, growing and growing, it covers the whole world.

It was this image of the little country in the glass ball which for some reason I remembered when I thought of writing this book. It was the country of my life contained in the globe of my head I wanted to let out. *That* country, as it was at that moment, the moment I wrote. I would check important facts, of course, but I would do no research, talk to no old friends, look at no old letters and use my journals as little as I could. Possibly, if I hadn't done this, a slightly different life might have resulted. Even a different person – though I think no more different than a different person looks back at you from different mirrors. But the life I wanted to write was the one I carried in my head as I lived it now. I have changed some names, a few times changed nationalities, but otherwise everything is as it was. As for myself, I have tried to be as honest and go as deep as I dared and was able, since to have any relevance to other people, apart from occasionally amusing or moving them, I believe something that Sartre once said: go deeply enough into anyone and you will find you are looking at humanity.

PART ONE

Childhoods

(1)

In the only production of Pirandello's *Six Characters in Search of an Author* that I've seen, the open stage was in semi-darkness. The six characters were sitting about in the gloom waiting. They lit cigarettes, walked about, said things to each other too softly for the audience to hear. Eventually, spots came up, someone entered back left and front right and said something or did some business or shouted to another person offstage. The play had begun. They could live again.

As written, *Six Characters* . . . doesn't start like that at all. I suppose I may have remembered the production I saw accurately, but I think it more likely I have altered my memory of it, though such a beginning fits certain aspects of the play.

Pirandello points out that in several ways a fictional character is more alive than a real one: ' . . . he does not have to worry about dying,' says the father in *Six Characters* . . . 'He never dies. Man dies, the writer, the natural instrument of nature dies, but the created character never dies. And in order to live eternally he need not be of exceptional calibre. Tell me, who was Sancho Panza?'

What a strange half-life, as they wait. And what were they saying, smoking, restless? 'Oh God, not again!' More likely, indeed that was one of the points in *Six Characters* . . . 'Hurry up! Begin!' Sometimes they wait for centuries, sometimes hardly at all. But even the most successful must have moments, even days, hanging around.

Hamlet, marching irritably to and fro in that ill-lit arrival-and-departure lounge where fictional characters are on standby, complains about having once again to exhibit his indecision. He *isn't* indecisive; he may have been once, but he has long ago learnt his lesson. Let's see what happens if I kill Claudius *at once*, as soon as I've seen the ghost.

Fortinbras or *Polonius* or *Someone*: Then we'd have no play.

Hamlet: Nonsense. We'd simply have a different play.

They never try it. Except, fairly recently, Guildenstern and Rosencrantz did so. Perhaps only the exceptionally unexceptional have such boldness.

But it was not the conceit, nor its implications, nor even Pirandello's ingenious working out of it that fascinated me. I'd forgotten the play completely. It was simply that I couldn't forget the image of those characters standing about before they were alive. And it was an active memory, recurring at irregular intervals. We are gripped like that only when something deep inside us has been struck. We alter memories for the same reason. Why had I altered my memory of the play? Why had that group stayed, why did it stay still, in my mind, frozen and significant?

(2)

Elements in one or two other fictional works have had that effect on me – the form of *Tristram Shandy*, for example, the end of *À la recherche du temps perdu* – but the strangest instance of something remaining active in the head like this was my knowledge, ever since I can remember, of the importance of nannies. It was almost like an instinct, something I was born knowing.

That I should automatically, instinctively, attach importance to these obscure beings was strange because I could remember almost nothing about my own nanny. 'A small, very kind, very sensible Scotch woman,' my Aunt Fidelity said. I had only two memories. One was of spectacles – but I may have got that from photographs (most early memories are induced). The second is of trying to make her be sick. She suffered from migraines and, at these times it seemed, loud noises could make her sick. I remember – it was at Snape so I must have been about four – slowly dropping my wooden bricks one by one into their box, looking closely at her while she sat with her head in her hands. Eventually, she was sick.

Nanny Paton. She was Scotch and came to us soon after I was born in Edinburgh, on 17 May 1933. My father Antony, then aged twenty-five, was a medical student there, but seems not to have watched or assisted at the birth because he told me years later that the doctor who delivered me was so appalled at my appearance he could hardly bring himself to let my father see me. I was born with a tail and was so dark the doctor thought I must be half black.

My father himself was not worried – at least not about the fidelity of his twenty-four-year-old wife Ruth. There was supposed to be black blood in her family, either West Indian or, more likely, from the then Belgian Congo. Certainly, there were faint signs of this. My mother had strong, Gauguinesque good looks and her wide, full mouth, high cheekbones, slightly slanted eyes and sloping forehead have often resurfaced in women I have loved.

My tail dropped off and my Belgian Congo colours to some extent drained away and now, when I look in the mirror, my father's sixty-year-old face sometimes glares back at me – especially when I have a hangover. At that time, in Edinburgh, long before he had been coarsened by age, drink and the foul-smelling, foul-tasting, home-grown, home-cured tobacco that killed him, he had a sensitive, handsome, almost feminine face – far better-looking than his three older brothers. He had fine, delicate hands and the well-turned calves of an Elizabethan courtier. I remember once, when I was about ten, and he was on a rare leave, standing peeing beside him and, as I glanced quickly sideways as all boys and men do, wondering anxiously even then, so important is that organ to us, if I would ever be able to match its prodigious proportions. Alas – though perfectly, averagely adequate in size – I never did. Luckily, the great parental pendulum has simply jumped a generation.

But of Edinburgh, like Nanny Paton, I can remember almost nothing. My father had to study there for longer than he wanted because he kept failing the chemistry papers. We lived in St Giles' House, Meadow Place. Meadow Place has since vanished. From the few remaining photographs, St Giles' House looks rather small, but it must have had at least three bedrooms: my mother and father's, mine, unless I slept with Nanny Paton, and that of someone called Nell who appears in the photograph album. I don't think my mother learnt to cook till after the war so perhaps Nell was the cook-housekeeper.

And I know I was taken for walks in my pram in the meadows nearby.

And that is all I remember of Edinburgh. But two significant things happened there. My mother followed Truby King, the Dr Spock or Penelope Leach of his time. Odd as it seems, King was an ex-colonel in the Australian army. He determined to impose military disciplines on the unruly world of the nursery. I, and millions like me, were fed to a rigid routine. Breast every four hours like clockwork – and *nothing* between, no matter how much the baby screamed. To this day, I find it almost impossible to eat between meals; whereas at the meals, I gobble.

The second significant event was at my christening. Someone put £25 into Post Office Savings for me. Throughout my childhood I was conscious of this wealth, my wealth, steadily growing in the background. I was also given five christening mugs.

I walked late, but had quite a large vocabulary at two, when my father's queer brother Eddie came to stay. He enjoyed teasing my mother in a mild way and used to say, 'Go into Mummy and say: "I am a bugger." ' From then on my mother seems to have been stalked by the spectre of my possible homosexuality.

My father graduated in July 1935. We probably spent some months at Snape before he took up his first practice in London.

(3)

Gordon Ambrose used to say that he found his patients often remembered the houses of their childhood more vividly and accurately than their parents or the other people in them.

The only constant in our endless wanderings (I never lived longer than three years in the same place until I was forty-two) was Snape Priory, six miles inland from Aldeburgh in Suffolk. It was, and is, a large, ugly, late-Victorian red-brick building, then with thirty acres round it, where my father's mother, Dorothy Cranbrook, moved in 1926 when her elder son Jock got married and *had* to have the big house at Great Glemham seven miles further inland.

There was a big beech and some oaks at one end of the house, a few tall firs at the other. A line of oak trees ran up the side of the little

estate beside the lane running down to Snape village. My grandmother had recently planted a little wood out at the back. There was
a mix of trees in about four acres, but a very cold first winter had
killed almost everything except the fir trees – but there is nothing
sweeter than the sound of wind in firs. No matter how gentle, their
myriad needles respond; great soft whispering waves flow through
them, an endless sighing, the sea on land. And oddly enough, when
they roar in storms, they are equally, indeed more soothing – as is the
sea itself, crashing on to the shore, or dashing against the shingle as it
does at Aldeburgh.*

I think I must have spent a lot of time at first with the servants. There
were four. Later, as my grandmother's money somehow evaporated,
they dwindled: to two, then one, then a series of eccentric often insane
temporary figures and finally to none, or rather to my aunt and uncle
who came to live there and look after her.

Four servants was in fact something close to a collapse. Not that
my grandmother minded. Such collapses stimulated her. But when
she and her husband first came to Glemham in 1915 they had
fourteen servants – ten inside and three gardeners and a boy outside.
Albert, the footman, wore livery, which was still quite common in
grand households into the 1930s. My grandmother liked to describe
how when she got dressed she stuck out her foot and said 'Stockings!'
and Macfarlane, her lady's maid, would pull the stockings up over her
plump legs. When the fire in the drawing room was getting low she,
or someone, would put out an arm and pull the bell rope. Maslin, the
butler, would come in and Granny or whoever it was would say, 'Put
some more coal on the fire would you please Maslin.'

I loved my grandmother's stories, which was just as well, since
they poured from her on an endless belt, repeated again and again
until I knew them so well they were really just soothing mantras: the
Strong Man of Tilwilly; ' "I'm always tired now," said the child';

---

*   There is a reason for this. When my daughter had her son Rudy, I gave her
    a tape of a recording taken inside the womb. It is what a foetus listens to for
    nine months and supposed to soothe little babies – and this it did. But the
    interesting thing about the tape is that the noise isn't some gentle rhythm
    of the pulse but a tremendous storm, crashing and roaring and surging like
    a gale at sea or a raging wind in a forest of firs.

'When gorse is out of bloom, kissing's out of season.' Then there was my Great Aunt Cilla. She had an emphatic extremely deep voice. One winter at Glemham Granny had been skating on the pond and came triumphantly up to her. 'What did you think of that Cilla?' 'At your *age* and your *weight* Dorothy,' boomed Aunt Cilla, 'I thought it was wonderful.' I saw Great Aunt Cilla once. She never married and all I remember is her big, gaunt, bony chin with several long hairs.

Maslin was one of the servants my grandmother brought with her from Glemham to Snape. I remember a balding, elderly male presence. Maslin was single and was in fact homosexual, but unable or too frightened to have any sex. Once Uncle Eddie said to him, 'Do you know what I'm going to do tomorrow Maslin?' 'No sir.' 'I'm going to go up to London, Maslin, and I'm going to pick up a nice, *very* good-looking guardsman, take him back to my flat and I'm going to *have* him Maslin.' 'You're a very lucky young gentleman Mr Eddie,' said Maslin gloomily.

But if Maslin is a shadow to me now, the others are not. Brown was the gardener and lived with Mrs Brown in a small cottage at the end of the short front drive. They were both Suffolk and both also brought from Glemham. Mrs Brown suffered from depression when young and Granny said she once had to pull her out of a rainwater butt by her feet. I remember a placid calm figure, in fact about the circumference of a water butt, whom it was fun to go and see on account of biscuits. Brown was short, strong, with a walrus moustache and the flat cap all country people wore. He did everything that needed doing outside, but his main work was in the enormous unwalled kitchen garden, with its little greenhouse, its cold frames and potting shed. He also tended the gleaming, glistening, beautiful engine outside the kitchen which he started twice a day to pump the water from the well and charge up the big batteries which provided electric light. Every day Brown and my grandmother had a long talk about asparagus beds or potatoes, or whatever the current problem was; problems often necessitating on-the-spot inspection. And every day he walked through the oaks to his kitchen garden and every evening he walked back. Soon there was a firm well-defined winding track known as Brown's path.

But Mary and Nettie were the chief actors, both Scotch (my

grandmother, also Scotch, said 'Scottish' was vulgar). Nettie had worked for one of the Boyles in Scotland and been seconded south as a first-class cook; Mary came from Perthshire and had answered an advertisement in *The Lady*. I remember Nettie as standing no nonsense and her hands smelling of onions. But she was kind and attractive (in her early twenties) and soon married Leslie, Brown's eldest son. Leslie was a butcher and immensely strong. Sammy, my three-year-younger brother, and I used to play in their sitting room on a battered sofa and I can remember my astonishment at the effortless ease with which Leslie lifted us high above his head, and the huge, bulging hardness of his biceps. I longed to be like Leslie. I was always very thin and not particularly strong. At this time, perhaps I was five, I several times, painfully but in vain, covered myself in a very hot, stinging menthol toothpaste to encourage muscles.

Mary never married, and never looked like marrying; she later cared for Granny on her own, slowly going mad and at last having to leave. But in the 1930s she was a lively young woman, completely indulgent to Sammy and me. She had very white skin, the floury, soft, dimpled texture of cakes made flesh. She was teasing and mischievous and liked to play jokes on us – like putting the stone hot-water bottles in our beds cold – when on her bap-like cheeks two tiny spots of colour would appear in merriment.

The hot-water bottles were needed. Snape, like most houses then, could be and often was absolutely freezing. In winter, people scurried from pools of warmth round the fires which were lit in every room until finally, under tons of blankets and eiderdowns, they reached the safety of their hot-water bottles. Chamber pots were an essential prophylactic against frostbite on the way to distant freezing lavatories. In our bedroom at Snape there was a black oil stove whose circular top with its round holes was thrown much magnified on to the ceiling. I loved lying in bed looking at this, telling myself stories, listening to the wind in the trees or, quite often, the thunder of the rats racing about behind the walls.

But of course the most important person at Snape was my grandmother.

(4)

She was the third and youngest daughter of the Earl of Glasgow, with three elder brothers and one younger. Born in 1879, she married my grandfather in 1899.

Bob, the uncle between my father and Eddie, used to say his father Gathorne was a gay. But Bob, gay himself, really thought, like many gays, that most men were queer. He thought the third Marquis of Salisbury was gay. He used to describe how Logan Pearsall Smith, whose amanuensis Bob was for many years, once saw the ageing ex-Prime Minister shuffling up St James's towards Piccadilly. A good-looking young man came towards him. Salisbury stopped and turned and followed the young man with his eyes. 'Obviously queer,' said Bob. 'But Bob, he might have been the son of a friend or he'd met him at tea the day before.' 'No no,' said Bob, 'queer as a coot.' His evidence for his father Gathorne's homosexuality was even more tenuous. There were two people on his father's staircase at Oxford whom Bob knew, or suspected, were homosexual. 'Pretty decisive don't you think?' It was pointless arguing.

I prefer to believe my grandmother: she said 'Gathorne and I had great fun in bed' and they had five children. At any rate, a good deal of sexual energy has flowed into our family from somewhere and I suspect partly through her. She remembered how she used to go into her mother's bedroom as a little girl and get into her bed. Her father was a naval captain in the 1870s and '80s and was often away. His disappearance apparently often coincided with visits from a young man, a cousin, aged eighteen. One morning my grandmother went in to see her mother. She found her completely naked (she must have been about thirty) sitting on the knee of the young man, who was also naked. Her mother turned round and they all stared at each other. 'Go away Dorothy,' said her mother. 'I'm busy.'

My grandfather Gathorne had to winter abroad at Hyères each year, to stem his TB, which he had caught the same year they had married; for the same reason he didn't speak at all for two years, conversing with notepads. Academics came to discuss philosophy with him like this. But he died when he was forty-five. My grandmother, aged thirty-five, was devastated and the symptoms of her grief reverberated for many years. She put on weight until she weighed sixteen stone. She developed various ailments: insomnia, asthma, breathlessness, mysterious stomach pains, a weak heart.

By the time I remember her she was fifty-five. Her ailments had gone. Her heart was in fact extremely strong (as proved by my father who, after he had qualified, made her run up and down stairs carrying a suitcase); she had lost weight and was about the same size as Mrs Brown. She had enormous energy. She conquered the middle echelons of county life: JP, Chairman of Snape School Council, district and parish councils, etc.; she electioneered (always Labour), she farmed her ten-acre field. Above all, she gardened. She created a rock garden in a deep dell in front of the house and with its terraces made a mini Hyères where she'd been happy with her husband. For many years she had a column in *Gardening Illustrated* – 'From a Suffolk Rock Garden'. Both Eddie and Bob were more or less professional botanists (as a result I can hardly recognise a daisy).

But my grandmother never married again and I don't think ever made love to anyone again, though she remained attractive into her fifties. She had large, firm, beautifully shaped breasts which, like the pendulum, surface now and again in the family genome. She fell in love several times and was several times proposed to – there was someone called Goffy I remember. Her uncle, Gilbert Hunter-Blair, was only ten years older than her and Gilbert's wife, my mother's Aunt Muriel, once caught them kissing in a rose garden, which led to a certain *froideur* between the two women. My grandmother used to say contemptuously that Muriel was a virgin and frigid. But Granny herself said the reason she herself never married again was because she had decided to devote herself to her children.

Which she did. She spoilt them and indulged them, was fascinated by them and forgave them everything and anything – and could be formidable in their defence. My Uncle Jock's first marriage was to Bridget D'Oyly Carte and was a disaster. She said he preferred his dogs to her, which he may well have ended up doing.

The trouble would seem to have been, not that Bridget was lesbian, as some people thought (and a number of women hoped) but that Jock was too highly sexed (my father, crouching expectantly outside their bedroom door aged nineteen, heard her say: 'Oh all right if you *must*'). After they divorced, which they soon did, Bridget worried that there might be something wrong with her. Practical, wealthy and secretive, a close friend of hers told me she paid an acquaintance well known for his love-making to fuck her – and to her surprise she enjoyed it. She had several male lovers during her life and one long-standing but secret male partner.

But it was the divorce that roused my grandmother. Clearly necessary, the whole thing, as it had to be then, being set up in Brighton, with Jock 'discovered' in bed with a hired woman by a detective whom he'd also hired. Bridget's father, Rupert D'Oyly Carte found out, told the court, and the divorce proceedings were stopped.

My grandmother was furious. She at once drove to the south of England where Sir Rupert lived. The impresario must have felt he had dealt with tougher figures than my grandmother, but within half an hour she had reduced him to tears. Her final words were 'And you call yourself a *Christian!*' The second divorce proceedings went without a hitch.

I don't think I ever saw my grandmother furious. I adored her and she adored me. She was an almost ideal companion for a small boy because she took his concerns as seriously as he did. She also, on the whole, preferred the male sex to the female. She was as interested as me in the little planes that seemed to buzz endlessly through the blue skies of the 1930s. Once, one landed in a field beside the road between Friston and Aldeburgh. As the wood grew at the back of the house, I grew with it. By seven or eight I could chop down and thin the little fir trees. We would discuss together where they needed thinning, my views given equal weight. As I carried the trunk to join the pile of cleared branches, my grandmother would tell me about the Strong Man of Tilwilly. This was a mighty forester of her girlhood whom the three sisters would encounter in the woods above Kelburn Castle, their family home, striding along with an entire oak or a great beech slung carelessly over his shoulder. Granny and I worked in the wood at Snape together for many years and we both agreed that when I grew up I'd plant a wood of my own.

She taught me to play cards; rummy, canasta when it arrived, but most often we played cribbage. She often let me win at first so that I wouldn't be discouraged. We played spillikins with delicate carved ivory spillikins – a parrot, a ladder, a billhook, lots of spears, little axes. And every night she read to me. I would climb on to her broad lap or sit on the arm of her armchair beside the fire and she would read R. M. Ballantyne's *Coral Island* or *My Dog Crusoe* or *The Just So Stories* and *Mowgli* or *The Railway Children* or any of dozens of Victorian and Edwardian children's books. The logs on the fire hissed, there was the sound of the wind faintly in the pines, and I could smell the lemon verbena she always wore in her buttonhole.

She kept all the presents I gave her and if they were objects – usually hideous – displayed them. She was particularly impressed by a clay horse and an alabaster fish I'd made at school.

I may never have seen her furious, but I certainly saw her cross. Unlike her own children, she did not spoil me. A felled tree had to be completely cleared of branches and neatly piled. I had to eat properly at table. If guests came, I had to talk to them as she had been taught to talk. When I was five I decided for a prolonged period to be a nurse. I dressed every day in a nurse's uniform and wouldn't do anything unless I was called 'nurse'. Commands to Jonny were completely ignored. 'Oh very well, time for bed *nurse*.' The only person who refused to call me nurse was my grandmother and for her alone I responded to my name.

All my life she gave me unconditional love, acceptance and tolerance, as she did her sons and daughter. She was far in advance of most people of her class and time as regards homosexuality. One might think that with two such extremely gay sons it could hardly have been otherwise (except that other parents then seemed to manage otherwise).

But to understand the dynamics of this, indeed of the whole Gathorne-Hardy family at this time, it is necessary to look at Glemham and the Big House.

(5)

One day when my Uncle Jock was seventeen he was being baited, as quite often, by his brother Eddie, aged sixteen. Losing his temper, again as quite often, he gave chase and slammed his fist with all his force into the billiard-room door behind which, quickly closing it, Eddie had neatly slipped in time. Jock broke two fingers.

This story, recounted to me merrily years later by Eddie, is revealing. Rivalries exist, sometimes rage, in all large families; they are considerably augmented in families split by primogeniture.

Primogeniture is the custom, particularly common in Britain, by which the eldest son – either by will or entail – inherits the vast bulk of the family money and the whole of the family estate where this exists. Its avowed object, indeed, is to keep estates and grand houses 'in the family'. This, of course, is manifest rubbish. It keeps wealth and huge houses in the possession of one member of the family. Everyone else is dispossessed; in a final twist of injustice younger daughters are often discriminated against in favour of younger sons.

Primogeniture may bite few, but those it bites it bites hard. The aristocracy and upper classes who initially fuelled the French Revolution were nearly all younger sons and in their fury at the practice of primogeniture it was one of the first things they swept away. It never returned. In France, you *have* to leave your possessions equally to all your children. Here, not only does the custom persist, it even takes place at quite low levels. Such families hope that by aping the aristocracy they will be mistaken for them.

It also throws a tricky burden on to the elder son. If necessary, he is expected to help his lesser siblings from his vast wealth: in my uncle's case land in Suffolk eventually amounting to about 1,500 acres, two properties in London (Chelsea) and, later, in the south of France, in Westmoreland (now Cumbria), as well as large stock market holdings. But when is necessary? How much is needed? My uncle was certainly not mean; on the other hand, he never went what you'd call mad with generosity. He trod an austere line.

Jock inherited his title – 4th Earl of Cranbrook – at the age of sixteen. Imbued with a stern sense of duty, a rather deficient sense of humour, an almost total lack of small talk, an authoritative, impatient, often bullying personality, these characteristics were steadily magnified by the power and pressure of his awesome Earlish responsibilities.

The family was thus split neatly in two: Eddie, Bob, my father and Anne versus Jock. I don't mean they disliked each other. They were fond of each other, on the whole; Anne loved my father and Eddie. They all respected each other, though when Anne, not a tactful or concise correspondent, tried to extract money for the spendthrift Eddie in later years, Jock was frequently exasperated beyond endurance. She usually succeeded, but at the cost of constant explosions.

The split was primarily due, of course, to the unequal division of money and other inherited spoils, coupled with Jock's pompous assumption of a Victorian paterfamilias. But homosexuality was an element as well.

Homosexuality was illegal with fierce penalties, the subject was shocking in print and generally reviled in conversation, yet in the circles Eddie and Bob moved in – the anachronistically but appropriately named Gay Young Things – it was not just accepted but fashionable. Since Wilde, and because of him, it was a sign of rebellion against Victorian/Edwardian conventions; a rebellion made thrilling by the very real danger of prison. Even in 1955, when Alfred Kinsey visited Wormwood Scrubs, thirty per cent were in for homosexual 'offences'.

Eddie was clever, amusing, but above all outrageous. Evelyn Waugh based the character of Miles Malpractice on him. He liked to shock – shock Jock, shock the county, shock anyone shockable. When the sweet little eight-year-old daughter at a party sweetly offered him her little bag of bulls' eyes he was overheard saying 'No thank you my dear, I only suck cocks.' He said 'my dear' a great deal which was a common affectation then. Bob wore a monocle (often Eddie did too). Bob was also clever, and he was a kinder man than Eddie and a talented writer, but he was afflicted with total recall. Whereas with Eddie people became exhilarated, with Bob they were liable to exhaustion.

I hardly knew my two gay uncles until well into my twenties, and remember little of them till some years after that, yet I must have realised quite early upon which side of the split I came. I think I must have modelled my accent on Eddie's, something that caused me trouble later. Nor do I really remember Glemham, the big house, at this time. I remember the smell of the trim, two-foot, head-high box hedges as I walked between them in the kitchen garden. I remember the hot moist air in the greenhouses and the heady scent of the white hothouse Muscat grapes – the best grapes in the world. My mother used to peel them, slit their green flesh with her long, polished, painted fingernail and place them, pipless, between my lips. I remember Nurse Norma, my cousin Gathorne's nanny, gouging disgusting nursery food into my mouth from my cheek where I was trying to hide it. She was much stricter than my gentle, unremembered Nanny Paton.

My uncles and aunt (and I when young) looked markedly Jewish. Anne had a theory we were really descended from Disraeli. My great-great grandfather was in the Cabinets of three prime ministers including Disraeli (thus beginning the rise from humble Mr Hardy, a Bradford solicitor whose father had been a gardener). Disraeli was notorious for infidelity with his colleagues' wives. Actually, thinking about it, I think Jock, Eddie and Anne look as much ancient Roman as Jewish. No doubt everyone in Europe carries ancient Roman genes. But I prefer this Roman/Jewish/black descent to the one I am confessing to.

Primogeniture, though unfair, doesn't usually cut the rest of the family off totally penniless. The three brothers and Anne were each left £5,000. On this my father Antony lived for some years, put himself through medical school, married, and finally, with what was left, bought himself into an expensive practice in Knightsbridge. We moved to London in 1937, when I was four.

(6)

We lived at 21 Milner Street, near Sloane Square, then, as now, quite a smart place to live. My parents must have been well off. Before the NHS, GPs' medical practices were even more like businesses than they are now. One bought a share for a sum commensurate with the current and potential value of the business – and at once began to receive dividends in the form of large fees.

The area around Harrods, which the practice covered, was indeed well off. The consulting rooms were at 26 Gilbert Street, a stone's throw from Harley Street. It had taken all the rest of my father's capital but it was worth it. Yet because it represented the entire assets both of him and his partner, Landale Clark, there was a clause in the contract by which if one died the other would buy his share (i.e. fully compensate the widow and family). Since they were both healthy young men the clause was academic.

My father was a good doctor, a particularly skilful diagnostician, charming, good-looking, and the practice flourished. He rapidly mastered the required medico-social arts. He employed a special undertaker who would come secretly and swiftly at any hour of the day or night to collect patients, always men, who had expired making love to the wrong lovers. He had several old, lonely, unhappy female patients who became particularly desperate in the evenings. My father, his lifelong trust in alcohol already well established, advised them to have a drink, a suggestion, he rapidly found, which horrified them. He therefore prescribed tincture of ninety-eight per cent alcohol, with two per cent of a suitably disgusting medicinal flavour. The results were dramatic and wholly beneficial. 'Might I have a *second* glass of the medicine sometimes, Dr Gathorne-Hardy?' 'You may have *three* glasses when necessary,' my father would say gravely. He was given expensive presents. I remember a Picasso drawing of a Pierrot in a red frame dated 1917, which always hung in the living rooms of our various houses.

Then there was my mother's contribution. My father would say, 'Your mother had £1,000 a year when I first married her.' I'm not certain about this: the only figure I can find is £350 a year.

I know too well where it all eventually went, but where had it come from? – all this marvellous money. Not from my mother's father. Arthur Thorowgood was a naval officer, eventually reaching the rank of commander. Nothing to be ashamed of, though nothing elevated, but he must have been a brave man since he got the DSO. His first wife, Agnes Watts, was the conduit. Her father, my great-grandfather, was Philip Watts. He joined the navy at the bottom as a boy aged fourteen in 1860, was noticed, put through the School of Naval Architecture in 1870, and thereafter rose steadily. Between 1885 and

1916 he designed, or had a hand in designing, and oversaw the
construction of many of the world's great battleships, including the
*Dreadnought*s, and was eventually knighted KCB.

His wife, Elise Isabelle, was Belgian, the daughter of Gustave
Simonau, a painter and lithographer who has a street named after him
in Brussels. My mother's Gauguinesque good looks came from her
(as does the suggestion of Belgian Congo blood) and she began her
career as a courtesan. My mother's younger sister, Mary, said that one
of her lovers had been Leopold II. This is quite possible. Leopold's
biographer, Barbara Emerson, speaks of 'various passing affairs over
the years' and money would certainly have been an element. Laure
Hayman, also the descendant of a painter, amassed a fortune from her
rich and sometimes royal lovers at about the same period and had a
house in the same street where Proust placed Odette, for whom she
was a model. Isabelle was apparently a formidable figure known,
somehow appropriately, as 'Go-Go' in the family. It seems likely that
not just black blood came flowing in with her but considerable sums
to augment those from making battleships. One of the many men
attracted to my mother, sensing something she had inherited from
her grandmother, described her as a bad girl gone good – not in fact
totally accurate.

I never saw any of these figures who had together made my
mother, but she I saw all the time. I find my mother the second most
difficult person to describe, since so much of her has been subsumed
into myself – who is, of course, the most difficult person of all to
describe.

(7)

My mother's dominant characteristics were her sympathy and her
humour. It was more than sympathy; something more like empathy:
she gave people the feeling she had completely entered their lives and
their dilemmas and completely understood and shared them. As a
result, all her life people from all levels sought her out to confide in
her, to tell her their troubles – and also to laugh with her.

In the 1930s, where I remember her as the person enveloping me in
a huge towel after my bath and singing to me, or telling me stories in

bed, or carrying me in her powerful swimmer's arms out over the freezing billows of the North Sea at Aldeburgh, others remember somebody very funny. She was popular 'because she brought laughter into the room', said my Aunt Fidelity, Jock's second wife. Despite swimming well, she didn't particularly like exercise, moving her long, slim legs in an odd stumpy step. She was, however, naturally good at tennis. She read a good deal, but what she liked best was talking with her friends. The telephone became her medium.

She was very quick, her humour partly deriving from acute, sometimes wicked observation; there was also a buried element of mimicry. Go-Go and Philip Watts used to entertain at their Chelsea Embankment house in the lavish Edwardian style which continued into the 1920s. Once they had Isadora Duncan to do her 'Greek attitudes'. When she had gone my mother, aged eleven, who had been watching from the top of the stairs in her nightie, rushed down and did all the attitudes again – to spontaneous applause. Her grandfather, no doubt remembering his courtesan days, also told her that it was vital a lady should like champagne. He paid her a guinea a glass until this was established, an inducement he would not have found necessary in later years.

She was a very anxious person, easily worried, something that excited a mildly sadistic side in my father. On their honeymoon he terrified her by leaving the train three minutes before departure 'to get a paper', got on at the back and waited ten minutes before rejoining her. Go-Go, as libertines do, saw to it that Agnes was brought up extremely strictly, and Agnes did the same for my mother – who was as obsessively clean and tidy as my father was obsessively the opposite, a dichotomy concealed for some years by the existence of servants. Her and her sister Mary's nursery toilet training must have been ferocious. It was part of a sort of bowel fever that raged across Europe and America during the period. The consequences of constipation were so dire that Mary actually had an operation to clear a blocked gut when she was eighteen. My mother was haunted by her bowels her entire life and eventually – Ambrose would have said as a direct result – they killed her. She had three operations for piles during the 1930s – the procedure then was medieval – and she became agonisingly over-sensitised. Yet even in the most painful and embarrassing moments she kept her sense of humour. Her anus would go into spasm and she once locked on to the probing finger of the surgeon. Unable to extricate himself, he idly flicked the pages of *Vogue* with his other hand while my mother lay in an agony of shame. After a while, no doubt to comfort her, he said, 'Funnily enough, Mrs Gathorne-Hardy, the last time this happened to me was with Noël Coward.'

My own toilet training was relaxed, perhaps because of her sufferings. Certainly this was true of her comments on my appearance. My mother, despite overwhelming evidence to the contrary, always thought she was ugly. This was one reason, said Fidelity, that she tried to be liked, to compensate, by being lively and amusing. (But doesn't everyone want to be liked? Don't most people try to be funny?) The belief that she was ugly had been drummed into her to prevent 'vanity'. As a result she not only told me the whole time I was good-looking, she told me if other people said so too. This sweet encouragement of my mother's was to have, such is the perversity of events and human nature, a quite different effect to the one intended.

I remember the sensation of her reading to me, the entangling, dreamlike fascination of it, but I can remember only one actual book, whereas with my grandmother I can remember very nearly all the books. Because they read to me so often and because I enjoyed it so much, I learnt to read very late (on Thackeray's *The Rose and the Ring* in fact). I also copied them by telling myself stories in bed about myself: 'He jumped on to his horse . . . ' What made my stories vivid was that they were accompanied by a rapid series of pictures, like stills from a film, illustrating the events. I can even see, now, that his horse was white. From this deep childhood base, much reinforced, grew, I think, the desire to write.

But my mother used to read the Bible to me, or rather she used to read about the crucifixion in a special, illustrated, simply but lengthily worded *Bible for Children*. This had nothing, or almost nothing, to do with religion but was connected to a curiously morbid trait in her nature. She loved to read about violent death. She used to cut out and keep the longest and most lurid accounts – usually from the *News of the World* – of all the celebrated murders of the day: Christie, Haigh the acid bath murderer, Neville Heath. She had a book called

The Düsseldorf Murderer, about a serial killer in the 1930s. 'He liked to hear the blood gush,' my mother used to say with grim satisfaction. I don't know where this side of her came from. Her father, Arthur Thorowgood, was apparently a cruel man who bullied her and frightened her. She never spoke about him except to say he was entirely responsible for her sister Mary's disastrous marriage. Perhaps she had fantasies of murdering him or him murdering her and appeased the violent feelings in this odd way; perhaps his violence had made her fascinated with it.

At any rate, it meant she read the story of the crucifixion to me again and again. In the picture of Christ being lowered from the cross into the adoring arms of Mary, he looked wonderfully, voluptuously inert, relaxed in the bliss of death. Years later, it suddenly struck me I might have identified with Christ when small.

When I was twenty I finally overcame the inhibitions and infuriating prohibitions, which could still be very strong in 1953, and made love to a girl. As I lay back in the hot churned bed in the darkness of that little attic room into the soft arms of my saviour, there flashed into my head the image of that voluptuously relaxed figure in the arms of his mother. I found myself thinking: *this* is the peace that passeth all understanding. It was an image and a phrase which was to recur again and again for many years.

I can see, or feel rather, my mother reading to me at Snape but not at Milner Street. I have very few memories of Milner Street. One is my parents coming back late at night. They are unbelievably glamorous. My father throws me the flower from his buttonhole and I can just smell the bay rum he put on his hair; my mother bends to kiss me and I am enveloped in her scent. I feel very safe because I am on a mattress in their bedroom, not in my own little room where some guest must have been put. I am already very frightened of the dark and in my room I have a light by the bed in the form of a lighthouse. It has a small luminous green button which I can press to release its beam if the uneasy ship of my sleep is attacked by monsters of the deep or crashes against the rocks. To this day, the luminous green of alarm clocks or of buttons in hotels glowing in the dark makes me feel odd.

Do I remember the muffin man with a bell and a tray of muffins on his head? I think this must have come from a book. But I certainly remember the First World War ex-serviceman, a Scotch piper, in his kilt playing his pipes along the fog-filled London streets at night. Nanny wrapped a penny in newspaper and I was allowed to throw it down to him.

I remember Nanny upstairs in our nursery at the top of the house. She was a sadist who disliked my brother. She used to put him behind the fireguard so that he ran to and fro crying in the heat from the gas fire. I later tell my mother and she is sacked.

But this nanny is a new one – she is called Bella Wildgoose. She is not my Nanny Paton, who has left. And a brother!

These were just two of several events that suddenly rocked my childhood. Childish events, on the whole, but vital to me – to me they are key memories; childish events except for one. This was a terrible calamity that was to change our lives for ever.

(8)

My brother Sammy was born in Aldeburgh Cottage Hospital on 31 August 1936. I can remember sitting astride my mother's flattened form and looking at him in the cot beside the bed. At his christening, he was given four silver mugs.

New siblings are always a threat to the young Crown Prince, but I was equal to it. I bullied Sammy ferociously, yet I loved him and defended him equally ferociously against outside bullying. We fought and played and fought, and when he was older – three to my six – I would climb into his bed, or he into mine, and I would tell him the stories I whispered in my head.

Sammy's birth must have been one of the causes of what now became quite disturbed behaviour. I grew, as I said, terrified of the dark, presage of the insomnia which has intermittently plagued me ever since. I became uncontrollably active. I also suddenly demanded to be kissed and cuddled all the time. At once, my mother became terrified. My insistence on being called nurse had sent a thrill of homosexual anxiety racing through her. I now compounded this by suddenly announcing, to her horror, that when I grew up I was going to wear my woman's underwear *underneath* my policeman's uniform. At once my demands for love became clear. The main cause of homosexuality was known to my mother, as it was to many of her generation: over-loving, over *physically* loving mothers fixated their sons, who became unable to attach to other women. My grandmother was over-loving: Eddie and Bob were homosexual. It was, inspired by Freud, as simple as that. Clearly, I was both demonstrating my potential homosexuality and, as it were, asking for it to be intensified.

My mother took me at once to a child analyst and asked if she should respond to my demands and if she did would I become homosexual? The analyst had some sessions with me – I remember nothing of all this – and said that, though I would be fascinating to analyse, it was not necessary. More especially, my mother should on no account reject me.

My mother temporarily relaxed, beyond beginning a long and losing battle to get my hair to part on the side (the middle presumably being 'sissy'). Yet why was her anxiety quite so intense? She might have wondered, if over-demonstrative mothers caused this disaster, why not Jock and my father? Nor was it that she disliked homosexuals. In fact, she had fallen in love with Eddie and then Bob before fixing on my father. She continued to love Eddie thereafter, and all her life she had numbers of close homosexual male friends. I think it was really because she thought homosexuals had a more difficult life.

I think my bad behaviour was also a response to a situation I learnt about only after my parents were dead. A year or two after they had settled into Milner Street, my mother was surprised to receive a bill for repainting the bathroom pink. But the bathroom hadn't been repainted, pink or otherwise. It turned out that my father had set up a mistress Go-Go-style in a flat in Marylebone. The pink bathroom was hers.

This must have been devastating to my mother. The letters that remain between them for the period before this show that she adored him and trusted him completely – as indeed, did he her. Yet the mistress idea was something very important to him, over and above the not unusual desire for someone else. My father was not exactly aggressively heterosexual, but he was obviously so. He sometimes said, only half-joking, that if my mother had let him sleep with her he probably wouldn't have married her. It was the intensity of his frustrated desire, frustrated for two years, that fused them together. Before her, there were hints about housemaids; also one of the Schreibers. After her, more mistresses – some clumsily concealed.

They eventually got over this one. But they were getting on very badly at the beginning of 1939 and I must have been aware of this. My grandmother said so badly that she thought they would have got divorced if the war hadn't broken out.

War – this was the calamity that changed our lives for ever. I can just remember some of the events at the beginning. Suffolk was much wilder then, some of the little sandy lanes still unmetalled. The twenty acres outside Snape and up to the church and beyond were still all common land. So were the sixty or so acres down to the river at the top of the lane which passes Crisp's farm and goes winding down to the village. This lane itself was lined with great elms, since fallen and not replaced by the insensitive farmer who now farms the land. My mother and I – it must have been May 1940 – were walking slowly up this lane under the trees when suddenly she stopped. 'Do you feel that thudding under the road?' She said, 'That's the guns in Holland.' It meant nothing to me but I've not forgotten it. It is feelings we remember, disguised as events.

Whether they would have divorced or not I do not know, but it makes little difference. Early in 1940 my father joined the navy and vanished into the war for six years. Nearly everyone born in the 1930s or early 1940s comes from a broken home.

(9)

We had given up 21 Milner Street in 1939 when it was clear war was coming and, as my father left, we went to Snape – my mother, me and Sammy, the little nucleus that was to be our family throughout the war.

At first, famously, nothing happened. Or rather, nothing happened as far as war went. But just before this my mother's stockbroker, acting one has to say with exemplary speed if slightly bizarre originality, had put half of her holding of shares into German war bonds and, as an equally original long stop, the other half into Japanese war bonds.

About eighty per cent of recovered artefacts and valuables in museums round the world are apparently the result of digging up things buried in emergencies. In 1939, all over Britain people dug deep holes and did what people have done for thousands of years. I stood solemnly watching my grandmother hand Brown piles of her best plates wrapped in greaseproof paper, bundles of silver cutlery and some packets of jewellery and the earth being shovelled back and then the hole being paced out from lines joining four trees.

But at Snape nothing else changed. It was a house that changed slowly. Twenty-five years after the war there was still a black-out lampshade hanging in the downstairs cloakroom. Ancient medieval diseases drifted up from the floorboards. I got scarlet fever. And Dr Collins came and felt me with his permanently warm fingertips. People never – or rather we never – went to surgeries then. Dr Collins – tall, kind, discreet, ancient – arrived in his car. There was an examination, murmurings, medicine. Dr Collins had a glass of sherry. Perhaps two glasses. I had to have a gland in my neck cut out and Dr Collins did the operation in the nursery on a table. As he bent over me, I think I can just remember smelling the anaesthetic, if that is what it was.

The pine trees among which my grandmother and I were tentatively working and were later to work much harder were growing taller. But Brown still mowed the grass leading a pony pulling whirling blades on a roller; a pony which was soon, between the shafts of a trap, to be my grandmother's sole means of transport.

When I compel Snape to surface from those last years there, I can see Sammy and me playing in the wood; I see the thin, fascinating yellow coil of my shit (or his) and smell the smell of it, not particularly unpleasant, rising from the damp earth and moss and the harshness and inefficiency of leaves as toilet paper; I smell the pine sap, sticky, translucent tree-blood; I hear the big bluebottles, as big as plums, buzzing and dying on the window sills; the sound of the cock crowing from the barnyard above the rock garden; the creaking of the floor-boards under the rather threadbare black carpet on the landing as my grandmother thuds down to have her morning bath, her long-haired dachshunds, who liked to warm themselves beneath it, scurrying behind her. But I must have realised acutely how the focus of our real life was changing and closing in on my mother's bedroom, because I can remember vividly playing on her bed. She had a collection of inch- and two-inch-long solid silver animals – a cat, a dog, a cow, a cockerel, a lion, a badger, about twenty – each of which fitted perfectly into its red velvet cat- or lion- or cow-shaped hole, like the simple wooden puzzles you buy for little children. I loved taking them out of their dark blue leather box and positioning them about her eiderdown and eventually, after endless muttered fantasies, pressing them home again into their luscious blood-red shapes.

Perhaps it was a reaction to this, to this awareness of our life changing, of my father gone, that now led me to run a temperature between 99° and 100°. This went on for weeks, to everyone's consternation and anxiety. Dr Collins could find nothing wrong. Eventually, he said no one was to take my temperature for a month. There was a green revolving hut in which my grandfather had slept for his TB and which Granny had brought from Glemham as a summerhouse. No doubt everybody feared I was inclining towards TB too and I was supposed to lie in bed in the hut all day.

This was impossible. I can still feel the great dynamo of six-and-a-half-year-old energy, the appalling block of frustration. I spent the whole time escaping and creeping – or if spotted, rushing – about the garden. Bella Wildgoose had gone, but my mother would run from the house shouting and waving her arms. Mary and Nettie would run, and my grandmother – they were all shouting, their arms waving above their heads like an illustration in *Struwelpeter*. Stop! Stop! No one could catch me. And now it is mid-1940 and there were evacuees. All boys my age. I leap from the green hut and chase one. I catch him and I can remember the feeling of savage triumph as I get astride him and am about to beat him up – when all at once he shoots up his fist and hits me as hard as he can in the eye. I am absolutely astonished as well as blinded.

My grandmother eventually had seven evacuees – all boys. She was the only person in the village, probably in rural England, who specifically insisted on boys. No girls please. But soon after this chastening lesson in East End, streetwise strength and skill, my temperature was taken again and found to be normal. And not long after that, about June 1940, we left for Scotland, evacuees ourselves.

(10)

Kelburn Castle lies between Largs and Fairlie thirty miles north of Ayr. It stands about two miles from the coast looking across to the island of Great Cumbrae opposite.

That part of south-west Scotland was far more remote then than it is now. But it was nearly not remote enough. Recently, while editing the wartime correspondence between my Aunt Anne and her book-seller husband, Heywood Hill, I came on some letters my mother wrote to Anne from Kelburn. She says that she and Sheila, Heywood's sister, have almost decided to emigrate to America with their children, 'for the duration', the expression people used for the period of the war.

Quite a number of middle-class families did this. In fact, when my mother wrote, the war was at last properly under way, but England was much more frightened and anxious at the start of 1940 when nothing was happening than it was when bombs began to fall and Hitler faced us across the narrow seas from Finisterre in a great sweep along the whole of northern Europe to Nordkapp in the north of Norway.

Kelburn Castle, spasmodically added to since about 1260 was, is – or at least as I remember it – with its turrets, embrasures, towers, keeps and battlements, a tribute to the accuracy of Disney's cartoon castles. I have the usual scattered scenes, those magnesium flares of memory that suddenly, momentarily, brightly, inexplicably and sometimes inaccurately illuminate the past. I slept up a winding staircase in one of the turret rooms. Kelburn was haunted, though fortunately the strange bumpings and slitherings the ghost made in its attic wanderings could not be heard in my turret room. (Someone later discovered that the ghostly sounds were made by owls sliding down the lead guttering in the angle between two roofs.)

Morning prayers were a feature of Kelburn, as of many big houses then. Servants filed in at the back. Everyone knelt. Either Uncle Patrick – that is, *Great* Uncle Patrick – or Aunt Hyacinth led the tiny congregation. I have very hazy pictures of these two. Aunt Hyacinth is wavery, anxious, her skin, no doubt under the influence of her

name, a pale blue. Uncle Patrick I see as George V or as the Earl in
Little Lord Fauntleroy. I am Lord Fauntleroy – a sycophantic, cunning,
sucking-up little creep. In the letter about going to America, my
mother reports a conversation between me and Aunt Hyacinth. I
start it: 'Aunt Hyacinth, what is that lovely prayer you say – not the
first lovely prayer, but the really *beautiful* one that comes second?' In
fact, what I remember about the beautiful prayers was their intolerable boredom and trying to mitigate it by tracing the pattern on the
green and blue velvet chair seat I'm kneeling at.

Sometimes we went out. The paddle steamer across to Cumbrae,
ploughing into the west wind so you were nearly blown off your feet.
Sometimes my mother used to take us to a *thé dansant* in Fairlie. At
forty or so little tables people ate scones and drank tea (or at our table
orange squash) and a few couples decorously foxtrotted or quick-
stepped to a band on the stage. There was a popular song in 1940
which I had learnt by heart and one day the band suddenly began to
play it. Should I tell them? I asked my mother and she led me, half-
reluctantly, half-excited, up to the band leader. I did indeed know it –
perfectly. I sang it the whole time, conscious how sweet I must seem.

> Oh Johnny, Oh Johnny, how you can love!
> Oh Johnny, Oh Johnny, heavens above!
> You make my sad heart *jump* for joy,
> And when you're near me
> I can't keep still a minute
> Because it's Oh Johnny, Oh Johnny,
> I love you so!
> You're not handsome it's true,
> But when I look at you,
> It's just Oh Johnny, Oh Johnny, Oh!

But on the stage, the microphone lowered, facing all those up-
turned faces, my mind went blank with terror. I simply repeated 'Oh
Johnny, Oh Johnny, Oh Johnny' again and again, until I was lifted
down and returned, agonisingly humiliated, to our table.

My father came on leave. He brought his revolver and we went
out to the burn rushing down behind the castle from the forests
through which the Strong Man of Tilwilly had once strode. Here he

fired into one of the clear, nearly still pools and the bullets flattened on the smooth, scooped-out rock at its bottom. I kept the flattened lead slug he gave me for years.

But the most glaring magnesium flares, the apparently most inexplicable, are in fact the most significant and glare fiercer because of that. It is in the bright light of one of these that I am standing outside my mother's bedroom. Sammy is inside crying. My mother is teaching him to read and, tormented by his inability to learn, he is crying bitterly. But she persists. I listen with quiet satisfaction and pleasure. A key memory.

Towards the end of 1940, France had fallen, the Battle of Britain, begun in August, was still raging and bombs had been raining down on London since September. We left Kelburn, not for America, but headed south for Shiplake, near Reading, not all that far from the eye of the storm, to join John and Sheila Hill and their two children Nicolas and Josephine.

(11)

Shiplake Grange, where we lived till the summer of 1942, is a square house, faced with stucco on the corner of the main Reading–Henley road and the lane leading up to the village of Shiplake Row. The rent was shared. It is opposite – or was, all this may be 'was', I haven't been back – a pub called the Plough. Few people had cars by now, and everyone travelled by bus or train or bicycle or pony and trap or horse. Five or six times a day the Henley–Reading bus would stop at the Plough and people clamber on or off. Sheila could remember my mother standing there and how the women from the village would cluster round her chatting before walking up the hill to Shiplake Row.

The house had quite a big garden and a four-foot brick wall facing both roads. When the class-war flared up, which it did intermittently and excitingly, we would throw stones at the village boys and they would throw stones back. We were heavily outnumbered but relatively safe behind our wall.

Nic was six when we arrived, seven when we left; I was seven and then eight; Jo his sister two years older than me, Sammy three years younger. I remember hardly anything of Jo or Sammy then, nor of the grown-ups. Little boys sometimes seem a different species, so totally do they become immersed in their imaginative lives. Someone read Nic and me Enid Blyton's *The Faraway Tree*, in which some gormless Blyton children climb a tall tree and find, cribbed from *Jack and the Beanstalk*, that it opens into a magic land. Nic and I located this at the top of a tall larch in the garden. The glimpses of the magic land above us as we laboured in vain to reach it, the feeling of it being there, even the sounds drifting faintly down from it, are far more 'real' to me now than, say, the cherry tree into which we also climbed and ate ourselves sick with the pink and white English-complexioned cherries.

Anything we did was real. We built an aeroplane – a cardboard box covered in feathers with cardboard wings and a broom propeller – and pushed ourselves off an old chicken shed. In my memory it glides a few feet before painfully crashing. Andrew Mylius, Peta Lambe's son by an earlier marriage, was a rather distant neighbour, but he was dumped on us by his stepfather admiral when Peta went to the Bahamas. He was younger than us and it was with him that Sammy played. Then suddenly, as the bombs came nearer, he was sent to Bermuda. Nic and I decided to visit him there and built a raft: a platform of nailed planks, a box on top to sit in, some old car tyres nailed underneath. This was tested on the Thames, a mile away, where we swam in summer. It floated, after a fashion.

As well as the village boys, we fought numerous other battles. Grown-ups were by definition enemies. This was especially true of Mr Barton who came three times a week to do the kitchen garden. We removed a manhole cover above some drain or soak-away and constructed a cover of sticks and grass and Mr Barton duly trod on it. Punishment was meted out – he 'might have' broken a leg – pity he didn't – which required revenge. We painted the seat of an outside lavatory he used with a mixture of glue and varnish. Did he sit on it? I know Nic and I crouched in a sort of space under the roof above it, helpless with giggles. Then I see Mr Barton, trousers round his ankles, straining to get off, then roaring with rage, shaking his fists, stuck fast.

We made cigarettes with grass and leaves stuffed in some long, elegant, card-and-Bakelite cigarette holders we'd stolen, and choked on the harsh herbal-cardboard smoke which tasted not unlike the tobacco my father was eventually to kill himself with.

Sealed inside the bell jar of boyhood, fused almost into one person, we hardly ever quarrelled. To remind myself that we must sometimes have done so I need to follow a final excremental detour that leads into the dynamics of our little group, a detour splintered as the war suddenly crashed in on us.

(12)

Little children are homogeneous, within themselves, with the world outside; growing up is a process of differentiation. Sex for children is just a part of play; by adulthood it has become an end in itself. I can remember watching from the door my two children Jenny and Ben in the bath aged six and four and a half. Ben was squashed up under the taps where Jenny habitually shoved him, but was lying back contentedly. Jenny was twiddling his cock with her toes. 'You like that don't you Ben?' 'Hmmm,' said Ben happily. 'But you like it even *more* when I do it with my fingers,' said Jenny. 'Yes,' said Ben.

This play and exploration extend as we all know into other body functions. Everything is tasted and usually eaten. There is nothing inherently disgusting about shit to a baby or little child; it is a sort of natural plasticine to be squeezed about or squashed against walls. But it is among the first of the differentiations. Sammy was still at the Snape-shit-fascination stage (he and Andrew Mylius used to drink each other's pee) but I had been changed. Jo says she remembers a game, initiated by me, of wrapping our shit in toilet paper and throwing it out of the window; it was, to us, daring, hysterically funny – and wicked. This meant it could now be used as a weapon. When angry, Nic used to taunt and shame me by saying, 'Your Mummy does squitty bigs.' My poor mother, wrestling with her bowels, wracked by anxiety, downing Ex-Lax or senna pods. But my riposte was the more devastating: 'Your mother hits you.'

Sheila Hill (Hill by birth and by confusingly marrying an unrelated John Hill) was in some ways a genius with children. She could invent amazing games and surprises, inspire wonderful outings, entertain and excite us. Here, she was a magician. She was also a genius with the store cupboard. Rationing was now quite severe and everyone kept a store cupboard of special things given, or got on the black market or, occasionally, sent from America. We each had our own small square of butter which we divided into seven squares to last the week. I remember Sheila once produced a huge *tin* of butter from New Zealand! Her tins of salmon were especially exciting. She was small, fair-haired, with attractively buck teeth, and her only defect as far as we were concerned was her temper. She could not control it and when she lost it would lash out. She never, that I remember, hit Sammy or me. I think my mother was frightened of her, though they got on very well on the whole. Jo inherited this temper and once in a rage locked all of us into the drawing room – a demonstration of power I did not forget. Jo also used to put large pieces of paper on the stairs, one on each step, saying 'I HATE MY MOTHER'. She told me she did this because Sheila never showed her the slightest affection and the evident affection my mother showed Sammy and me made her both angry and jealous.

My mother's bedroom now became of cardinal importance. It was the only room in the house with her furniture in it and it became our own small home within the larger one. In it, we were safe. Her arms about us, she read to us or told us stories; it was almost the only place Sammy and I played together. The little silver animals came out again and inhabited the eiderdown.

By an unfortunate coincidence, in both the households where we lived till 1946, the husband spent much more time at home than my father away at sea. Although of course I knew the reason, very early on I resented this. It seemed increasingly unfair and I blamed the fathers present and my absent father equally. John Hill was a catering officer in the RAF at Stradishall Camp near Bury St Edmunds. From time to time he got weekend passes and, twice, a whole week. I wonder now if the cornucopia of Sheila's locked store cupboard owed something to a catering officer's position.

John was a tall, anxious, rather cadaverous, humorous and gentle man who later developed stomach ulcers. He was an extremely gifted painter and was prevented from reaching the heights of which he was certainly capable only by an intense money anxiety which kept him slaving as an interior decorator all his life. Yet the anxiety was entirely unnecessary: he was a very rich man and when he died in 1988 in his eighties, left two million pounds – to everyone's astonishment.

But we did see my father once. He started the war as a surgeon lieutenant on the warships guarding convoys across the north Atlantic; his ships gradually became bigger until by the end he was an acting surgeon commander and PMO (Principal Medical Officer) on air-craft carriers. He was sunk once, in June 1940, on an armed merchant cruiser, HMS *Carinthia*, in the north Atlantic. Wherever he went and whenever he could he sent us presents: knives from the Medi-terranean, assagais and knobkerries from Cape Town, boomerangs from Australia, kukris (a Gurkha weapon) from India, and knives and krises from the Far East. Almost always weapons, partly because he knew we'd love them, partly because they frightened our mother. He sent only two harmless presents: a small tourist statue of a black woman with very long breasts, and a polished double coconut with a fuzz of coarse black hair between the two truncated thighs of its stained black lobes. 'Really,' as my father typically put it, 'it's a coconut cunt.'

I don't remember his single visit, but I remember just after he had left. My mother came into my room that night and sobbed bitterly sitting on my bed. I put my arms around her and tried to comfort her, and I remember the feeling of her taut shaking shoulders and how she couldn't be comforted and how inadequate I felt.

My father's long and repeated absences had two profound effects. First, I felt I had to be the father in our family because he was away. To this day, if Sammy and my son Ben are with me together I will call Ben Sammy and Sammy Ben. Emotionally, at a certain level, they are both my sons. (Indeed, I will call Nic Sammy in these circumstances so I suppose I took him on too.)

The second effect was in fact to intensify something already existing. My father was nine when his own father died, already having been seriously ill for some years. He could not have been a very effective father. My father had had no father to copy, he was in any case a busy GP beginning to make his way. And then, the war. For many years without an effective father, I too found it hard to be one and if I have failed as a parent it is here. I might have made a better mother. My father's absences also meant I was brought up by women: my nanny

and my mother, my grandmother, with later subsidiary figures like
Sheila and Fidelity. It is not surprising that later on I always, on the
whole, preferred women to men, to talk to, to be with. Also, we realise
today that feminine gender characteristics are often shared by men, just
as masculine ones are shared by women. In the 1930s this recognition
was not so common. I seem to have sensed extraordinarily early that
quite a number of things in my character were more in tune with
women than men, and that I might have to conceal this – my women's
underclothes underneath my policeman's uniform. It was this element,
not my sexual orientation, that was behind many of the things my
mother, in her terror, saw as latent homosexuality.

My father left for his war. Our war, in a mild way, now intensified.

(13)

Over a number of nights some time early in 1942, the Germans
dropped bombs on Reading, about five bomber-flight miles away.
That long drone of night-time aircraft engines for me is one of the
sounds of the war, the muffled solid sound of the explosions, then
distant fireworks flickering in the sky. Once we watched excitedly
from the garden, untouchable.

In fact, not untouchable. One morning we found a burnt-out
incendiary on the gravel at the back of the house. A few nights later
the house was shaken by a tremendous earth-quaking thump. There
was a large crater among Mr Barton's vegetables, seventy or so yards
from the house. The bomb was so big that it had plunged down
through the Berkshire clay and vanished. ARP wardens in blue hats
arrived, peered at the crater, and put up a notice: 'DANGER.
UNEXPLODED BOMB'. What would have happened if it *had* exploded?
So far as I know, it was never removed or detonated. No doubt it lies
rusting there now. One day the reverberations of lorries will set it off
and Shiplake Grange and the Plough will be flattened.

When we went to Snape, which we very occasionally did, the
underground in London, the backs and sides of buses, would be
plastered with posters: CARELESS TALK COSTS LIVES, COUGHS AND
SNEEZES SPREAD DISEASES, DIG FOR VICTORY above a huge boot
driving a huge spade into the earth. The Pathé News in the cinema,

with the facetious commentary in that extraordinary, rapid, metallic upper-class voice: 'At Braysend in Cornwall a ten-foot marrow shows even Land's End can Dig for Victory . . . ' This huge, all-pervasive war in which we were enveloped – its progress every hour reported on the BBC, the thin daily papers containing almost nothing else at all – embraced all our little wars and made them part of it. The village boys were Germans at whom we threw grenades, just as we were their Germans to whom they did the same. Mr Barton had been dropped by parachute and was a spy. Even 'the mothers' as Nic and I called them became outposts of the German army if they behaved badly enough.

And as the war continued and rationing tightened, I developed an expertise in organising a mini-rationing on each plate of food: the minute piece of meat or bacon or sausage we were allowed, the two eggs a week, were divided up and shared with each mouthful. And in the homogeneity of childhood, where the boundaries between reality and imagination, between you and the outside world are still blurred, the meat, the potato, the peas were also, as it were, people; I felt a certain sympathy for that fragment of cabbage without its share of bacon. I still divide my plates of food in this way; and at some level I retain that sympathy with inanimate objects – the clock inherited from my Uncle Bob is grateful if I remember to wind it up, the shoes thank me for feeding them with polish.

And this, in my case, ramified out. One of the treats at Shiplake was to be taken to the pantomime in Reading. There was always – perhaps still is always – an interlude of ballet. To *Swan Lake*-like music the Sugar Plum Fairy or Fairy Daffodil would enter, dazzling on her points, and twirl about for seven minutes. I was electrified by this. Responding to the often barely sublimated sexuality of ballet, the wonderful flying freedom of its movements, I thought I had never seen anything so beautiful or so exciting. I now wanted to be a ballet dancer.

To become the thing you love, to fuse with her (or him), isn't that the dream of every lover? Thirty-four years later I was left by someone I loved. Anna. I soon found long-entrenched habits changing. Still responding to wartime school demands, I had always up till then had shallow speedy baths. I would begin to feel guilty if I stayed in a bath longer than ten minutes (the prescribed time at Port Regis and

Bryanston) or if my bath was deeper than six inches (the prescribed depth). On the other hand, like most men, I liked to spend twenty minutes or so on the lavatory, reading. Anna was seldom more than four minutes – alighting and departing like a bird; while her baths were never shallower than the overflow and often above it, and she remained there hours, enveloped in scented steam. Now that she had left, I found myself spending longer and longer in deeper and deeper baths. I began to spring off the lavatory seat as off a trampoline. In a hotel bedroom in Rheims, driving back alone from Italy, where I had finally realised what had happened, I suddenly found that I smelt like her. In my agony, if I could not possess her at least I could turn into her.

My solution to my desire to be a ballet dancer like the Sugar Plum Fairy was based on observation. Her extraordinarily long, strong yet perfectly shaped legs were clearly the result of spending so much time on the tips of her toes. One of my mother's oldest and closest friends, Helen Woolley, had ballet dancer calves. Here the cause was obscure, but I could see the ballet dancer mechanisms at work again in the legs of the young women, all then wearing wedge-shaped very high heels. Accordingly, I bought a large quantity of cheap rubber Phillips heels and hammered them one on top of the other on to the heels of my own shoes.

I was allowed to totter off in these to Cane-End, the little private school we all went to (a school run on progressive lines – hence the name, hence the tolerance). I remember only two things about this permissive little school. I was chosen as Puck in the school play. For weeks I pretended I was learning the (truncated) part but did nothing. The hideous truth emerged six days before the performance when I was forced to stop reading from my script. In this emergency, the geography and games mistress, an unsuitably big, middle-aged woman who had played the part as a girl, was hurriedly drafted in. Instead of the nimble dainty boy they had envisaged putting a girdle round the earth, a heffalump lumbered round the stage. I was deeply humiliated and for many years had dreams about not learning a part.

The second was an act of cruelty. Schoolchildren often seem to turn instinctively on the feeble like a primitive tribe expelling a potentially weakening member. One of these at Cane-End was

Helen Billo, a very thin, sallow, nervous creature with a flat face. One cold winter's morning she was standing next to me on a bench at assembly. With a shudder of disgust, feeling she was crowding me, I suddenly dug my elbow sharply into her side. This coincided with Helen Billo's falling sideways, fainting from feebleness and cold. I can still remember my guilt. She smelt of mouldy tennis balls.

I suppose we must have done lessons. At least I could read now. But the shattering pile-driver of middle-class private education was not to start smashing down on to my head until we moved to the White House Farm in Suffolk, which we did in the summer of 1942.

(14)

White House Farm was near the big house at Great Glemham, now full of troops, and also belonged to Jock. We spent the rest of the war there with him and Fidelity and our five cousins: Gathorne (five weeks younger than me), Juliet (then eight), Sophie (six and a half), Tina (two) and Hughie (six months).

The house was a typical, rambling, timber-framed, sixteenth-century Suffolk farmhouse with the steep pointed roof which came from once being thatched. (Steep so that rain ran quickly and easily off the thatch.) It had one low storey, six small, low-ceilinged bedrooms, the two largest of which were my mother's and Jock and Fidel's. The upstairs bathroom was for grown-ups, the downstairs for children. There was no electricity, an Aga, a coke boiler for hot water. With its beams, its uneven wooden floors, its steep crooked stairs, the house creaked in the wind and at night.

The ages between nine and thirteen are vividly remembered. All our clothes were bought with coupons at Martin Bros in Sax-mundham. Vacuum tubes ran up and down all over the shop and sucked small canisters of change with a sharp *Crack!* at the speed of bullets. Fidelity, with typical invention, said that my mother saved money by cramming my feet into tiny shoes for far too long – despite the x-ray machines in which we endlessly looked at them. We were left alone – today it would be seen as dangerous – to play for hours at a time together. There was a tiny garden, but we played on the farm.

In the semi-light of the cavernous big barn we hid or fought or just slid about on the sweet-smelling hay. We made long tunnels deep into the stacks of threshed straw and then up to the top of them. The herd of Red Pole cows ambled in every morning and evening and in the evening one of us would have to get the milk. George Pendle, the stooped, gloomy cowman, clanged the pail down on the concrete floor under the swollen, heavily veined udders, tucked his stool under his bottom, pushed the cow over with his capped head, directed two long jets of milk out into the disinfectant-smelling cowshed to clear the teats and then swiftly and rhythmically – left hand right hand, left hand right hand – spurted them down into the warm, foaming, filling pail. One would wait till he was ready.

I watched. I watched when the bull serviced the cows. Sometimes he was led by the nose snorting and dangerous and randy into a small pen. Here, because of his great size, he needed help. Quite often a rather grand land girl called Hermione Potts would come over from the stud farm (also Jock's). Hermione, who loved Sammy, had a chinless face, a voice like the Queen's, and popped-out eyes. Her face would flush, her plummy voice deepen, and her eyes pop out even further as the bull trembled and sweated and she wrestled with its huge penis. Finally with both hands she managed to slide it home like a torpedo into its tube.

In fact, many things were still done by hand, as they had been for hundreds of years. Muck spread, beet pulled and stacks stacked, all by hand; instead of weedkiller all the men went out with hoes, and instead of fertiliser and nitrates, as well as muck, crops were rotated, fields left fallow and clover planted.

A walnut avenue led down to the white farmhouse, then came the farmyard, scattered with hens, the straw stacks in the stackyard, the milking shed and pig shed and barns and stables; and then the long strait which went past the oval pond with its ducks on the right; and the nut grove with its rectangular pond on the left and then on and on it seemed flat for miles but in fact about three-quarters of one; past some isolated oaks, a stretch of distant willows in one of the fields, on down to the stream which marked the eastern boundary of Jock's land.

In summer we would run or bicycle down this track over the grass and, slipping off our clothes, swim in the stream. Or rather, for a year or more, simply play about in the reed-and-watercress cold-running shallows where minnows or sticklebacks darted. There was a pool, too dark and deep to see its bottom, whose great depth could swallow a man. Suddenly, one summer, some soldiers turned up. We explained the dangers of the deep pool. But after a slight pause in the summer heat, they too stripped off and plunged in. To our astonishment this phenomenon of the river world, this black monster-concealing abyss, turned out to reach no higher than their upper thighs. I can remember their white naked bodies and bronzed faces and forearms and how they larked about laughing, splashing and ducking each other and shouting: 'Fuck off you . . .' splash, shout, duck. Thereafter we used it ourselves and it was there I taught myself to swim.

At the end of the summer, the harvest. In hot sun the tractor would circle one of the small hedged fields, the reaper and binder beside it. Gathorne and I would stand at strategic points and shoot the rabbits with our .410s as they raced from the dwindling stand of corn. I once shot fifteen. The whirring reaper would cut and the binder would gather the corn together and bind it into armful-sized sheaves with binder twine and dump them out on the field. The men would pick them up and lean them upright together in a stook, five or six to a stook. As the sun fell, the long black shadows of the stooks slanted across the stubble.

The tractor, open to the air, then, as all tractors were, always pulled the reaper and binder round. But it was the only one on the 350-acre farm and petrol was severely rationed even for something as vital as farming. A lot of the heavy work was done by the two Suffolk Punches. These big strong animals are direct descendants of the chargers that went into battle at Agincourt and Crécy and carried the armoured knights of England through the Middle Ages. That is why they are the only carthorses not to be encumbered with great tussocks of hair round their hooves. There was nothing they couldn't do. They pulled the plough over the fields, then the harrow over the plough, and it was always one of them that pulled the big cart into which the stooks were collected, once judged dry enough.

One, two, three, even four of us would ride astride them, their bare, broad, chestnut-brown backs warm under our bottoms and between our thighs as they moved and stopped, moved and stopped, steadily up and down the field. They moved as easily and powerfully and steadily as machines, machines whose vein system seemed all on the outside like moving Pompidou Centres. But they were very alive, noisily blowing out their lips, shaking their big heads crossly at the flies, swishing their tails or lifting them to extrude a few big sausages of dung, great glossy creatures, groomed smooth and with that wonderful strong animal sweat smell of hot horse like – like what? Like fresh toast, like ironed sheets, like a woman's warm skin, but really only like itself.

One man stood in the cart with his pitchfork, calling out to the horse when to move or stop, arranging the sheaves as they arrived. Two or three others pitchforked them up. It must have been hot, hard work, but they were very strong. None stronger than Ted Cobbin, the foreman. This kind, humorous, nut-brown man had muscles of iron. He could single-handedly lift a five-bar gate. Many years later, when he was over seventy-five, I heard him describe, like a character in *The Woodlanders*, how in old age he could identify by an ache here, a twinge there, some feat of his manhood on the farm.

And later still, some while after the sheaves had been stacked – threshing. We would hear the traction engine's iron wheels rumbling down the lane as it came slowly into view pulling the threshing machine, belching smoke. It would rumble down between the walnuts and take up position by the stack to be threshed. The threshing machine would be joined by an endless belt to a wheel on the engine, coal would be shovelled in, the big iron wheel start to spin, the men would pitchfork the sheaves into the clattering thresher, chaff would fly, sacks fill with grain and be hauled away, and we would all rush about with sticks smashing the heads of rats and mice which shot out of the stack and were trapped by the netted barrier which had been put round it. It was hot, noisy, exciting and there was beer for the men to drink.

I have memories of us shooting the rats as we did the rabbits with our 4.10s, but I think this is imposed. Several people would have been killed. But I loved shooting. We learnt at first by shooting sparrows in a big thorn tree at the corner of the farmyard. Jock was at his best in this situation, tending little boys. He would have been an excellent schoolmaster. He became kind and jovial. He was infinitely patient, he knew when to let you loose, when to correct, when to praise. Later on, I became quite a good shot – I once got a left and a right of a pheasant and a woodcock. I remember standing at the corner of one of the woods by the stream and shooting six pigeons one by one as they swooped swiftly out ahead of the beaters, the sharp clapping together of their wings eventually to be ruined for me by Bayley at Bryanston. Little boys are instinctive hunter/gatherers – especially hunters. I certainly had no scruples at that period, except once when I shot a hare and it screamed. When I was twenty-one, Jock and Fidel gave me a finely chased 12-bore shotgun, an extremely generous present – though it may have been partly prompted to compensate for a distressing event which they knew was to follow soon after my birthday.

There were a number of ponies on the farm – three or four at various times – and we all learnt to ride. I enjoyed this too, but it was shooting I enjoyed most. Horses are unpredictable and can be frightening. People are always being killed or breaking their backs hunting, though somehow I managed to survive three or four of these events. Fidelity, however, was nearly badly hurt when her horse, an old racehorse inappropriately named 'My Happiness' and given her by Bill Astor, suddenly died under her as she was cantering down the field beside the walnuts. The dying horse convulsively half-rolled on her and she was concussed and badly shaken. Dr Collins hurried out. My mother, who loved Fidelity, hovered anxiously. Drama.

Loved Fidelity. That she certainly did; but not only that.

(15)

Fidelity's conversational style, which meshed well with my mother's, was one of inspired exaggeration. It worked best on, or creating, disasters. Quite small mishaps would rapidly be inflated into hilarious catastrophes. She was very quick, so quick that she could get things wrong.

She was an excellent mother for children; less sure with adolescents. And she came from a family of Quakers. The Seebohms were a very clever family. Fidelity's niece, Victoria (later Glendinning), was to become, in my view, one of the best in that astonishing recent flowering of British biographers. Her father Freddy, Fidelity's brother, was chairman of Barclays France and later Barclays D.C. and O. Another brother, George, a very successful stockbroker – but with Fidelity her Quaker upbringing induced a certain frugality of spirit. Later, when my mother began to drink more and more, Fidelity hated it. No one liked it, but she *disapproved*. Fidelity had not had to go through the things my mother had to go through. This in particular, but also the difference in their social and financial positions, the fact that Fidel was very busy, a JP, chairperson of this committee or that institute, then of the Aldeburgh Festival, while my mother was none of these, led to a distancing. I had the feeling that my mother sometimes felt deserted by Fidelity.

But none of this obtained at White House Farm. This was the high point of their friendship – and it went very high. Both were in their early thirties and extremely attractive. Fidel's looks were quite different from my mother's: much more English, even Scandinavian. She had a fair, speckly complexion, a wide quite thin mouth, level grey eyes, a broad forehead, a perfect, delicately pointed nose (which I longed to have too and tried to obtain by squeezing), and the fine, spun-gold hair which never goes grey. And yet this frugal Quaker was also capable of abandon.

War, it is well known, whirls countries and peoples into a maelstrom of sex and love. Indeed, one of my teachers at Cambridge, Peter Laslett, had a theory where an aspect of this explained the social upheaval and altered behaviour which also famously follow war. The closeness and intense camaraderie of fighting fuse armies and navies into something that can be legitimately viewed as a great love affair or close conglomeration of many little love affairs. When peace disintegrates these unions, the psychological disturbance and erratic behaviour which is known to attend the break-up of love relationships take place on a massive scale. Someone should explore Laslett's idea.

But, at another level – husbands are away for months at a time or far busier than usual; the manhood of the country is being destroyed and must be replaced; while, since they may, too, soon be dead, the men still temporarily here or on leave or come to help from abroad, will all soon go away again, so nothing is serious and all of them have the glamour of that imminent death; they deserve to be made love to – there must have been a sense here, from all this, of Fucking for Victory.

Temporarily here and tinged with that glamour were, as far as East Anglia went, the GIs – screwing as many willing Suffolk war widows, and non-widows, as they could get their hands on. Jock's land above the village three miles away had been flattened to make an air base for Flying Fortresses. I remember an atmosphere of laughter and flirtatiousness and excitement at the White House and GI officers arriving with bottles of whisky and nylons. One of them taught us how to lasso. Another, particularly dashing and good-looking, told my mother he always insisted on having his revolver under the pillow when making love in case some husband unexpectedly returned. Whether my mother ever slept with him or any of them I don't know – though she later described to me how a big black American sergeant who used to help her with the salvage at Saxmundham once came up to her from behind, enveloped her in his arms and said, 'I could eat you dirt and all.'

My father used to intimate without saying straight out that my mother was less keen on sex than he was, more inhibited and faithful and so somehow not quite satisfactory – either to explain and excuse his own infidelities if I ever discovered them (which I did) or perhaps to encourage me to follow his example. I felt saddened by this picture, but I was pleased to discover when they were both dead that it wasn't entirely accurate.

In fact, I partly discovered this before my mother died. I was poking about in their furniture, which by then was stored in a stable at the big house – I must have been about twenty – when I came upon a bundle of letters to her from John Nash. They were love letters: ' . . . those warm kisses under the trees at Snape . . . ' etc. I read them riveted. That evening, back at 18 Hartington Road in Aldeburgh, where we had finally settled, I said suddenly, in a special drifting sensitive voice, 'You know Mummy, I don't know why, but I always felt, somehow *sensed* I suppose, that there was something, some love or attraction or *something* between you and John Nash.'

My mother looked up sharply and said equally sharply, 'You've been reading my letters.'

'No no,' I said, 'no no no – it was, well, just something I sensed, you know.'

My mother did know only too well. Before she died, she asked Gathorne to burn all her letters including the ones from John Nash, which to my irritation he did, though I suppose he had to. Later still, I learnt that it had been a great deal more than warm kisses. That randy, humorous, extremely alive, tiny, gifted painter, with his deeply lined face, black, protuberant eyes and melancholy wife, had made love to my mother as often as he possibly could. They once, Fidel told me, made love in the rock garden at Snape – tantamount to making love on the altar at Sandringham when the Queen is expected any second.

My mother had another affair during the war with a man called Harry Wetherall. He was an amusing, glamorous figure then, rich, competing at Wimbledon, frequenting nightclubs. Oddly enough, I met him several times long before I discovered his role in my mother's life. He said he used to go and listen to Fats Waller play in London during the war. (I wonder if he ever took my mother.) One night he and the pianist were the only two people left in some club at 5 a.m., Fats as usual with a large tumbler of whisky balanced precariously on top of the upright piano. As they left together, Fats said, 'You're a proper gentleman Mr Wetherall.' Keeping up this status required a huge quantity of drink, which cost a great deal of money. By the time I met him, Harry had drunk all his money and all but destroyed himself.

Their affair must have been conducted in London; and as it became safer we, too, would very occasionally go there for treats, staying always with Anne and Heywood or ballet-legged Helen. In April 1943, for instance, my mother and Sheila – both keen on the star Jack Buchanan – took us all to see *The Merry Widow*. I thought I had never heard anything so beautiful as its famous waltz. My ballet dancing ambition was now at its height and the two became entwined. I was always practising and I remember prancing and pirouetting about on the grass one summer while my mother and Fidel gossiped above the music from the wireless and praised me and tried not to laugh too obviously.

Today, I might have been encouraged. I would have gone to one of the boarding ballet schools. At that time, in my family, it wasn't even considered. It was bad enough that I became a writer. Although I was always good at dancing, especially when it became wilder in the '50s and '60s (yet oddly enough, or perhaps not odd, I can never do the waltzes I fantasised about then), the real dream, the dream of a would-be ballet dancer, sank out of sight.

(16)

Port Regis, the little prep school I was sent to aged ten, with Nic aged nine, in September 1943, had just been moved from the potentially dangerous south coast to a place of 'safety' about fifteen miles as the bomber flies from that same south coast.

This was into a wing of Bryanston School at Blandford, the school to which its pupils often went. Port Regis was a conventional school but it was, in a mild way, progressive, and I went there partly because of my father. This was the only part of my childhood upbringing in which he played a significant role. He had been beaten cruelly both at this own prep school and at Eton and he was determined Sammy and I should not suffer the same brutal and senseless humiliation. Port Regis had no fagging, hardly any hierarchy except for head boy and dormitory captains, and no beating – there must have been punishments but I can't remember what they were. Not that it was in the least chaotic; it was ordered, disciplined and the teaching was effective, but the regime, largely because of the headmaster John Upward – JMU – who shared its qualities, was kindly and humane.

Thanks to a boy aged about twelve called Christopher Newhouse I was flung more or less at once into experiences I had no idea existed. Newhouse, it was said, had been dropped on his head as a baby. And there was a scar to prove this. Under wild spiky hair, he had rather wild eyes which he blinked a great deal. He walked with a long bouncy stride, and had the most enormous genitals anyone had ever seen. It must, I learnt later, have been a condition known as Infant Hercules in which, due to an andreno-cortical disorder, the genital developments of manhood are thrust prematurely on to someone much younger. Newhouse's huge genitals required him to masturbate six or seven times a day. He would often do this, feverishly excited, lying on his back on the dormitory floor with his bony knees up. We would gather round and watch in astonishment – until, sometimes crying aloud, Newhouse ejaculated. He told us that his mother, seeing him tormented by his endless erections, had taught him how to do it.

Under Newhouse's instructions we rapidly learnt to do it ourselves – and do it to each other. Every night, after lights out, we would get into someone else's bed and do it. (But never, thank God, with Newhouse. He took his relief – it hardly seemed like pleasure – alone. I shudder to think what might have happened had he clambered, with his huge engine, in with one of us tender ten-year-olds.) I remember one boy called Redwood with a bulgy rather red face who must have had sadistic fantasies. He used to hiss in my ear as his transports reached their climax, 'Smash your balls on a marble slab, smash your balls on a marble slab.' He became a distinguished executive of a recording company, Decca I think; and in the late 1950s I used to see him striding about, still rather red but only his eyes bulging, among his cables at the Aldeburgh Festival. I wondered if I dared, and didn't dare, call out, 'Smash your balls on a marble slab Redwood.' Newhouse was also a precociously good pianist and used to play boogie with a similar frenzy. He looked as if he was masturbating then, too.

Adults are frightened of child sexuality because they equate it with their own, but they shouldn't be because it is different. With children it is part of, a form of, play. With adults, as I said earlier, it becomes an end in itself. At Port Regis, aged ten, we were on the cusp. For instance, I never fancied any one boy more than another – though I was sometimes apprehensive that Redwood might get totally out of control. (I did, however, make one stipulation – and I blush to confess it. There was a boy called Boyd whom I regarded as lower-class; I *therefore* always asked him if he'd had a bath. If he hadn't, I got out of his bed or turfed him out of mine.) But, class prejudice aside, our sex was a form of play – at the same time it was beginning to move into adult areas. I remember us lying next to each other in our separate beds masturbating and waiting to come together, 'Are you ready?' Already I was learning that the essence of sex was shared desire, shared pleasure and excitement and that *their* desire and feeling was the most important. 'What no one with us shares,' wrote Coleridge, 'scarce seems our own.'

I have always been grateful to Newhouse for introducing me so early to these pleasures and many years later I put him in a long short story which I in fact called 'Infant Hercules', but when he left we for some reason stopped getting into each other's beds.

By then I was learning to cope in the jungle. I rapidly found that, though very energetic, my spindly body was physically weak. If I fought, I lost. I developed strategies and weapons to defend myself and to become popular – all of which still operate to a greater or lesser extent. After lights out, when we weren't tossing each other off and later when this had stopped and we just tossed ourselves off, I told the dormitory stories. I also discovered what was both a defence and popular – making people laugh. Finally, I learnt to wound with my tongue. As I became adept, this gave me a sort of guilty pleasure and I would do it for pleasure alone. I remember a big, gentle, soft, myopic boy called Webb. He had tame rabbits at home which he loved (actually, he looked not unlike a rabbit). Sitting next to him in the dining hall, I asked him how his rabbits were. Very well, said Webb, smiling happily as he thought of them. Are you *sure*, I said, you know how often rabbit hutches catch fire? No they don't, said Webb. They do, I said, it's well known. The fire starts slowly smouldering in the straw, the rabbits smell the smoke and run and huddle against the end, suddenly flames spring up, the hutch soon catches, flames leap higher, the rabbits go mad with fear, then their fur catches, they scream . . . Poor Webb's face twitched and reddened, his pale much-magnified eyes filled with tears. I didn't stop till his rabbits were charred, cooked corpses – or did I have pity and say it was only a story? Your rabbits are fine. I hope so. Either way – forgive me, Webb.

I was too light for football and hated the heavy, mud-sodden ball, just as I was terrified of the hard cannonball fired at me in cricket. But I discovered I was good at tennis. I practised for hours and eventually I became school champion. Thus I was saved by my mother's tennis gene from being branded the games-fearing wimp I really was.

But one other sporting event had an extraordinary and extra-ordinarily formative effect on me. Sports Day included something called a flower pot race for junior boys. You were given two flower pots turned upside down on which you stood. Balancing on one, you moved the other forward, stepped on to that and, again balancing on one leg, moved the other flower pot forward and balanced on that one, now moving the first one forward again. So you slowly progressed. If you fell off, you began again. I kept falling off. In my memory, all other events are long over. Dusk is falling, taxis taking parents to the station. I am still battling with those bloody flower pots. Suddenly, out of the gloom appears Mr Pringle, whose younger brother taught us Latin. He watches me fall off and wearily go back and start again. 'Well done Gathorne-Hardy,' he says, 'well done. You've got stamina.' I never forgot this. I had stamina.

My Cranbrook cousins thought I was jealous of Gathorne's future earldom and wanted it for myself. At Port Regis in 1943, with all its competitive and extremely snobbish little boys, such things were certainly useful. Against the ace of family wealth (was it his father's *diamond mines* Roper casually told us about?) I played the ace of class ('No *no* – a viscount is the *son* of an earl'). But my anger later at the injustice of primogeniture had nothing to do with titles: it was to do, at a superficial level, with money. As the *zeitgeist* swung until most of the middle class was half ashamed, or more, at what it was – I swung too. My name and accent were bad enough and the various earls now hung round my neck like millstones. To have *been* one would have been horrifying. What I wanted in my past were miners.

The aristocrat I really wanted to be then was not an earl, incredibly exalted though that high position undoubtedly is, but the first Duke of Buckingham. In 1944 the school moved to Gorhambury, outside St Albans, where Francis Bacon had lived. Port Regis moved into the requisitioned home of the Earl of Verulam. They didn't even bother to board up the extensive series of van Dyke portraits among which James I's lover, with his white insolent face above its elaborate ruff, his long fingers emerging lazily from their lace, was easily the most intoxicating. I stared at him and stared at him and wrote his name again and again in my essay book – George Villiers, Duke of Buckingham, George Villiers, Duke of Buckingham . . .

It was at Gorhambury that my insomnia first became the problem it has remained intermittently ever since. Night after night I lay awake listening to the sounds of the sleeping dormitory in a rising panic that I would never sleep again. A temporary solution was stealing ether from Matron's surgery and breathing deeply from ether-sodden cotton wool until I swooned. I soon discovered that an added sedative was masturbating under its influence in swooning, much-prolonged bliss. But soon the surgery cupboard was locked. Eventually I became so distraught that I was put to bed in the afternoons. Now I lay awake hearing afternoon school noises, watching the jackdaws swooping and playing in the air and listening to their curious cry which is so difficult to describe – like children or recordings of dolphins or kisses or like toys being squeezed. Sometimes I dozed off.

In September 1944 an entire division was dropped at dawn by parachute over Arnhem in the Netherlands. The steady drone of their flight above us seemed to go on all night. Hour after hour they droned until the droning became a torture. But this was only the noisiest manifestation of the all-embracing war. The Mickey Mouse gas masks of Cane-End had been replaced by little adult ones – in which we suffocated for half an hour's practice each week. There was a French game called 'L'Attaque'. Two-inch cards in tin stands had tiny pictures of 'C-in-C', 'Colonel', 'Lieutenant', 'Spy' and other troops. You had your small army of these cards on a board with various terrains, and played by advancing one of your cards against your opponents': 'Colonel' beat 'Lieutenant' but 'C-in-C', of course, beat both. Only 'Spy', who wore plain clothes, and 'Mine' could beat 'C-in-C' ('Mine' was beaten by 'Sapper'). It was a prep-school game from the First World War and had hardly needed dusting off.

We trooped out and picked hips to make rosehip syrup which, with the malt extract twisted in sticky brown loops round the spoon, supplemented our wartime diet – the watery, crumbly dried egg scrambled egg, disgusting tinned pilchards, margarine like gun-grease. The dining hall at Gorhambury looked on to the ornamental Elizabethan garden now planted with vegetables by three land girls. The Latin master, the younger Mr Pringle, red-haired, very tall and lanky, with intense blue eyes staring fixedly from behind thick lenses, must, I think, have fallen into unrequited love with one of these bosomy creatures. He looked madder and madder until one Latin class suddenly veered off into the Facts of Life – verbs and nouns were swept from the blackboard and penises and vaginas and ovaries replaced them. This happened the next class too, then Mr Pringle disappeared.

Teachers were always arriving or leaving. Mr Basildon was carted off in a blue van and we eventually learnt that he had been a deserter from the RAF. (Mr Basildon was the scout master and had irritated and humiliated me by inexplicably – I knew all their silly knots – refusing to let me pass my 'tenderfoot' tests to progress from cub to scout. I gradually became the oldest cub in the history of scouting.) Mr Chapman arrived *from* the RAF to teach boxing and gym. He was small, bald and tough, with cauliflower ears and a pulped nose. He also added an element of his own not in the curriculum – wrestling. Mr Chapman used to come and sit beside me watching while I practised my scales on the piano. Gradually, he sat closer and closer and, finally, a few terms before I left, he would, after a while, take one of my hands and hold it in his bruiser's callused nicotine-stained fist. The real Facts of Life lesson was given by JMU, smoke billowing from his pipe, at the end of your last term. My mother and my father had told me these regularly more or less since I was born. I couldn't remember not knowing them – or some of them. Despite Eddie's flagrant behaviour and my mother's anxieties I hadn't yet cottoned on to what was driving Mr Chapman, and I don't think JMU dwelt on it either. A friend of Auden's and brother of the autobiographical novelist Edward Upward, he was a sensible, civilised man and, as far as his boys went, didn't mind what they did in this respect; but he would certainly have minded what his masters did. Indeed, that is probably why Mr Chapman, too, abruptly left.

On the whole, I think I was happy at Port Regis. Yet writing these few pages from the artesian well of memories spouting up, I have several times been overwhelmed by a terrible feeling of desolation and despair. I remember sitting alone in the kitchen of Anne's house in London, 10 Warwick Avenue, on my way to Waterloo and the school train and thinking, 'I will never be as unhappy as this again.' Nor have I been; or rather all unhappiness since has just been echoes of that moment, since the greatest pain comes from losing or leaving or being left by someone you love. The suffering of being torn too young from parents and home (unless they themselves are very unpleasant) is the most profound thing about boarding schools. Most people who go to them – and all who write about them – finally forget and bury their pain, but I never forgot that moment in Anne's kitchen. When I myself eventually wrote about them, this retained knowledge enabled me to untangle one of the sources of their curious power.

At Port Regis I dealt with this pain by reading. Literature – novels and stories in particular – is unique in that one of its functions is to provide escape. The role is sometimes sneered at but it is an important one. I now began to read for hours at a time. I read anything and everything – Biggles, Buchan, Rider Haggard, Arthur Ransome, the Scarlet Pimpernel, the Wizard and *Beano*, Richmal Crompton's Just William books, Enid Blyton, Sherlock Holmes . . . but with Conan Doyle I much preferred his four historical novels. As I got a little older I read all of Scott's Waverley novels.

The stories I began to write were always historical. (I remember a countess – Countess of Buckingham? – being besieged in a castle.) Writers, good and bad, are made, not born, and most have some such genesis. Early and copious reading (to escape pain or loneliness) and praise. My dormitory laughed or became terrified at my stories. Chet – Miss Chetham – my English teacher, praised what I wrote. Miss Chetham! – as precise as a pin, merry, wonderful ballet-bulging leg muscles emerging from sensible but swirling skirts. I once exasperated her beyond endurance fooling about and she slapped me with her gym shoe. I was astounded. Miss Phillips smelt of lemon soap and indeed looked rather like a rounded cake of pink and yellow soap with spectacles. Three times a week she read aloud from a book she'd chosen. And she praised my brief history essays. But I think I'd already begun the process earlier. I must have already taken in that Bob was a writer and that he fell into my side of the family split. If he and Eddie and even Jock had all been ballet dancers – a pleasing image to those who knew them, which would have produced into the bargain the first dancing earl – things might have been different.

But the books that had by far the most influential effect on my behaviour and development were Edgar Rice Burroughs's Tarzan books. These effects operated most strongly at White House Farm.

(17)

We were forced to write home once a week to our parents and, desperate for something to say, I had mentioned *en passant* how that nice Mr Chapman used to come and hold my hand while I practised my scales.

My casual reference went off like a depth charge in my mother. It was compounded by the coincidence of a similar incident between Gathorne and a master at his prep school. Anxiously, the mothers conferred. Jock must explain things. Reluctance led him to postpone this till winter was approaching, when he took us out at dusk one evening to shoot duck on the marshes. I remember the long wait, the dyke behind which we were hidden growing black against the sky, the cold. I don't remember any duck.

When we got back, my mother asked me with false easiness how it had gone? Did Jock talk to you? Not much. Didn't he tell you about – well, various things? No. But didn't he mention Mr Chapman then? No. Gathorne was similarly blank.

I don't know how they resolved our incomprehension, but I do remember the winters at White House Farm. Summers are famously hotter in childhood, winters colder – but in fact there was as a matter of record a run of very severe winters in the last half of the 1940s. The farmhouse had several large cast-iron radiators which ran off the boiler, and with its thick walls and small rooms it was never cold. Heat came from the oil lamps too, which every evening had to be filled, their glasses cleaned, their wicks trimmed and then lit and carried round the house. Some of us had candles. At the same time, the thick curtains had to be drawn tight so that no light escaped. Black Out. The Aga distributed heat, especially to the two radiatorless rooms above it. One of these, the cat room, was left empty because the cats used it to shit in. The sitting room had a deep nine-foot-wide fireplace which burnt huge logs.

The two ponds would freeze over and Fidelity found several tight, elegant, high-buttoning women's skating boots from Glemham around 1910 into which we crammed our big feet and wobbled on to the ice and finally skated. Once, we found about fifteen eels in the bank of the nut grove pond under the ice. Jock cut off their heads and we watched amazed as they continued to writhe and undulate, swimming headless round and round the bucket in the kitchen.

The ground froze and became too hard for riding. The miniature countryside of Suffolk is not much good for sledging. But there was still shooting. Winter transformed shooting, making it an aesthetic experience as well as a hunting one. I would stand transfixed by the beauty of the bare woods against the snow, against the icy blue sky; transfixed by the silence; every breath fanning out in the cold air, when at last the beaters came nearer and nearer banging their sticks against the trees and suddenly a scarlet pheasant would come flying out whirring higher and higher frantic for safety until violently stopped and turned into a tumbling, downward-hurtling bundle of feathers.

In fact, I think I have imposed the self of three years later with that transfixed by beauty. Children of eleven, twelve, thirteen don't exactly feel or think like that. But I had in fact, in those Suffolk woods, begun the transition to such feelings – and it was Tarzan who led me.

(18)

My reading of the Tarzan books happened about the same time that I was given a puppy, a mongrel collie/spaniel. A tiny furry marmalade-coloured armful, he was called Teddy because that was what he looked like. After some initial training by me, Teddy accompanied me on the Burroughs trail.

Like Stevenson with Dr Jekyll and Mr Hyde, and indeed not dissimilar, Edgar Rice Burroughs had hit on an archetype of considerable power, that of the beast that remains buried in civilised man. Certainly, the beast within me became a slave to his books. With Teddy at my heels or more often, at first, dashing with puppy over-excitement into the impenetrable undergrowth, the knobkerrie sent home by my father in hand and, as my feet hardened, barefoot, I took to the jungles round White House Farm. We did in two years manage to trap one rabbit and at once I 'threw back my great head and gave vent to the wild and terrible cry of the bull ape that has made its kill' (*The Beasts of Tarzan*, the only survivor on my shelves of those wonderful books). The little rabbit was taken home and I skinned it and 'so invidious is the virus of hypocrisy' I let it be cooked. Like Tarzan had in a moment of weakness, I ate burnt flesh, while 'he [me too] would have much preferred it raw and unspoiled, and he had brought it down with arrow or spear [knobkerrie, in fact] when he would have far rather leaped upon it from ambush and sunk his strong teeth into its jugular; but at last the call of the milk of the savage mother that had suckled him in infancy rose to an insistent demand – he craved the hot blood of a fresh kill'.

But actual killing was in fact almost irrelevant to the fantasy; all that was needed was more Tarzan books and luckily the prodigiously productive Burroughs had written a great many. The savage mother that had suckled me fed them to me one after the other – *The Return of Tarzan, Tarzan and the Jewels of Opar, Tarzan the Untamed* . . . the end of *The Beasts of Tarzan* promised that 'The further adventures of Tarzan and his son are told in *The Son of Tarzan.* Tarzan's son inherits his love of the jungle . . . The lore of the jungle comes easily to him, and he battles mightily.'

The lore of the jungle: *that* was the point. Teddy and I crept through the woods until we knew them better than Paternoster the gamekeeper. Crept because 'Grim beasts would stalk him, as they had stalked him in the past, and never would there be a moment, by savage day or by cruel night, that he might not have need of such crude weapons as he could fashion by hand.' I, of course, had my knobkerrie, but I learnt to spot the smallest movement of the beasts in an instant – the savage pheasants and ferocious rabbits – and note the slightest sound – the plop of alligator or water hen in the stream, the rustle of deadly snakes through the nettles or bracken – the smell of some dead kill under the leaves and in the brambles, and after a while I could walk barefoot without snapping a twig, skills so vital to survival in a jungle.

Burroughs, at the height of his powers between 1914 and 1930, though he continued to produce long after that, had to write with such speed that there was a good deal of repetition. Tarzan was always 'melting into the jungle' or 'merging' with it, or becoming a beast again, 'one with the other beasts', and as he did so I melted and merged and became one with them too. To merge like this, to concentrate so hard on not snapping twigs or listening for possible savage beasts in the ordinary rustles and movements of an English wood is not just very exciting, at eleven and twelve you can't think of anything else. What I loved about the woods was that feeling of being completely taken up and absorbed by them, oblivious of anxieties about school or Jock or my absent father or indeed anything at all but them.

And to consciously and deliberately merge into the trees and brambles in this practical way is, or at any rate with me became, the first step towards a more aesthetic and mystical merging. It was really an elaboration of my feelings climbing the Faraway Tree. I suggested then that growing up was a process of differentiation within the homogeneity of childhood, a series of developments as we condense out of the amorphous self. This identifying with nature, being moved by nature, which was to become very important to me, seems to be universal. We are animals and we are part of nature. Everyone has his own route to this awareness; mine was Tarzan.

And Tarzan lingered for many years unchanged under his more ethereal manifestations. By the age of seventeen my feet were so hard I could walk painlessly on new stubble or Aldeburgh shingle or on hot tarmac in summer. At twenty-five I was thrown out of the Savoy for not wearing shoes. Today when I walk alone in the woods of Norfolk or the forests of Spain and Italy I am often, still, really Tarzan in the jungle.

(19)

The domestic arrangements at White House Farm consisted of my mother and Fidelity and a shifting gang of supernumeraries, two at a time. Fidel cooked breakfast and supper and one of the local women employed at that time cooked lunch. My mother couldn't cook anything at all. She would help as they chatted. Fidelity said that just after we arrived my mother asked her which end of a potato you should peel first.

As they chatted. Almost my greatest pleasure while we lived with our cousins was to sit in a corner of the kitchen while the endless skein of gossip and description and mimicry and speculation and analysis and memory and laughter wound about and weaved and wandered and doubled back as the potatoes were peeled and carrots chopped, pots and pans put on the Aga and taken off and the two women forgot me sitting, listening, trying to be invisible. Sometimes, breaking from their absorption, they would suddenly remember me – '*pas devant* . . . '. It was a feeling of entrancement, of being enveloped by an only half-, even quarter-understood but fascinating and mostly humorous world that has, in fact, continued to fascinate me ever since – the world of women, of women talking about their feelings and their doings and their friends and enemies and men and children, women gossiping, going back and forth together, with their acuteness and nuances, their sudden ribaldry, their appreciation of each other, their cattiness; all so far richer and more interesting and more sympathetic than male talk – or at least than any male talk I had heard then, and indeed was to hear for many years. I could listen to my mother and Fidelity for as long as they chatted together.

We all made our beds and tidied our rooms and washed up, and one of the local girls came twice a week to help clean. My mother's contribution in this respect was defined, Fidelity said, precisely. She spent a lot of time in her bedroom 'which was *her place*'. She cleaned it every day. (She was later, as I said, as obsessively clean as my father was obsessively dirty and messy. He rarely had a bath.) 'Ruth, as her *general* contribution,' Fidelity added in her customarily pointed way, 'did the stairs.'

I don't think Fidelity quite appreciated the significance of my mother's bedroom for her or for Sammy and me. Once again, it was the only room where the furniture was all ours and once again, but more so, it became our home within a home. More so because, where at Shiplake the house and its expenses were shared, now we were interlopers into someone else's house, there on sufferance, the poor relations. No amount of tact and care and 'fairness' and not mentioning – and there was all of that, especially the not mentioning – could disguise the basic fact of the situation. In her room, my mother would read to us, and read aloud my father's letters which were numerous, and again, although aware I was now too old, I would take the silver animals from their red velvet beds.

And it was along to her room through the frightening darkness of the creaking farmhouse that I felt my way at night when I couldn't sleep. Individuals, just like groups, pick on some particular way to express their anxieties and neuroses. Victorian young women suffered from neurasthenia; today they have anorexia. I, as I've indicated, had picked on insomnia. My mother would wake and uncomplainingly soothe me. She would hold me close to her in her hot, sleep-smelling arms and I would feel the cold-cream on her cheeks, then she would give me an aspirin and I would creep back through the sleeping house and go to sleep myself.

One night, Fidelity came and woke me up. My mother wouldn't get into bed unless I undressed her. I came and did so. Although she was drunk, it wasn't too difficult, except she kept toppling over. But it upset me and frightened me and I remember I cried. Perhaps my father had written to say he wasn't coming on leave after all.

(20)

Once again, I remember my father coming only once, though he must have had several leaves during those three years. This, too, I associate with drink. He had managed to get a bottle of whisky – something extremely rare during the war. Juliet was allowed to carry it into the house. She dropped it. For three days, the adult contingent of the household was plunged in gloom. I also remember his letter after he'd got back to his ship. As a good officer should, he'd let his junior doctor inspect him along with the rest of the crew. He was the only man out of the one thousand five hundred to have fleas. I didn't really appreciate the enormity of this – the PMO with fleas! – since we had them all the time.

I can remember hearing earlier that his ship, HMS *Carinthia*, had been sunk but that he was safe. My mother, Fidelity and Jock listened to the BBC news two or three times a day. That thread which connected them to Alamein or Gallipoli or Singapore vibrated in us too.

On the whole, I loved the war. From the wall charts at school, I knew the outlines, the silhouettes, sideways and from underneath, of all our planes and all the Nazi ones; I knew from the same source the

insignia of all the ranks in the navy and the wavy navy, the RNVR –
Royal Naval Volunteer Reserve – which my father had joined. The
gold bands of rank round their cuffs undulated as opposed to being
straight. My father's ranks, first Surgeon Lieutenant, then acting
Surgeon Lieutenant Commander, would leap out at me. Even today,
if I see these charts yellowing in a museum I get a curious feeling, as
if the past had brushed the underside of my mind.

My fantasies were bloody and all about invasion. I would fight
them on the strait leading to the stream. Galloping on one of the
ponies, hanging low on one side, I would fire my .410, wheel and
gallop away.

England has always been vulnerable along its eastern coast because,
almost as close to the Continent as the southern one, it is flat, cliffless
and rockless. It was here the Vikings invaded. In the 1580s the coast
was armed against the Spanish, but the Armada was swept past on
southern gales. Similar precautions were taken against the Dutch in
the seventeenth century. During the Napoleonic Wars the ring of
Martello Towers was continued way up beyond the Wash. The flat
beach at Aldeburgh – and for miles and miles on either side – was
defended by great concrete blocks against Nazi tanks, and long coils of
barbed wire against Nazi soldiers. That is why we had to swim at Iken
or in the stream. My fantasies, that is, were not totally far-fetched. At
the height of the war you needed a permit even to go to East Anglia.

Troops were everywhere. The importance of Jock's war work –
secret, or at least nameless – meant we were given a small petrol
allowance, but nearly all of it was used by him. We went by bicycle
or else pony and trap. Fidelity was taking us in it to Iken one day,
when we were chased by a tank.

And one night we were violently and terrifyingly woken by a
tremendous explosion. A Flying Fortress had been shot down as it
took off and had crashed into the trees lining the wall round the big
house at Glemham. A hundred yards to the left and it would have
flattened the village, a mile and a half to the right and it would
have flattened us. Its full bomb-load, on fire, continued to explode at
intervals through the night. We hurried to see it as soon as we were
allowed and clambered over the shattered bomber. You could sit in
the pilot's seat (no blood) and we came back with chunks and lumps,

including some unfired bullets. Today the scar of paler bricks in the wall is still visible and the trees behind it noticeably younger.

(21)

My grandmother, too, went everywhere by pony and trap. On my visits to Snape, which were for a week or so every holidays, I would run behind the trap with Tarzan-like bare feet to harden them. The trees in the little wood were now taller by seven or eight foot than I was and serious felling became necessary. The Strong Man of Tilwilly staggered out of the wood and dumped the trunks beside the green hut for later sawing and splitting. I had decided that my wood, which I'd plant when I grew up, would also be mostly pine trees.

Sometime now I first met Benjamin Britten. He and Peter Peers had a converted windmill in Snape village to which they returned from America in 1942, sharing it with his sister Beth Welford. He and Peter, but particularly Ben, became friendly with all of us, later especially with Fidelity and, for a while, me; but now with Bob and my grandmother.

Homosexuals were often drawn to my grandmother because of her sympathy for them. And they, like everyone, also valued her robust common sense. One of these was Siegfried Sassoon. He had briefly been a lover of Bob's and for a longer period a lover of Bob's lifelong companion Kyrle Leng. It was possibly about his marriage or about some love affair that he arranged to see my grandmother in Aldeburgh. I was asked as well. Anne became very excited. 'You are about to see someone *very famous indeed*,' she said. 'You must remember *every detail*.' I do remember some details – an aquiline nose, craggy eyebrows. We had lunch in the Wentworth Hotel. Then Sassoon said to his son, about my age, 'Now George, you go out and play for a while. I have to talk to Dorothy Cranbrook.' Appalled, I realised why I'd been asked. 'You go with him Jonny.' My acquaintance with the great has often been like that.

During the war England, particularly rural England, returned in some respects not just to what it had been in the 1920s but to the 1890s. Private cars almost vanished from the roads, which were empty except for sudden tanks or long convoys of army lorries. As with my grandmother, for many people horses became a recognised way of getting about. Before the maniac Beeching, the railway was not just for major arteries; the countryside was veined with little lines often carrying people to quite small villages. Windmills still ground corn. I remember my grandmother and I going over the windmill at Friston two miles or so from Snape. The air was full of flour and dust and the clatter of machinery; the tall white clapboard structure shook in the wind and strained as the aptly named sails went rapidly round and round with a steady thudding. The maltings at Snape, long since boutiques, cappuccino kiosks, craft stalls and antique shops, was still a maltings where barley was processed for beer, and my grandmother, as a further contribution to victory, had Crisp, who farmed the land all round her, come in and plough and plant with barley the big ten-acre meadow at the top of her little estate.

You could see the Crisp farm across a shallow declivity under half a mile away. Sammy and I were staying at Snape in 1944 towards the end of the war when once again we were woken during the night by a terrifying and violent explosion. One of the latest flying bombs – doodlebugs – had landed on the Crisps. By some miracle, no one was killed or even hurt and the family came and sheltered with us. All the windows along the front of Snape had shattered.

We saw doodlebugs several times at White House Farm. They spluttered like motorbikes through the air above us, the flames of their exhaust orange against the night. You waited for the engine to cut out, but this never happened and they simply spluttered on towards London leaving us to wonder where they would land, what and whom destroy. Did I think that then? I can't be sure. I think it now but, despite missing my father, despite narrowly missing being blown up three times, despite all the other obvious manifestations, the anxieties of my mother, the war still often seemed unreal, more like an adventure in a book.

(22)

Towards the end of our time at White House Farm, when I was thirteen, I began to be attracted to girls. The first was a visitor, Leila Barry, also about thirteen. Leila was American and so, at thirteen, more or less fully developed. Wide-mouthed, slant-eyed, large-breasted, slender but ballet-muscled legs – for her three-day visit I felt a desire quite different to my feelings at Port Regis. I now had the cleaned-up cat room above the kitchen as my own room. Leila slept in the room next to it and after she had gone (alas – for ever) I got into her bed and smelt her intoxicating smell of American cleanliness. I also masturbated by lying face down and rubbing my cock against her sheets, imagining I was making love to her.

Thus I replaced the primitive, if coarsely effective Port Regis hand method by one far more sophisticated and sympathetic to fantasy, later extended to pillows, bolsters and similar soft and feminine objects. Many years later, I discovered that I had accidentally joined an elite. Alfred C. Kinsey, the American entomologist and sex researcher, found that only two per cent of his nine thousand male sample masturbated in this way. They were almost always Jews. In the Talmud, the prohibitions against, and penalties for, masturbation are even more ferocious than those against pre-marital sex. They are couched in terms of not putting hand to penis and to avoid this Jews have had to evolve my system – and this apparently extends even down through three or four generations of non-practising, non-believing Jews. I say I accidentally joined this elite, but it could of course simply have been my Disraeli genes kicking in.

Other genes which were also definitely kicking in at this time were those responsible for the size, shape and timing of female breasts. I have mentioned my grandmother's breasts, but Fidelity too had fine ones; from both sides, therefore, splendid breasts had poured into Juliet and Sophie's blood and these had started to have an effect. It coincided with a sudden increase on my part of an embarrassing and uncontrollable tendency to erections. Practising my ballet gave me erections. So did riding. I remember being naked and having to leap off the seesaw in the garden and run into the house bent double to conceal an erection. It was now that the sharing of baths with my two burgeoning cousins was abruptly stopped.

On the whole we got on very well together. The five Cranbrook children were, at that time, emotionally, my and Sammy's brothers and sisters. But seven children was like a small school. Alliances and enmities would form and break up. Gathorne and I would sometimes fight – once over the existence of God (I said he didn't exist, Gathorne that he did). Rumours would suddenly sweep the school. For instance, one was that it wasn't necessary to chew meat so we swallowed it whole in choking lumps.

Jock's petrol coupons were saved and every summer we drove to another property he had, this time in Westmoreland, a hill farm near the village of Ravenstonedale. I later placed the 'Infant Hercules' story in Westmoreland so that I could write about that beautiful place – about the smell of sheep and the endless sound of trickling, bubbling, running water, about the sheep-cropped trampoline turf, the wind off the fells, the grey curtains of rain that drifted in succession across them, raining in more and more of the soft water, filling the peaty tarns, then lifting and vanishing into sunlight, about the clumps of hard, dark green rushes which could be peeled to their soft white pith; write about mountains like Wild Boar Fell rising into that great inverted ocean of air in whose immense depths one could then, in the mid-1940s, sometimes see a golden eagle, a speck, circling in vast sweeps; about the sudden outcrops of gorse in the valleys whose yellow blossom smelt like crushed moths. We slid on a tray or our bottoms down the long grass of the slope that led to the beck, always full and still perpetually fed by thousands of glinting, gurgling tributaries and running noisily below the squat white farmhouse with its outside stone stair, the beck where I learnt to tickle trout.

It all sounds idyllic – and so, to an extent, it was. But I was by no means always happy.

(23)

This was partly to do with the temperament of my aunt and uncle as they affected me. Jock was a clever, dominant and aggressive man with a quick temper. He was in many respects a natural soldier, and had indeed gone to Woolwich in 1918 as a gunner and rapidly became an officer. But because of a mysterious 'clot', whose origin and danger I could never quite fathom, he had been invalided out. For many years he tried to get back and every year was rejected again because of the 'clot'. His uncle, Frank Gathorne-Hardy, was a general (and was later, thereby, to cause me some trouble) and Jock may have felt that he too would have reached high rank – and he was probably right. The war, in which, had he been a serving officer, he would have played a part, frustrated him intensely and exacerbated his military qualities until as far as I was concerned they became defects. He had with us, as he had with his brothers, an over-developed sense of duty and discipline, something chilling and un-pleasure-loving. He didn't drink (or couldn't – the clot again). His talk was all fact, in the male way. We could quite easily have made butter and cream for ourselves as practically all dairy farmers did in the war, but Jock said we must live in this respect like the rest of the country – something that struck me as ridiculous.

I said Fidelity's style of conversation was one of inspired exag-geration. It was also one of inspired sarcasm and ridicule. She employed this with devastating and often very humorous skill against Jock. She told my mother that she did this deliberately because she was aware of his dominant aggressiveness and was determined he would not damage their children.

But the main reason, even the real reason, all this affected me so much was because of our situation. It was, as I said earlier, bad luck that while practically every other father in Britain was at war I happened to live with what, to me, seemed the only two who weren't. But at least John Hill had only been at home intermittently and was in any case a gentle and uninterfering figure in my life; Jock was neither and was there all the time. My sense of unfairness was compounded because in disciplining and correcting me he was not only presuming to take my father's place; he was also at the same time usurping my own place, since I was the father in our family.

Then, though no doubt there was truth in Fidelity's self-justification to my mother, I think she also exercised her skill because she was very good at it. She enjoyed it (rather as I had enjoyed teasing Webb about his rabbits). Some years later when she helped run the Aldeburgh

Festival this was a facet of her character which appealed to Benjamin Britten, who had a waspish side himself. He loved to hear her sarcasm and he used to let off steam about everyone and everything in short often vitriolic letters to her which, I think mistakenly, she later burnt. Mistakenly – and also by so doing joining another still more infamous relation, Sir Francis Hastings Boyle, the man who actually put Byron's journals on the fire at Murray's.

Fidel loved my mother, loved her I think more than anyone else outside her own family, but she nevertheless sometimes exercised her particular verbal skill both on my mother and me. I'm sure I was often a maddening little boy – I 'showed off', rushed frenetically about, talked all the time, my voice was shrill, but there is nothing more humiliating for young people than sarcasm and when she did this to either of us I minded and secretly hated her. At these times, shooting invading Germans as I hung low on my galloping steed, I often killed Fidelity as well. And this, too, was compounded by our situation. As I grew older, I became more and more conscious of our inferior position, poor relations in the house of rich cousins, as in some Victorian novel, and interpreted things in this light. I would lie awake at night in the cat room and imagine I could still smell shit. Remembering the few times we hunted, I could soon recall only the one where, for reasons I forget, I had to ride a worn-out hired hack while Gathorne galloped ahead on one of our sprightly ponies. Fidelity's sarcasm was a part of all this. Nor was it simple. Gathorne was to go to Eton, I to Bryanston. I resented this. But I didn't want to go to Eton myself. On the contrary, I would have refused. My father had not only forbidden it, he had told Sammy and me on numerous occasions that it had taken him ten years to get over Eton – for reasons which, since nameless, were the more menacing and terrifying. But I simply knew that Eton was smarter, grander, snobbier than Bryanston and that was that. It was part of the pattern.

Resentment is an ugly, demeaning emotion and I don't like feeling again what I felt then (though I suspect that many of these feelings I suppressed at the time and they emerged – or perhaps were added – later). I am aware, too, that I am being unjust to my cousins and in particular to Fidelity and Jock. They were perfectly aware of the delicacy of the situation and took care about it. My being given my own (completely clean) room and my own dog were evidence of this. They often spoke about how when Gathorne and I were twenty-one we would have a huge joint party together at Glemham. The occasional flicks of Fidelity's tongue were as nothing to the efforts she took on our behalf.

As for Jock – what else could he do? There was no obligation on him to have us. He did so out of kindness. He was a just man and certainly treated me no differently from his own children. He was also a more complex and interesting man than I have sketched from my child's perspective. With women who attracted him he could be charming and, even, amusing. He had considerable intellectual integrity. Despite being strongly in favour of the death penalty, when the subject was debated in the House of Lords he read everything he could about it, decided he had been wrong, and voted accordingly. Baulked of the army, he became an extremely competent self-taught botanist and zoologist. Towards the end of his life, like many bullying and aggressive men, he became much gentler. He was called 'Carper' (a grandchild's mispronunciation of 'Grandpa') and used to go fishing with John Nash. I wonder if, as the fish rose, they ever discussed my mother.

There is often an arrogance in large families, in upper-class families often a class arrogance as well. They are self-sufficient, don't need outsiders, and feel it and show it. There is a concomitant sense of warmth, of solidarity and safety. Sammy and I shared in all this for a while. Then the war ended and once again our lives changed, this time, in the end, more fundamentally than when it had begun.

PART TWO

Youth, First Love

(1)

Although my mother's money, thanks to her mad stockbroker, had received a blow from which it never recovered, didn't even begin to recover, we had entered the war with the Knightsbridge practice intact and waiting, still potentially rich, or relatively rich. We left it relatively poor. Against all expectations (or rather hopes) the other partner Landale Clark had been killed. My father was legally bound to pay his widow half the value of the practice. He felt the most sensible course was to sell the practice for what he could get (in fact considerably less than half its pre-war value) and remain in the navy.

He said later that he would have done this anyway, and since staying on was not the only course I think this is true. My father loved the navy. As a boy sailing on the Alde with Anne at Slaughdon, a mile from Aldeburgh, he had fantasised about being a sailor. At Eton, he'd tattooed a tiny anchor on to his arm with a compass point and ink which lasted all his life. When he was twenty he went to Liverpool and signed on as purser in a merchant ship. The ship's doctor was an Indian and my father got on with him so well he was asked to help out in the surgery. The work fascinated him. At one point the doctor had to do an appendectomy in very difficult circumstances, helped by my father. It was his experiences on the merchant ship that decided him to become a doctor himself.

And he loved the navy as a life, both during the war and when he took to the sea again after it: standing on deck at night before sailing, the lights of the port twinkling about him, excitement – a voyage ahead; the ship being towed from its moorings and then the sudden increased throbbing of its engines and the wind freshening on his face

as the twinkling lights receded and vanished, his family vanishing
with them. He would go below for a whisky in the wardroom, or
take one in his cabin. Like us in my mother's bedrooms, he became
adept at making a tiny home in his cabin with photographs, weapons,
the piles of the *Leiston Gazette* he had sent out during the war. He
never loved my mother so much as when away from her (a common
element in service and other marriages I imagine) and was a gifted
letter writer. He also liked the chance to have affairs. (Apparently I
may have an Indian half-brother/sister.) He had hobbies, which
really became accomplishments, skills: he made exquisite belts and
purses out of red and white string; he became more than adept on his
tin penny whistle. All this, with the danger during war, the endless
possibility inherent in long voyages, the camaraderie of the wardroom, the emergencies of medicine far from hospitals, was far closer
to things which were important and which stirred him. Because my
father also said he could never have stood all the superficiality and
flattery and charm inseparable from a practice like his, the necessary
London social life, the selfishness of spoilt rich patients, the unreality
of it all.

Certainly, our life now and hereafter on a series of Royal Naval air
stations was real enough. The Arch, on the air station at Culham near
Abingdon, was the old lodge of the estate that had been taken over.
We had half. This consisted of one room at the top going across half
the archway for Sammy and me, a short twisting stair to a room
below for my parents and another short twisting stair to the living
room below that. Attached to this a small outroom had been built on
for the cramped kitchen and, on top of this, a bathroom, just big
enough for a bath, an Elsan and a basin.

It was the tiny kitchen which eventually brought my mother to
her knees. To cook she had one of those small Baby Bellings with a
single solid plate and a minute oven/grill. But she had to rely
principally on the black cast-iron range. This was the original
Victorian one, with one big oven and a small one. The coal fire also
heated the water in a cylinder above and to the left of the stove. This
stove she came to hate.

It had probably worked very well under the conditions for which
it had been designed. But in order to make an airfield about thirty

acres of undulating, wooded parkland had been gouged out and bulldozed flat in front and on both sides of the Arch, so that we perched about eight feet above the runways sixty yards ahead. Across this metalled plain ferocious winds would race – or else we would be suspended in flat calm. There seemed to be no alternatives. In the wind, the usual state, the stove would roar, hardly to be restrained by its various dampers, its plates would soon glow a dull red, the kitchen became intolerably hot, the cylinder jumped and rumbled as the water in it started to boil and would have to be run off in clouds of steam from the hot taps. In a calm, it would refuse to light or teetered on the verge of going out. My mother, red-faced and blackened with coal from fighting with it, would use the Baby Belling and boil water for us to wash in.

Yet, if cooking was primitive, we now at least had electricity and the chore of cleaning, filling and lighting oil lamps was over. But this was balanced by the Elsan. The boredom and effort of emptying it meant my father always put it off. As a result it was extremely difficult, even helped by me, manoeuvring the over-full, awkward, smelly object down the twisting stairs and out to the pit.

There were other difficulties, but since they were shared by most of the country in 1946/47, and certainly by everyone on the station, we didn't see them as such. Rationing and other wartime emergencies continued until 1953. Few people had cars then (we didn't have one till 1961). Shopping was done by naval bus into and out of Abingdon once a day. Occasionally my father was able to swing a car – 'Send transport to the Arch would you. PMO.' We bicycled. The fridge was a meshed cupboard nailed up outside. My mother did the washing in the kitchen sink and hung it to dry in the gale which seemed to perpetually envelop the house. It was often noisy. Fighter planes landed and took off a lot of the time and about half a mile away the main London train pounded through a deep cutting, invisible but audible and followable in billowing clouds of smoke.

I see now how extraordinarily difficult it must have been for my mother: she had never cooked; despite routine anxieties, always had enough money, a servant or two, her two children looked after or diluted with other children; the husband whom she loved but had been expected to leave gone . . . suddenly, nearing forty, she'd been dumped with the lot, plus the stove. It was now that her blood pressure began to worry my father.

Yet, although the stove did eventually get her down, we were happy at the Arch. I also see now that continually living in other people's houses, continually beholden, had imposed a strain. In our little living room with its coal fire, probably clothes drying some-where, my mother in her habitual position on the floor, legs out, back against the wall which eventually had a patch there, it was as though her bedroom, so long our home, had suddenly expanded to embrace an entire house – or half house. For the first time we were a family – a family whose ingredients I now rapidly began to learn.

(2)

Drink was prominent among its features. My father, at bottom not a confident man, had always to an extent relied on drink, and in later years did so entirely. He also saw it as a medicine. He'd used it with his old ladies in London, and he used it during the war. He found that his young pilots flying missions quite soon, if they weren't killed, reached a high state of tension. The only way to relieve them was to get them drunk so that they would spill everything out to him. It was easier to get them drunk if he got drunk himself.

Drink also received an imprimatur from on high. The *Carinthia* had been sunk in the north Atlantic. It was June and for days the sun shone. My father developed an inflexible routine. Like clockwork, every day from twelve to one he would sunbathe on a hatch amidships. One day his hangover was so frightful he couldn't manage it and simply lay in his cabin. At 12.30 exactly the torpedo which sank them struck underwater directly below the hatch, blowing it to pieces. 'If I hadn't had such a bad hangover,' my father said, 'I'd be dead.'

Money was more insidious. I couldn't properly understand why we never seemed to have any. My father's ranks during the war had always been 'acting'. After the war, when he transferred from the 'wavy navy' to the Royal Navy proper, he began again as a lieutenant. Fairly soon he was a lieutenant commander, and he received a bit more as a doctor; but not till the 1960s' reorganisation of the NHS did service doctors, along with GPs, get substantial rises, by which time it was too late for us. He must still have been paying off the debt on the London practice. No doubt expenses at White House Farm had been considerably buffered by Cranbrook money. Drink, a major item on the budget, was relatively more expensive than it is now. But undoubtedly by far the greatest expense was two sons at private boarding schools.

My parents began to sell things – a large oak table with leaves you slid in. The silver animals in their scarlet beds went. The christening mugs went one by one till only two were left, one mine, one Sammy's. It was like being in a shop with a hopeless turnover. Hopeless in other ways. They were always being cheated. A man came to look at a splendid Edwardian silver salver, embossed and entwined. He offered £20. My mother, aghast, said why so little? Surely it's solid silver? Oh no, love, said the man, turning it this way and that to show there was no silver mark. At last my mother said we needed far more. She'd have to find something else. When my father came back that evening he found the silver mark easily enough. The man had kept his thumb over it. This went on, at a diminishing rate as things to sell ran out, for the rest of their lives. The one thing my mother refused to sell was the 1917 Picasso drawing in its red frame of a Pierrot.

An anxious woman anyway, from now on my mother channelled many of her anxieties into worrying about money. She had good reason. We never went hungry, but food was usually bought on account and bills often postponed or paid by degrees. From the age of thirteen anxiety about money slowly and unnoticed permeated me until it reached the marrow of my bones.

I think about money too much and may even talk about it too much. I am all right if I have money in hand. But if I haven't, or if prospects are bad, I panic automatically – only the relief of paying household bills sometimes overcoming the fear of shelling out. If faced by a choice of purchases I invariably choose the cheapest. As a result all our radios, fridges, washing machines, etc., crack up before they should. All large expenditure terrifies me, and quite small sums appear large. When I bought Nicky's engagement ring twenty years ago (not particularly expensive – about £170) I

suddenly felt extremely sick in the Bond Street jeweller's. I sat down
and began to pour with sweat. It took several minutes, attendant
fluttering, before I was able to write out the cheque. This allergic
reaction to expenditure has not been helped by my eventually
choosing to earn my living solely by writing books, a decision still
only forming at the Arch, but which now received a considerable if
unwitting shove forward from my father.

(3)

It took several months before I stopped feeling shy with my father
when we were eventually all together again. And he was shy of us. I
came to admire him and love him, but I think at a deep unreasoning
level I never totally forgave him for leaving me. Yet in many ways he
was an ideal father for young boys.

For one thing, he was not particularly grown-up himself. He was
almost as messy and untidy as Sammy and me, not only to irritate my
mother but as a relief from the impeccable behaviour and turnout
expected of the PMO. He could sympathise with our fantasies and
enter into them because he was a fantasist himself. He always shaved
with a cut-throat razor, and had a percussion cap, muzzle-loading
shotgun and a signal cannon from one of his ships, HMS *Wolf*, which
fired golf balls. He tried to create a garden in the arid red soil left by
the bulldozers, but became obsessed by his compost, which he fed
dried blood. He had nearly as many penknives, swords, spears and
other weapons as we did.

We had to behave, but he had a much lighter touch than Jock –
and eventually no touch at all. When he came home in the evenings,
he would tell us about cases which interested or amused him. In my
memory, they were all about sex. A petty officer had a length of thin
plastic tubing vanish up his penis. It seemed inexplicable, till my
father remembered, and looked up, a similar case in one of his *Lancet*s
or *BMJ*s. In some men the urethra is an erogenous area which can be
excited in this way. A rating came with one of those large, glass,
pyramid-shaped Gloy pots of glue up his rectum. 'You'll have to go
to hospital,' said my father. 'I can't get it out. How did it get there?'
'I sat on it, sir,' said the rating.

Then one of his own ratings in the surgery kept on falling asleep on duty. My father had him in and it turned out his new young wife was setting the alarm for quarter to five every morning. 'She wanted him to fuck her,' said my father, a note of envy in his voice.

I don't know how long he and my mother went on making love but they didn't have separate bedrooms till about 1956, when we were at 18 Hartington Road in Aldeburgh. They were certainly still doing so at the Arch, because my mother became pregnant with Rose there. But I think he was also having an affair with the sister on his staff. Or, to put it as it was, fucked her from time to time. Barbara Bailey had thick black eyebrows which met in the middle and was always particularly sweet to my mother. I once saw my father kissing Barbara in the back of a car. He was probably referring to this when, as we were lying side by side in some long grass outside the Arch, my father rather drunk, he suddenly said, 'You're like me Jonny. You'll always want to have a mistress as well as a wife.' I think what he meant was that he wanted me to be like him.

On a similar occasion we discussed me writing. 'I think we are about the same cleverness and intelligence,' said my father (true). 'I wanted to write when I was young but' – and this was the shove – 'I realised you have to be very clever to write well and I wasn't nearly clever enough.'

(4)

Patrick, one of the young pilots, and his small, pretty, sexy wife Susan, lived in the other side of the Arch with their first baby. We would have supper with them or they would come to us. Everyone drank too much. My mother and Sue gossiped. Pat and my father would play 'Are You There Moriarty?'. Blindfold, they lay flat on their stomachs holding each other's left hand with a rolled-up newspaper in the right hand. Pat would say, 'Are you there, Moriarty?' and my father would answer 'Yes' and quickly roll left or right or lie still while Pat tried to whack him. You were allowed one whack. If Pat missed, it was my father's turn. When he was hit my father would cry 'Arseholes!' and have another drink.

Or else we would go for meals or drinks to the other officers' quarters, two rows of Nissen huts beyond the surgery. We could have lived there and my mother would have been far happier. But my father, ignorant then of the stove's temperament, had been seduced by the eccentricity of the Arch. Also, he could fire his muzzle-loader or his cannon without disturbing so many people.

And people came to see us from outside. Juliet came once. I remember my Great Aunt Muriel coming to tea. She was my mother's father's sister and it was she who had caught Granny kissing her, Muriel's, husband Gilbert in the rose garden. Although apparently 'very good' with the young sailors she'd befriended during the war, she was a prudish, snobbish, 'formidable' Edwardian lady and my mother was frightened of her. She cleaned feverishly. The living room had light blue underfelt (carpet had been too expensive). Large oily stains of Elsanol, made before my mother realised newspaper had to be laid down for my father to lurch across, stood out blackly. These were concealed. The Elsan was freshly emptied, quantities of extra Elsanol lavishly poured in. Aunt Muriel arrived. Nervous talk. At length, 'I wonder if I might go to your bathroom Ruth?' She was away a long time. When she returned, she was looking extremely displeased. 'Ruth – I think you should know that there's a hornet in your Elsan.'

I think it was at the Arch that my father first planted an extra-ordinary variety of vine he'd discovered. This vine was not concerned with grapes but growth. It was excessive in a way my father appreciated. In a good week its tendrils and shoots could put on six or seven inches.

By the time we left, I knew the station intimately. Between the Arch and the surgery and officers' quarters, there was a wood where Tarzan hunted with his hound and knobkerrie. We bicycled every-where and as the sons of the PMO were waved in and out past the guard at the main gate, feeling important. To this day, I cannot see an army or air force camp, catching sight through the meshed perimeter fences of their huts or hangars or tanks or fighter planes, their concrete roadways and painted signs, without that brush of the past and a feeling that, if I drove in, I'd somehow be welcome.

At night, the almost perpetual wind that my mother came to hate almost as much as the stove, soothed me in the same womb-like way as the wind in the pines at Snape. Sometimes it would drop, and I would hear the trains go past, muffled by the cutting; sometimes my mother and father would be murmuring downstairs. Going back to school was terrible.

(5)

I don't really remember the end of the war. The newsreels followed the Allies as they overran Germany. I do remember, too vividly, the brief, violent glimpse of piles of emaciated corpses at Belsen, before we were hurried from the cinema at Saxmundham by my mother and Fidelity. I was pulled through the door, staring back at the screen.

By chance I was at Snape when Brown and my grandmother paced out the lines from the four trees, fortunately all still standing, and Brown methodically dug down. It was as exciting as buried treasure. Eventually, he reached the bundles of plates, cutlery and jewellery. The greaseproof paper had been useless. The middles of all the plates fell neatly out as they were taken from their parcels. The silver was so tarnished and encrusted with silver rust it was clearly ruined. Only some of the jewellery survived.

And I remember my last term at Port Regis. I was head boy. The winter of 1947/48 was another ferocious one. From November to March it was always snowing somewhere in Britain and there were drifts up to fifteen feet high. The whole school was sent out to get wood from the grounds at Motcambe, near Shaftesbury, where we'd just moved. Someone found a huge stack of peat, twenty feet long by eight feet high over which grass had grown. Every fire in the building burnt peat, including the boiler in the basement, and for a while the school smelled like an enormous nineteenth-century Irish croft.

In the spring of 1948, aged fourteen, and nearly a year before we left the Arch, I went to Bryanston near Blandford in Dorset.

(6)

The headmaster at Bryanston then was Theobald Coade, in the last years of his long reign. In the mythology of public schools – especially of course as promulgated by Bryanston – T. F. Coade has become one of the 'great' headmasters. Brought in, in a hurry to replace the first headmaster, a man called Jeffreys who turned out to be too homosexual even for those homosexual days, he must once have possessed some sort of fire. He had clearly had the gift of choosing (or keeping) talented masters (less sure on mistresses, of which there were few). But by the time I arrived the fire had long been doused by routine, age and corrupted by years of sycophantic praise. Sensibly, he had decided to devote his last years to producing plays. In so far as he still had contact with the boys he was, at least as far as I was concerned, a pompous, self-important, unsympathetic, uninspiring, distracted man continually delivering incomprehensible and irrelevant semi-sermons in the manner of nineteenth-century cleric headmasters. I was overheard calling Nic, who came a year later, a sod. The prefect reported me to Coade and I was hauled in. To me sod was a simple, meaningless term of abuse. I suppose, pushed, I'd have said a lump of turf. Coade assumed I was brazenly foul-mouthing Nic as a bugger. After his half-hour harangue I knew I'd done something frightful but hadn't the faintest idea what. Another time, rebelling against hair an inch long, Nic and I stopped going to the school barber. Coade forced us to cut each other's hair. He stood over us while Nic obediently hacked me into the inmate of a concentration camp, but then he left while I snipped a few stray strands above Nic's ears. I blamed Coade for my horrendous appearance.

He looked rather like Tyrone Guthrie, and may have identified with him, but his fierce concentration on directing plays had two beneficial effects. First, he left his staff to themselves. The first two years of secondary education are of course spent hammering in basic information and basic skills. Mr Royds, for instance, the history master who went on to become headmaster of some other public school and chewed so many Megazones to cover halitosis he smelt like a chemist's shop, had a sort of genius for teaching order and method to chaotic minds. Every book I've written (or will write) was constructed by an evolved Royds system. But it was not till later I realised what it could mean to give inspiring men like Wilf Cowley or Andrew Wordsworth their heads.

The second result of Coade was more subtle and pervasive and made what was otherwise a perfectly conventional minor public school of its time untypical. Since the headmaster, an obsessed figure but still admired and supreme, clearly regarded acting as all-important, all artistic endeavour was elevated and other goals shrank in proportion. Thus Coade's wife had a literary society which I joined and finally helped run, where we read aloud our stories and poems. The *Saga*, under Wilf Cowley, was as much a literary and illustrated magazine as a report of games matches and societies. Gifted artists were engaged to teach us. Roger Hilton, sober then, or mostly sober, taught art. Don Potter, aptly, produced generations of gifted potters and sculptors. (It was really his skilled hand that had shaped the clay horse and alabaster fish which so impressed my grandmother.)

But it was games that, while regarded, shrank in comparison with many other public schools, many still, as they had been in the 1920s, largely institutions for teaching sport. After the first year, you didn't have to do any of the three official games – hockey/cricket/rugger. You had to do *something*: rowing, athletics, and if you were good enough some recognised ball game like squash or tennis, or else you could spend your afternoon 'pioneering' – vague moping-about jobs in the school grounds or buildings, which everyone had to do once a week. Pioneering was run by another obsessed figure called Briggs. Eventually his obsession overwhelmed him and he forced the whole school to build a Greek theatre – no doubt egged on by Coade.

But in the first year you had to do the big ones. The ferocious winter of 1947/48 was still continuing when I arrived and the woods and rounded downland hills in which Bryanston is set were covered in snow. I was going through a phase of wearing black, skin-thin, skin-tight kid gloves, useless against cold, indeed seeming to induce it. Even after chasing the iron-hard hockey ball over the iron-hard turf I came off feeling I had frostbite. At least in hockey you had a defensive weapon or could avoid or flee the cannonball; in cricket, where it was fired even more violently, you were often expected to let it smash into your unprotected hands. But it was rugger that terrified me. I was so light and spindly a tough forward could easily have drop-kicked me over the crossbar. I feel this may indeed have happened. Thank God, in the second week of the autumn term, a branch snapped as Tarzan sped through the upper levels of the forest and snapped my arm with it. I never touched a rugger ball again.

After that, I rowed in the spring and autumn on the winding Stour as it flowed swiftly past Bryanston on its way to Blandford, four miles away, and then on to the sea. In its icy, castrating waters we had to bathe naked. I sculled alone upstream under the drooping beeches. When summer came, I played tennis.

Tennis! The gigantic building which houses Bryanston is set in woods and seems from a distance to be made of red and white rubber Mini-bricks – the 1930s/40s version of Lego. At its back a broad terrace stretches the length and below this, just before the woods and divided by a round pond, eight grass tennis courts stretch its length too. On either side of the steps which lead down from the terrace, long grass banks, mown to a crew cut, also overlook the courts. It is an amphitheatre.

In my memory, when I first stepped out one fine early summer Saturday afternoon in 1948 on to one of these smooth, green, embedded billiard tables (so good were the courts, so effective the amphitheatre, that the Dorset County Championships were often played there), there are, on this afternoon, at first only a few people strolling on the terrace or lounging on the banks. But not long after I begin to play, a sort of electric buzz runs round the school. More and more people run out to watch. The banks become crowded. Who is this stripling, this Mozart of tennis? Now the terrace starts to fill . . .

Tennis didn't save me from anything – even playing no games at all had a certain cachet at Bryanston. But it gave me great pleasure. Nic, who was as good as I was, played as my partner. In my second year we were in the second VI; for the last two in the first VI. I became the secretary, also running the tennis courts, and enjoyed the minuscule power. At Port Regis I had spent whole weekends banging a ball against a wall with a white line on it. Now I practised for hours on those superb courts and played matches on them which continued long into the summer evenings. Afterwards, team tea with a great many cakes and being polite. We went by taxi and played at surrounding schools, stopping for cider on the way back.

However, we were in fact no more than average good schoolboy players. Also, in the end our game – my game at least – suffered as a result of grave character defects. I could not stand losing. Sometimes this made me lose my temper with Nic, a more phlegmatic character than me. Or else, I had shameful recourse to the weapon I had evolved for attack and defence – my tongue. *Sotto voce* taunts and sarcasm, sneers, jokes – since psychology is even more important in tennis than other games such tactics could work. After losing a match, one school wrote that they would not play Bryanston again if I was in the team.

Nic and I played at Wimbledon twice. The first time we were knocked out in the first round. The second time we got through this and had a walkover in the second. But the third round – Bryanston had never got so far – revealed another grave character defect: Nic and I had hangovers. Our defeat was somehow compounded by my white kit, beautifully ironed by Anne with whom I was staying, having turned bright pink – owing to her inability, as yet, to master the new launderettes, just appearing then.

Tennis was run by Wilf Cowley. This small, bald, nut-brown, humorous man, who was to have considerable influence on me, was in his last years and left when I did. Writing, these long drowned figures suddenly float mysteriously up from the depths, their features blurred and distorted but gradually steadying and defining as they wobble up, until they break the surface and there they are clear and sharp, alive – even frightening. Wilf is narrowing his small eyes rather sunken in flesh and making that curious S-shaped movement of his body as he serves at tennis again. Not frightening – though in a year I am to join his house, Portman, reputedly slack. Not frightening, though he quite often lost his temper with me. But Carpenter-Jacobs, who rules the junior house (a mistaken appointment) in which I am now, *is* frightening. Sardonic, sarcastic, saturnine, he looks like Charles II with short hair but has the temperament of a Cromwell. He remarks in his first report that I seem to veer contra-dictorily between a frenetic, over-active, over-excited social life and hours of solitary reading. But he praises me for reading. He gives me the feeling that it is good for me, it nourishes me. I have never lost this, and it is an added pleasure, rather as we eat today partly (some people entirely) to improve our health. There is the same element in my feelings about music and in response two new figures bubble up:

P. D. Rodgers and Timothy Beamish. Rodgers is small, balding, alert, precise as a metronome. Twice a week, instead of lying on our beds after lunch for a quarter of an hour, we go to the music room and Rodgers feeds us Mozart, Delius, Richard Strauss, interfering with our imaginations by gently imposing his own – 'Imagine we are in a moonlit grove . . . ' Beamish is known to be a composer and is not precise at all, but vague and distrait and indeterminate and almost certainly homosexual. He lives with his mother and willows limply about like an artist in a Wodehouse novel, taking a few music classes and teaching the piano.

As quickly as they surface, these figures sink back. I am alone again in the vast junior house dormitory, with its long windows overlooking the terrace and tennis courts and twenty-seven beds jammed together. And here, of course, there is sex again.

(7)

Boys who had been without the benefit of Port Regis's sexual Socrates, now discovered masturbation. Listening in the night to the muffled rasping and creaking of springs, an orchestra of solitary surreptitious sexual activity, we fuelled each other's desire. And now, as we became older, the thud of ejaculation was added to the shivering ecstasy of orgasm, and the flood of hormones added to this, so that, though some vague effort was made out of modesty and embarrassment not to make too much noise, it was often impossible. A boy called Bayley made such a racket that suddenly someone leapt out of bed and stripped off his bedclothes. Caught *in flagrante*, his pyjama trousers round his ankles, Bayley was in his frenzy quite unable to stop and I remember the loud slapping his hand holding his cock made against his stomach. Even today when a pigeon darts out from a wood and I hear the sharp clap-clapping of its wings, I sometimes seem to see Bayley flying out behind, still grotesquely active.

It is quite difficult now, as these powers diminish, and seem about to vanish, to remember the urgency, the dominance of need, in those adolescent days. Almost anything turned you on. Looking up words in the dictionary for instance – 'coitus', 'sexual intercourse', 'vagina', 'masturbation'. The large Oxford dictionary in the library fell open at these entries. Some boys were in a more or less permanent state of erotic arousal and sexual fantasy. A friend of Turner's met him in the woods one hot summer afternoon wearing his raincoat. Asked why, Turner opened it to show that he was almost naked, wearing only his shoes and a spongy rubber bicycle handle grip round his unusually long cock.

Though my father and mother had impressed on me that masturbation was harmless, one official line still being put forward by the well-meaning but excessively dim school chaplain, the Rev. Jarvis, was – yes, harmless, but not if done *too much*! How on earth could you tell what was *too much*? For a while, I tried to restrict it to Saturday night and Sunday morning, but was forced to flee the history room or changing room showers bent double so frequently that I gave up.

I wonder now how poor Newhouse coped when hit by this fresh deluge of testosterone. Did his mother, having saved him once, now teach him to make love to her? A version of this eventually became my solution to this rather esoteric problem. Hermione Potts, her art honed on the bulls of White House Farm, could have handled it.

Already, I felt the solitariness of all this a terrible waste. I furnished it out with fantasies. These were vivid. From pictures of girls or of girls seen, particularly of the sluttish girls who slopped about the kitchen in clogs and did the washing-up. Leila continued to play a dominant part, occasionally joined by Sophie and Juliet, but then fantasy was suddenly powerfully fuelled by the *News of the World*. This contained a report of how a fourteen-year-old public school boy had been seduced by the matron. How I *longed* for that matron. Forty years later, in a somewhat remote way, I was able to make love to her. 'The Infant Hercules' joined my memory of Newhouse to my longing for the matron and I had Newhouse seduced by his prep school matron. Though about their physical passion, in the story the matron without realising it falls in love. At the end, she receives a letter bringing the association to an abrupt end and, running desperately down the Westmoreland hill away from the letterbox, suddenly hears a terrible cry from someone behind her. But the cry – a cry of shock at her realisation both, at once, of her love and of its end – comes from herself.

I put this cry in the novel *Particle Theory* as well. It happens when pain or grief are too great to be acknowledged as one's own and are projected outwards. A similar phenomenon was described to me by Mark Culme-Seymour when he was dying of cancer. He said that, before they increased his heroin, he had had an image of his pain as a white-hot brick in the corner of his hospital room. I only once heard myself the cry I described.

But in fact, at Bryanston now, psychologically the most noticeable expression of sexuality was older boys falling in love with younger boys – primarily, it seemed to me, with me. On the whole pretty young boys were girl substitutes and the feelings aroused were romantic and very strong – as I discovered later myself.

I found the romantic love longings of older boys upsetting and oppressive. Aware that I was being transformed into a girl contradicted my desire to grow into a man, which was, at fourteen, already strong. It was made more intense by my spindly limbs. Also, my voice refused to break. We spent a whole term learning *The Messiah* (music, I was to discover years later, that went deep). After that, I left the choir. To show how manly I was, how unsuitable as an object of desire, I pretended my voice had now broken.

At the same time, confusingly and also contradictorily, I reacted as I imagine attractive girls do react as they discover this. I was flattered by the attention. I felt a curious excitement as I became aware of a power. When the desire was truly homosexual, which it very occasionally was, I was nervous, impatient and I think disgusted. This period, lasting about one and a half years, had a profound effect on me. It affected my attitude to popularity. I more and more disliked it when my mother told me I was attractive or good-looking. All this was the more confusing because I was soon to fall seriously in love for the first time myself.

(8)

We continued to see a certain amount of our cousins. Shortly after the end of the war we all went to the south of France. My great aunt, Jane Gathorne-Hardy, who died in 1943, had had a villa near Vence with some hectares of land which she planned to give to my father but at the last moment, mesmerised by the daft imperatives of primogeniture, felt she ought to add it to Jock's other estates.

My parents, Sammy and I stayed in a hotel in Vence. I hold a few of the brief flashes with which memory illumines patches in the blackness of the past: the oily smell and the green of the bean salad at the hotel meals, the alternating bars of bright sun and shade thrown by the Venetian blinds, heat, walking in the heat across the disused rail viaduct that led to the villa. My mother made friends with a racy and amusing French widow called Doris Décar, with hennaed hair and raddled neck, who said she got great pleasure from suckling a little rough-tongued kitten and that my mother should try it. Doris's companion, a man, was homosexual and sixty and had hennaed hair too. I was with them listening one afternoon by the viaduct when a gust of mistral suddenly lifted his hair into the air. He was completely bald except where the hair had been grown two foot down from the back of his neck and which he carefully and artfully coiled to cover his baldness. As his hair rose up, he tried to grab it with one hand, tried to cover his head with the other, gave a loud shriek and took to his heels, his hair streaming out behind him like a flag.

For many years, we spent Christmas at Glemham. Once again, my parents' bedroom became our temporary home. They always kept a bottle of whisky there for tanking up, sometimes two. On Christmas Day we went round the farmhands and tenants where Fidelity gave out scarves and pullovers and we in turn were given glasses of cherry brandy or neat whisky. How my father was able to stand at the end of these rounds I don't know, but he was one of those heavy drinkers who hardly ever appeared drunk. Gradually, every cell in his body became filled with alcohol but he remained unchanged. My mother at this time was still quite circumspect.

I would be able to go riding again and also shooting. I still loved shooting, except for one thing. I found trying to talk to the men Jock had asked to shoot absolutely excruciating. This had to be done walking between drives or when just standing about. I had realised when very young that the whole adult male world was a secret society. But it was one betrayed by a large number of secret signs — special ways of standing, with crossed legs or one foot in advance of the other or one foot tapping; sometimes they would slowly rise on tiptoe and sink back or pull their noses or put one hand behind their back. I thought if I did these signs I would conceal the fact that I wasn't a member of the society; I might even somehow get in. It was really just a later version of my policeman's uniform. So I would now once again, regressed, stand about in agony, pulling my nose and crossing my legs and coughing in a special way.

But these occasions were sometimes enlivened by my father who came out with his percussion cap muzzle-loader. Every now and again the deep rumble of his broadside would echo across the woods like something in the Napoleonic Wars. The discharge of flame, smoke and wadding would disperse in the wind and be immediately followed by a frenzy of reloading – powder was poured down in reckless quantities, shot and wadding ramrodded in, the flint adjusted, the pan primed, my father, well tanked up, his hair on end looking like Captain Haddock and pheasants, meanwhile, sensing safety, streaming above him. He never hit anything.

We also went to dances. Cider cup and eightsome reels, Sir Roger de Coverley, Strip the Willow and the Dashing White Sergeant. But not only, as time passed, such innocent merriment. Now that young people can on the whole make love together if they are attracted, they dance so far apart they might as well be dancing alone. In those days, if you were middle-class, one of the few places you could come anywhere near touching a girl, anywhere near anything like sex, was on the dance floor. We moved clamped together in semi-darkness, hot, excited, frustrated. But it was a good way of discovering if someone really fancied you.

One Christmas, when I was about fifteen and a half, we went to a dance at Poynders End, near Hitchin, the home of Fidelity's brother Derek Seebohm and his wife Patricia. Their daughter Jennie, aged fourteen and a half, was already a wide-mouthed, slant-eyed beauty, one of those girls already sexually almost a woman, whose sensuality had developed so early and so strongly that already all her perceptions and reactions were seen in relation to it and, as it were, filtered through it. One of the dances was a Penny Dance where you had to dance holding a penny between each other's cheeks. Clutching each other tightly, our cheeks pressed together, we circled the floor. That night we slipped out to kiss upstairs in her bedroom and then returned shaking and breathless to the dance floor, to slip out separately and meet in her bedroom again.

Wherever I went I was attracted to some girl or other, but I was in love with Jennie for about five years. She taught me to French kiss. I remember her guiding my hand inside her dress and up under her bra to her breast in the back of the car as we were driven back from some dance or other. I remember the desperately urgent, clumsy, blunt, hot physicality of our passionate embraces in the spare rooms or attics of different country houses while Strip the Willow or a quickstep floated faintly up from below. What we really wanted, what it was clear to me even then should have happened, was that we should go to bed together. But, allowing much, this Jennie somehow didn't seem able to allow. I discovered years later that Patricia had, in the strongest possible terms, 'warned her against me'. In fact, the entire Seebohm family seems to have been put in a state of panic by the Penny Dance. Freddy's daughter, Vicky Seebohm, told me she too was warned how dangerous I was in this respect. Alas, I was never in a position then to test her resolution. Perhaps it would have faltered.

It was against such strictures that our world was beginning to rebel. Jennie could not quite escape. If she had, our two lives might have been quite different – and perhaps happier. Certainly, mine would have been both. But even today when I think of her then – and of her sister Alison who possessed the same miraculous sensual-sexual magic – my heart beats faster.

Before we left Glemham, we would discuss mine and Gathorne's still distant twenty-first birthday party, plan future visits and dances, and then set off by train for the Arch again – and, later, Lydford. Or else, my parents and Sammy would go, and I would stay a few days at Snape.

(9)

It was about now I began to see much more of Benjamin Britten whenever I came to Suffolk. The basis of our friendship was tennis. If I was staying at Glemham he would drive over and we would play on the field-like grass court there. If, more usually, I was at Snape he would pick me up in the Rolls (or perhaps it was later they got that), and we'd play on one of the municipal hard courts at Aldeburgh, and he'd drive me back. Sometimes, and gradually more frequently, we'd play later and then go to Crag House on the front where he and Peter now lived and both have a bath. Sometimes I would stay and have supper with them and Ben would drive me back afterwards.

I remember the atmosphere of those early encounters clearly; it was not entirely simple. At one level he had an extraordinary empathy. He was gentle, intuitive, clearly moved by our poverty, anxiety about which I was starting to express, interested not just in my ambition (at that time to be an actor) but in my feelings. The expression of this empathy, which he showed to quite a number of young boys and which was no doubt one spring to the genius he had writing music for them, was often almost Enid Blyton: facetious, boys together, Ben – teasing, ironic, jokey, slightly flirtatious – the older, just. He returned, I'm sure, in a deeply sentimental way to his own adolescence and, when he smiled with his lopsided rather soppy expression and put his arm affectionately round my shoulder, he was also putting it round himself.

In contrast was his ferocious competitiveness. I took games off him but I don't remember ever beating him at tennis, nor at squash, which we played later. And being beaten by Ben was quite literally like that. Later on, it made me think of Peter Grimes.

He was not an altogether easy companion. There would be awkwardnesses, sudden fleeting tensions, silences; Peter was a much more relaxed and obviously charming character. But, apart from something almost sadistic in his cool destruction on court, there was nothing remotely threatening about Ben, his kindness was self-evident, his sympathy felt. A public schoolboy of my generation, especially one now thoroughly over-sensitised in this respect, could tell if someone desired them in about four seconds, and I was of course perfectly well aware he was attracted to me. I was not nervous; nevertheless I was already rehearsing a variety of responses. I also suspect that, as at school, I could not help flirting slightly – or perhaps the awareness was itself a form of flirting, and Ben (himself returning to public school mode) was conscious I was aware, or wondered if I was in fact and to what degree, and it was the whole edgy tension of it that stimulated him.

(10)

On the first day I returned from Bryanston at the start of our last seven months in the Arch, my mother was in the bath.

'I suppose you think I'm looking very fat,' she said, which I hadn't been thinking. 'Well, I'm pregnant.'

She was forty, about to be forty-one, and tried to shift the baby with gin but thank goodness failed. They left the Arch in early April 1949, when I was about to be sixteen. My mother went to Glemham, my father went to HMS *Heron*, the Royal Naval air station at Yeovilton in Somerset, Sammy and I were at school. We had been promised a Nissen hut whose layout we could dictate and had drawn a great many plans. My mother had always longed for a girl and Rose was born on 18 April in Ipswich Hospital.

When we came back in July, my parents were well settled into our new home at Lydford. And now there was Rose.

(11)

Lydford was a small collection of houses, not really a village, at a crossroads on the Fosse Way, about four miles from HMS *Heron*, itself about four miles from Yeovilton. Our house was called the Poplars.

It was square and plain like a big council house, with plenty of spare outside wall to take the explosively growing vine once the cutting, brought from the Arch, got going. The house had four bedrooms and quite a large garden behind a few poplar trees. As far as my mother went it was a huge improvement on the Arch. Lavatories (two) with plugs to pull, an Aga, she also had fifty-nine-year-old Mrs Buckle in to help twice a week for two hours. On her first day, Mrs Buckle had looked lovingly at three-month-old Rose asleep in her pram. 'What a sweet little thing,' she said. 'I couldn't harm a hair on her sweet little head,' which my mother thought rather an odd remark. Not till we were leaving did she learn that Mrs Buckle had served twenty years in Broadmoor for killing, in an attack of madness, her own two little children with an axe. 'They might have told me,' said my mother.

Nothing happened, and I imagine if she had been told, Mrs Buckle would have had to go – but she was needed. To start looking after a baby, effectively for the first time, at forty-one cannot have been easy. Then, though he had obviously fiercely reined in his desire for bizarre dwellings, my father hadn't noticed that all the water in the house had to be pumped up to the attic by hand. There was again no fridge, though there was a big larder.

But, desperate in her anxiety to keep the home clean, we were still my mother's main burden. As Sammy and I became more adolescent, we became just that. And the biggest adolescent of all hadn't grown up much. Events in the final years of his life suggest that he still needed, unconsciously, to rebel against the nursery disciplines of his childhood, the beatings of his prep school – but the recipient, now and later, was my mother. In the garden he grew tobacco. This was harvested and hung to 'cure' in the garage above his mushroom beds. He would eventually cut it with cheap naval shag and roll it into untidy cigarettes. It was like smoking old jeans and he emitted clouds of unpleasant-smelling black smoke like a rubbish tip on fire. But the soft dampness of Somerset meant that 'curing' often took place above the Aga, much to my mother's irritation. I also remember him making 'Bovril' on the Aga, which involved boiling a smashed-up calf's head for hours. He made beer, but bottled it too early in order to give it a good head. Stored in the larder, one of the bottles exploded, then another, then another. Visiting the larder became hazardous, but couldn't always be avoided. Even one of his main occupations, knotting exquisite belts and purses out of thin but very strong red and white string, which he'd learnt in the war, made a mess.

My mother was a victim, and victims choose partners who will victimise them. My father fitted the bill, but usually not too grossly. He was a kind man and also completely dependent on her. There was also a strict limit to my mother's need to be a victim. She could be sharp. If the limit was exceeded badly she would clench her jaw and not speak to us. This was unendurable (it could last all morning) and we would soon all do whatever it was we hadn't done – wash up, help pump water, tidy our rooms, clear up Bovril or tobacco mess – and things would relax again.

As at the Arch, my father's adolescence made him an ideal companion. They were neither of them religious (my mother had been, and perhaps at some level still was; my father attended naval services in the line of duty), nor have I the faintest idea of their political views – if they had any. I would guess usually Conservative. I often read in the evenings, as did my mother, while my father worked at his latest belt, but he was perfectly happy arguing about the existence of God, or if democracy worked, or anything else that school and reading made me bring up. As it got later, and my mother went to bed, he and I drank more scrumpy, the lethal local cider, which he alternated with whisky, and our talk would wander to his past or the war or some fracas on the station or what we would do if we were rich. We'd try and invent a system of pulleys and hammocks that would take us upstairs and tip us into bed without us moving or undressing. Sammy remembers my father asking him one Saturday night to get him three jugs of scrumpy and a chamber pot and how furious my mother was to find him there in the morning, the jugs empty, the pot full.

But my father's mess-creating activities had another purpose. Aside from the convenience, the well-off run up bills because they can pay them; the poor try not to because they can't. My parents often couldn't but they were unable to kick the account habit. School bills *had* to be paid and overdrafts were strictly controlled, but things like pub, garage and village shop bills grew inexorably. The chief figure here was Mr Maggs, who seemed to own or run everything in Lydford. Quite soon my father began to owe easy-going Mr Maggs considerable sums. I remember one morning seeing the ashtray beside his bed piled five inches high with ends from the cigarettes he'd smoked from anxiety during the night. The tobacco, beer, perhaps even the Bovril, were all partly attempts to deal with this. More effective were the continuing sales – the second (and last) silver salver, bits of my mother's jewellery, an oak tallboy. Then one day they came to me. My Post Office savings had slowly accumulated into £100. Could they cash these in? I felt extremely proud of this, which I like to think temporarily cleared everything off.

The Maggses' son Peter was my age and we used to do things together, principally spending hours spying on a path hidden by a

hedge where local couples went to snog. We always hoped to find
them shagging ('snog' and 'shag' both new words to me), but I don't
remember we were ever successful. As at the Arch, a railway line –
the main London–Exeter – ran about 200 yards from us passing over
the old Roman Fosse Way which ran immediately behind the
Poplars. It was down there, Tarzan now starting to give way to, or
rather amalgamate with, Keats and D. H. Lawrence, that Teddy and
I set off on long walks.

(12)

Peter Maggs and I liked each other. Class only slowly reveals itself
and impinges on children. The village boys Nic and I had fought at
Shiplake had not been class enemies so much as Germans. I was not,
therefore, aware of the 'classlessness' of wartime, except that may
have been what delayed my awareness of the class attitudes and
antagonisms in England in the 1940s and '50s – and which are still
here now, if slightly disguised and muted. That, and the fact that
everyone got on with my mother. But I do remember noticing how
the papers more and more reported things other than the war or
things related to it. I remember thinking how trivial they'd become.
I was aware, that is, of the dispersing of unity, the vanishing of a
common aim, which is something different – or perhaps another way
of looking at the same thing.

I was also aware, even if it didn't seem to involve us, of the
growing enrichment during the '50s. I didn't like it. It seemed
somehow wrong. I suspect many people of about my age feel that –
the induced puritanism of those brought up in the war. It may sound
odd, from someone always anxious about money, but I have also
never wanted a great deal of it. My anger at primogeniture was not,
fundamentally, about money – though it was sometimes expressed
through money – but about unfairness.

(13)

Nevertheless, some of the growing wealth must have trickled down to us. My father at last bought some transport, a small motor scooter called a Corgi, crude ancestor of the sleek modern Vespas and mopeds. It had been patchily developed from those dropped by parachute in the war and was still essentially the same as them. He would putter off to work on it and would tow Sammy and me in line on our bicycles to Sunday services on the air station, fulfilling both his duty and his role as the eccentric PMO. He also rode the Corgi back from station cocktail parties – he called it 'Coming home on George' ('George' was slang for automatic pilot) – and it had an almost miraculous power of carrying him safely home half-drunk.

Once I was sixteen I could ride it too and did for two hours or more at a time, skimming low along the undulating lanes, intoxicated by its effortless speed, up and down, up and down the rolling billows of Somerset downland until I felt I was flying. People came to visit or to stay. Betty Richards came quite often. She was a rich friend of Heywood and Anne's and, when we knew her, tall, heavily but still somehow elegantly built, and amusing. As Betty Fletcher-Mossop she'd cut a considerable swathe through literary and social London in the 1920s and '30s. She had a London house, but now spent much time, first in a small but perfect early-eighteenth-century house near us, and later in a large country house with park and lake guarded by high walls more or less in the middle of Yeovil. Her voice had deepened and roughened with time, gin and cigarettes, and her face was round and red and her black eyes popped out, but she had been a beauty. Before her marriage to Nigel Richards, shot down and killed in 1943, I think she must have had a good many lovers; at least that is what I imagine she was inferring when she tossed out 'drenched in spunk' as I stepped on to a thick white sheepskin rug in front of a fireplace in her smaller house.

As well as witty in the slightly outrageous way typical of her period, she was something of a maverick. She didn't mind what she said or to whom and, not caring if her behaviour shocked people, could cause considerable chaos. At the Aldeburgh Festival once, wanting to pee, she heaved herself on to the basin in her large, expensive bedroom in the extremely stuffy Uplands Hotel. There was a brief pause, then the whole plumbing system was ripped from the wall, sending hundreds of gallons of water plunging down to the rooms below. Betty thought it monstrous to have had such a flimsy appliance installed.

She was very intelligent, very quick – and also extremely generous. She came to see us because my mother made her laugh and she admired my father, but she was also upset by their evident hard-upness. With an abrupt, embarrassed gesture, going even redder, she would stuff handfuls of those large floppy old fivers down my mother's bosom. Sometimes, long after she had left, another would turn up thrust deep.

I came in for some fivers too – and more. When, still shy of her, I first stayed alone at her big house, I couldn't find my only trousers, the ones I'd come in, after my bath the first evening. I searched frantically, and then, very embarrassed, with a towel round my middle, went and told Betty. Enquiries revealed that her butler Alfred had come and said, 'What should he do with the young gentleman's trousers?' Betty had said, supposing he meant should he iron them or have them cleaned, and imagining more than one pair, that he should do what he thought fit. Alfred had thrown them away. I borrowed some for supper and next day we went into Yeovil and she bought me not only new trousers but a new suit and shirts.

In love with Jennie and more and more aware all the time of attractive girls, my fantasies entirely heterosexual, my memory now is that my mother's hysterical fears about homosexuality had left me untouched. But this, again, is the magic of Ambrose casting itself back twenty-five years. The truth was quite different and was revealed by something which happened when we had another visitor. The events took place, unfortunately, the night before I was due as godfather at the christening of Andrew and Harriet Wordsworth's son Oliver in Dorset.

Biddy Harrisson resembled Tallulah Bankhead in more than her wide-mouthed now disintegrating good looks. She had had dozens of lovers and several husbands but kept the name given her by Max Harrisson, the anthropologist who invented Mass Observation. She was likeable, louche, and my parents were fond of her, enjoyed her sense of humour and the general panache of her bad behaviour, but now slightly dreaded her drinking. They had been asked to a station cocktail party and explained to Biddy it wasn't possible to take her. 'Never mind dear,' Biddy said to me, 'we'll have our own little *tiny* cocktail party.' She sent me to the pub to get two jugs of scrumpy and a bottle of gin. Most of what followed is now hazy. I remember Biddy telling me that the great thing about making love was that you could do it anywhere. By the time my parents returned, I was very drunk. I somehow inveigled them all into the larder and locked the door (it was the period of exploding beer bottles). Apparently, my mother told me afterwards, I then shouted out several times, 'You think I'm a bugger but I'm not, I'm not.' I remember my father putting me to bed, my being sick, then him being sick (vomit always had this effect on him, an odd trait in a doctor you might think – except I suppose nurses usually do such tasks).

The next morning, I had my first major hangover. I had to get up at five to catch the buses (the journey involved several changes) to Childe Okeford where the Wordsworths lived. I took my last christening mug and, feeling terrible, set off. I was sick again waiting in the dazzling sun for one of the other buses. My christening mug was greeted with amazement. When I got back I found that I had grabbed Sammy's by mistake and had to ring and ask Harriet Wordsworth to send it back.

(14)

The Wordsworths' friendship did much to ameliorate my last two years at Bryanston, but, although I was fond of them, I don't think they had any particular influence on me beyond this. Coade, whom I was not in the least fond of, had more.

For a variety of reasons, all schools encourage acting but at Bryanston, because of Coade, it was elevated into a major school goal. For two years I wanted to be an actor. In my second term I was the Winslow Boy. I acted in several of Coade's productions: Anouilh's *Antigone*, Sophocles' *Oedipus Rex*, Shaw's *You Never Can Tell*, *The Lady's Not for Burning*. This was the heyday of Christopher

Fry. Coade did several of his plays and loved intoning in the portentous nasal style he affected that eclipsed the man's often, to my ears then, moving verse. We took *The Lady's Not for Burning* to Bournemouth and London. I also acted in several of the plays my friend Terence Mullins put on. Mullins wanted to be an actor too and we became close. At the end of two years it became clear he was a far more talented actor than me. The actor, like the dancer, sank inwards – but was not entirely lost. Writing, at least some of the writing I have done – history, fiction, biography – often involves a sort of inner acting.

But since Jock was already writing me letters about how vital it was I chose a job with a pension, and since acting was notoriously fickle in this as in every other aspect of a sound career, I also seriously considered becoming a doctor. My brief incarnation as nurse when five at Snape indicates, if obliquely, that I, like all the children of doctors, had early had intimations that I might perhaps join my father. Now science started to reinforce this.

The biology labs had been built in the old stables near the squash courts and the gym-theatre. Dogfish, waiting for dissection, swam to eternity in the formaldehyde whose curious smell pervaded the long chart-lined rooms. There was something magic about having oneself explained and positioned in life and having its extraordinary mechanisms revealed in Mr Harthan's methodical classes. What was magical was that I could understand them. My brain sent electrical messages to my fingers which then closed. There, stretched on their small racks, severed frogs' legs twitched when current was applied. My Adam's apple was growing next to the site of my thyroid gland and in response to it. In that tank, fed on thyroid tablets, tadpoles in a speeded-up film became minute mature frogs in a week. Worlds more miniature still, sliced and stained, pulled into focus under microscopes. The light often became dim from the plants growing up the windows.

A second Mr Potter laid down the inflexible laws of physics. He was a powerful thumping man with the small, red, wet, sensual mouth of Henry VIII, and he too had the gift of clarity. Except when someone forgot to light a Bunsen burner, his labs smelled of nothing. Prisms, mirrors, thermometers, pipettes, calipers, scales, slide rules, graphs – light, colour, temperature, mass, density, weight, sound; there was something exhilarating in the inevitability and inflexibility of those laws. If the answer was different, you were at fault, not they.

I would have followed science and might indeed have become a doctor if it hadn't been for Miss Wilson. Perhaps my father had had a Miss Wilson too. My Miss Wilson was one of the few women on the staff and she had grown large and masculine, her furry face grey with smoking, in order to conceal this fact. She made chemistry incomprehensible and if you tried to untangle what with screeching chalk she'd scrawled across the blackboard, she answered with such glaring and scorn you didn't try again.

It is difficult, looking back from what took place, to know how serious these ambitions were. I feel now that I always knew I would be a writer, a process I located beginning in the stories I told myself as a child. Once started, I followed everything that encouraged this and rejected anything that didn't. Rejected, or transformed; my father's joint put-down, that neither he nor I was clever enough to be a writer, had made me determined to prove him wrong while at the same time secretly fearing he might be right. Perhaps acting and medicine, that is, were needed as disguises behind which my real ambition was able to become so much part of me it could not be eradicated or evaded.

But there is a sort of instinctive determinism in the way we view the past – our own, other people's, other countries'. Whatever is, was inevitable. Surely, if my family had been ballet dancers, as I said, if Terry Mullins had excelled at rowing or at nothing, if Miss Wilson had had a stroke or, more likely, been murdered, would my life not have been very different?

(15)

Something else now came into play which also had its origins far back, back in that homogeneity of childhood I referred to: the childhood fusion of self, imagination and the outside world whose complex elements condense out as we grow up – or grow older. One of those elements whose power to absorb I had already experienced via my own peculiar route – Tarzan – now took on the status of an elemental force. The woods round Bryanston ceased to be jungles and became, with the great green ocean of downland, with the currents of air which endlessly flowed across it, tossing the cowslips and orchids and pouring down into the valleys and occasional fields of undulating wheat or oats, with the river sliding like a serpent swiftly between them, suddenly possessed of the most extraordinary power. In winter I would sit entranced by the branches of the enormous beech trees outside my study, black against the grey sky, intricately entwined and interlaced and sighing in the wind till I became entwined in them myself.

These feelings were confirmed (and perhaps created) by reading. I now began to have love affairs with a succession of writers – that is, I would read all their books, sometimes two or three times, and then read everything about them. I spent all my pocket money on Penguins or second-hand books in Blandford. But it was on my mother's shelves at Lydford that I discovered for myself Virginia Woolf and, that writer above all to fire adolescent pantheism, D. H. Lawrence. Two of my mother's favourite writers, product of her sense of humour, were Thurber and the Grossmiths of *The Diary of a Nobody*, which I enjoyed but which did not become passions, perhaps because they weren't my discoveries; but nor did Ivy Compton-Burnett who was. Next to her (the shelves were chaotic) was *The Real Life of Sebastian Knight*. I was intrigued, but my literary love affair with Nabokov did not begin till eight years later, two years before I worked for Weidenfeld and briefly met the author. As intoxicating – and sometimes as stylistically fatal – as Scott Moncrieff's Proust (another later affair) I was in thrall to Nabokov for several years. Yet the strange thing about these obsessional literary love affairs is that, once over, the writer seems to have been consumed. I still admire these four, and several others; I cannot bring myself to reread them.

My passionate feelings for nature, my reading, had a number of effects. I was never particularly religious, at Bryanston or anywhere else, but I considered that these nature experiences were in fact religion. Indeed, I later reversed this and wondered whether all religious experiences weren't actually derived from, or disguised, intense feelings about the natural world. Mystics, even ordinary believers, talk of the need to 'transcend' the self. I don't think I felt I transcended myself in the sense of becoming or reaching something higher – but I could easily think I had done this if I had wanted to. Even at seventeen it did not seem surprising that we could feel absorbed by, possessed by, one with, the natural world – since we were so obviously part of it. I realised it could have been my severed limbs not a frog's twitching on the rack in the biology lab. That we are animals and how much so has become clearer and clearer. The culture dictates the forms of the identification and absorption, but it has existed at all times and worldwide. In fact, that it is also the root of religious feeling and therefore of the belief in God was proved to me when He manifested Himself to me and told me so Himself – at least that is how I eventually interpreted a rather mysterious event that took place years later.

The fact I could have these tremendous feelings made me feel special, chosen. Peter Levi, in *The Frontiers of Paradise*, suggests that this is an important ingredient in the make-up of certain artists (Rimbaud for example) and may be connected to awakening sexuality – 'the emergence of repressed sexuality without object'. It may be so. There was certainly a good deal of awakening sexuality about, though not particularly repressed and not without object. Nor was I alone. I think most of Bryanston felt special in some way or other. And we were right to feel that.

The forces that burgeon in adolescence are very powerful; what they promise is wonderful and for a while seems possible. Bryanston, like all groups of young people, particularly the encouraged 'privileged' groups at public schools, was full of geniuses. The only difference between those who became writers or painters and those who didn't is that something like this, the memory of it, continues to be necessary to artists to sustain them in their solitary pursuit, just as the fires of romantic love are now necessary to fuse couples for the long haul of marriage.

Under this impetus I began (again with most of the school) to write poetry. I remember an exalted Lawrentian poem that began 'Today I was the lover of a tulip'. Since the Arch, I had found that back yards, railway sidings and derelict areas and allotments seen from trains, kitchens, washing-up, dustbins – the ordinary in fact – were just as moving as the more obvious beauties around Bryanston, and I wrote a poem to express this – Wilf Cowley told me T. S. Eliot felt the same – called 'Behind the Face of Houses'. Nick Tomalin, three years older than me, couldn't read my handwriting and thought it was 'Behind the Face of Horses', a subject so original he at once thought he would publish it. I have never hero-worshipped anyone, but I admired Nick Tomalin because, among other things, he was editor of the *Saga* (actually, as I write, I think I did almost hero-worship the immense wedge-shaped spread of his black pubic hair glimpsed sometimes in the shower room). Later tragically killed in the Israeli-Arab conflict, he was a gifted journalist and a man of great attractiveness. The timbre of his voice had a peculiar charm, as did his slightly cynical, quizzical, often humorous comments, made with his head on one side. Sometime after he'd left, Wilf made me editor of the *Saga* and I was able to publish anything I wrote.

Charles Handley-Reader had a class once a week broadening the minds of those in the sixth form who wanted this. He had pale red hair carefully brushed back in tiny, rigid wavelets like sand after a departing sea, sand-speckled fastidiously gesturing hands and a clear, strong mind. Freud, Darwin, Jung, determinism/free will, child-upbringing, modernism in art and literature – in his brief, dazzling lectures a kaleidoscope of new intellectual dimensions flashed in front of us. He later killed himself in a horrifying way (he cut off his penis in the bath), and it is true there was a tension, at that time creative.

Then there was Mr Gillett, the senior French teacher. Mr Gillett, both cynical and kind, was an existentialist; Sartre-like, too, in his acne, his Gauloises and his brilliant mind, the density of his massive brain seeming to make his head almost too heavy to support. He lent me his rare edition of *Ulysses* but, apart from not understanding it, I spilt Nescafé on it and fifty of the expensive rice-paper pages fused together. I returned it silently to his shelves a few days before I left.

As a result of these two, I became fascinated by intellectual speculation. Mullins and I prepared a paper – 'Man as a Pattern-forming Animal'. I can't remember what was in it precisely, but it took weeks and was delivered jointly to the Da Vinci Society. This was an honour. The Da Vinci Society, run by Andrew Wordsworth, was usually addressed by distinguished visitors, often writers. I can remember Stevie Smith standing on a chair to deliver one of her poems and making herself giggle so much she nearly fell off.

Mullins had bright red hair, small quick-moving light brown eyes, a wide mouth and the difficult stimulating temperament of the Celt. We shared a study and argued and went smoking together in the Hangings – as the woods above the Stour were called. He would take offence and get over it more or less simultaneously. He moved oddly, his limbs splayed.

What has happened to him? What has happened to all of them – to Woodstone, for instance, or Newhouse? What has happened to the boys I loved?

(16)

Actually, I did try and find Mullins once. I got rather drunk in London (Carlton Mews) two years after leaving Cambridge and at two in the morning rang up all the Mullinses in the directory, causing some annoyance. I didn't find him, though I remember one odd fact. Terry had never told me, or I'd forgotten, what his father did, but out of about twenty Mullinses two were chimney sweeps.

Woodstone was small, hunched-up and, at seventeen, still completely undeveloped – beardless and pubic-hairless, ball-less, his voice still piping. He was teased over this, but fired back with such good humour he seemed scarcely to mind. Then one day all the tadpoles' thyroid pills vanished from the biology lab. Woodstone had clearly minded a great deal and the theft heralded a nervous breakdown. Yet, showing considerable courage (was it foolish or wise of his clergyman father?) he came back six months later, I can't remember in what hormonal state.

As for the boys I loved – I don't want to know what happened to them. I prefer, when I think of them, which I do by chance about once every five years, that I should see them as they were, embalmed in the amber of my past desire.

Yet – what sort of desire? Martel, aged fourteen and with a *gamin* face, had green eyes, light olive skin, lightly freckled, light brown hair growing low on his neck, and long beautifully shaped legs upon which he moved with an awkward grace, his feet slightly turned in.

In love with him, too terrified to show it, I would now stand for a quarter of an hour at the end of a corridor down which I knew he might come – as I suppose love-sick youths of eighteen must have stood hoping to see me three years before. I would place myself so that I could stare at, devour, his beautiful face without him being aware of it, filled with a yearning part pain, part ecstasy, part tenderness, part sadness. If we accidentally brushed against each other when he came to book a tennis court (he played tennis) my heart would hammer for ten minutes.

Did I want to have sex with Martel? The obvious, psycho-analytically inspired assumption would be that I did but that the taboo on homosexuality was so strong that I suppressed the desire and transformed it. That in fact all male public school loves – the situation was universal – were disguised homosexual love. Certainly this was sometimes so. There were lustful encounters which were really just expressions of, outlets for, pure sex. But these were usually between contemporaries. This did not happen to me. The situation I was in – along with practically everyone in those highly (and absurdly) artificial, single-sex, youthful environments – was more complicated; in the end more extraordinary. Nearly all the youths of seventeen, men of eighteen fell in love with boys in place of girls – since there were no girls. This was the aspect I had sensed earlier and hated. But to create the illusion, they had to be younger – thirteen, fourteen; to preserve it, they had to be chaste. Chastity, in turn, created the peculiar form of the love.

It was, essentially, the chaste romantic love cultivated for its intensity of feeling by the Muslim countries of Arabia in the ninth century and, from them, at the Court of Eleanor of Aquitaine in the twelfth. If Eleanor had come to Bryanston, or any single-sex public school then, she would have seen at once what was going on. Nor was it or is it negligible. It is the same chaste but all-consuming passion that runs through Hazlitt's *Liber Amoris* or *Eugene Onegin* or, less refined but no less strong, it is why Mills and Boon books are read and why young girls fall in love with pop stars. That yearning, that unconsummated, not to *be* consummated, never-ending longing *is* an extraordinary feeling.

Masters at public schools at that period panicked at the intense current of passion swirling between the young men and the boys but there wasn't much they could do. Some of them shared in the passion, since the best schoolmasters of boys often have a homosexual element. At Bryanston, Cranborne Chase, the girls' school at Crichel was, I suppose, meant to mitigate our longings – or at least transfer our fantasies. Certainly, I lusted after one or two, distantly seen, but Crichel (as it was always called) didn't succeed in this because Coade was terrified of any real contact. Crichel girls, for example, were banned from joining the weekly dancing classes, where they could have played a mutually useful and harmless role. Instead, we danced with brooms. The class was taken by Mrs Lethbridge, a beautiful creature of twenty-seven. After she had demonstrated a new move in the quickstep, a neat reverse chassé, say, she would put on Victor Silvester and call out lightly, 'Now, collect your partners.' We would walk over to the bundle of long-handled brooms stacked against the wall and shuffle round, the dust-laden bristles against our cheeks. For a brief moment, Mrs Lethbridge, lithe and strong but light as a feather in the hand and with that marvellous feminine capacity to lead while seeming to be led, would take each of us in turn. Then, her fragrance still floating in the air, it was back to your broom.

Of course, boys and girls at mixed schools have equally intense feelings for each other, but these merge and blur into later, consummated, passions or are, today, soon consummated there and then. The public school loves of heterosexual young men in the past were never repeated – and were never forgotten. These love affairs flung far into the future 'a spell', wrote Disraeli in 1844 in *Coningsby* 'that [could even] soften the acerbity of political warfare'.

Cyril Connolly, about whom I was later to have rather ambivalent feelings, was at the theatre with Eliza, a mutual friend, when he suddenly noticed a large red-faced man with a nicotine-stained moustache and stared at him fixedly for several moments. In the taxi going home he suddenly burst into tears, sobbing, until at last he blurted out, 'At school . . . he . . . used . . . to . . . smell . . . of . . . tangerines.' And wept bitterly and unrestrainedly – for what? Lost youth? Lost love? Lost dreams?

I too saw one of the boys I'd loved again. I was about twenty-seven and suddenly met Martel pushing a bicycle towards me on the pavement near Piccadilly Circus. He had on a backpack, hefty climbing boots and he had a moustache. I don't know how I recognised him. Perhaps, as he thumped towards me, his climbing boots turned in. But that is not how I remember him.

(17)

I left Bryanston in the summer of 1951. I see the thin figure of eighteen, about to join the army for National Service, not as a coherent character, or even collection of characters, but as something unstable and contradictory, struggling to make sense of a series of accidental distortions and inhibitions and haphazard accretions.

Anxiety about money has now been firmly stuck on. So has a love of wind in pine trees. So has an attitude to clothes. Clothes rationing (continuing till 1950) meant that not only did I seldom have new things but that, shorter than Gathorne, I often had his cast-offs. To this day, I find it almost impossible to buy new clothes. I depend on presents and, still, on cast-offs – from my son and stepsons and, more recently, the dead. Yet the odd thing is that, at heart, I am a dandy.

The war and privations which followed it went on for years. Bread rationing was brought *in* in 1947 and this and some food rationing did not end until the early 1950s. These and other privations had still further effects. I can't bear to throw away soap and often find myself trying to wash with something the size of a lozenge. I was able to give up smoking but now, warned about cholesterol, I can't give up butter. Our fridge is always full of ridiculous scraps I've saved on saucers.

My reaction to Jock taking the place of my father, the fact that I may have unconsciously blamed him for my father's absence, probably meant I would always have had difficulties with authority. This was considerably compounded by various idiocies at Bryanston. My dealings with authority figures remain tricky to this day. And not just obvious authority, but the 'authority' represented by what is expected, what is generally accepted or popular.

The main punishment at Bryanston was runs. On your free afternoon and every Saturday afternoon you worked off the runs you'd accumulated. Each run was six miles and took most of the

1 My mother and father engaged in 1930. For me, what is interesting in view of what I later discovered about him is the sensitive, almost feminine face of my father.

2 1931 – the wedding.
Left to right: Eddie and Anne, my father's elder brother and younger sister; on the far right is my mother's younger sister Mary Thorowgood, long before her downfall.

3   1933. My mother holding me aged a month or so outside our little house in Meadow Place, Edinburgh.

4   Nanny Patton with my brother Sammy and me outside Snape Priory in Suffolk, my grandmother's house. About 1937, just before Nanny Patton vanished.

5   Brown, my grandmother's gardener. It was Brown who had to tell her that the other gardener was having sex with one of the pigs.

6   A recent view of Snape.

7   In an apple tree at White House Farm in Suffolk, where we spent most of the war with our Cranbrook cousins.

9   Tarzan of the Suffolk woods with his hound Teddy – an important relationship.

8   Sammy and me walking in Fairlie. My hair is pinned to one side by a Kirbigrip. A centre parting, where it naturally fell, was regarded as sissy.

10 Kelburn Castle, near Fairlie, Ayrshire, my grandmother's childhood home. My mother fled there with Sammy and me in 1940.

11 The Arch, from the airfield side. The left half was ours: Sammy and me across half the arch, our parents below, the sitting-room below them. The little bathroom and kitchen were in the stuck-on addition.

12 Jock's farm Banks, near Ravenstonedale, Westmoreland.

13   Glemham – the family home of our cousins.

14   The Poplars at Lydford, Somerset. My father's Corgi is in the foreground. I'd forgotten the imposing urns.

15
The Nissen huts at Carnoustie in Scotland into which we moved in 1951. It was this move which finally made my mother insist they buy a fixed home.

16   Biddy Harrisson, louche, amusing, outrageous friend of my parents, who gave me my first major hangover when I was sixteen. Husband Tom on her left.

17   Ben Britten and Peter Pears outside their house in Aldeburgh in 1950. This and the preceding three or four years were those of my friendship with Ben.

18   Betty Batten – a formidable, quite difficult, very funny and very generous figure who used to stuff five-pound notes down my mother's bosom.

19   The RSF mess in Berlin in 1952. *Left to right*: Basil Johnston, David Ferguson, the General's niece, Ian Gordon, Peter Cartright, David Cameron, fire, Harry Thompson, Malcolm Fleming, Jimmy Williamson, Lillo (dog), Colin Simpson, Major Cunliffe-Cave.

20   Nell Dunn, about ten years after I first met her – but just as beautiful.

21   1955. With my cousin Caroline Jarvis (later Cranbrook) at San Fiz in Northern Spain, where I first met Eliza.

22   With my sister Rose in my bedroom at Number 18 Hartington Road.

23   Eliza rented a primitive cottage at St Simon in the Lot in 1956. This was the bath.

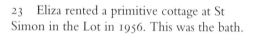

afternoon. I ran many hundreds of miles. Running, apart from the addiction to endorphins, became the penance that dissolved guilt. I continued to run two or three times a week until I was sixty and my ankles began to crack up.

I remember worrying about the superficiality of some of my friendships at Bryanston. I thought friendship should be profound – or not at all. I resolved this by seeing that one could have what I called 'squash friendships' – that is, people you got on with well enough but on the basis of a single interest or two. But this sensible, obvious observation and decision was to cause me trouble later on.

The effect of Bryanston on love, on the having and expressing of strong feelings in general, was more insidious and more profound. The pain of being sent away from home very young, in my case ten, can be great, so great that most people find it pleasanter to forget. But it has long-lasting effects. If my mother and father love me how could they send me away? Is it safe to love anyone? The expression of strong feelings is always disruptive in close communities like boarding schools, but if feelings can also be so painful, should I have any deep feelings at all – or, if I have them, at least should I not bury them out of sight and out of mind? Perhaps sexual feelings are the only real feelings – or the only safe ones. I only slowly resolved all this. For instance, it was not till eight years later, when an equally sharp emotional knife – which struck when I left someone I loved – sliced through me to that deeply buried pain and confusion, that I slowly began to feel strongly again at all. At least, this is one way of looking at it.

(18)

My father's posting after Yeovilton was to Scotland – Carnoustie near Arbroath. The Nissen hut he'd promised Sammy and me before was now at long last to become a reality. Aghast at leaving the comforts and luxuries of the Poplars for another ramshackle dwelling, my mother can't have been much comforted when my father arrived back excitedly with this news.

Alas, I was to see little of our new home. About to be called up, it was decided I should stay at Snape until this happened, while Sammy, Rose, and my parents settled into the Nissen hut.

My grandmother and I, too, settled into a routine, one dominated for a while by my exercise programme. I had elected to join the Royal Scots Fusiliers, a distinguished old infantry regiment based at Ayr near Kelburn. Someone or other in the family knew the colonel-in-chief, Major General Hakewill-Smith, and I thought, absurdly, I might gain some advantage from this. The RSF was reputedly very tough and I was nervous I wouldn't be able to take the training. I went for barefoot runs along the lanes. I chopped down trees and split logs. I played tennis.

My friendship with Britten and Pears had continued on the same lines as it had begun, only now our contests were invariably followed by supper at Crag Path before Ben drove me back. We corresponded a bit – postcards on holiday, a letter from me asking if 'Johnny' in *The Little Sweep* could be spelt 'Jonny', which it now is (all the characters were named from our family). But as my stay at Snape became prolonged I began to see much more of them than usual.

One late afternoon, after I'd been beaten in a particularly hard game of tennis, I was standing in their bedroom with its large double bed, wrapped in my towel and looking out at the sea, when Ben, whose baths (in my water) were extremely rapid, came through in his towel. I remember the intent but soft look in his eyes and the familiar sentimental expression on his face as he advanced towards me across the thick, pale blue carpet. Somehow keeping his towel on, he put his arms gently round me and kissed me on the forehead.

I had long rehearsed what I would do. I put up my hand between us and said solemnly – 'No Ben – it is not to be.'

Ben must have been slightly taken aback by this opera-like response, but he did not falter. I think he retreated for a moment, then he advanced again and put his arms round me once more. Once more I put up my hand – 'No Ben – I'm afraid I can't.' And that was that.

Such was his skill and gentleness – combined with the fact that I was fond of him and had long known something like this would happen – that I remember no awkwardness. We went down and had our usual Martinis and wine. I would have got slightly drunk. I don't know what we talked about – but they were among the rather few people to whom I could say that I now wanted to write. But I said to

Humphrey Carpenter, when describing this incident for his excellent biography of Ben, that had I responded at all to the advance, I would quite soon have been in the double bed.

I think this is probably true. But I was eighteen. It could hardly be called paedophilia, which has become a highly charged subject in the last fifteen years or so. Despite this, it has to be recognised that there are boys of thirteen, fourteen, fifteen who enjoy sex with older boys and men and pursue it. The possibility that Ben made the most of such circumstances, or analogous ones, is raised at one point by Carpenter: 'After Britten's death, John Evans was told by Pears that Britten had "needed an active figure (Peter) to his passive, but he also needed to be active to a boy's passive. And I've always had the impression that Peter meant that both types of relationship had been consummated."' Certainly, the intensity of his reactions sometimes when the likelihood of overt sex was clearly impossible would support this.

And when this impossibility was clear, as it was in my case, and with many of the other young boys he is known to have loved or been attracted to (the number is quite large) he was delicacy itself. I was fourteen when I first met him and, though at once aware I attracted him, as I said, I never felt remotely threatened. David Hemmings, who had similar experiences, quite often slept in Ben's bed with him – and felt, and was, perfectly 'safe'.

It is clear that Britten's complex feelings for these young boys were a central element in his complicated genius. Because of what had happened I was aware of this element whenever I saw or heard his work thereafter – nor does it require great perspicacity to see that innocence, a fascination with the corruption or destruction, some-times sadistic, of innocence, or a symbolic representation of this, are behind some of his greatest works – *The Turn of the Screw*, *Peter Grimes*, *Billy Budd*. These complex feelings – tenderness, part parental, part the longings of romantic love, identification with, and a return to, feelings of his boyhood, lust and guilt at lust, frustrated desire – also gave him the insight into sin and longings for redemption which enabled him to write such marvellous music for churches. In this sense, that collection of young boys, of which I was briefly one, were among his principal muses.

I also told Carpenter that from now on, though with great subtlety and tact, Ben very gradually saw less of me. This, too, is true, but I think unfair to him. I had begun to leave home. I saw much less of everyone connected with it. I continued to write to him, see him and play tennis and squash for several years.

I remember one particularly horrific occasion early in 1957. Ben had invited me and, unusually, my parents, to the first night of his ballet *The Prince of the Pagodas* at Covent Garden. My parents were both shy and extremely nervous – my mother as much about my father as about meeting the rich and famous. Ben and Peter were there and I think the Harewoods. My mother made my father sit at the back of the box behind everyone else and near the tray of smoked salmon sandwiches. I expect she hoped he might eat them, since he'd brought his flask to sustain, as he put it, 'flying speed'. He did this so successfully that he soon took off into heavy sleep. There is a point some way into the ballet – another work about sexuality and the corruption of innocence – where a lot of parasols cover the stage and are whirling round to tinkly, Bali-esque, Eastern-sounding music. Perhaps some pagodas are whirling too. Suddenly, there came a tremendous commotion from the back of the composer's box. Loud, hoarse cries, shouting, the noise of plates of smoked salmon crashing to the ground. People in the stalls looked up in astonishment. My mother sprang up and rushed my father out the back and away to a taxi. I think she showed considerable courage reappearing at the interval. My father later explained that he had been dreaming he was back in Hong Kong. Suddenly, something had woken him and he had found to his horror that he had actually been transported there. Terrified out of his wits, drunk, his reactions had been both flight and fight.

I remember Ben with affection. He was the reason I called my son Benjamin.

(19)

In fact, my games of tennis and squash came to an abrupt end that year anyway at the end of September, just days before I was due to leave for Ayr. Crisp was cutting a very late stand of barley in the field across the lane. I was chasing a rabbit which had run out before the reaper and binder when I caught my foot in a rabbit hole. I was flung violently forward, there was an audible sound of snapping and a moment of agony. The men took the gate into the field off its hinges and laid me on it (something I'd read about but never believed actually happened). They carried me to the house and lifted me on to the sofa in the drawing room. I remember I was suddenly sick with shock.

Surprisingly quickly, Dr Collins was there. Once more, I felt eleven. He examined my swelling knee – and with his permanently warm fingers bandaged it up. Then he had his usual glass of sherry.

I had badly torn the ligaments in my left knee. The leg was encased in plaster from groin to ankle. A telegram was sent to Ayr, followed by doctor's letters.

My damaged leg interfered with but, apart from exercise, did not alter the routine Granny and I had established – and which was essentially the pattern for all my visits to Snape. Mornings were for work. I was now actively writing short stories. Also, I had got into Cambridge (not particularly difficult then) and had decided to read history. I had been sent a long reading list and had begun to plough through it.

My grandmother was sixty-two and still very active. She called herself a good cook, by which she didn't mean she could actually cook (I never saw her even boil an egg) but that she was very good at thinking up meals and dishes – and certainly this is a useful skill. Nettie had long gone, living nearby with her family. Mary lingered on for a while, gradually going mad. Then there came a week when she served up four suppers of cabbage on toast and nothing else. Soon after, she returned to Perthshire. Eventually, quite a number of the long series of my grandmother's servants were certifiable, but I think this particular stay was in a period of stability during Elfreda's tenure.

The trouble with Elfreda is that I put her in a novel – *Particle Theory* – and I can't now distinguish between my Elfreda and the real one. She was a refugee from Latvia, about thirty-five, heavily accented, voluble, subject to mood swings, noisy and something of a slattern. She was good-looking in rather a lippy way. I suspect she drank. She had a pretty, goody-goody daughter aged nine with blonde plaits, called Ousjima. But she was an intelligent woman and an effective cook. In any case, my grandmother had to put up with what she could get now, though I think Elfreda's loud voice and loud laugh sometimes got her down. Also, she broke things. While I was in the army, I received a letter saying Ousjima had gone to friends and Elfreda had suddenly fallen ill. My grandmother had had to feed and look after her. Interested, I wrote and asked what she'd cooked. Easy, answered my grandmother, she'd looked up Latvia in the *Encyclopaedia Britannica* (1916 edition, kept in the dining room) and it said Latvians lived mostly on raw fish. So she'd bought raw fish, put it on a plate and, because Elfreda was infectious, pushed it over to her with a broom. I saw this scene so vividly I eventually put it into *Particle Theory*, but as I write now – did my grandmother *really* just shove it in? Certainly, the raw fish is accurate.

As darkness began to fall earlier and earlier, we would hear the first two or three pheasants in the little wood 'cocking up'. About once a week I would wait until it was almost dark, then slip out and walk as quietly as I could up the drive – now lumbered with my plaster – carrying the .410. Once my eyes had adjusted, I'd move very slowly into the trees. The black silhouette of a pheasant would suddenly be outlined against the night sky. I would stop. Slip off the safety catch. Fire. There would be a cacophony of frightened pheasants taking off – the wood was full of them – but I would collect mine from the ground and take it back to Elfreda to hang in the larder.

Then I would rejoin my grandmother for praise at my skill and our pre-supper two glasses of sherry and chat. At quarter past eight I would unfold the small walnut-veneer table in front of the fire and help carry in whatever Elfreda had cooked. After supper we'd read or, more usually, play cribbage – hard-fought contests since cribbage is to an extent a game of skill and we were now equal. I would have a glass of beer. Sometimes, for old times' sake, we'd get out the spillikins.

But quite often, both before and after supper, we'd listen to the wireless, as it still was, nearly always the Third Programme, as it too still was. At the beginning of the week we'd go through the *Radio Times* ringing what we liked – interesting talks, plays, Schubert/ Mozart/Beethoven etc., and, of course, anything of Ben's. My grandmother had a measure for the moving power of music – did she get gooseflesh down her spine? She said this was very rare, but an infallible guide.

I agree with her as to rarity. How often is one *really* moved by art? I very much enjoy music, but I remember only one moment of true ecstasy. Edwin Fischer, a pupil of Schnabel's, came to play at Bryanston. When he'd finished I suddenly found to my astonishment that, without realising it, I had leapt on to my chair and was wildly cheering. Opera, theatre, film – OK, strong feelings certainly, but often somehow tricked from one by some technical alchemy, cinema especially. With painting, again I remember only once. I'd gone round the Uffizi and ended up at Botticelli. As I stepped in front of 'La Primavera', stared at it, I suddenly, again to my astonishment, burst into tears. I am most easily, most widely and most often deeply moved by prose. For a long time poetry frightened me – would I understand it? (I know not necessary, but necessary to me.)* This is probably because, like a lot of people, I was made to read poetry too young – especially Wordsworth. To me, Wordsworth is to poetry what Brahms is to music. Only recently have I begun to read poetry again and enjoy it. Some people can't read poetry till they are sixty.

Anyway, Granny and I would sit on either side of the fire, the pine logs spitting, bubbling, hissing and flaring, music pouring from her large wooden wireless with its knobs and fretwork face, and wait for gooseflesh – and once or twice we'd agree it had come. We would go to bed around eleven. I would read, then lie listening to the wind in the trees till I fell asleep.

I would pluck the pheasant the morning after I'd shot it, my grandmother would clean it and then Elfreda, who refused to touch it till then, cooked it. The weekly or twice-weekly pheasant was a useful, almost necessary, addition to the Snape economy. I never understood my grandmother's money, except that there wasn't now quite enough. Gradually a crisis would build. How much she'd get for her barley would become vital. She would sit, smoking cigarette

* Céleste Albaret to Proust after he had given her the obscure poems of Paul Valéry to read: 'But are you quite sure that these are poems? Aren't they more like riddles?'

after cigarette and flinging the ends into the fire, piles of bills on her ample lap. Eventually, Jock would arrive. They would be locked in conference. Jock would leave, my grandmother looking rather chastened. Most of the largest unpaid bills would have been paid, though never the drink bill at Hunter & Oliver in Saxmundham which, because of its periodic and violent inflation whenever Eddie stayed, Jock always refused to pay.

Another thing we did was teach ourselves to respring armchairs. All at least fifty years old, obese, collapsing, we soon hauled in and tacked fast their great sagging corset-less stomachs, taut and trim, with new webbing and tightened springs. We even tackled a sofa bought in Maples in 1899.

It began to grow cold. We had an oil stove in the big drawing room as well as the fire. My plaster came off but my leg was so weak I had to go into Saxmundham three times a week for the kneecap to be jerked electrically. The pony trap was hardly ever used now, though Freya the pony roamed destructively about (the 'Shut Gate – Pony Loose in Grounds' card on the drive gate once had 'Tiger' substituted by someone in the village. No one noticed for months.) My grandmother drove me in, in her small Ford.

My parents and Sammy came down from Carnoustie for Christmas at Glemham. My mother fussed anxiously about my imminent departure and gave me a small travelling iron to press my uniform with. Ben gave me Ronald Firbank's eight novels in one volume. Thus equipped for the trials ahead, on 5 January 1952 I set off for Ayr. Scotland, when I entered it, was deep in snow.

(20)

I had had no idea that there was more than one Jock in the world before I came to Ayr. I thought there was just my own, solitary, imposing uncle. Soon after I arrived at the bleak RSF barracks, carried by taxi (the last of many such luxuries for many months) through the swirling snow, I found there were dozens of them; my uncle had suddenly multiplied thirtyfold and in pigmy form since they were all, with the striking exception of Davie, minute. They – all the privates, that is, and me, since I was one – were now all Jocks.

Standing outside our barrack room, I heard Second Lieutenant Marr say, 'Get the Jocks out on parade will you please Sergeant.' 'Aye sir,' then sticking his head into the big room – 'GET Y'FUCKIN' ARSES OFF Y'FUCKIN' BEDS YOU FUCKIN' SHOWER AND OOT ON FUCKIN' SQUARE THE LOT OF YOUS.'

'Fucking' – the all-purpose adjective.

Sergeant Sinclair, a grizzled Glaswegian, had, first thing, asked me something I was now always to be asked, was I any relation to General Gathorne-Hardy? Adding that I didn't look as if I could possibly be. I had said I supposed I must be since all Gathorne-Hardys were related. I wrote to my grandmother and soon learnt that General Frank Gathorne-Hardy had been, as I mentioned earlier, my father and Jock's uncle.

Perhaps, at the end of the two weeks I spent at Ayr, class may have been a factor, but I think at first it was just complete, continual, mutual astonishment operating between me and all the other Jocks. For one thing, we could hardly understand what the other said. I spoke in my usual upper-class, public school way. These tiny, tough men were all Glaswegians – a few, or possibly all it seemed to me, just out of prison or borstal. The Glasgow accent, famously, has the glottal stop – the swallowing of word endings. Only Arabic and Cockney share this, of which the mildest is Cockney. Glasgow and Arabic are about equal. I had not yet got used to the glottal stop; while my own fluting tones . . .

Then, they clearly had never seen anyone who wore pyjamas. Despite two sluggish radiators, the long room with its thirty close-pressed beds was cold. I rapidly evolved a night uniform as bulky – with sweaters, socks and pyjamas – as my day one. Were they really so tough that the same skimpy, dirty grey underclothes they wore all day would take them through the night? What they thought as I clambered heavily into my bed – some deep-sea diver of the dark – I can't imagine.

Yet they were not really, or only, tiny tough men. They were boys of eighteen. Many, except for those who'd been at borstal or in prison, had never left home and were visibly homesick, for me a long familiar pain, but now fleeting, soon dulled. Shaven like convicts, woken at six and marched to 'ablutions' through the dark, we were all equally bewildered by the mad new routines of blancoing, polishing, ironing, marching, drilling, being shouted at. There was a huge, five-pound industrial iron we shared. I might as well have been ironing a tent with my mother's dainty travelling iron for all the impression it made on the coarse thick folds of my khaki greatcoat. It could hardly cope with the four army-issue khaki handkerchiefs. I threw it away. I lost Firbank. I tried, and failed, to buy a hot-water bottle in the Naafi.

I also asked the Naafi girl for some soap. She shoved across a large yellow rectangle like a chunk of cheddar. 'Don't you have bath soap?' I said, adding humorously, 'I'm not a floor, you know.' The Naafi girl looked at me, she looked at my accent, then she slapped my face.

After two weeks, I was told I would go to Edinburgh for potential officer/NCO training. A group of six Jocks decided they would black my balls and cock with boot polish as a gesture of farewell. I don't know if this was the Helen Billo effect or an episode in the class war, but perhaps I was saved by the latter. Cowering in the toilet where I'd fled, my tormentors outside, I suddenly heard the deep voice of Davie. I didn't know Davie at all, except to have seen what no one could fail to see – that he was enormous, and enormously strong. 'If any o'yous touches him, yous'll have to reckon wi' me.'

They sensibly decided not to reckon with Davie. Was it some feudal echo – or simple pity? He was rather shy when I thanked him. The next day, 20 January, I was taken by truck to the station and left to catch a train to Edinburgh and dreaded Dreghorn Camp, notorious for the 'hard men' who were its NCOs and instructors, the roughness of its recruits, and the severity of its training.

(21)

The barracks was at the south-western edge of Edinburgh at the extreme limit of the trams, still running then, and at the eastern edge of the Pentland Hills, whose first outcrops rose above us, where the rifle ranges were and where we often trained.

The ranks of Nissen huts, two hundred or so of them, in lines stretched out on ground sloping gently down towards the distant and invisible city, looked bleak under the snow; bleak but also bleakly beautiful – austere, abstract, sad.

And cold. My birthplace can be cold and that winter, following the pattern set up, it was very cold indeed. In fact, the potential officer/NCO platoon was housed not in a Nissen hut but in the Sally Anne. This was an old wooden hut which had once been used by the Salvation Army. It was said to be colder than the Nissen huts. The wooden sides were split and cracked and the wind moaned through them at night. It was heated by a single, big, cylindrical cast-iron 'Tortoise' stove, which we stoked till it glowed red hot. The trouble was, the coal ration often ran out before the end of the week and we couldn't always steal enough to keep it going.

I spread my greatcoat over the bed and increased my night uniform by a scarf, gloves, and thick underwear I kept for the night only. I must have looked odd, but no one commented. There were others now in pyjamas; besides we were all fighting the cold. Every morning the top sheet was frozen hard from our breath. It cracked when you moved and you felt you were having to break out of bed. The painted fire buckets, standing some way from the Tortoise stove, never thawed and the ice on them was two inches thick. It was said a man in the intake before our one had died in his bed from the cold. He was told he was malingering but in fact had pneumonia. Rumours of this sort abounded: suicides, imminent posting to zones of danger, of sergeants who buggered their recruits. If a recruit refused – endless jankers (which I underwent later), even beatings-up. 'You should'a seen poor bastard's fuckin' heed – and the fuckin' blood! Jesus fuckin' Christ!'

I say 'our' intake, but in fact Ayr had sent me too early and for a week I was the only member of it. Early each morning in the dim light of winter thirty companies, about three thousand men, marched in their platoons out on to a parade ground swept clear but often already lightly covered in snow again. Eighty-nine squads of thirty men wheeled out on to the square with one squad in the middle consisting of one man – me. 'Platoon – 'alt' yelled Corporal Langland as he and I arrived somehow, it always seemed, in the front of the parade. I'd stand rigidly halted. Eventually, rotund Captain Parks would arrive and walk slowly round me. 'Stand the platoon at ease

Corporal.' 'Platoon – standat – *eyse*,' yelled Corporal Langland, and I'd stand at ease.

My memories of the eleven weeks at Dreghorn rush past in an exhausted blur out of which sudden shapes, like my first parades, loom and then vanish. Reaching for the first cigarette before getting up. A Woodbine, but an end – for the reviving harshness and that moment, still, of dizziness. Cigarettes bound us together – lighting from someone's lighted end (a Dutch fuck), passing them round, taking one from an offered pack, stubbing out and keeping the ends. There were breaks for a smoke. Finding that, after a while, I could make the Sally Anne laugh. Three of them helping me dress in the incomprehensible tangle of webbing and weapons and catches and clips. Waking one night, snow still falling, and hearing loud panting and grunting and seeing huge shadows, thrown by the Tortoise stove, leap round the Sally Anne. Big Jimmy MacClaren had tried to pull a sock through his rifle to clear rust and it had jammed up the barrel. In a panic, he was repeatedly heating a length of thick wire in the revved-up red-hot stove and thrusting it down the barrel as hard as he could, trying to burn the sock out. Even from my bed, I could see he was just ramming it further in. 'Push it in the other end Mac.' The remnant of charred sock fell out at once. Yet he was right to panic. A sock up his rifle! It could have meant the glass house. Certainly jankers, which was *not* pleasant. It meant CB – confined to barracks. The only times I escaped barracks, on a weekend pass, I spent with the Watsons. Close cousins of my father, and a generous, kind couple. I would rattle into Edinburgh on the tram and they would let me have baths, feed me and let me sleep. On Sunday evenings I would rattle back, dozing and waking, watching the tram driver whirl the horizontal brass wheel to start and stop. But I reached the peak of exhaustion after my own jankers. One of the PE sergeants disliked me. He said my neck was dirty. Sensibly not going into my simian and Belgian Congo antecedents which explained this, I nevertheless said my skin was naturally dark. 'Don't give me that shite.' Two days later, up on a charge, I was marched in front of Captain Parks. 'Any relation to the General?' My relationship clearly compounded the crime. 'Seven days confined to barracks.' Jankers was hell. Up at five to report to the duty officer. Then throughout the day and into the night reporting and doing any dirty work that could be found – seriously blocked toilets, filthy kitchen surfaces and floors, mincers clogged with fat, rubbish, distributing coal or painting stones, a military obsession. All-day training – drill, bren gun lessons, map exercises, etc. And still, at night, my uniform to press, my belts and brasses and badge and rifle to clean and polish. I was often not in bed still ten or eleven – and up at five again. I continually fell asleep blancoing and polishing. I remember falling asleep over my rifle out on the firing range, probably a glass house offence. Yet I was in fact the cleanest man in Dreghorn. Baths had always meant love; now they meant warmth as well. I discovered I could get into the sergeants' bath house a few huts down from the Sally Anne. I would slip out when everyone was asleep. The moon would be up, my footsteps silent in the snow, the whole camp smelling of snow. Wonderful steaming hot gushing water. Then hurrying back through the moonlit snow, hugging my heat to me for the Sally Anne. Four days after my jankers ended, the PE sergeant again said my neck was dirty. Once more I was on a charge. That same afternoon, Captain Parks passed me in the lines. 'How's it going Gathorne-Hardy?' I said it wasn't going well at all. I told him about the new charge. I told him my skin was naturally dark. To my horror, I suddenly found my voice was breaking. Captain Parks didn't say a word. He just nodded and walked on. But the charge was dropped and thereafter the PE sergeant laid off me. Food swims up out of the haze. Disgusting food, but we were so hungry we ate it. Long Lizzie – five feet and nine delicious inches – Long Lizzie in her clogs in the vast dining hall. The entire camp lusted after Long Lizzie. She just tossed her beautiful sexy head and dismissed them. Fuck off. Head in air. Clogging off into the kitchen whose stinking, grease-coated great cooking vessels I'd lately tried to scour clean. At last the weather broke, though not always improved. Rain drummed on the Sally Anne's corrugated iron roof and poured off the Pentlands and that arrogant, lanky, sadistic bastard Second Lieutenant Mitchell yelled and swore at us and hit us with his stick to get us deeper into the mud of the assault course. He, I suppose, was hard, and the PE sergeant was certainly one of the hard men, and our own sergeant could be tricky – but I liked Corporal Langland. He wasn't hard at all, though he could act so if necessary. He was small, about thirty, a Yorkshireman and looked like T. E. Lawrence. As the rains stopped and spring now streamed down from the Pentland Hills he and I would sometimes climb up away from the camp, ostensibly on some exercise, but really just to sit somewhere and smoke and talk. I would lie stretched out, my pack under my head, and Corporal Langland would stretch out too, his head on my stomach, and talk about his life in the army, and before as a boy in Yorkshire. He was a kind, rather lonely man and I think probably homosexual. How few people remain: of our lot, only Jim MacClaren's leaping shadow; Montgomery – clever, with pink cheeks and thick spectacles; and Leeming – handsome, saturnine, cynical, thinking entirely about girls. Eventually I was sent away to WOSBI – the War Office Selection Board. I passed – I would become an officer. Everyone was astonished except me. The advantages of being thought hopeless, stupid and inefficient were so obvious that I'd been all three. Captain Parks was amused, Second Lieutenant Mitchell openly and rudely aghast. Now I was made lance corporal. I couldn't stop looking at, couldn't stop *feeling*, that single v-shaped stripe glowing on my arm. Emboldened by this, but still terrified, I asked Long Lizzie if she'd like to go out with me. A film, Saturday night. She looked at me – and said yes. *Yes!* This really did astonish me. Long Lizzie wasn't known to have gone out with anyone, not even Leeming. We'd meet at the main gate outside the guard room. Five-thirty. Then the army struck. As usual, since there were no real emergencies, they had to invent one. I was summoned to Coy HQ early on Saturday morning. I was to leave for Mons Officer Training Camp in two and a half hours. I must pack at once, hand in my kit, and report back. I rushed up to the cookhouse but there was no Lizzie and no one knew where she was. I left messages, but as the tram rattled me away from Dreghorn towards Princes Street, my kit bag between my knees, I wished I could have told her. I have wished that, at long intervals but from time to time, ever since.

(22)

Officer training took four months. It was both slightly easier – better food, warmer huts, etc. – and harder, since the training was harder. I had been sent to Mons, near Aldershot, because the army had decided to transfer me either to the artillery or the cavalry. The army then existed largely to bugger recruits about and I had been buggered about, but for some reason I found this particular arbitrary interference intensely irritating. I therefore wrote to Major General Hakewell-Smith. Perhaps he decided I must be a relation to the general. At any rate after two months I was transferred to the infantry training camp at Eaton Hall near Chester. I was once more a Royal Scots Fusilier. Before I left to join my regiment in Germany I was given ten days' leave. I had fittings for my new uniform in London, then took the night train to Arbroath. At last, I would see our Nissen hut.

(23)

In fact, there were two Nissen huts joined in the middle by an umbilicus, like Siamese twins. I can hardly remember the huts (though I remember the little vine cuttings brought from Lydford), but in convenience, from my mother's point of view, they were midway between the Arch and the Poplars. They had once been two dwellings and we had the luxury of four lavatories, rows of two in each hut.

The air station, HMS *Condor*, was near the sea and also near a famous golf course. I remember walking on the golf course's wind-swept edge and finding a despairing question on the wall of a lonely public toilet: 'Is there noboddy queer in Carnoustie?' Seven years later I put it, changing the town, into my first novel *One Foot in the Clouds*. Karl Miller said that the spelling of 'noboddy' was a brilliant touch. I agreed, but in fact I can't spell and thought that was how it should be spelt. The sad figure from Carnoustie had probably scrawled 'nobody'.

It was at Arbroath that I began reading Alfred C. Kinsey's *Sexual Behaviour in the Human Male*, which my father had bought when it came out in 1948. This, as far as I was concerned, was simply erotic literature of great power; it also confirmed, among many other things, that I should be sleeping with Jennie.

It was on this short visit that I discovered my mother was unhappy. It was not the new camp. As usual, she had made friends easily and the Lambes and other old friends like Helen Wooley came to stay (Peta Lambe in fact had a miscarriage in one of our many lavatories). But the strains of the war, the incessant moves during and after it with, latterly, two adolescent boys, the incessant anxiety about money, then giving birth to Rose at forty-one, increasing drink and my father's domestic intransigence (I can't remember him washing or drying up so much as a teaspoon), all this had begun to exact a toll. Her blood pressure was so high, my father said that had she been a rating he would have had her invalided out. She was becoming dependent on Nembutal to sleep. (It was not discovered till after she died that persistent use of Nembutal causes depression.) She was forty-three while I was there and told me that, were it not for Rose, she would see no point in living.

I seem (I read from the journal I had just begun to keep) to have taken my mother's account of her despair as something temporary, a momentary attack. But the difficulties of her life multiplied, as did her illnesses, and this despair, which may also have had deeper roots, came again and again. In the end, it wasn't momentary at all.

(24)

On my way to the regiment I stayed one night in London in Helen Woolley's little basement flat off the Old Brompton Road.

I had arranged to meet Jennie in Kew Gardens. Autumn was early that September 1952 and we lay clamped tightly together by desire, hot-faced in the drifting leaves. While Jennie's teeth chattered in an agony of frustration, her mother's grim, forbidding shadow loomed (as I now know) successfully over us while I came in my nice new Erskine tartan officer's trews – fortunately leaving, as far as I could detect, no outwardly visible stain. I left for Germany next morning.

(25)

The Royal Scots Fusiliers were stationed at Wuppertal, about twenty miles east of Düsseldorf. And it was here that Elvis Presley was to arrive amid scenes of frantic excitement.

My own arrival was less auspicious. It coincided precisely with that of our new colonel. This is an extremely important moment in the life of a regiment, especially perhaps for officers. The whole morale and atmosphere of the regiment derive from him. He is all–powerful. More particularly, all future promotion for officers depends on his recommendation. The importance of what was about to take place was impressed on me almost as I entered the barracks. The colonel would inspect, that is meet, the officers tomorrow. I was at once assigned a batman. He was to start cleaning my dress uniform immediately.

The following morning we were lined up in the officers' mess in a hollow square (that is, a square with one side missing). The regular officers were in blues, the National Service officers in their light khaki service dress, with leather Sam Browne belt across chest and round waist, and their tartan trews. We looked and felt incredibly smart. The atmosphere was tense.

As the most junior officer I was last to be inspected. Lieutenent Colonel Thompson was a big man with, I had learnt the evening before, a formidable reputation. There was dead silence as he moved slowly from officer to officer. Each had a few words. At last he was standing in front of me. I noticed he had long red hairs on his pale but powerful wrists.

'Gathorne-Hardy. I see. Any relation to the general?'

Stiffly to attention, I said clearly and sharply, 'Yes sir. A niece sir.'

There was an appalled silence while we stared at one another. Then I said, 'I mean a nephew sir. I'm sorry sir. A great nephew in fact, sir.'

But it was too late. I had said I was the niece of the general. Colonel Thompson walked briskly from the mess. A few moments later, the assistant adjutant came up to me. 'That was not in the least funny, Gathorne-Hardy.'

This incident was never forgotten exactly, but I lived it down. In fact, I came to like Colonel Thompson and especially his attractive wife. Later, I used to play tennis with them. And eventually I made friends with a number of officers. But for two months or so I was more lonely and more bored at Wuppertal than at any other time in my life.

It was partly because there was a custom of not speaking to new young officers for about a month. I gradually began to feel I was losing not just the power of speech but my wits as well. It also seemed to me that even without this most of the talk was of that relentlessly masculine, relentlessly practical sort that had often made shooting at White House Farm so painful. (Most men don't converse – they tell you things. When men talk together they take it in turns to give each other information.)

And I had nothing to do. I had no platoon and was seconded to that of Colin Simpson, a regular subaltern. I rapidly realised, as bizarre tale followed bizarre tale, that Colin was a fantasist. He had charm and was a competent officer, but soon left the army to become a journalist on a succession of papers where the drama of the 'story' was more important than strict accuracy. Then I lost sight of him, until all at once, forty years later, there he was on television. It was a series, with Michael Buerk and a lot of 'reconstructions', about fantastic escapes. Colin had apparently survived a ten-foot pointed wooden pole being driven through his back and out four feet in front of his chest. Something like one of his tall stories had suddenly actually happened to him and he had looked understandably startled.

But, at Wuppertal, Colin was clear he didn't need any assistance running his platoon. I wandered about the camp still getting amazed pleasure at being saluted and saluting back. I spent hours in my room, writing my journal and to Jennie.

Camp cinema twice a week; mess nights once a week (dress uniform, the regimental silver, of which they were extremely proud, along the table, the piper, drinking the King's health as the port goes round, and at last able to go and pee, eventually staggering to bed drunk); every morning marching with Colin in front of the platoon for muster parade; every night listening to the British Forces Network on a wireless bought on the black market for cigarettes by my batman — it was a strange, inflexible, totally enclosed, self-sufficient little British army world. With one exception, I almost never left the camp and had no contact at all with what was going on outside it. Nor did anyone else. We might just as well have been on the moon as in West Germany.

(26)

The regiment had six horses, and the sole escape from my incarceration was when I went riding.

The countryside round the camp was beautiful — rolling, often steeply rolling hills and scooped-out valleys, most thickly forested. The autumn leaves, in which Jennie and I had so lately and so passionately kissed, blew along the rides as I galloped down them. I returned shaken and wind-blown myself, the smell of hot, lathered horse rising round me.

The young National Service doctor, Simon MacIntyre, might have become a friend, but he was about to be demobbed. Once, just before he left, he came riding with me. As we trotted under the trees, he tried to explain Einstein's Theory of Relativity. Simon was an egghead — literally; his head was shaped like an ostrich egg and he was almost bald. I can remember the odd feeling of my mind reaching its limit. I followed him step by step then suddenly — incomprehension. 'Let me go over it again,' he said patiently, our horses now walking. You understand this? Yes. And that this leads to this? Yes, I see that. That was clear. Then, and *therefore*, it means this. No. I couldn't see how it meant this. I was suddenly in a fog. On a graph, you could have pointed to the precise point where my stupidity began.

The forest opened on to the long grass field before the camp and we cantered back.

(27)

The assistant adjutant, Freddy Stimpson, had never quite forgiven me for saying I was the niece of the general. Or rather, he felt I should have been punished in some way. About seven weeks after I arrived his chance came. I was told to report to his office.

There was a four-day boxing course for officers in Hamburg. One officer from each regiment. I was to represent the RSF.

'Do you mean I'll have to get into the ring and fight sir?' I asked, aghast.

'That's right.'

'But sir, I've never boxed in my life. I'll be massacred.'

'Nonsense Gathorne-Hardy. Get your tickets from my sergeant and book yourself some transport. You'll do fine.' He looked at me with satisfaction. I could see him thinking – this'll knock the niece out of him.

The 250-mile north-west overnight journey to Hamburg has vanished, obliterated by fear no doubt. The train would have been hot and swift, my first-class sleeper extremely comfortable. My uniform according me attention if not respect.

But I remember vividly my enormous relief at discovering next day that Freddy Stimpson had been mistaken. It was a course to learn how to *judge* boxing, not how to actually box. There would be no *question* of my clambering into a ring.

The actual course was rather fascinating. I had never known what to win 'on points' meant in boxing. In fact, it is very simple. The front of a boxer is essentially a target defined by an imaginary line drawn across the top of his (and now her) head, down through the ears, across the shoulders, down the side of the body and across the waist where the belt goes. Anything below or behind this line is off target and doesn't count – indeed is a foul. Every hit on the target counts a point. You watch the two fighters, note how many hits each lands and score accordingly. There are nuances, most of which I've forgotten. You have to judge the force of a blow – it's no good just tapping the target, you can't hit with an open glove – and so on. We watched a great many fights – boxers had been brought in from camps all over Germany – our cards were examined and criticised. At the end, I was qualified to judge boxing up to some very low level – inter-battalion I think. Unfortunately, my new skills were never put to use, but ever since I have watched boxing on television with a more interested eye.

There was quite a lot of time not watching boxing. I explored the Reeperbahn – the street of prostitutes. Losing my virginity was probably my single most important and urgent preoccupation, but it wasn't going to happen on the Reeperbahn.

One evening I went to a performance of *The Merry Widow* and remembered seeing it with my mother in the war. Yet it was not just remembered – I felt comforted as if in some way she had held me for a while in her arms. She was to arise from my subconscious like this and comfort me at a much more troubled time many years later.

But most of all I talked. In the same hotel and on the same course was a young subaltern called Edward Tankard. I hadn't been with someone I could really talk to for nearly a year. Nor, I suspect, had he. Good-looking in a louche, *fin-de-siècle* sort of way, amusing, cynical (I think probably from Eton), ribald, flippant, intellectual, keen on drink, we talked till three or four each morning. I have never seen him since and have never forgotten my gratitude for the sense of release I felt talking to him.

(28)

Hamburg in fact marked a more general release. As though I had come through some unadmitted probation, my fellow officers began to talk to me. Freddy Stimpson, while understandably disappointed that I hadn't been systematically beaten up, nevertheless felt that something had been exacted and turned out to be friendly enough.

Other characters began to emerge from the hitherto silent ranks in the anteroom (the name given to what was in effect our large sitting room). Billy Whamond, a small regular officer, who had seemed preposterously affected, was in fact funny, kind and brave. He suffered from a crippling congenital lung condition and his life was a constant and painful battle against it. Another regular subaltern was David Cameron, an intelligent, lazy, handsome, loping figure who spent most of his time in pursuit of girls, as I would have done if I'd dared or known how – or indeed had there been any girls. Cameron shipped them over from England and they put up nearby.

My closest friend was another National Service lieutenant called Basil Johnston. A small, jumpy man, Basil arrived after me and initially liked me because I ignored the probation. I was drawn to Basil by his sense of humour and his intense anxiety about most things military. He concealed this, more or less, but it would suddenly surface. One of the junior officer chores was collecting the money for the battalion's weekly wages from the military bank in Wuppertal. The sum involved was about twenty thousand pounds (say half a million now) all in the highly coloured Monopoly money with which the British Army of the Rhine – BAOR – was paid. So, though a sum worth stealing, it was in a form of limited value to anyone outside the army. Like everyone else, I would take a single soldier with me, though he was armed, as was I. Basil took his entire platoon and they were all armed with live ammunition. He also took three sten guns and a bren gun.

It would have taken a sizeable contingent of Force X to get the battalion wages off Basil. Force X (or Y or Z or the Blue Army – for some reason Russia was never actually named) was 'the enemy' and provided our sole *raison d'être*. I didn't, personally, think war with Russia was likely; at the same time, in 1952, it didn't seem impossible.

My job was to train my platoon in the simple military skills I had learnt at Mons and Eaton Hall. I had never expected I would be able to command and control thirty men but the weight of military discipline backing me up was fearsome. Also, on the whole I got on well enough with them – or most of them. My sergeant, Sergeant Dalgleish, was an intelligent, amiable, rather lazy long-serving NCO and together we ran the army equivalent of Wilf Cowley's Portman House.

But there were hours of boredom. Some I would spend in my small, hot bedroom, reading or writing short stories in my journal. Or else sit in the anteroom, the stifling silence broken by rustling newspapers or Billy Whamond suddenly calling to the mess waiter 'Would you mahnd *awfl*'y getting me a *huge* gin and tonic Martin?'

There was a big billiards table and I became good on it, preferring the elegance of billiards itself to the more complex snooker. There was also billiards fives, which consisted in slamming the balls from end to end with the flat of the hand – I forget to what purpose. This got me into trouble. There was a certain tension between some of the older officers and the National Service ones. These senior officers thought, rightly, that we didn't take army matters seriously enough. Chief of these figures was Major Ferguson. Chinless and mustachioed like Ruggles in the *Mirror* strip, embittered at not being made a lieutenant colonel, Major Ferguson hated me. He had been infuriated and alerted by the niece incident. Several times he sent me out for wearing slippers in the mess. He used to tell Basil and me not to laugh so loudly. One early evening I was playing billiards fives when I hit the ball too hard. To my dismay it took off, soared across the anteroom and went like a cannonball sideways through Major Ferguson's *Times*, whipping it from his hands. He made the most tremendous fuss but he was lucky, as I tried to point out. A foot to the right and it would have struck him on the temple, probably killing him. I had to do a week's orderly officer – the officer equivalent of jankers.

The weather grew colder. Then it was announced that at Christmas the battalion was to be posted to Berlin. Weeks of packing and logistical work began, but I was due leave and was told I would miss the move. Basil, to his horror, was put in charge of the regimental silver. This was no light responsibility. Despite occasional English snobbery towards Scottish regiments, the Royal Scots Fusiliers was one of the most senior and distinguished regiments in the British Army. It was 4th of Foot – the fourth infantry regiment to be founded. During the centuries it had accumulated vast quantities of silver; everything from elaborate set pieces with cannon, flags, silver soldiers with raised swords and silver bodies on silver stretchers to single silver pheasants, horses, plates, machine guns and so on. Fanatically cleaned, this gleaming mass covered the table on mess nights; the sergeants' mess had similar heaps.

The value, according to Basil, was incalculable. He was in a state of barely controlled panic. He insisted that the armed guard he'd been detailed should be trebled. I was to go on leave the day after Basil went to Berlin. The day before he left he came to me and said he'd ceased to sleep. He hadn't slept for two nights. White and clenched, he looked ghastly. I gave him two of the yellow Nembutal capsules from the emergency supply my mother had given me and taught him how to open them and pour out some of the bitter white barbiturate if he didn't want a full dose. But next morning he told me that, desperate for sleep, he'd taken both. He looked calmer, or at least drugged. That evening he drove the silver to Wuppertal station and supervised its transfer to the train. He then went to have a pee or get a coffee or a paper or something. Ten minutes later the train left – without Basil. It transpired afterwards that, perhaps still groggy from Nembutal and confused by the uniformity of Wuppertal station, he'd passed the Berlin platform and got on to another train which, by chance, pulled slowly out a few moments later on its way to Vienna. All I had time to hear before I left for England was that a message had come from the sergeant in Berlin. The silver had arrived safely but his officer had vanished.

(29)

When my father was told at Arbroath that his next ship was to be HMS *Centaur*, an aircraft carrier going to the Far East, my mother said she refused to move again. They must buy a house.

They bought 18 Hartington Road in Aldeburgh, Suffolk. It cost two thousand pounds and Jock lent them the money. Although my Bryanston fees had ceased, repaying the loan replaced them. It took my father fifteen years. He was, of course, still paying Sammy's Gordonstoun fees.

Number 18 Hartington Road is the last house at the eastern end of a short terraced row of small red-brick houses in a street directly above the High Street. Aldeburgh since then has become to a considerable extent middle-class. Our home, for instance, is now the holiday house of a London businessman who comes in the summer for the Aldeburgh Festival and to go sailing at Slaughden. But then those little houses were quite humble and were the homes of small shopkeepers, fishermen and the like. Mr and Mrs Miller, who ran the minute but excellent stationers in the High Street, lived at the end farthest from us (about seven doors up). There was a family of mouse-like Plymouth Brethren opposite.

Our house too looks small but it is roomier than you'd think. Basically two up, two down, there are in fact three tiny bed-sized additional rooms upstairs, one of which was Rose's, one Sammy's, one the bathroom. Downstairs, there was an additional small kitchen and a room called the 'Beetle Room'.

I had the second largest room upstairs next to my parents'. From here, between and over the roofs, you could just see the sea about a quarter of a mile away. And in any sort of strong weather the house was enveloped in its womb-music, like the wind in pines, as the waves fell in great arpeggios slantwise upon the shingle. Arpeggios which have gradually sucked away the shore till the Moot Hall on the edge of the shingle beds now stands where the centre of the little town was in 1550. In 1953 these enormous broken chords overwhelmed the concrete sea defences and waves rippled along the High Street. As global warming takes hold no doubt this will become a regular occurrence. Aldeburgh will be like Venice.

Moving so much had (and has) made me very conscious of possessions, as conscious as the Bedouin are. First in my mother's bedrooms, later, and still more, in the Arch, the Poplars and the Arbroath Nissen huts, our pictures, clocks, armchairs and sofa had been what made each place our home. Number 18 Hartington Road was our final family one and I loved it.

I loved it for its size for one thing. Those possessions, which had stamped each temporary camp as our own, had now been so reduced by the intermittent but steady depredations of their sale that they could all be fitted into the small house. The few that couldn't be placed were piled in the Beetle Room (my father's latest hobby was entomology).

The patch of grass below my window and the single but quite large earth bed were ample for the vine and my father's erratic gardening (my mother, who had a Hiroshima touch with plants, wisely left it well alone). It could take his vine, but was too small for his tobacco needs. Tobacco was now grown and cured at Glemham.

I liked the closeness, the way that, after my mother had stumped with *café au lait* ready mixed and toast to me in bed ('This is the last time I'm doing this Jonny'), I could lie half-reading, half-listening, as I had with her and Fidelity at White House Farm but now fully comprehending, to her endless conversations on the telephone at the bottom of the stairs with her friends and her friends who were often her patients.

Above all I loved my sister Rose. Now nearly three, extremely active, bright, talkative, funny and in every conceivable way as charming and edible as it is possible to be at that delicious age, she would climb into my bed, my bath, on to my knee or any other part of me she fancied climbing on to, and for several years I was really her father.

Not that my father was not also her father. In fact, he was more effectively and emotionally so than with either Sammy or me. But he was away in the Far East until just before – or just into – 1956 and I filled the gap. (Shortly after he left Rose found a beetle. She placed it carefully and proudly into one of his insect bottles and put it into the Beetle Room for his return. It was in fact an apple pip and its total immobility eventually began to worry her.)

My parental role was probably good – certainly it was enjoyable – for both of us, but it was quite difficult to readjust to a more balanced position when she grew up. The way we achieved this was rather unusual, and despite it I still – as I do with my son Ben and Nic – muddle the names of my daughter Jenny and Rose when they are both together.

My leave was quite short, about ten days. In fact, I don't remember if my father had already left for HMS *Centaur* or left after Christmas. This was no doubt spent at Glemham and nor do I remember that, though I know the weather was still quite mild. I do, however, remember an incident with a French letter.

I always carried one of these in my wallet in case – or rather, in hope. Lying in bed a few nights before I had to go, I suddenly realised I ought to practise with it. I unrolled it, fitted it on and did so. Then I threw it out of the window.

I was having breakfast downstairs rather late next morning when my mother came in.

'You'll never guess what I found on the lawn,' she said, a look of distaste on her face.

'What?'

'A used French letter! One of the Americans must have come in with some tart during the night. It's too disgusting.'

I felt myself go crimson and began to sweat. 'How really *disgusting*,' I said, bending my head low over the toast. 'What did you do?'

'I had to use the tongs. I don't know what we can do. I don't want the lawn ankle-deep in used French letters.'

'No.'

The next day it grew abruptly colder and the day after that, when I left for Berlin, it was snowing.

(30)

For some reason, the journey was unusually slow, and it continued snowing all the way from Paris, snow on snow, until, near nightfall, I was fairly near the East German border. I forget the station – it may have been Osnabrück – but here I had to change on to one of the German-run military trains.

Going into East Germany then was tantamount to entering Russia with whom we were, as far as the army was concerned, virtually at war. I felt too excited to sleep, and after a while put on my greatcoat and scarf and walked back down the carriage. It was the last one and outside the back it had a small balcony or viewing platform with an iron rail. There was a gush of cold air as I opened the door on to this.

It had stopped snowing but the train sped through a flat white world, white even though it was night. Wide white fields, dark blocks of woods, single strokes of black trees against the white, all of a sudden a house crouched black. Once, the fleeting orange dot of a light. The air was biting and I turned up my collar and put the scarf over my head and ears. The train made a soft rushing sound and a great plume of snow spurted up behind it, an endless fountain like the wave behind a speeding ship.

I stood for a long time, at first oblivious of the intense cold, on the platform at the back of the silently rushing train – racing deeper and deeper into enemy territory. Eventually, now freezing, I went back to my super-heated first-class sleeper.

The RSF barracks were out near Kladow on the western outskirts of Berlin, indeed in terms of distance nearer Potsdam. Berlin was then divided into four zones: British, French, American, Russian. The fenced perimeter of our camp was directly against a pine forest in the Russian zone. From time to time we would see the grey figures of the Russian soldiers against the snow, patrolling distantly through the trees, like wolves.

Berlin has a Continental climate; that is, very cold in winter, very hot in summer, with quite lengthy and pleasant interludes in spring and autumn. That winter, the temperature regularly registered fourteen degrees Fahrenheit – what my grandmother called eighteen degrees of frost. But our barracks were superbly equipped – both for officers and men – far better, I suspect, than anything in Britain then. All the windows had tightly fitted second windows screwed in at the onset of cold, the heavy radiators were furnace hot. I took my platoon skiing among the woods and miniature hills of the Grünewald and we skated on the Havel. The intense cold seemed appropriate to our frightening isolation so far from the rest of the Allied forces in Germany. Appropriate, too, to the looming pine forests where once or twice I actually thought I did see wolves. Late at night, as the last post – that unbearably haunting lament for four hundred years of death and bravery – echoed across the frozen barracks, I sometimes thought I heard wolves too.

Army life went on everywhere and always: parades, inspections, training, exercises, football, camp cinema, mess nights . . . Probably all military establishments have a culture of drink. Our German predecessors certainly had. Next to the urinals in the basement of our much larger and more attractive mess there was a line of fat bowl-shaped porcelain receptacles to vomit into, each projecting from the walls between two stout stanchions to hold on to. Drink was absurdly cheap for the occupying army and so were cigarettes. I started to smoke Balkan Sobranie.

More names float up: Donald, the amusing new doctor; Neil, amiable but rather over-talkative in a barrister-like way, who would lie on my bed and try and provoke me into arguing with him while I tried, rather ostentatiously, to write. But my companion remained Basil. He had more or less got over the fiasco of the regimental silver. He said he realised almost at once he was on the wrong train; and had learnt nearly as quickly that the express to Vienna was not going to be stopped, much less put into reverse as he had at first somewhat hysterically demanded, for a very junior British army officer. He eventually got back to Wuppertal and then Berlin. 'Of course, they didn't punish me,' he said, 'because it could have happened to anyone.' It seemed to me it could have happened only to Basil, but his distress must have been evident.

The snow melted and gradually it grew warmer. I had again been made stables officer, in charge of the six horses. They generated a good deal of manure and I asked my new batman, Rae, to dig a small terraced garden along the bank outside my room in the junior officers' quarters. My old batman, Marshall, whom I was fond of and in whom I used to confide, had been irritatingly transferred to Basil's platoon, but I persuaded Basil to make him his own batman.

Once more wrapped and double-wrapped, swathed and suffocated in our military cocoon, we did now have some very brief, very slight, superficial contact with the outside German world. I sold sacks of manure to Berliners living nearby. I arranged and paid for (and never took) three months of German lessons. Every so often we drove into the city, for what Basil called 'a thrash', in the very old, battered second-hand van we'd bought in January for almost nothing from an officer, Captain Bone, in a returning guards regiment. Basil, full of hope, called it 'The Passion Waggon'. Bone had also given us the address and telephone number of a 'marvellous' brothel run by a 'Madame Kitty', which Basil and I noted down with beaming gratitude and knowing laughter – terrified.

A thrash meant doing a round of nightclubs, ostensibly in search of girls, or at least some sort of good time. These evenings were excruciating. They were expensive, even with the ludicrously favourable rate of exchange. I dare say some of the hostesses might have been persuaded into bed with money and effort but they certainly weren't particularly keen and seldom very attractive. The only time we went to a club where they were both and I began to press forward I soon discovered to my astonishment that they were all men in drag. We would return late, exhausted, fairly drunk and much poorer.

I remember reading somewhere at that time that youths and young men thought about sex every four minutes – or something equally rapid – which seemed both amazing and also perfectly reasonable. Basil and I discussed our terrible dilemma – the lack of any possible partners at all. Though the solution was obvious we shrank from it. David Cameron had another of his girls, Jean, with her friend Sharon, out from England and somehow got them into Berlin. He begged me to help him by taking Sharon on. Jean was exquisite, but the phenomenon of the very plain friend is notorious. I even had to get into bed with the unfortunate Sharon, quite pointlessly for both of us, in a very expensive hotel paid for by David.

Finally, Basil and I grasped the nettle – if that is an appropriate metaphor. At the end of June, five months after we had heard about her, I rang up and made an appointment for us both to go and see Madame Kitty.

(31)

Madame Kitty's centre of operations was Pension Zamett, 61 Giesbriecht Strasse. She had told me, in a slightly chilling phrase, that 'hours of business from three till ten is'.

We drove off as late as we dared, cold sober after two beers. The Passion Waggon was not only uninsured and unlicensed but delivered its exhaust in clouds through several holes under our feet. The hot summer air swept in through the open windows as we rattled and banged into Berlin. Basil kept combing his hair.

Giesbriecht Strasse was just off the top of the Kurfurstendam and was still, like much of Berlin, half-wrecked with bombed buildings. We stopped at number 61, rang the bell, waited. The door opened and we were shown into a long corridor. From somewhere deep in the building came very faint, muffled dance music.

Halfway down on the left was a door with a glass sign 'Pension Zamett' glowing dull red. A heavily lined elderly face peered round.

'*Ach so* – from Captain Bone. Yes I remember. Come in.'

She led us into a small, high-ceilinged room off a small hall. There was a long, red plush sofa, a chandelier, a bookcase with false-looking leather books. The entire wall opposite the sofa was taken up by an oil painting of seventeenth-century Puritans in black. I sat on the sofa to wait.

Basil was now in a state of considerable agitation, walking up and down smoking, combing his hair again, not listening. Suddenly he said, 'I think I'll wait for you outside. I can't do this. Here, take my money.' We had drawn the equivalent of fifty pounds each. He poured all his Deutschmarks into my lap and fled, leaving me, equally nervous, alone.

Madame Kitty returned with three of 'my lovely young girls'. I chose Barbara; small, golden-haired, eighteen or nineteen. Madame Kitty shooed out the other two and, delicately, left us alone. Barbara spoke excellent English and, after some rather aimless exchanges, I said it might be nice to have a drink.

'Wait a minute. I'll ask Madame Kitty.'

It was Madame Kitty herself who returned, alone, serious-faced. 'So you think Barbara a nice girl? How much would you like to pay for her?' We settled on fifty Deutschmarks, which I fumbled over to her.

'I was wondering,' I said. 'I wonder if we might have a drink?'

'What would you like?'

'I wondered if you could bring a bottle of whisky and a soda syphon?'

Madame Kitty gave a wizened cackle. 'Only one drink is in the fifty Deutschmarks.' She cackled again, called through a door, '*Komm' hier*, Barbara', and turning, suddenly said, 'But where your friend is?' When I explained, she said, 'I thought he looked too young. Yes. It is probable he has never had a woman. It is not good to have your first woman here.'

I followed her and Barbara along a further corridor, past a tiny kitchen and into a red-papered, high-ceilinged bedroom, discreetly lit. A large bed with a pink satin cover filled it below another huge oil painting, this time of some big naked nymphs sporting heavily round a fountain. Next to the bed was a green screen in front of an alcove. Madame Kitty brought in two ridiculously minute glasses of brandy and two glasses of Coca Cola and left with a friendly, wrinkled smile. We swallowed our inadequate drinks and then Barbara disappeared behind the screen. As if the fountain had begun to play, I heard splashing and the running of a bidet. Soon after this we were rolling together on the bed.

It became clear after a while, as might have been predicted, that nothing was going to happen. All Barbara's sinewy wiles could do nothing and, suddenly overwhelmed by despair and shame, I put a stop to them.

'Don't worry. It doesn't matter. You are not the first. It often happens, especially in a place like this.'

As we lay and smoked she went on comforting me. I noticed how large the aureole was on her small pointed breasts. She told me she had a daughter aged seven months whom she had to bottle feed 'for business reasons'. She would like to see me again. If we wanted to go to bed together it would have to be in a hotel. 'You understand, my home and this place are two different places.' She wrote her name and address in lipstick on my cigarette packet.

Basil was smoking when I joined him outside.

'What was it like?'

'Indescribable.'

We drove back through the hot Berlin night in silence.

(32)

I doubt places like Pension Zamett are often the locale of such initiations today. But from the mid-nineteenth century to the mid-twentieth century this was a classic, clichéd introduction to sex. Quite often, in books, the middle-class hero got VD, and suffered physical agony and (deserved) tortures of conscience. Sometimes he simply had sex and just suffered the deserved tortures of conscience. More rarely, as for me, it was a sort of rite of non-passage.

But just because something is a fictional (and biographical) cliché doesn't mean it can't be painful if it happens to you. To have wanted to make love to someone for so long, to have tried so often, to have fantasised about it, dreamt about it – and then to fail so humiliatingly! To be impotent! Probably *never* to make love at all ever.

I brooded on this and like this for a long time. I determined to succeed at what had become – once so simple and so necessary – Mount Everest. Determined to succeed; terrified I would fail again. I also brooded in secret. I told no one. To try and exorcise it, I wrote it up in my journal. Basil, sensible, wise but almost equally humiliated, begged me to describe it. I therefore also wrote a *Fanny Hill* version which I read out to him.

I quite often read aloud from my journal. I had begun it to practise writing. Wilf Cowley had taught me that good writing should come close to the vernacular. I knew my writing was stilted and artificial and I hoped keeping a journal would loosen it and make it more real. Eventually, I think it did do this.

But, of course, it rapidly also became a repository for all my woes, a riskless means to revenge and, in the end, if asked why I kept it, I would have replied – lest it die. As to whether I thought it would be published, I believe most journal-keepers secretly think this — certainly, all journal-keepers who are writers do. That is why, paradoxically, they may, like Larkin, ask for them to be destroyed after they are dead. But it is quite possible to hold two (or more) diametrically opposite ideas at the same time. I also knew (and know) my journals never would be (nor will be) published.

But, skimming the pages after Madame Kitty, I can see that, though recurrently miserable about the fiasco and determined to reverse it, I in fact quickly recovered. Our life in Berlin was very busy. I never did guard duty where Nazi war criminals like Hess and Doenitz were still doing time, but there were many other inter-zone duties. (Doenitz, incidentally, was to give me a lot of trouble later.) I was seconded to a French regiment for three weeks. We had endless parades.

I got into trouble. Basil went on leave and asked me to take Marshall temporarily on again, so I enlarged my garden and put him to work. By chance, David Cameron went on a course and asked me to do the same with his batman Stewart, so I told them to extend the flower beds still further. Unluckily, a visiting general came to take a salute at a parade. Walking through the mess with Colonel Thompson on his way to lunch they met Rae. 'So, what do you do young man?' said the general. 'I'm Mr Gathorne-Hardy's batman, sir,' said Rae in his soft Edinburgh voice. Next they came across Marshall. '. . . Mr Gathorne-Hardy's batman, sir.' Finally, they met Stewart . . .

Then, while driving in Berlin, a wheel came off what Basil, despite now overwhelming evidence to the contrary, persisted in calling the Passion Waggon. Fortunately, neither we nor anyone else was hurt as the van skewed across the road, but all our non-existent or illegal documentation came to light (I had found a lot of old German military swastika and eagle stamps in drawers, and stamped them all over my provisional licence). This row rumbled on for weeks. I was saved by Cambridge.

Because of my knee injury chasing rabbits, I had joined up four months late. I therefore applied to leave four months early to take up my place at university. The delay was agonising and it looked as if the row over the Passion Waggon might keep me in. In the end, they relented and at the end of September I was free to go.

But what really made my last months quite enjoyable was that I had come to like many of my fellow officers and they to like me. When I left, nine of them came to the station to see me off. The general's niece had finally been accepted.

(33)

I had been sufficiently well educated at Bryanston to take the Higher School Certificate (now A-level) history papers at S-level – scholarship level. I managed to reach this and was thereby encouraged to apply to the Suffolk County Council for a scholarship.

I was given a major county scholarship, though the chief education officer and his committee cannot have been entirely unmoved by the fact that my uncle, the chairman of their county council, had driven me into Ipswich and was waiting for me outside. The chief education officer asked me what career I had in mind. I said with sincere, serious but at the same time disarming frankness, that I was considering a career in county education.

The scholarship paid for my education but not for my keep. Up till then my father had given me a small allowance of ten pounds a month but this he now said he couldn't continue. (I don't know why. Their finances always underwent wild swings, usually downwards.) Jock very generously said he would give me £225 a year. This would have to cover everything, in term and out. Running up a few debts and supplemented by Christmas and birthday presents, I just managed it (it didn't even occur to me then that I could have worked in the vacations).

Thus buttressed, I went up to Cambridge on 15 October 1953. I had tried for Corpus Christi because Gathorne was there and because it was a college where, once again, Jock had influence. But it was full and he was unable to get me in. Trinity had room so I went there.

I lived far out in the suburbs, in a single, small dingy room with a gas ring. The only heating, apart from the ring, was a tiny, black gas fire with a single bay window of seven fragile white ceramic towers which when lit hissed and turned red, then glowed white and if, with gobbling meter, left on for hours, eventually heated the room. It took twenty-five minutes to reach my lodgings by bicycle and this, with my shame at its dinginess and smallness, meant I hardly ever asked anyone out there. Instead, I spent most of my time with Gathorne in his rooms in Corpus. But I was often lonely in my first year and as a result I worked. I found I enjoyed history. In particular, I enjoyed lectures.

Most actual learning at university is done by reading, writing essays and in tutorials (at Cambridge, famously, just you and your tutor). But the books can be dull and so can tutors. What good lecturers can do is inspire.

Two of my tutors were like this. Peter Laslett, teaching English history, did so by paradox, originality, sudden insights and daring speculation. He compelled you to question every accepted cause, every assumed effect. He was amusing. He was very good at current scholarly feuds – at this time particularly centring on the Civil War. Yet he told me that when he'd begun he was a hopeless lecturer. Like Churchill, he had laboriously taught himself how to speak in public.

Herbert Butterfield (not a tutor) had a course on European history from (I think) 1450 to 1850. Always interesting, with Napoleon he suddenly electrified us. I remember him describing how Napoleon had extraordinary gifts quite unrelated to generalship. He could look at one of the metre-wide ledger pages detailing the equipment of a regiment and *at a glance* spot a discrepancy between stirrup irons and saddles, say, or cartridges and bandoliers. Governing his vast empire, he would dictate orders and take decisions for two days or more at a time, stopping only for meals or an hour's sleep. He sometimes found it necessary, in order to calm his racing mind, to do this from a tepid bath. A short, stocky man, with increasingly wild hair, Butterfield in effect *became* Napoleon and for two weeks, twice a week, kept us intoxicated with the great Frenchman's rise and fall.

But the most astonishing figure in this respect was Professor Ullman, my medieval history tutor. Ullman had fled Nazi persecution before the war and when it began had joined the Pioneer Corps as a private. He was discovered labouring here by a surprised Cambridge academic who knew his reputation. There began a process of extracting this internationally renowned scholar from his unsuitable situation. A position was found for him at Cambridge, but even here he met with a good deal of prejudice. It was many years before he was a full professor and when I was being taught he was always given distant and cramped lecture halls. Yet he was a profound and gifted historian, an excellent teacher and an inspired lecturer. It is not difficult to make medieval history extremely boring. Ullman made these complex, intricate, turbulent centuries live in all their complexity and turbulence – and would then explain them with vigorous and fascinating clarity. I remember one lecture in some distant chemistry lecture room he'd been assigned. The small room was packed, as always, with undergraduates in the aisle, on the broad window sills, standing at the back. Ullman strode up and down his platform in front of the blackboard, his long gown streaming behind him. At one dramatic point he flung his arm up and out and his gown billowed over the ranks and stacked piles of glass test tubes, bottles, bell jars, crucibles and retorts heaped on a table by the last lecturer. Ullman paused, then swept his arm down again, sweeping with it all the test tubes and crucibles. The noise was tremendous and any other lecturer would have lost us. Not Ullman. He strode back down his platform, continuing his lecture, and completely ignoring the crashing – and so did we. It could simply have been a sound effect of the clashing and smashing of suits of armour arranged on purpose to illustrate his discourse.

With teachers such as these, and time to study, I went into my exams at the end of the year – the prelims – moderately well prepared and, in fact, I got a first. Unfortunately, the results of prelims don't count in your degree.

But even if I hadn't been hopelessly distracted and seduced by what, to me, were more important things, I would never have got a proper first. I have not got, in that invidious, dated, exam-centred, university-centred phrase, 'a first-class mind'. I have met first-class minds and the difference is noticeable at once – there is an effortless quality in the rapidity and logic with which they think, a genuine surprise at your inability to grasp some point or other. It is as if their brains were made of different material.

Gary Runciman, at Cambridge with me, has a first-class mind; so, oddly enough, did my Uncle Eddie. I think my cousin Gathorne probably has too. I am always slightly nervous in the company of first-class minds and try and shelter behind humour; in life I compensate with my most useful mental quality, which is persistence – Mr Pringle's stamina, I suppose.

Anyway, stumbling through Cambridge with my second-class mind, work was not, as I say, all-important. Far more important was my desperate desire to prove I wasn't impotent by losing my virginity and the sexual frustration that went with it. And just as important as work was my writing.

(34)

Before I'd gone up to Cambridge, Nick Tomalin had asked me to have a quick drink with him in Soho. In a brief outburst of intoxicating and outrageous flattery (I remember still the inaccurate but thrilling words 'You'll go through Cambridge like a knife through butter') he said he was already in the process of deciding who should edit *Granta*, then the leading university magazine, when he left at the end of the academic year. Nick said that, on the advice of Wilf Cowley, he was considering me. Would I write a piece for them?

I wrote the piece; it was heavily edited and published, but I heard no more about being made editor of *Granta* – somewhat to my relief as well as disappointment. Nevertheless, one reason as far as I was concerned for starting a magazine was to jog Nick's memory – or frighten him with competition. Also, of course, to publish anything I had written.

Chandelier was edited by about six people, including Gathorne, Sophie, me and our friend David Gribble. It was financed by David's father, who gave us a hundred pounds.

Our strong point was shameless exploitation of friends. Ben wrote 'Advice to a Young Composer', which would bear reprinting today. Stephen Potter, forgotten now but famous then for his gamesmanship books, did a gamesmanship piece. I also wrote to Ivy Compton-Burnett, whom I'd met a few times because she was a friend of my Aunt Anne and her bookseller husband Heywood Hill. We printed her reply, notable for succinctness.

Dear Mr Gathorne-Hardy, I'm afraid I only write novels.
Yours sincerely,

IVY COMPTON-BURNETT

It was fun rushing about soliciting advertising, arranging displays, getting people to sell it, launching issues with parties. But, though Mr Gribble's money ran out, the extraordinary thing, given its quality, is that *Chandelier* sold surprisingly well.

At least, it was surprising until a few years ago. Then, while Nic Hill was helping clear out the Hill family house near Aldeburgh after his parents had died, he opened an obscure floor-to-ceiling inset cupboard he hadn't noticed before. He was, he said, quite literally knocked flat by the avalanche of nine hundred *Chandeliers* which poured out on top of him, untouched since they had been bought forty years before.

(35)

I had decided I must prove I wasn't impotent before my twenty-first birthday. (I thought 'impotent' was being unable to sleep with a woman. In fact, I continually had ample – too much – proof that I wasn't impotent at all. I remember writing a poem, or rather an embarrassing and opaque set of verses on the subject in my nearly full journal at this time with the title 'My Mistress is a Mattress'.)

Girton and Newnham were there; for several years the only colleges that took women, but there was a large teacher training college (where Sophie and Juliet went), secretarial colleges and technical colleges, and there was no real shortage of girls. I kissed them and entwined myself passionately round them, under them or on top of them on sofas and beds and cars, danced clamped against them in hot, pitch-black rooms and eventually, agonisingly frustrated and rather drunk, returned alone to the thin, hard, sheeted, icy, unresponsive body of my leaden mistress. Almost all of the middle-class female sex, including foreigners, seemed determined not to sleep with anyone until they were married or thirty.

Almost all – but not quite all. There were brave exceptions. One was Claire, Nick Tomalin's beautiful partner. Each year at a university seems to have its Zuleika Dobson, its Long Lizzie. She is the most beautiful and attractive girl in the world and all the men desire her. Claire was that girl in my first year. In reality, in a university of ten thousand graduates, each group had its Zuleika (all circles of young men do). But the editorship of *Granta* was a position of exceptional elevation and prestige and Claire was (and is) quite exceptionally attractive. Many people were aware that Nick had a real mistress (still a word one could easily use then) and it made him seem even more sophisticated and successful.

There were others. There was Thompson, a rather red, bulging figure in Trinity who went up to London and had a black prostitute. He returned, as if from Venus itself, to amazed admiration. I remember he said he hadn't had a bath for a week and could still smell her on him. It was all we could do not to ask him to strip off and let us share this extraordinary phenomenon.

In my second year Jocasta Innes was Zuleika. I got to know her, and the rest of Cambridge – or my bit of Cambridge – desired her intensely, though in vain. I discussed the problem of girls not sleeping with men and she said there *were* girls who did and she would introduce me to them if I liked. Eventually she did, to one, but by then it was too late.

Then Nic said he had met a beautiful girl he wanted me to meet, or rather support him meeting one weekend.

(36)

Nic had picked up Nell Dunn in an art gallery. She had invited him to stay and he had asked if he could bring me.

He did this, not because he thought Nell would suit me – he thought she would suit him – but because her mother Mary, then Mary Campbell, used to have what amounted to a salon on irregular weekends at her house, Stokke, near Great Bedwyn in Wiltshire. Nic was too nervous to go alone; indeed we were both so nervous even together that on the train from London we bought a bottle of red wine. We had finished it just after Reading, when a thin, middle-aged man in a suit came over to our table in the restaurant car.

'Forgive me interrupting you two young men, but I couldn't help noticing the pleasure with which you polished off that bottle of wine. I am an ex-alcoholic and it gave me great pleasure too. I wonder if you would permit me to buy you another bottle?'

We said yes, but had to drink quickly because Great Bedwyn isn't all that far from Reading. As we got off I pulled the communication cord and, from the top of the bridge over to the next platform, we watched the kerfuffle as the guard rushed up and down the train before, eventually, it steamed out.

We were met by Mary Campbell, in trousers and with her Land Rover. Mary, about forty, was very attractive then, and indeed for many years, with a round, open face and dark eyes with which she looked you straight in the face, blinking a lot. Everything about her seemed straight, honest, lively and above all *interested*. Her skin was so delicate that it was a while before you noticed the network of extraordinarily fine lines like the lines that come and go on the delicate skin of boiled milk.

But her daughter Nell, aged eighteen, looked quite simply wonderful – with golden curls, a boat mouth in a Botticelli face, a slim-legged figure that looked as if cream had been lightly poured over it and set firm and very rounded. She had Mary's rapid blinking, but with Nell's blue eyes it looked as if she had just made some faintly wicked and delightful suggestion. Laughter cascaded out of her and rippled away and then came cascading out again.

I can't remember exactly who was there, apart from Robin Campbell, Mary's second husband, and Freddie Ayer. I think Cyril Connolly and Laurence Gowing came the second time Nic and I were there. Possibly it was Eduardo Palozzi or Laurie Lee or Tom Matthews and Martha Gellhorn or Woodrow Wyatt, all of whom used to go to Stokke, among many others.

Nic and I were put together in a room with a large repaired patch in the ceiling. Mary said it had been made by Philip Toynbee. He had announced melodramatically and drunkenly that he was going to kill himself. When no one took any notice he rushed from the big sitting room, grabbed a shotgun and thumped loudly up to our bedroom. Shortly afterwards everyone was startled to hear, muffled from upstairs, the sound of shooting. They did now, of course, as he'd wanted, take some notice – notice rapidly diluted by the fact he'd fired both barrels into the ceiling.

In fact, I remember only three things about the weekend. I remember Nic and I coming down to the large, L-shaped sitting room to find everyone sitting round a small but functional Tortoise stove with a long chimney in the base of the 'L'. Mary asked me if I could make a Martini. I said of course. Would I fix one for all of them, please. I went over to the small table of drinks, filled a cocktail shaker half with gin, half with Martini, rammed some ice into the top, shook it about and was about to pour when Mary called across the room that she wanted to taste it first.

She did so and instantaneously, to my astonishment and horror, in full view, spat it out all over the carpet. She went over to the sofa full of Freddie Ayer or Laurie Lee or Martha Gellhorn or whoever it was, opened the window and poured my Martini into the garden. I learnt that a proper Martini was something like nineteen-twentieths gin and one-twentieth Martini and had to be ice-cold but not diluted.

Three or four tumblers of what now amounted to aviation fuel succeeded in soothing this social humiliation and also thrusting back the effects of the bottles of red wine gulped into an empty stomach too quickly on the train. It was a Pyrrhic victory. The second thing I remember is finding myself in an argument with Freddie Ayer, towards the end of supper in the Aga-heated kitchen and after another bottle or two of red wine, about free will and determinism. In my memory it is like my first appearance on the tennis courts of Bryanston, but now as David against Goliath or Christ against the Pharisees or the young, very young Duns Scotus taking on the ageing Aquinas in a set-piece medieval scholastic disputation – and holding him at bay. Gradually, astonished, the whole table fell silent. 'But surely Freddie, if you allow the *first*, how can you *not* allow the second?' And then suddenly, in mid-sentence, I felt a tide of alcohol sweep through my cerebral cortex like an anaesthetic tsunami. I not only lost the thread, I couldn't even remember what we were talking about. I had to confess this and shortly afterwards Nic helped me up to our room. During the night I was sick several times into a rather pretty tin waste-paper basket beside the bed.

I sometimes saw Freddie Ayer again over the following years but was really hardly even an acquaintance. It was another Siegfried Sassoon relationship. But I liked him because he treated young men as his equals. I remember staying with him at my Jarvis cousin's house in Lincolnshire and how he tap-danced expertly the length of their long dining hall with his very pretty daughter, his feet as nimble as his mind. We had one more discussion during our non-friendship.

Talking about the psychology of the mind, he said he never saw mental images of something he was talking or writing about. I, who see nothing else, couldn't believe it. How could anyone think like that? He insisted. 'But what happens when you think of a cow, for example?' Freddie thought for a moment, then he said, 'I think I see the word "cow".'

The last thing I remember about the weekend is how well I got on with Nell. Although it was Nic who had been invited, and although she was even-handed, it was becoming clear it was me she really fancied. She, too, was going to be a writer (and indeed became a far more successful one than me). We talked about our future writing intensely and enthrallingly. I returned to Cambridge glowing with her.

(37)

Despite this socially fairly disastrous start, I was asked to Stokke, along with Nic, very soon afterwards, about three weeks later, probably at the instigation of Nell. This time Cyril Connolly, Laurence Gowing and his wife Julia Strachey were staying. It was a briskly cold, early spring weekend, the wind strong, the sun shining.

Cyril could be tricky socially. Suddenly gripped by depression or irritation or because he felt he wasn't getting enough attention he'd tilt back his head, shut his mouth, his moon face would become a bowl of porridge, and he'd spread an enormous *Silence*. But not at Stokke and not this time. For one thing, he was very fond of Robin Campbell. Robin was a curious, very human combination of flawed vulnerability and calm strength of character: he had great common sense, wisdom even, humour, kindness, was a warm and comforting father figure; at the same time he was one of those people you wanted to help. A man of great courage, he had lost a leg in a daring raid to capture Rommel and been a prisoner of war. It was said he felt he'd paid his debt to society and was therefore justified in not working, but instead tried his hand, not very successfully, at painting, sculpture and even music. Mary, on the other hand, had the hostess's gifts for encouraging the brilliant guest (also, incidentally, for protecting the nervous one) and creating the atmosphere and good food necessary for Cyril to shine.

And that weekend he did shine. The moon became the sun. He would turn his head from side to side, his eyes twinkling, to see how he was going down. The tragedy for the conversationalist – and on form Cyril was as good as you can get – is that people are usually too amused, too engaged, to record anything. And this is especially true of those creative fantasies peculiar to his genius which would suddenly burst in Cyril and fountain from him like fireworks for minutes at a time. A piece he wrote for *Encounter* – 'Bond Strikes Camp' – is the nearest he came to demonstrating this gift in prose (and in this failure to recall he showed himself less studied, more spontaneous, than Wilde, whose equal he could be, in that Wilde, who often rehearsed what he said, remembered enough to furnish his four great plays).

But, to follow this digression, I thought I had once recorded one of Cyril's extraordinary displays. It was when I was with Eliza in 1956 or '57: Cyril arrived for lunch one Sunday, for some reason irritated by a long account by Arthur Koestler, covering several pages of the *Sunday Times* review section, of a trip he had made in a canoe down the Rhine. 'Have you seen that article of Koestler's?' Cyril said crossly. We agreed we had. There was a silence, Cyril staring glumly ahead. 'Imagine it,' he said in his flat voice with its slight edge, 'imagine having to go down the Rhine in a canoe with Arthur.' And then all at once a sudden glimmer of expression went across his large fat face. 'I'd be in the back,' he said, 'Arthur in front. After a while, Arthur would say, "Cyril, you're not pulling your vate" . . . ' And for about fifteen minutes their trip got wilder and wilder and funnier and funnier, until the conventional phrase 'helpless with laughter' was completely accurate. So vividly did I remember it, I thought I'd written it up in my journal. I'd looked before, but when I went again to find it for this book – nothing.

Buoyant in our laughter, Cyril continued in amiable vein towards everyone all weekend. Not yet having any reason to feel irked by me, I was included, though it was rather evident he was much more interested in Nell than in Nic or me.

But then, I too was much more interested in Nell than anyone else there. Once again, we talked intensely about our writing, mutually impressed by all the things we hadn't yet written. Before supper I asked Nell if it was easy to get from the Philip Toynbee room, where

Nic and I had been put again, to her bedroom. Nell said it was and showed me, thereby, or so it seemed to me, implicitly accepting my implicit suggestion.

Eventually, everyone started to go to bed. I lay, pyjamaless, cold, tense with longing and terror, and at last the house was quiet. Then I got up, put on my dressing gown, and said to Nic I was going to see Nell.

'What for?'

Big, ramshackle, seventeenth-century, pitch-dark Stokke creaked in the wind like White House Farm used to; the stairs creaked as I tiptoed up them, feeling my way, to Nell's small chintzy attic room at the very top of the house. I pushed open the door and whispered, 'Nell.'

'Yes.'

'Can I come in?'

'Yes.'

I sat on her bed and talked a bit. Then I said I was getting cold and could I come into her bed for a moment.

'Yes.'

When my middle stepson, Noa, lost his virginity at the sensible age of sixteen, he said he was both surprised and disappointed. He had known what would take place fairly precisely: there would be a sudden surge of romantic music, lights would flash, the room would tilt and whirl and he'd almost certainly glimpse waves surging up and dashing against rocks – and none of this had happened.

I wasn't disappointed at all. I thought it was marvellous. I was amazed how naturally we fitted and slid together, how easy it was, amazed I could ever have found it difficult. We lay in each other's arms in her tiny, soft bed, while the wind blew and the attic creaked and for the first of many times ahead, to the words the peace that passeth all understanding, I had a sudden image of the crucified Christ, of my being the crucified Christ, lowered and lying in the arms of Mary. Then we made love again and I slipped out and crept back down through the sleeping house.

Nic was awake and very upset. He said, 'I've been talking to the wallpaper.' We went on talking for some time, while I told him about Madame Kitty and how I'd been sure I was impotent, things I had told no one.

The next day I kissed Nell goodbye in front of everyone as if nothing had happened and, our love-making enveloping me like a cloud – I'd be like Thompson, I wouldn't have a bath for weeks – returned to Cambridge.

(38)

I saw Nell – sweet, golden, laughing, cream-covered Nell – quite a lot for a few months. I discovered Biddy Harrisson had been right, you can make love anywhere – on camp beds, on the Wiltshire downs, in linen cupboards, in baths, in the toilets of trains . . . But we were never in love, which is probably why I had suddenly found it was all so easy. We stimulated and excited each other, attracted each other, made each other laugh, and I was profoundly grateful to her – but that was all. Not long afterwards she married the man she did really love and I, having taken that first plunge, swam away. But she is still one of my closest friends in that *amitié amoureuse* way which is one of the best forms of friendship in the world.

The fraught and frustrating nature of my long delayed passage had considerable effect on me. I felt a sort of fury that I'd been denied what it had long been clear to me shouldn't have been denied. I felt I had to catch up and it was twenty-five years or so before, fortunately inheriting something of the Boyle and Go-Go's energy, I decided I had caught up. It was not so much a question of how many girls or women I could get – though perhaps most men (and probably women) can't help, however faintly, a feeling of notching up – but that whenever I was without someone to sleep with I would get in a panic that I'd never find anyone again and take over-frantic steps to find someone – which led to one or two disasters. Some of my friends would probably say I used to be too interested in sex. I don't actually think this is possible, at least until about fifty, but certainly it has often fascinated me. Madame Kitty has meant that I have sometimes been impotent the first time I sleep with someone though, unless I have to leave at once, it has always been all right in half an hour or occasionally not till morning. And for many years, most of my life, Madame Kitty vanished completely – only now, as either the Great Silence or Viagra looms, does she stalk me again.

And perhaps I should repeat, in case this brief confession does give an impression of *number*, it would be the wrong impression. I have been seriously involved with five women, of which the last has been, still is, the most serious, the most important (and the best). I have often wished I found it easy, but I've found it very difficult, and usually impossible, to be unfaithful in these circumstances – which of course means a considerable diminution in number. What that is precisely, or even roughly, I don't know – I would have to read all of all my journals and that, as I explained, I can't face; but I'm sure it wouldn't prove in the least exceptional.

All this, the weaving and working out of it, stretches ahead over the future. When I got back to Cambridge in the spring of 1953, having met my deadline by the skin of my teeth, it was to my ludicrous twenty-first birthday and the explosive events which followed it.

(39)

Although I had always been told that Gathorne and I would share our twenty-first birthday party at Glemham, it had become noticeable, then very noticeable, that this plan hadn't been mentioned for three years or so. When something to do with you is so resolutely not mentioned it becomes almost impossible to bring it up yourself. All the same, because for a long time I had been told this was what would happen, had then assumed it, I was paralysed from arranging anything else. Besides, I couldn't afford anything else.

In the end, my twenty-first birthday was marked by a lunch in the Taj Mahal in Cambridge. Jock, Fidel, Gathorne, Juliet and Sophie came and I think possibly my mother. A few days later the Taj Mahal was prosecuted for serving tinned cat food as the basis of its curries and shortly afterwards had to close down.

However, Nick Tomalin now told me that he wanted me to be editor of *Granta*, starting in October, and that I must get to know Julian Jebb, my fellow editor. I returned to Suffolk, considerably cheered by this news after my gloomy coming-of-age celebration, to preparations for Gathorne's.

For several years a party was given every June at Glemham for the Aldeburgh Festival. There was a bar and you paid for your drinks but anyone could come and nearly everyone did. Jock and Fidelity had decided, with sensible frugality, to combine the two parties, and accordingly asked a number of guests for Gathorne. I don't remember my mother being there – it was not the sort of thing she really liked – but I came over from Hartington Road to stay the night since I knew I'd be too drunk to drive back.

At least, I'd hoped I'd be too drunk. But I soon realised I hadn't enough money to buy more than two or three drinks at the bar. I also began to feel a seething resentment, faint before this, that what I'd always been promised had been so easily and completely forgotten. I suddenly expressed and assuaged both anger and thirst when I remembered the cellar key. This hung on a special nail which opened the door down to the cellar where Jock stored quantities of wine, some of it very good indeed. It didn't take long to carry up a lot of bottles and start opening them in the kitchen.

The first Jock and Fidel knew of these events was when some woman came up to them and said, 'Oh *so* clever of you to have special drinks served for the twenty-first party guests in the kitchen.' Hurrying there, they were appalled to find a large, grateful, happy crowd milling densely around me as I dispensed open bottles of Château Margaux or Château Latour or whatever it was I'd brought up. It was a party, growing bigger all the time, clearly impossible to stop.

The next morning I had the most frightful hangover. There was a long larder then next to the kitchen and I was trying shakily to get some ice from the fridge, when Jock came in. He looked grim.

'Jonny, I want to talk to you about what you did last night.'

I found I was feeling an odd mixture of terror and anger. 'I'm not going to talk about it Jock. And if you ever mention it again I shall never speak to you again, and I'll never come to Glemham again.' Jock didn't answer, and I walked trembling from the larder.

The hero, wrote Freud, first defies the father, then defeats him. Jock was not my father but he was, to me, a much more frightening man than my father. I had defied him, but I hadn't defeated him. There hadn't been, there never was, any need. I had behaved badly, perhaps very badly, but then Jock and Fidel hadn't behaved very well either. Perhaps they were aware of this, or at least aware that I had reason to feel as I did. At any rate, Jock continued to pay my allowance, continued to write me letters about jobs with pensions, neither of them changed towards me and the incident was never referred to again. I think that was magnanimous.

The summer passed at 18 Hartington Road and Snape and in October I returned to Cambridge to take over *Granta*, work if there was time, and get to know Julian Jebb. I had met him briefly at the end of term and I hadn't liked him.

(40)

Julian was quite soon to become one of my closest friends and remained so for over twenty years. He was my best man when I married, and before and after that lived in the flat immediately above us at 18 Warrington Crescent. So immediately and so often did we go up or he down we might as well have been in the same flat. We stayed with each other's parents, went abroad together, I introduced him to many of my friends and after a while he was often more intimate with them than I was and I and they were drawn closer by this.

At first I was frightened of him. He seemed too smart, too sophisticated, too quick; I was also disconcerted by his appearance. He was very small (on the form rejecting him for national service, he'd managed to glimpse, he told me, the phrase 'of dwarf stature'); he had yellow hair, a pale, unhealthy-looking complexion and a puckered, elfin face a bit like Truman Capote's. I remember once going round Malaga fish market with him and by the end we were being followed by about thirty children staring in amazement at this odd creature which might have slid off one of the slippery marble slabs.

But these impressions vanished in a few days. He was quite simply one of the most amusing and stimulating companions in the world. Gerald Brenan said seeing Julian was like drinking a bottle of champagne; this was true and often led to the drinking of several bottles. He had a gift for developing a fantasy almost equal to Cyril's, but where Cyril took off alone, Julian and you did it together. He was an actor and a mimic sufficiently accomplished to succeed in the Footlights, a particularly talented group then. Above all he was sympathetic and interested in what you did, remembering what you'd done, cheering you on and up. If I'd started to die at

Cambridge, or later, I'd have sent for Julian. And if all this involved a good deal of flattery – who cares? (He was perfectly aware of this attractive trait, incidentally. Staying with Barry Humphries, filming, in Melbourne, he quoted him saying, 'Well, Julian, I don't think you've pushed the flattery cassette in quite hard enough – and try getting the volume up to eight: I think I can take it.') He was recklessly generous and extremely kind. If there was someone too shy or too young or left out at a party or on holiday, or a weekend, Julian would talk to them, if necessary for a long time – something rare among good conversationalists, especially one who liked to catch, and did catch, the great and famous: Alison Lurie, John Betjeman, Elizabeth Bowen, Elaine Dundy, Antonia Byatt, Caroline Blackwood, Paul Theroux, Melvyn Bragg, V. S. Naipaul, Frances Partridge, Germaine Greer, Patrick Leigh Fermor . . . I could unreel Julian's later friends over several pages. My own relationship with him might have been complicated because he was gay and for a number of years was in love with me. But this seemed to cause us no difficulty beyond the recognition that our feelings for each other were different, though I think it may sometimes have given Julian secret pain. In fact, aspects of this were probably true with many of the people he knew. Because his love-life was rarely satisfactory, he invested his friendships with the strong feelings usually reserved for love. Much later, this meant he could be demanding, set tests or take offence, and this was eventually accompanied by the emergence of other sides to him – more self-destructive, sadder, darker.

But none of this was evident at Cambridge while, helped by art editor Martin Newall, we edited *Granta* together. Our magazine, as all university magazines should be if they are sensible, was almost entirely frivolous and Julian's two great gifts as an editor were an inspired, often satirical frivolity and an ability to get almost anyone to write for us. If we needed a bit of weight, whether frivolous or not, he would get in clever young dons or, if necessary, clever older ones. We tried to get good short stories and poems. As far as I am aware, I didn't really have any gifts as an editor. But our task was made easier because *Granta* had reached its apogee under Mark Boxer two years earlier. It had declined after that and declined again under us, but the momentum of success carried us on. I think there were three issues a term or perhaps four and we usually sold between one or two thousand copies, but the advertising revenue was so huge we didn't have to sell one. Each year we made a profit of about £200, which we spent giving parties.

I now had lodgings in Trinity Street with Mr and Mrs Wells. Mr Wells was small and thin, arthritic, acned, irritably anxious and could be seen off. Mrs Wells was enormous and a tougher proposition – for Mr Wells as well as me. Julian was running through some inheritance or other and people came to his King's College rooms for drinks most of the time. But without *Granta* money, I couldn't have afforded to entertain; however, because of *Granta*, my social life improved dramatically.

For instance, I was elected to the True Blue Club. This was, is, the oldest dining club in continuous existence in England. Founded around 1732, its purpose was not political but 'good talk', though I remember only a lot of drink. The new member had to drink a pint of claret as fast as he could. Some people downed it in seconds, something I refused to do. Actually, I do remember one incident – my first and only physical fight. The dinner that night was in King's and towards the end Karl Miller and I had an argument, about what I've forgotten. Really, it was just more pints of claret on top of initial pints of claret. Before long we were rolling and struggling along the corridor outside the dinner room and bumped by chance against E. M. Forster's door. He opened it politely and must have been surprised and delighted to see two handsome young men in passionate embrace. Perhaps he thought for an instant, as Frankie Howerd would have said, that his luck had changed – but we rolled fiercely on. Fiercely, but harmlessly. Even sober I doubt Karl and I could do each other much damage. Full of claret, tangled like two wildly waving, drunken daddy longlegs, we could do none. After more rolling, we were exhausted. By chance, I ended up on top and have since counted it a victory. The following year I became president, perhaps because of this triumph.

I tried to work and did so to an extent. One of my tutors at Trinity now was Jack Gallagher. He was a brilliant historian and a teacher who would, by outrageous propositions, force you to think. 'So – what's so monstrous about starving Africans eating babies who'll die anyway?' and you would have to explain. He was inspiring in other ways but I must have been frustrating for him because my essays were frequently late and were often scrappy.

At the end of the 1955 summer term Julian left. For our last *Granta* party for the non-existent last issue (all the proofs had fallen into the river) we hired a large boat with a large cabin and puttered down the Cam. I then set off on a long vacation which was to change the focus of my entire life for the next few years – and in some ways for ever.

(41)

One of my friends at Cambridge was another cousin, Caroline Jarvis. Her parents, Ralph and Coney, had asked if I'd go to Spain with her for three weeks. They'd pay my fare; I would protect Caroline from rapacious Spaniards. Of course I said yes.

The holiday was with Ralph and Frances Partridge and Eliza Simons, as she then was. They had together taken a large house for the summer in the village of San Fiz near Betanzos in northern Spain not far from La Coruña. Ralph Jarvis had just returned from there and before we left he took me out to dinner in London.

About forty-five, a banker in Hill Samuel, he was clever, subtle, devious, a man of urbane humour and extraordinary charm. He charmed me, flattered me, and soon began to astonish me. He revealed that he had been obsessively in love with Eliza for some time, but that recently their affair had begun to torture him, especially on his recent drive down with her and short stay at San Fiz. During the day, Eliza had been irritable, distant, cruel. At night, as passionate as ever. As he talked and talked I became aware that he was really begging me not to sleep with her myself. 'But Ralph – how could I? You said she was thirty-three?' Ralph clearly didn't see this as the insurmountable objection which, in my innocence, I then did, and he continued to try and charm me on to his side.

Fatal precaution. The journey out was a nightmare; some crash in Madrid had paralysed the entire Spanish railway system and we spent three days and two nights in our non-sleeper, second-class compartment in stifling August heat. But I arrived, on 21 August, intensely curious about Eliza and, at least partly, in a way I certainly wouldn't have been if Ralph hadn't, in effect, suggested it.

The house at San Fiz was tall, lumpy and ugly like most Galician architecture, with a big, dried-up garden and big iron gates, no electricity or plumbing (water from a well) and three Spanish girls and a cook to look after everyone.

I was eventually to get to know most of that 'everyone' very well indeed, but at first they all seemed rather daunting, enviably civilised and clever and somehow very un-18 Hartington Road. Desmond Shawe-Taylor was staying, about to go. He had the face of an impatient cherub, a rattling quick mind, and used to sunbathe naked on a patch of parched grass in front of the house behind the gates. Crowds of ragged, barefoot village boys (poverty in Spain was terrible then) used to gather and stare in wonder at the distinguished music critic's pale, sun-creamed body, which was no doubt what he wanted. (Desmond, among his many intellectual and human attainments, was extremely highly sexed. I remember him saying, when he was sixty-five, that he would still invariably get an erection from the movement travelling on top of a bus.)

A few days after Caroline and I arrived, Gerald and Gamel Brenan turned up. Gerald, I was told, was author of the best books ever written on Spanish literature and the Spanish civil war. What immediately caught me was his conversation. In particular, I had never heard anyone talk about books like he did, as if they and their characters were real life – only often more important and interesting. Thirty-two years later, to my astonishment, I was asked to write his biography, which I did. Even at this first meeting, I might have come to hero-worship him, except that it isn't, wasn't, in my character; also Gerald was too human, could make himself too ridiculous. But I came to love him. Gamel too – with her caked white make-up to mask the ravages to her beauty (she was approaching sixty), her despair at wasted talent, her quick, gentle – with Gerald sharp – sense of humour and her odd habit of miaowing as she crawled up the beach out of the rolling Atlantic.

The routine at San Fiz was ordered and we swam regularly in that Atlantic. Expeditions would sally out to beaches: Eliza's three little girls – Nicky, Georgie and Rose; Rose, two, round and chubby, accompanied by a silent and colossal blown-up replica fifteen times her size – nanny; Caroline; Burgo, Ralph and Frances's son, who could be rather difficult but who I got on with; for a while the Brenans and Ralph, Frances and Eliza. Ralph had only five years to live but his weak heart was impossible to detect or even imagine in his big, strong frame. One beach had a sandbar, a few feet below the water and about two hundred yards out, to which Ralph would swim. Once, as he heaved himself upright out of the water to stand on it, a school of dolphins appeared and played about him and he stood, dripping, slightly bowed, looking like a god.

I was shy of him because he seemed both quick and formidable, and all men of his age reminded me of Jock. But one of the most sympathetic aspects of Bloomsbury was their concern with youth and their treating young people as their equals. Virginia Woolf's journals are always wondering – what does the *younger generation* think of this or that? I used to get flustered then, I still do, when asked what I *thought* of something – but with Ralph and Frances, and Gerald too for that matter, this aspect manifested itself in listening with interest, questioning, drawing out. Frances, in particular, with her sense of humour and silvery cascade of laughter not unlike Nell's, was particularly adroit. In our regulated life, the sherries before lunch, the drinks before dinner, but above all the meals that stretched out were as much a time for talk as for eating – though they all seemed to like eating, especially Ralph. Drinking was moderate.

Occasionally there were expeditions. Ralph took us all to a bull-fight in La Coruña and paid for a box. Franco, who had been born nearby, was in the one next to us. I thought, if I'd brought a grenade with me I could change the course of Spanish history. Litri had come out of retirement to fight for him. I remember the great bullfighter half-kneeling, one thigh against the ringside so that he was trapped, and the bull whirling past him and tossing up the cape.

But the person who more and more fascinated me was Eliza. At twenty-two, or to me at twenty-two, a woman of thirty-three seemed impossibly much older; and though now both twenty-two and thirty-three seem little different (young men who fall in love with an older woman will find they eventually catch up), it is true in some ways the gap can be very wide to start with – especially between an attractive woman who had already had two husbands and a good number of lovers and me who was, in Christopher Fry's phrase, as near a virgin as makes no difference. Yet, Ralph Jarvis hadn't thought it was impossible. But it never occurred to Eliza at first, I think, until she and I, Burgo and Caroline went on a four-day expedition into Portugal. By this time, I was literally in a fever, running a temperature of about 100°, proof, if proof is needed, that even the beginning of obsessional love is not like but actually is the onset of an illness. I must have said something, or just looked something one night when she put her head into my bedroom in some Portuguese hotel, and said goodnight. I remember the sudden speculative look that crossed her face.

The first night we were back at San Fiz she came down late into my small bedroom at the bottom of the house and got into my bed. After that, I crept up to her big room at the top of the house every night and got up and went back down to my own room before breakfast, which everyone except Ralph and Frances had in Eliza's bedroom. Then there were the long siestas, as the sun moved slowly round and I was perpetually amazed, so new was it all still, at the peace which passeth all understanding and my continual descent from the cross. And no one knew; no one even suspected.

On 18 September Caroline and I went back to England in the train. Eliza had said she'd get in touch.

(42)

However, she didn't. I heard nothing. And I felt too proud, or too nervous of being humiliated and raising the distant, cold voice Ralph Jarvis had described so vividly, to ring or write myself. I realised it had been what people called a holiday romance and that was that.

Back at Cambridge, I soon embarked on one of those over-precipitous replacements which often caused me trouble. I had now got to know Jocasta Innes. Really, I longed to seduce her, but instead I went to bed with one of her friends, Sophia. (A common pattern with men, incidentally.) It didn't really work for that reason, but one day Sophia – a beautiful Hungarian who looked like a blackberry – said she was pregnant. Our panic over having a child drew us together in a way engendering it had not. I remember talking to a young man one windy, winter's day in a boathouse near Chiswick and getting an address. Another contact, in Half Moon Street, a louche, middle-aged, pouch-eyed doctor, smelling of stale brandy, said, 'Look Gathorne-Hardy – do nothing. In my experience, when a girl gets pregnant, her back really *is* against the wall – leave them alone. She'll make damn sure she gets rid of it.' In the end, we found a doctor and hospital and borrowed from a generous friend of Sophia's the equivalent of £2,800; which I was still paying back five years later.

Julian had left and, marking a further stage in its decline, we had made Nic and David Gribble editors of *Granta*. I slightly missed what passed in that tiny world for fame, but must have retained a sort of afterglow, because a rather strange thing took place. I said I couldn't temperamentally hero-worship, and this has been true despite an absent father and resented would-be father figures; I was also not someone people chose as hero – for much the same reasons they didn't choose Gerald Brenan. But now this happened to me. I realised a metamorphosis had occurred in the way one of my friends, David Spanier, was regarding me. The distinguished journalist and poker genius no doubt eventually lost the need, but at that time he had a series of heroes. Suddenly, briefly, inappropriately, I was one. He came for advice to my rooms in Trinity's Whewall's Court. He hung on my words. The climax, and my unmasking, came when he arrived and said, 'Jonny – I have crabs. What should I do?' I looked at him. Crabs. What on earth did he mean? Was this – unlike him – a foray into Nerval territory? Did he mean should he buy some tiny leashes or little dog's leads? Or was it some culinary venture? After thought, I said, 'David – if I were you I'd do absolutely nothing.' Soon after this he attached himself to worthier metal – Jonathan Miller, I think, or perhaps it was Rory McEwen.

At the end of the October term or it may have been the start of the first term in 1956, I got a letter from Eliza. Would I like to come and have supper with her in London at 27 Montpelier Square?

From then on, I went up to London every second or third weekend. This change of focus, which is what it became, was not helpful to work, though I did as much as I could. For the second part of the Tripos, I'd changed to English and I'd wished I hadn't. I find it hard to explain why. Certainly, I found writers I might not otherwise have done and became passionate about them. The

Samuel Butler of *The Way of All Flesh* I would eventually have read, but probably not Pope, for example. There were some very good lecturers – I remember David Daiches on James Joyce. I went to one of Leavis's lectures. He strode in, gown billowing, good-looking but grim, jaw set, at that time the embattled Zwingli or Calvin of English literature, and I remember his analysis of Shakespeare's verse – how, for instance, in *Measure for Measure* 'In thrilling region of thick-ribbed ice', the intense cold was conveyed by the repeating rrr's – was itself thrilling. I became fond of my tutor, Theo Redpath, whose habit of turning up an hour or more late for tutorials dictated the form of my third novel *The Office*. He was perceptive, but so clever, so able to see all sides, he found it almost impossible to reach a conclusion; in the end, though often stimulating and illuminating, this led to a feeling of paralysis, of stasis, in his students as well as in him. Leavis was certainly inspiring but his followers, of whom there were many, were so maddeningly doctrinaire I couldn't bring myself to go to more of his lectures. I now wish I had.

As the terms passed, I went up to London to see Eliza more and more often until I went practically every weekend. I also seem to have begun doing something else at this time – or possibly a little later. My Aunt Anne, who reminded me of it recently, can't remember exactly when but she told me that about now we had arranged to meet for lunch in Swallow Street. She arrived very late and was told no one called Gathorne-Hardy had appeared. She sat down and eventually had lunch alone. Meanwhile, I was doing the same at a different table. It turned out I'd given my name as Hardy.

This was an early, rather minor, response to the social reactions I'd first become aware of when the Naafi girl in Ayr had slapped my face over my accent and her huge cake of yellow soap – and it was to recur many times. Should I disguise my voice, hide my past (or some of it) and pretend to be what I was not – or not?

Today, this would not seem to be in the least surprising. Over the last twenty to twenty-five years a great many children of the middle and upper middle classes have been trying to do precisely this – with accent, clothes, attitudes, a studied vagueness about parents, schools, sources and amounts of money. But in the late 1950s it was slightly in advance of its time. Except that I suspect that as regards social change the '50s were a more significant decade than the '60s. An indication of this was revealed, incidentally, by the recent massive research into British sexual behaviour (the research Mrs Thatcher tried to stop) – the 1994 *Sexual Attitudes and Lifestyles*. They found 'no evidence of a sexual revolution co-terminous with the decade of the 1960s'. All the changes supposed to have taken place then in fact took place in the '50s. Median age for first intercourse, for example, fell in the '50s as much as it was to do over the next thirty years. The real pioneers were not the Stones or the Beatles or the flower children, or the hippies, but, among countless others, people like Nick and Claire Tomalin, me and Nell and Sophia. What happened was that in the '60s people, especially the media, woke up to what had already happened. The nervous reactions of the Seebohms at my attraction to Jennie were partly due to their anxiety about changes they could sense starting to take place all around them.

I don't, therefore, remember any of my contemporaries being particularly shocked by my affair with Eliza. Except, it seemed, for one. Gathorne came to me and said a lot of people were deeply upset by my behaviour. It was felt I was dragging the family name in the mud and I should stop. The entry in my journal which reminded me of this is laconic and sharp and no doubt echoed what I said to him. I thought then he was jealous, which he may have been, but I think I was also probably being unfair to him. He was almost certainly responding to what he was hearing in his family and genuinely felt he should warn me.

The combination of Cambridge social life, *Granta* and Eliza made me very nervous about my degree and it seemed quite possible I might not get one at all. In the end, I got a 2.2.

My allowance came to an end with the last day of August, but I had already moved to London. I hadn't the faintest idea how I'd earn any money, except it was unlikely to be in something with a pension.

London, life – and now, like everyone at that age, those Peer Gynt skins and the patterns they embodied, laid down by childhood and youth, skin wrapped round skin wrapped round skin wrapped round skin, would go on working their way out for decades, until the results became intolerable and I had to try and change the patterns. Peel the onion, and find – what? Peer, of course, found nothing.

PART THREE

My Life! My Life! My Life!

(1)

The temptation in writing one's life, or the desire, is to find significant patterns. But suppose there are none? This is not the moment to revive Pirandello (I am aware that that distant introduction still needs explaining) but perhaps it underlies my fascination with Sterne, which I also mentioned earlier. I have often copied his way, in *Tristram Shandy*, of writing in short sections. Readers today – reading only in bed at night or on trains or planes or beaches – need such aids. So do I. Short sections turn an impossible mountain into a series of conquerable hillocks. But what I thought had interested me in Sterne were the workings of a mind made concrete, his endless digressions, his wandering and meandering off the straight narrative line for pages, chapters at a time. However, what I may really have sensed was that this apparently aimless meandering was in fact a metaphor for life, or for my life.

If I sliced off the top of my head and emptied it on to the table, looked at neutrally that is what you might see – an enormous heap of incidents, dreams, emotions, accidents, desires, fears, successes and failures, the jumbled contents of a thousand films, two thousand TV and radio programmes, 20,000 books and 100,000 newspapers and magazines and advertisements, the massed array of the past: Nanny Paton, Mary and Nettie, my mother and my father and my grand-mother, Fidelity and Jock, Sammy and Rose, Nic and Julian, Eddie and Bob, Mr Pringle and Mr Pringle's sex-crazed brother, Newhouse, Basil, the colonel I told I was the general's niece, Hussein, all the women I've ever made love to and all the women who have refused me . . . ; all this and far more, just a huge, formless, seething heap, material for endless Sterne-like, truncated narratives, diversions and speculations. But nothing else or more. Not in the least significant.

In fact, at this point an odd aspect of memory makes it easier to use the material in this way. At first, life is a narrative or at least a chronology; as time passes and enough of it accumulates one can see it and experience it as a picture. As a result it becomes possible, in memory, to leap about in our past lives; order and linearity increasingly disintegrate – or can be made to.

And this freedom brings into play other aspects of memory, of written memory. Take Heisenberg's Uncertainty Principle. Until the 1990s the Uncertainty Principle stated that it was impossible to measure both the *position* of a particle and its *momentum* at the same time. The reason was that to measure either of these you had to use light and photons of light exert a pressure, albeit a minute one. If you measured the *momentum* of the particle, photons of light bounced off it and changed its position. If you measured its *position*, the photons of light struck the particle at random and altered its momentum. That is, the physical act of measuring exerted a force and altered the thing you were trying to measure.

The same is true of memory. Add in its capriciousness and you get the Uncertainty Principle of writing autobiography. The act of writing alters what you are trying to write about. As I began this book I received by chance a letter from a reader of my long short story 'The Infant Hercules'. I hadn't thought about Newhouse for years; the letter brought him vividly back to me. And not just him but the whole train of events with which he was associated. As a result, the racket Bayley made masturbating had already been revived in my head when I began the book. He therefore reappeared when I came to shooting pigeons at White House Farm. I don't mean what I wrote wasn't true, only that I might not have included it. An accident had introduced a bias, whether distorting the truth or revealing it, whether beneficial or not, I'm not sure.

And indeed, as I write at this very moment, another echo is set up. After leaving Weidenfeld and Nicolson in 1959, I was tutor for three months to five children in a seventeenth-century farmhouse on a remote and isolated part of Dartmoor. The husband, a businessman, was away all week and often for a fortnight at a time. The wife, Yvonne, aged I suppose thirty-two, did not fall in love with me exactly but I reminded her of her youth. She had actually *been* a ballet dancer. She talked about it and took to dancing about the house, pirouetting and *entrechat*-ing and suddenly doing the splits, to my admiration. One lunchtime she spun into the larder and I suddenly heard a loud *thunk!* – then silence. Yvonne did not reappear. After a while, I went into the larder. Pirouetting light-heartedly into the air, she'd struck her head violently against one of the old beams and knocked herself out. I had not planned to include this incident, since it had no significance. On the other hand, books are held together, given structure and resonance, by such echoes. Perhaps I should include it after all in 1959.

This introduces another uncertainty. The imperatives of art are different from those necessary for a straightforward and accurate self-portrait. But these impulses are inseparable from writing a book, just as memory is inseparable from the imagination. The two sorts of truth resulting are not contradictory but they are not the same. But perhaps this is the way to resolve the temptation I started with. Even if the life itself does not really hold any significant pattern or indeed significance of any sort, the book might. You can try and make an autobiography a work of art. In fact, what this all means is that it is now, writing my autobiography, that I realise most strongly that *all* writing is fiction.

There is another odd thing about memory. Childhood memories are just 'me': me in my mother's arms after my baths at Snape, me halfway up the Faraway Tree at Shiplake, me/Tarzan stalking through the woods at White House Farm; but adult memories are of things that happened to me. There is a difference of point of view, of feeling, of texture. This, too, allows freedom when recounting. It also has to be registered.

What was about to happen to me now, in September 1956, was my first appalling experience of work – and of course the intensification and complication and eventual destruction of my affair with Eliza.

(2)

During my first three years in London, where I was to live for almost thirty years, I learnt a number of lessons which were to be continually reinforced.

First, I was astonished by how rich most of my friends turned out to be; even the quite humble daughters of an accountant, for example, or the son of a GP. A lot of middle-class guilt is soundly rooted in actual handed-out or inherited money, as well as in the ability to earn it. I also noticed how consistently they lied, or remained silent, about the huge sums golden-fisted fortune had doled out to them – and would augment when their rolling-rich parents died. Were I in charge, it would be compulsory by law to deposit each year a complete statement of assets, income and expectations, figures freely available for inspection personally, in Somerset House or on the internet. It is interesting that when Solon was called in to reform the constitution in Athens in 591 B.C. one of his first acts was to make compulsory the public declaration of all sources and amounts of wealth.

Not that I have anything to complain about. For one thing my friends were on the whole very generous and I frequently benefited from their wealth by way of meals, weekends, rooms, sometimes even flats and holidays. At various periods I have relied on the three or four suppers I could solicit every week. And in 1975, and again in 1978, I suddenly and unexpectedly came into some money – not quite enough, as I saw it, but none the less a lot.

But at this point, in 1957 and for the next twenty years, not having money meant a job was essential and urgent. I had only two ideas – journalism or copywriting. I tried to get a job on *Picture Post*, backed by my old tutor Jack Gallagher, but I was turned down; possibly because of my *Granta*s or perhaps the rolled umbrella I borrowed to impress – or both. I have since done occasional hack reviewing and written a few articles, but I am not good at it and it takes me a very long time. I think I might eventually have learnt to be a journalist. I would certainly have been better off and probably better known, but journalism seemed to me to have one huge disadvantage. I wanted to write books, if possible novels, and journalism was too close to, often actually was, 'real' writing. Advertising was not. My friends were split between (hopeful) writers/painters, the media and layabouts, and bankers/business or just being rich – and all of these secretly despised advertising. But advertising had a second great advantage. I had a vague idea I could perhaps work part time at it.

Both suppositions turned out to be accurate, but at considerable cost. My first advertising job, as a trainee copywriter, was two years with S. H. Benson. I like to think I got it as a result of the little pile of *Grantas* which I once again nervously flourished – but there was no way of telling. P. L. Stobo, the creative director, was a man of few words. He flipped the pages of my *Grantas* silently and, it seemed to me, sightlessly. 'We'll let you know.' I think the fact that Bobby Bevan, the chairman, was a friend of my parents, probably did it.

In the 1920s and '30s, would-be writers usually chose prep schools. In the 1950s and '60s they chose advertising. I eventually ended up on what amounted to the Parnassus among ad agencies – Ogilvy, Benson and Mather. But even Bensons then had Gavin Ewart and John Yeatman – one of the authors of *1066 and All That*.

Despite the intoxication of earning money (£600 p.a.), I hated those two years advertising. I found writing copy almost impossible. I had to learn, not just an entirely new way of writing, but a new way of thinking. There was an early meeting, me sitting in, to discuss the problems of jute. The main problem, apparently, was that no one knew about jute. No one. It didn't show up at all in the research. Suddenly, I had a brainwave. Why didn't we (how quickly one becomes 'we' in a new job), why didn't we run a campaign on the headline 'Jute the Obscure'?

I soon stopped making such suggestions. And my difficulties were much compounded because I had just begun to read Proust, the writer above all who for a while transforms both how you see the world and what you feel, while his prose, especially refracted through the elaborate, serpentine sensibility of Scott Moncrieff, transforms the way you write – or try to write.

Longing to write like Proust, I was being forced not to write at all. Everything I did was rewritten fifteen or twenty times, and then turned down. I remember that Linguaphone was running a series of advertisements in the *Reader's Digest* at that time. Instead of the seventy to a hundred words you usually had to clamp, screw and grind your brain into, these advertisements needed two thousand. It was felt this might suit me. Over two weeks, I rewrote the same Linguaphone advertisement nine times – and was then told to give up. It didn't seem to me that there was the faintest difference between what I'd written and what eventually appeared. I was simply being gratuitously tortured.

But even worse was the sense of imprisonment. No one warns school and university leavers of this. For eighteen or twenty years you have relatively free and varied conditions of work. You have about four months' holiday a year. Suddenly, you are shut up in a small box or small area in a large box eight hours a day. You have two or three *weeks'* holiday a year. After five months at Bensons I would sometimes go to the echoing toilets and sit weeping with frustration. I would go up on to the flat roof and stand, blown by the wind, looking down at the traffic in High Holborn or away down Kingsway to the Aldwych and imagine the big building suddenly setting off and smashing everything in its path – a fantasy I sent up so often and so vehemently into the ether it was eventually picked up and put into a Monty Python film.

People were the only compensation. On the whole the so-called 'creative' workers in advertising, particularly the copywriters, are, or were then, pleasant, civilised, intelligent and literate companions. They were usually cynical, amusing, gregarious and not infrequently kind. Gavin Ewart was a kind man, with gentle humour and infinite patience with the dotty stuff we had to write. Yeatman was really a prep school master, ironic and detached. John Mellors, a laconic Yorkshireman, was my boss and another sympathetic figure.

I was put into the little office of Joan Kennedy, an attractive Scotswoman of thirty-five. She had some big lorry account and had to bang out reams of technical copy. She was a gentle person with a quick sense of humour, but her pretty face was often sad, and it was becoming possible, in a certain roughness and high colouring, to detect drink – but then everyone drank too much. (Julian worked nearby, either at Thomas Aske the literary agency or at *The Tablet*, I forget which. We often had lunch together and had, by trial and error, discovered that a Stingo, a barley wine and a large sweet sherry, were best and cheapest for producing the muzziness that got us through the afternoons.)

Joan and I both soon learnt to leave the room when the other's telephone calls got tricky. Joan's were with Derek, a reporter on the *Mirror*, her hard-drinking, amusing, unfaithful lover of several years who couldn't commit himself. I would return sometimes to find her cheeks wet with tears.

My own conversations were with Eliza.

(3)

Although I had been seeing Eliza as often as I could while at Cambridge, when I came to London it was not to move in with her. Although this was what I really wanted, it did not take place for a year. The delay was partly the result of the paradoxes which underlay our affair, both intensifying it – and eventually destroying it.

Gerald wrote once that, since everyone knows that romantic love cannot last, there is always a sadness hovering at the edges of a love affair. In our case, it was more than the edges. We both thought that what we were doing was – in any permanent sense – 'impossible'. The fundamental reason was my conventionality – at some point I wanted to marry and have children and a family which I supported. Eliza couldn't have any more children and, thanks to massive alimony, was rich while I was poor.

There were peripheral reasons. Gathorne had not been right about my dragging the family name in the mud, but as year succeeded year I was aware that my mother became increasingly agitated – though the agitations of parents over what they see as their children's unsuitable liaisons usually serve to cement them. Eliza, too, came in for disapproval. By chance or inclination, her men before me had usually been ten or so years older than her. Jealousy is the last emotion to die, and these (as I saw them) aged figures in their mid-forties resented my arrival. Perhaps they felt threatened by what Montherlant (was it?) called the insolent avidity of youth. There were those who had not been lovers but had hoped to be, and now the way was blocked – or made more difficult.

Cyril Connolly, in particular, seemed to find my new role an

increasing irritant. I remember Eliza coming back very upset once
after he had attacked her. *How* did he attack you, I asked. 'Well, one
thing he said was, if all I wanted was sex out of a toothpaste tube . . . '
said Eliza, nearly crying. I could see this was insulting, both to her and
to me; at the same time I felt vaguely flattered. 'Do you suppose he
was thinking of those new large-size Colgate tubes?' I said. 'What do
you mean?' said Eliza uncomprehending. 'Nothing. Nothing. Doesn't
matter.' We went to stay the weekend with Arthur Koestler and, after
a good deal of drink, his aggression became evident. Indeed, I'm not
sure jealousy *ever* stops. Ralph Jarvis, who died in 1973, never spoke to
me again. And with one or two of those men who have survived, now
truly ancient, into their eighties, and though it all took place over
forty-five years ago, I am still sometimes aware of latent hostility.

We went to a performance of *Der Rosenkavalier* at Covent Garden
and I remember looking at her and seeing tears running down her
cheeks and knowing why – and it made the opera more painful,
more poignant and more powerful. And so with everything else.
Besides, I couldn't, then, bear to leave her. Why, after all, *should* our
affair be so 'impossible'? I was in love – obsessed and fascinated; and
fascinated also by everything we did. In my brief holidays from
Bensons, we went to France and Spain and Morocco – none of
which I knew. Her whole way of life was totally unlike the Arch or
18 Hartington Road; and my finding it new and exciting made it new
and exciting for her again.

I lived, when not with her, in a series of temporary dwellings. The
first of these was in Lennox Gardens. My grandmother had given
birth to Jock in Lennox Gardens in 1900. After a while they kept a
cow in the mews to supply milk. But I was lent a capacious flat by a
Cambridge friend, Robert Loder, at the top of the Loders' family
house. I was living here when I saw Pirandello's *Six Characters in
Search of an Author*.

The play fascinated me. I remember going up on to the roof of
the Lennox Gardens flat and talking to someone – perhaps it was
Robert – nearly all night. I remember the dawn rising over the roofs
and the milk float with its clinking bottles doing its round far below
under the trees. But what eventually intrigued me far more was
how I soon forgot the substance of the play and gradually created

what I saw as my own memory of the beginning of it, the actors wandering near the dimmed stage waiting to go on. It was this play, my play, I never forgot.

After Lennox Gardens, I rented a series of small bedsitters or sometimes just bedrooms. Not till I joined a friend, Richard Williams-Ellis, in Carlton Mews, was I settled.

I went to Montpelier Square several times a week, often quite late after spending the evening somewhere else, and Eliza and I went away for weekends. I introduced her to Julian and she became one of his closest friends. But I had many other friends and of course I went down to 18 Hartington Road and Snape.

(4)

In 1957 my grandmother was seventy-eight and though, as a result of cancer, she had had one of her large breasts removed five years before and, at the reappearance of cancer, radiotherapy to her neck in 1956, she seemed exactly the same, except for the rather baggy simulacrum of a breast that, when she remembered, she constructed out of rolled-up stockings and handkerchiefs.

We still worked in the wood together, still planned the wood I would one day plant, played cribbage in the evenings and went for drives in her car, though now I usually drove. There were slow changes to the countryside. Gradually, the common land round Snape was ploughed up. First, in stages up to the church, the common opposite the side gate and next to the field where I'd torn the ligaments in my knee; later on most of the common just before the village went, a common which had once stretched down to the river. The mill at Friston had long since ceased to work, so had the Maltings. And year by year hedges were ripped out and the little fields amalgamated into the gross prairies which now disfigure Suffolk and Norfolk. But the real difference in the house itself lay in the succession of women who came to cook and, it was hoped, perhaps tidy and clean a little.

Elfreda had eventually left (by some miracle a man had appeared) and was, despite her shortcomings, now revealed as a high point of efficiency and sanity. Indeed, with an exception at the very end, I can remember only one other sane helper after her and that was Mrs Dalton. She was eighty-three, two years older than Granny when she arrived, but very tough and very Yorkshire. She had been 'in service' all her life and as a result they got on extremely well. In fact, they were very alike, except that where my grandmother bustled, Mrs Dalton walked with a rolling gait like a mate of Long John Silver.

A nadir of some sort was reached with a lonely and deeply depressed figure called Mrs Hunt. Many years before she had been the women's golfing champion of Kent but had fallen on hard times. She arrived with all her clubs and an extremely old dog, a black, smelly, wheezing heap, her only companion and love. My grand-mother inclined to be sympathetic to people who liked dogs and when this repellent object fairly soon died took some time to comfort Mrs Hunt. 'I had Brown bury the body outside the kitchen', she wrote and told me, 'so she could look at the grave while she washed up.'

By chance, I came down to Snape for the denouement of this tragedy.

On the Saturday morning Brown had come in for his daily talk in the drawing room about what was going on in the garden and what to do about it. I was reading and didn't pay much attention until I realised that Brown, with some difficulty, was trying to explain something that had nothing to do with his garden.

'What do you mean Brown?' my grandmother said rather briskly. 'What are you saying? *What* is Mrs Hunt doing?'

'Done, she have done already m'lady,' said Brown. 'That were done three days ago.'

It appeared that Mrs Hunt, in her grief, had dug up her dog's body and returned it to its bed in the kitchen.

'Come with me Jonny,' said my grandmother, at once stimulated. I followed her into the kitchen and there, sure enough, was the black heap back in its basket. There was quite a strong smell of decomposing dog.

'Now Mrs Hunt,' said Granny, kind but firm, 'we really can't have this you know, can we. Jonny, go and get Mrs Hunt a large tumbler of sherry.'

When I came back, as instructed, with about half a pint of sherry,

Mrs Hunt, her big, lugubrious face already red from crying, was crying again. My grandmother was sitting massaging one of the golfer's hands and talking soothingly.

'Go up to my bedroom Jonny and in the bottom drawer of the chest of drawers you'll find some old dresses I keep for things like this. Bring one down.'

I didn't particularly want to touch the corpse, but my grandmother didn't mind things like that. She lifted the dead dog on to the dress, Mrs Hunt watching miserably. 'Drink up Mrs Hunt, you'll feel better after some sherry. Come on Jonny, take the other end.'

I followed my grandmother out of the front door, the heavy load in its green and pink flowered shroud swinging between us. We buried it in the orchard, putting the turf back carefully and firmly so that it was impossible to see where. 'We don't want more exhumations,' said my grandmother.

This was not the only time Brown had had difficulty breaking awkward news to her. Anne remembered how in the early 1930s, when they kept pigs and employed three men on the little estate, his morning visits were already routine. One day he'd come in and talked incomprehensibly for some time. Finally, after repeated questioning and a good deal of misunderstanding, my grandmother understood he was saying that Goldsmith, one of the other men, had been having sex with one of the pigs. Eddie, who was, as he was compelled to do at various times in his life, sponging off her for a few weeks and was usually bored stiff by the minutiae of Snape, perked up at this. 'Which one Brown?' Brown explained. 'Oh no – not *that* old sow,' said Eddie.

But my uncle was a very different man then.

(5)

The most productive period of Eddie's life, at the risk of adopting the tone of an obituary, was the ten years he spent as an antiquarian bookseller with Elkin Matthews. During this time he gradually came to know as much as, and often more than, anyone in England about, in particular, seventeenth-century books and book-making: about the minute differences – a reversed initial capital, an absent frontis-piece, a dating error etc. – which distinguished rare editions; about

seventeenth-century printer/publishers; about the obscure authors of
the sermons popular then; about the endless pamphlets and pam-
phleteers – in fact about the whole complicated, to Eddie fascinating,
world of the scholar-bibliophile. Despite his habit of helping himself
from the till, which complicated their accounts, he was apparently an
extremely valued member of the small team at Elkin Matthews,
which included his brother Bob. And just as very attractive young
women assistants will draw custom into a shop, so Eddie drew people
in because he interested, entertained and amused them. He also read
what he was selling. He read voraciously all his life, particularly
poetry. I have a number of seventeenth- and eighteenth-century
volumes of poetry he bought – or took – from Elkin Matthews, often
annotated in pencil in his small, idiosyncratic handwriting.

Elkin Matthews went bust some time in 1936. There followed
several years of sponging – as much as he could squeeze out of Jock,
my grandmother and his rich friends. When he had money he was
generous and instinctively extravagant. One of his ways of getting
about Europe, for instance, was to buy a second-hand car at Dover
and sell it, always at a loss, in Gibraltar or Nice or wherever he
needed to end up. Among others, Bobby Pratt-Barlow, a very rich
American homosexual who spent a great deal of time in Sicily,
wanted to leave him money, but Eddie could never be bothered to
sustain the attention needed to fulfil this pattern – a common one
among homosexuals.

In 1939, while in Athens, he joined the Diplomatic Service,
spending the war in Cairo and, after it, serving in Beirut. But these
years, and especially the first sponging years, were also spent in
lengthy and strenuous botanical and zoological expeditions in
Greece and the Middle East. He became as good a botanist and
small mammal zoologist of these regions as he had been bibliophile
and for years he sent the fruits of his explorations to the Botanical
Gardens in Edinburgh. These Middle Eastern expeditions also
suited him sexually.

It always amused Eddie and Bob that, though they were the
homosexual members of the family, it was my father and Jock who
had been notorious at Eton. They enjoyed telling me about them and
I remember Bob, no doubt joking, saying once did I know that Jock

had been held down while the Duke of Gloucester buggered him. I asked Eddie if this was true. 'Perfectly true, my dear, perfectly true,' Eddie said, 'except he wasn't held down.'

Bob, though he had casual sex, also had a homosexual marriage with Kyrle Leng, which lasted over twenty years until Kyrle died. But Eddie never had anything like this and preferred a great deal of sex with numberless youths and boys from fifteen upwards, usually working-class. This was much easier and safer round the shores of the Mediterranean. Or relatively safer. He got syphilis once from one of these transient partners. 'Entirely just retribution, my dear, for buggering an Arab boy on the shores of Lake Galilee on Christmas Eve.'

I have sometimes wondered why Eddie achieved so little. He had no ambition to succeed in a worldly way at all, though he certainly wanted to be liked and to enjoy himself – and 'enjoy' included his botanising and his reading. Laziness is sometimes disguised fear and I think at some level life, engagement, did frighten him. Yet he was gifted; quite apart from his wit, he spoke French and German, he had, as I said, a 'first-class mind' with a retentive memory, but his enormous reading, his considerable learning, only produced a single eight-page anthology – though this was almost perfect of its kind, which was unique. *Inadvertencies* was eventually printed in a limited edition of 200 copies in 1963 by Bob, who had a printing press.

Though it was published later with a less subtle title by the Bodley Head, both versions are rare. Puerile to begin with, quite quickly you find yourself laughing, and the predominantly homosexual flavour (or queer, as Eddie's generation would have said) is less because of his own inclinations but because the words queer, balls and bottom and to an extent tool are susceptible to the inadvertencies he was concerned with (that is to say, inadvertencies from authors who were, with one exception, famous in English literature). In fact, his approach was catholic. I'll quote five of them:

William Makepeace Thackeray
> The organ 'gins to swell;
> She's coming, she's coming!
> My lady comes at last.   (*At the Church Gate*)

. Charles Dickens

She touched his organ; and from that bright epoch, even it, the old companion of his happiest hours, incapable, as he had thought, of elevation, began a new and deified existence.

(*Martin Chuzzlewit*)

George Eliot

A boy's sheepishness is by no means a sign of overmastering reverence; and while you are making encouraging advances to him under the idea that he is overwhelmed by a sense of your age and wisdom, ten to one he is thinking you extremely queer.

(*The Mill on the Floss*)

By the author of Little Dot, My Mates and I, Saved at Sea, etc.

Poor old Treffy was in bad spirits this evening. He felt that he and his organ were getting out of date, things of the past. They were growing old together. He could remember the day when it was new. How proud he had been of it! Oh, how he had admired it . . . But when he had eaten his cake and taken some tea which he had warmed over again, old Treffy felt rather better, and turned as usual to his old organ to cheer his fainting spirits. For old Treffy knew nothing of a better comforter.

The landlady of the house had objected at first to old Treffy's organ; she said it disturbed the lodgers.

'No,' said Christie, 'you mustn't think of it, Master Treffy. Let me see, what can we do? Shall *I* take the organ out?'

Old Treffy did not answer: a great struggle was going on in his mind. Could he let anyone but himself touch his dear old organ?

(*Christie's Old Organ*)

Henry James

Then she had the equal consciousness that within five minutes, something between them had . . . well, she couldn't call it anything but *come*.

(*The Wings of the Dove*)

In 1956, when Eddie was fifty-five and the oldest, if most amusing, third secretary in the Diplomatic Service, he was unexpectedly axed.

He was given a tiny pension and so began the second period of sponging which lasted until his death in Athens aged seventy-eight. This meant increasing and often prolonged visits to Snape which, despite her pleasure in having her adored son, were sometimes testing to my grandmother. They were often very testing to Eddie.

He used to seek relief with my mother at 18 Hartington Road. They would sit and drink and gossip and complain, for example, about how *tiny* the glasses of sherry were they got offered at Glemham. But my mother loved him and these visits refreshed him. As did my visits to 18 Hartington Road refresh me when I could escape from London.

(6)

In July 1956 my father had returned from his long spell of duty abroad, burdened, among other things, with the buried memories of Hong Kong which a year later, as I described, were to burst explosively to the surface.

During this tour he was at last made a commander, something we had all been very anxious about. I think the long delay must have been due to a number of adverse reports during his naval career. My father said because there were relatively few doctors compared to other professions in the navy, to become a surgeon commander was like anyone else becoming a captain.

My father also returned in love. His ship, the aircraft carrier HMS *Centaur*, had undergone extensive manoeuvres in the Mediterranean while based on Malta. There he had met an attractive Irish woman, a schoolteacher, Mary Smartt. She, too, returned to England in July 1956, now thirty-nine, joining a school at Ashford. My father, after his leave in Aldeburgh, was once again posted to Yeovilton, though now without my mother. He and Mary used to meet at Salisbury for weekends. For the next eighteen years my father led the stable double life – wife/mistress – for which I think he had always longed and which he had suggested to me that time we'd lain in the long grass outside the Arch. An element he particularly enjoyed, and which he thought, mistakenly, he'd achieved with consummate skill, was the secrecy.

But, underlying this, my father's ill health, which was to become catastrophic from 1964 onwards, first wobbled in 1958 when he began to run high temperatures. As he became worse, he was moved to the naval hospital at Gosport. The source of the trouble seemed to be his right lung. Cancer was suspected. My father described four doctors round his bed discussing his symptoms – one of whom was himself. He realised afterwards, he said, that he had felt completely detached. His body was just a case, nothing to do with him at all. In the event, his own diagnosis – a badly infected lobe, not cancer – proved the right one.

It necessitated a fairly extensive operation and he came to 18 Hartington Road to recuperate, which he did sleeping in my room, now his. I think it must have been now, with Mary's advent, that my parents stopped making love – and to that extent it wasn't, perhaps, quite the ideal wife/mistress set-up of my father's early fantasies. Whether my mother minded the cessation I'm not sure. I think she was probably both relieved and also did mind. Just as when she discovered about Mary, which of course she did several years later, she was glad sometimes to share the burden he had by then become, glad to get him out of the house, perhaps pleased for him – and jealous.

It took two months for my father to regain his health, something he gauged by his ability to drink large quantities of whisky again and once more smoke lots of his disgusting cigarettes. Here, the White Horse, in the High Street below 18 Hartington Road, was important. My father went there every morning to drink whisky chasers, and roll his cigarettes in the small back room and talk to Bert Allen, the publican. Bert, a little older than my father, a squat, shrewd, almost toothless, amusing man, deeply Suffolk, matching my father in drink, gradually became a close friend, along with Mrs Allen.

It is indicative of the difference between my mother and my father – often, perhaps, the difference between men and women – that while he had only two real friends and few acquaintances in Aldeburgh, she was friends with half the town.

(7)

There were no supermarkets then, but the High Street contained all the shops necessary for life and death within a hundred yards; nevertheless, going shopping with my mother could take at least two hours. Every few yards, someone would stop and engage her in chat. When Rose was small, she would stand waiting, gently tugging at my mother's skirt to get her to move on. Later, she would run off to play with Lizzie Cook, her best friend, whose father owned and ran the main men and women's clothing and haberdashery shop next to the chemist. From this vast acquaintanceship, and also from Mrs Gooding who came in once a week to clean and gossip, my mother came to know everything that went on in that Dylan Thomas-like little seaside town: that the fishmonger was having it off with *both* the post office women, both bearded, sisters, for instance, or that it had been the county surveyor who had been stealing underclothes from washing lines.

Her main friends – five or six – rang in for long sessions on the telephone. These, too, could total an hour or two each day. But other friends rang too. Often they would be in trouble and talking to my mother, her understanding, her common sense, her humour were all therapeutic. Not infrequently she performed the role now taken by counsellors and psychotherapists.

And another pattern now gradually emerged which hadn't had time to form before because of the relatively short periods we had spent on each Royal Navy air station. Friendship is a form of love and raises many of the same feelings. So much did my mother enjoy it, so concentrated was her attention on each acquaintance or friend, so intensely interested did she seem, and indeed was (while they were there), that quite often one or other would feel she was *their best friend* and that they were hers. They were hurt – angry, jealous – as they discovered her 'best friends' were numerous.

But my mother's closest friendship in Aldeburgh was subject to none of these strains. This was with her younger sister Mary. Though not as attractive as my mother, my Aunt Mary had also been beautiful as a young woman. She fell in love with a handsome young subaltern

called Bobby Lamont, whose brother became a brigadier. Bobby, my
mother told me, was clearly a 'rotter'. Everyone could see that,
including Arthur Thorowgood, who forbade the marriage. Incensed,
Mary married the rotter and her father refused to see her or speak to
her again. Unfortunately, the general judgement of Bobby Lamont
seems to have been accurate. My parents had to bail them out several
times, once, in the '30s, lending Bobby the equivalent of £5,000
which was never paid back. This sum would sometimes still surface
in conversation, tinged with horror.

Eventually, after the war, Bobby, who had been seconded for bad
behaviour from the Royal Scots Fusiliers to some regiment in Africa,
embezzled an enormous amount of money from the army. He was
cashiered and sent to Wormwood Scrubs. Mary, almost penniless,
went to live in Aldeburgh with her two children in a small two-up,
two-down rented terrace house along from a pub on the front. My
mother – whom Mary called Roo – used to give her small sums of
money when she could afford it.

I was very fond of Aunt Mary. Though she was eventually crushed
by poverty and misfortune, it was fun going to see her. She was a
gentle woman but with a quick and lively sense of humour. I
remember the particular smell of their cramped little house, a smell I
recognised and which moved me. It was not a smell of dirt exactly;
on the contrary its elements were partly those of excessive washing:
of damp dish cloths, washing powder, boiling clothes, torn linoleum
still damp from scrubbing; it was the smell of kitchen, the smell other
rooms took on because they were so close to the kitchen and had
become impregnated with its smells; it was the smell of anxiety over
too little money, the smell of too old material – worn carpets, worn
curtains, worn chair and sofa covers; it was the smell of scoured skin
on hands, of untidy greying hair; the smell of tiredness; the smell of
being poor.

It moved me not just because Mary moved me, but because it
reminded me of the Arch. I sometimes smelt it at 18 Hartington
Road. Yet Mary, from the same wealthy background as my mother,
had become *déclassée*, if one can still use the term, in a way my
mother never did. On a simple material level, 18 Hartington Road
and my parents' living standards slowly improved. Whereas Mary's,

if anything, declined. Until 1967, our house was heated by a motley collection of oil stoves, open fires and tiny antiquated electric fires; then central heating was put in, if rather sparsely. In 1961, my father bought their first car since before the war, a Morris Minor beetle. He had it souped up with extra carburettors and special headlights to dazzle anyone who didn't dip. He used to teach Rose to drive on the old aerodrome at Glemham. Rose, aged eleven and rather small still, sat on a cushion. 'Faster Rose, faster,' my father would shout.

But, like his, my mother's health also began to deteriorate. Her blood pressure still required constant monitoring and bizarre diets. I remember meal after meal consisting only of boiled saltless cauliflower. But far worse was her psoriasis. This had started in the early '50s and gradually, inexorably, spread over her whole body – elbows, then arms, into her bush, her back, her knees and ankles – eventually almost everywhere except her face – though her scalp and ears and eyebrows were affected. To relieve the infuriating itching she took tar baths and Rose used to help rub Betnovate into her back every morning. Rose bore the brunt. She can remember, aged nine, sweeping up with dustpan and brush the flakes of skin beside the bed which my mother, maddened beyond endurance, had torn off during the night. My mother must have done this semi-conscious. In order to sleep with her exacerbated skin, to obtain oblivion, she had had to increase the amount of Nembutal which she had already taken for several years. The result was that if Rose went to my mother's room for any reason during the night she couldn't wake her. From about 1957 on, Rose would often hear a curious hissing noise as my mother, drunk, pulled herself up the stairs. It was the sound of her hand sliding up the banisters to get a new grip but to Rose it sounded like a snake. Blissful together during the day, she had a fantasy during her childhood that at night her mother turned into a witch who might kill her.

I did not realise, till much later, how bad things had been. I feel I should have done. No one knew the effects of long-term barbiturate use at that time, but the continual anxiety, year after year after year, about money (which was to get worse), the unremitting, unrelieved, incurable march of psoriasis, with its endless itching, pain and often bleeding, and the humiliation of disfigurement, the worry about her blood pressure – I knew about these. I should have taken in what they were doing to her. I should have remembered the cumulative strain of the war, the Arch, the Nissen huts.

Later on it all became obvious, and one reason I didn't notice then, was because my mother concealed things. She was so stimulating, and so stimulated by talk and company that usually, though less often as time went on, these kept her buoyed up during the morning and early afternoon. She seemed the same as always. Also, she was ashamed of her drinking and tried to stop. I remember one of the books she bought – *Tomorrow Will be Sober*, a title which made her laugh. She didn't sit down and drink too much at any particular time, but took swigs throughout the day. My father had bought a small wooden barrel – three bottles, say – of rather good sherry. This rapidly went, but the idea was you could fill the barrel with disgusting cheap sherry and it would metamorphose into delicious sherry. It didn't, but the barrel, always ready on the sideboard, was ideal to take from. My mother would tipple and swig, swig and tipple and suddenly topple over into a state of slurred speech and a curious sideways squinting look as if aiming up a cue into a pocket in a corner of the ceiling and you'd know you'd had it. No more of the talk I enjoyed so much with her.

But I suppose the real reason I didn't notice it all was that I didn't want to. Also, it is true, I was obsessed with my life in London.

(8)

By July 1957 I was sleeping at Montpelier Square practically every night of the week and by November I was living there.

This significant move, more significant than I realised since I'd never done it before, was described by Eliza, who had and did realise, as my 'digging in'. Achieved with a mixture of my determination and her apprehension, it was paradoxically made possible only because in July I also finally found somewhere else I could live permanently – or for as long as I liked.

Carlton Mews, reached through a narrow entrance off Trafalgar Square, was an enclosed square, or rather rectangle, built about 1820, probably by Nash, to house the horses and carriages of the houses of

Carlton House Terrace. It has now been coarsely and completely obliterated by the Anglo-American Bank. One of the stables, number 5 Carlton Mews, had been converted by the architect Elizabeth Denby just after the Second World War. The large drawing room had been panelled to four feet, tiled a further four and then plastered to the ceiling, and there was a kitchen off it. A circular iron stair led to a large bedroom, two minute bedrooms, and a bathroom with an antique gas geyser. Richard Williams-Ellis, a friend from Cambridge, had, with the flair of his uncle Clough, discovered this beautiful, peaceful place out walking one day and had taken over the lease from Elizabeth Denby. He had the large bedroom; I had one of the small ones. There were gas lamps spaced along the wide, horse-wide balcony outside and a man still came each night to light these and each morning to put them out. Apart from the inside transformation, invisible from the outside, Carlton Mews must have looked much the same in 1957 as it had in 1820. Though I wasn't often there, I could have been at any time during the next three years.

Only when I didn't have to live at Montpelier Square, when it was possible, if things went wrong, for me to drop out at any moment into the safety net of Carlton Mews swinging beneath me, could Eliza and I allow ourselves to do what, still, at an unspoken level, we regarded as 'impossible' and still also felt, well, why *should* it be impossible if we both wanted it, which we did?

One reason our life was difficult for me was also a reason I enjoyed it so much. 'Look!' Cyril remarked cattily at this time. 'Here comes Gathorne-Hardy – with all the gaiety of a kept man.' This wasn't quite true. I was still a trainee copywriter at Bensons now earning the equivalent of about £8,000 a year, but taxed and out of which I had to pay my Carlton Mews rent. I occasionally paid the drink bill, or some of it. But if I wasn't *totally* kept – and Eliza was very skilful and tactful at disguising this – I soon began to feel that I was. Combined with this, we saw only her friends. Apart from Julian, my friends seemed to have been frightened off.

Then, Eliza was eleven years older than me, but for five months of the year she was twelve years older. Ignoring what I felt, I thought I *ought* to be living with someone of my own age or younger – like my contemporaries. Also my contemporaries – or so it seemed to me –

were sleeping with a great many of these younger women. I had, so far, only had Nell and Sophia, and two one-night stands I didn't count; not only did I want more, I thought I *ought* to have more. The figure I picked on to embody these fantasies was the beautiful one of Jocasta Innes. In fact – and this demonstrates how closely entwined the process of living with Eliza was with leaving her – I had first slept with Jocasta the same month that I had moved into Montpelier Square.

A third element was my continuing anxiety about homosexuality.

(9)

My mother, in the face of what was becoming overwhelming evidence, had ceased to worry about my homosexuality, though fussing endlessly about every other conceivable aspect of my life. I, on the other hand, had now begun to worry that, though I didn't seem to be homosexual, I ought to be. This was not a simple anxiety. I believed then like a lot of people and as I think I still do that everyone had elements of homosexuality or a potentiality for homosexuality or at least for homosexual acts. This was often hidden, *repressed*, by fear and various cultural pressures. *Repression* then, as now, was more or less a sin. It was likely that my mother's terrors, the taboo imposed by school and society, had led me to *repress* that side of me. I must find out if this was so and if it was *unrepress* it. Besides, though it might be true I was perfectly content not being homosexual, I might never have homosexual desires or fantasies, was it not my duty to discover as much as I could about myself, to explore and experience as much as I was able and brave enough to do? Just to ask the questions was to answer them.

The figure I chose for this exploration was someone I'd met at Cambridge. Hussein Sherrif was descended from the Prophet. He was the grandson of the Mahdi, the royal Sudanese leader against the British. He was also the most beautiful person I had ever seen. He moved exquisitely, with the languid grace of some supremely confident highly strung animal, his black liquid eyes, in his fine glowing black handsome face, sardonic and lightly lidded. He was sensuous, sensitive, sophisticated, witty, ironic, smoked with a long cigarette holder and was promiscuously, discriminatingly bisexual. If I had been a Roman emperor he would have been a permanent member of my court so that I could have looked at him all day.

In February 1958, I see from my journal, Richard and I gave a party at Carlton Mews. Eventually, around two o'clock in the morning, everyone had gone except Richard, me and Hussein, who was gyrating elegantly by himself to whatever music had been put on. I was quite drunk. I drank several glasses more and then got up and began to dance around him. Before long we were dancing clinging together. Richard, becoming embarrassed, went up to bed. More drink. Now we were simply entwining to the music, only pausing to change records, have another drink, and re-entwine. 'Feel this,' said Hussein, putting my hand to his crutch. His erection, barely smothered by his very tight trousers, did cause a sudden surge of desire. Yet when we finally pulled ourselves drunkenly up the circular iron staircase and were squeezed together naked and hot in my extremely narrow bed I could feel nothing at all, try as I might. I remember Hussein's very thin, hard, almost bony prick like an over-long, over-active propelling pencil – but over-active in vain. At last I said, 'It's no good Hussein, I'm too drunk. We'll make love in the morning.' I got up, very carefully, at eight to bicycle to Bensons by nine. Hussein didn't wake. I was interested to see that, with a hangover, his usual vibrantly black skin had taken on a dull grey tinge.

This episode didn't change anything. I realised I'd made the mistake of choosing not someone I fancied, who attracted me sexually, but someone I found beautiful; either that, or the taboo and fear were too strong and needed further battering.

Shortly after our encounter Hussein had to go back to the Sudan. I didn't try and find another man, despite vaguely thinking I should. In fact, as I've hinted, not until I saw Ambrose in my late youth or early middle age or middle youth or whatever you now call forty-three, did I finally resolve all this.

(10)

In February 1958 I began my first novel, eventually called *One Foot in the Clouds*. I had recently finished Proust and embarked on Nabokov – tricky, even dangerous spurs to a young writer starting out, but in fact it was a painful humiliation that made me begin.

A year earlier Eliza and I made a trip to Tangier from Spain. Although I told everyone I was a writer, all I wrote (or had written – I didn't count *Granta*) was my journal. Against 'Occupation' in my passport I had therefore put not 'writer' but the more honest 'journalist'. Morocco had recently come under scathing attack in British newspapers and the regime had furiously banned anyone connected with them from entering the country. Ridiculously, I hadn't noticed the obvious ambiguity in my occupation and the moment 'journalist' was spotted, I was seized and hustled away under guard to await the next ferry back to Algeciras. It took a lot of embarrassed explaining that I'd only meant I kept a diary – I had to produce the wretched thing from my case – before I was finally, reluctantly, released into Tangier.

This incident produced a minor crisis. For years I had told people I was a writer, yet I couldn't write anything, or nothing I thought any good. I decided I would abandon the whole idea. Very rapidly, I realised I couldn't. Since I was three or four, during the time my character was forming, the hearing and then telling of stories, first to myself, later to others, had gradually formulated itself into the desire to write them. The two had developed together more and more entwined. 'Being a writer' was part of the structure of my being.

It struck me that all as it were instinctive ambitions, 'vocations', must have a similar genesis – and that this was what my novel would be about. It would be about the son of a doctor whose character and idea of himself as a doctor became similarly entangled. Then something would lead him to give up medicine. The book would end with him realising that the self-destruction necessary for this was more than he could bear, or in fact accomplish. After a few chapters, I saw that, though I could sustain a would-be doctor hero, I knew this psychological mechanism best as it operated in me. I therefore started again with the hero a writer.

Early in *Speak Memory* Nabokov describes the effect of writing autobiography on memory, how 'the amnesiac defects of the original – blank spots, blurry areas, domains of dimness . . . the neutral smudge might be forced (by intense concentration) into beautiful focus so that the sudden view could be identified, and the anonymous servant named'. I reread the passage while looking for an observation, which I roughly remembered, that he had in fact made about the effect of writing *novels* on memory. I couldn't find it (I didn't try very hard) but, to save me reading the whole book again (and how elaborate, over-elaborate, that once adored prose seems to me now – and yet how catching it still is) let me invent an appropriately Nabokovian metaphor. He said, let us suppose (or perhaps after all I remember it accurately), that there were blanks in his memory like those pale, square patches against the wall from which pictures have been removed, where he had extracted some incident from his life and put it into one of his novels. I found something quite different. In *One Foot in the Clouds* I had made the doctor, and later the writer, live in Carlton Mews. I made the hero Robert (me, of course) be seduced by the heroine Sonia (Jocasta) in the big bed in the big bedroom. But I never slept with Jocasta or anyone else in that house – unless you count Hussein. Yet when I think back to that time now, there is a new picture on the wall which I can't shift, the memory of me and Jocasta together in Richard's bed at Carlton Mews.

Novels you write create memories. Even odder is how other people's memories can, via a novel, become one's own. The painter Tim Behrens described to me how he and his Italian lover Raffaela made love one winter's night in the boiler room of a hotel in Italy (the rest of the hotel was full and a bed was rigged up for them there). After a while they began to *steam*. I put this in a novel *Madaleine* (unpublished for a curious reason) where the hero Daniel (me again of course) made love to Madaleine (Anna) in similar circumstances. But Anna and I never went to Italy. The novel is mostly based on actual events which took place in Spain. I've never slept in a boiler room, alone or with anyone else. But now it has become a memory of something I did myself. I can see the boiler room vividly. I can see the steam rising off our bodies. But these events all took place, or in the case of my steaming in the boiler room did not take place, long after those first years in London I'm still describing – fifteen years after them.

(11)

Throughout 1958 my life with Eliza became more and more agonising for both of us. The sort of thing that would happen would be this. Life would be rolling along, week after week, stimulating and apparently happy. Eliza would take us to the opera again, and would have paid for my suit to be cleaned as well as my shirts, she would also have paid any expenses caused by our week-ends, one, let us say, to the artists Dicky Chopping and Denis Worth-Miller at Wivenhoe, except I would have bought the three bottles of wine we took; we would also have just had six of her friends, and now to a rather shallow extent my friends, to supper. I might have struggled slightly here, but on the whole enjoyed it. Then the following day she would, very mildly, have asked me to fill the log basket or get some wine from the cellar. Suddenly, I would find myself exploding – how *dare* she order me about. I was already completely smothered by her money, her friends – all twenty or thirty years older than I was – by her house and her car (a Mercedes) and from having all my clothes constantly cleaned. Quite apart from being wounded, Eliza hated rows and confrontations.

One solution seemed to be for her to sell Montpelier Square and for us to set up house together in the country. Weekend after weekend we drove round Wiltshire and Berkshire deep in this fantasy. Eventually we found a more or less perfect eighteenth-century house under the Downs, within reach, but not smothering reach, of the Partridges at Ham Spray and the Campbells at Stokke. Eliza asked me if I liked it. I *did* like it, but couldn't say so. To say yes would mean being committed. Besides, I wanted to stay in London almost as much as I wanted to get out of it.

The reason was that London was full of the girls and young women, one of whom I felt at some point I ought to marry and all of whom I wanted to sleep with in much larger numbers. Like smothering, I wouldn't think about these girls for weeks at a time – then suddenly the longing for them would overwhelm me. Although I tried to conceal this, Eliza was no doubt painfully aware of it. Yet, typical in the dynamics of love affairs, while at first when I had tried to dig in she had resented me, now that I wanted (or thought I wanted) to dig my way out, she wanted us to stay together.

Eventually, in August, we decided we must separate. She was very sad as I drove her to Heathrow to catch the plane to Spain. I felt calm and rather excited. I hadn't told Eliza, but I had arranged to meet Jocasta the next day.

Driving back into London, I suddenly found I couldn't see through the windscreen, which was completely obscured by rain. I turned on the wipers, but they didn't seem to work. I had to stop the car and then discovered that it wasn't rain but tears pouring from my eyes and blinding me. Not for the last time, I found I had no idea what I was really feeling until the moment I felt it.

(12)

Having spent the past few months thinking incessantly of getting off with Jocasta (among others), all I now wanted was to be back with Eliza. Except – that was *not* all I wanted. I imagined myself back in Montpelier Square, I once more longed to be in some remote cottage beside the North Sea – something I had in fact arranged – with Jocasta, whereupon, walking hither and thither distractedly while the sad, grey, snot-coloured sea rolled in beside me, I would find I was crying again, desperate to fly out to Spain.

If I hadn't been in this dilemma, which I was to be with her several times, I think I might well have fallen in love properly with Jocasta, married her and lived happily ever afterwards. She was intelligent and funny, and her curious inability to meet one's eyes gave her an elusiveness which I found particularly fascinating, probably as a result of my recent immersion in Proust.

She was also what used to be called a good sport. I took her to 18 Hartington Road after our weekend in the North Sea cottage. My father was there because the next day was Rose's ninth birthday. He was invariably immediately attracted to anyone I brought down but at this point usually exerted some self-control. My mother and Rose were over at Glemham all day so my father had booked us for lunch into a nearby café, a boring, prissy establishment on the High Street called Greensleeves, run by two elderly sisters. Our task was to prepare for the birthday by filling balloons with gas via an enema attached to the stove. A lot of gas escaped, adding heady fumes to those of the disgusting sherry which my father was drawing by the tumbler from the little barrel.

At ten to one we left for Greensleeves Café because the sisters stopped admitting customers promptly at one, though food was served and eating tolerated until two. We arrived at three minutes to one and the elder sister refused to let us in. We showed our watches, all telling the same time. But now the other sister came up and reinforced the first.

When we got back to 18 Hartington Road, my father said we must teach them a lesson. We got a dozen tie-on labels and wrote, 'If you want a good fuck go to Greensleeves Café, High Street, Aldeburgh. Tel: Aldeburgh 254.' We tied the labels to twelve balloons and released them. 'With any luck some will make it to the US base at Martlesham,' my father said.

My copywriting life, which I had to continue during the week, had gradually improved. That is to say, though I loathed it more than ever for interfering with my struggle to write my novel, I did become slightly more competent. At last I was given my own account. I had always hated Marmite and still do but, as John Mellors said, 'You seem to have mastered the corny Marmite copy. You'd better have the account.' The Marmite account was also the cause of him paying me, unwittingly, what was at that time the greatest compliment possible. Most of the ads required fifty words of copy plus slogan, which I've forgotten. But one, a special space in the holiday pages of the *Hastings Gazette*, needed 350 words. Spreading my wings, I took a great deal of trouble over this and carried it in with pride to be vetted.

John read it, then he read it again. 'This is bloody useless,' he said in his blunt North Country way. 'This is really crap Jonny. What have you done? We're right back to square one. This isn't advertising copy, this is . . . this is more like . . . well, this might have been written by Proust for Christ's sake.'

After three weeks I couldn't stand what I was going through — what I was putting Jocasta through — any longer. I wrote a letter to John explaining briefly what was going on and telling him I was resigning from Bensons at once and flying to Spain to sort things out. I bought my ticket, sent a telegram to Eliza to meet me at Gibraltar and set off soon afterwards. At that time you still flew to Gibraltar in Dakotas adapted for passengers and pulled slowly through the air by propellers.

(13)

The first thing I did in Spain was to confess, in far too great detail to show how open and honest I now intended to be, everything about Jocasta. *Not* what Eliza had expected or wanted to hear. We then went to Tangiers.

We returned and I worked out my notice at Bensons as John had asked me to do in a most tolerant and charming reply to my abrupt and slightly hysterical letter of resignation (his letter began 'Oh dear'). I then embarked on a torturing and endless seesaw of indecision.

I sometimes wonder now if the influence of Proust, in particular the influence of the Narrator's indecision about whether or not to propose to Albertine, made me feel I *ought* to be indecisive. But I don't think so. Books don't usually affect one so directly. But perhaps Proust made me observe more closely, as he did, what was happening and also made me more attracted to the literature of indecision. Prominent here were Benjamin Constant's *Adolphe* and his journals, both heavily concerned with his indecision about continuing with Madame de Staël or not, a decision which took him, something with which I sympathised totally, about twenty years.

I found, like him, that being indecisive about something so central spread indecision like a staining ink through my entire system. I dithered about seeing Julian or not, or going to 18 Hartington Road or not, or even what shirt to put on. At one point I actually thought of calling my novel simply *16*. This derived from Constant's habit, so invariable were his many indecisions, of giving them a number in his journal to save him having to write out all the details again. One number, say sixteen, was 'Indecision about everything'.

I also noticed the operation of another curious psychological law. Together again for four months, then separated, then together again for two months – each successive and shorter period of reconciliation led to repeating, but faster and faster, each stage of what had happened in the past: tentative meeting, awkwardness, fascination and excitement, intimacy and love, first suggestion of friction, actual friction . . . the last time I was with Eliza, nineteen months later in Spain, the entire affair, which had lasted one way or another for four years, played itself out over three days.

I won't dwell on these months. Indecision (unless in the hands of Proust or Constant) is as boring to read about as it is agonising to undergo. But to keep my end up when with her, and to live off when I wasn't, I took another job. This was with the publisher George Weidenfeld.

(14)

Weidenfeld and Nicolson at that time occupied a warren of little rooms on the first and second floors of number 7 Cork Street. I had been engaged, George would explain, as 'the most brilliant copy-writer in London'. My responsibilities were advertising and related promotions, PR, blurb and catalogue copy (the same usually), entertaining (that is, George's parties), and a vague suggestion I might be 'involved' with novels. I hadn't the faintest idea how to do any of this except, I suppose, as the least brilliant copywriter in London, blurbs and advertising copy (I didn't know how you bought space or where or how often or anything else to do with advertising).

But the huge advantage, for me, was that I was to work only four days a week; in return I had to give W & N first refusal of my novel to which, George said with an extremely meaningful expression, holding me for several seconds with his large eyes, they would give very special attention, very special *indeed*.

Those big, marble-like eyes – marbles which, when George entered some social gathering, could roll with almost inconceivable rapidity round an entire room, an entire *ball*room, pausing for an infinitesimal moment to register someone it might be worth talking to before speeding on – those prominent, hypnotic, persuasive eyes were turned on me again two days after I arrived. I had been summoned to the only large room in the warren (also the only room with wall-to-wall, indeed any carpeting), George's office.

'Jonny, this is a very important year, very important, for our publishing,' he said, his voice still holding a trace of the Vienna from which he'd come as a youth. 'I want you to pull out all the stops. *All* the stops. We publish this spring the most important book Weidenfelds has ever published – the Doenitz war memoirs! The war memoirs of Admiral Doenitz! The last Reich President! You can imagine the impact. Make no mistake Jonny – this is going to be a very big publishing event indeed.'

'Goodness George. Right. What sort of thing did you have in mind? Showcards . . . ?' I couldn't think of anything else. George at once looked impatient. 'Showcards, showcards, of course, of course. *All* the stops. Brilliant copy. PR. I leave it to you. Barley will give you some photographs.'

Back in my tiny office, which I shared with the sales manager Geoffrey Ritson, at the very back of the building, both galvanised and at a loss, I tried to work out a 'campaign'. Where to place ads I could get from the files, but showcards – how many? Twenty thousand? Thirty thousand? Determined to be careful at this early juncture of my publishing career, I ordered a hundred two-feet by three-feet showcards.

These huge Doenitz showcards were to haunt my first five months at Weidenfelds. I managed to place two; the other ninety-eight towered above my filing cabinet, jutting out into the room. Whenever I could, I would smuggle one out when I left in the evening, half concealing its angular bulk under macintosh or coat, forcing it at Carlton Mews, now become a neo-Nazi cell, into the inadequate dustbin.

I soon discovered that George chose three or four books a year as great, pull-out-all-the-stops publishing events – and in this he resembled every publisher. To maintain their own confidence and generate enthusiasm in the workforce, they have to psyche themselves up to ridiculous levels over what are often quite ordinary, even boring books – like the Doenitz war memoirs. Advertising and probably most commercial ventures are the same; George's pop-eyed excitement was justified far more often than that of his rivals.

I was at Weidenfeld and Nicolson a year, finally resigning a few days before I was fired. I never got to know George particularly well, but from my humble, as it were carpet-high view, I observed him. That impatience with showcards was typical. He had great intelligence but always 'from an embracing and summarising point of view, disregarding every kind of detail', as Casanova wrote of the Duc de Choiseul. Volatile, capable if necessary of great charm and subject to sudden glooms, he was easily bored, especially by the mechanics of publishing. Reading bored him and he was adept at skimming and getting the gist. Sometimes not even that. 'I can judge a book by its weight,' he once said, only half-joking, holding out a volume on his plump palm. In his little kingdom, reputations rose and plummeted. Newcomers were invariably high for a while, and just as invariably fell. At first George and I would from time to time have breakfast together in his rooms in Albany. Austrian breakfast: rye bread, smoked ham, salami, liver sausage, liver pâté, pale hard cheese, cucumbers.

On these occasions, after talking about whatever party or book promotion which was their cause, or excuse, he would sometimes become philosophical about his life. Should he have been an academic? Why had he not gone into real big business, steel, say, or coal? He could have gone into steel. He would have been much richer, much more powerful. I think I could have told him. For one thing, George was a snob and publishing gave him a *cachet* and an *entré* into a far wider, more distinguished and more interesting world than big business could ever have done. Also, he was extraordinarily successful with women (or perhaps it wasn't extraordinary. Mirabeau, one of the ugliest men in France, was also very successful. Or Kissinger. Power – or the feeling of power – is the clue.) W & N published quite a number of books to get George into some drawing room – or bed. Then, if in a strict sense steel would have made him more powerful, it would not have been power as George liked it – via the ear of prime ministers and presidents, owners of newspapers, millionaires. Nor would he have had the endless prospect of new schemes, new deals, new hook-ups and tie-ins, the continual injections of adrenaline he loved so much, and which were perhaps needed to keep those moments of gloom at bay. He would certainly have been richer in steel at that time. But without his books, his schemes, his parties, to what end? It is true W & N regularly teetered on the edge of financial collapse, saved at the last moment, sometimes by a marriage, sometimes by transfusions of new business partners' cash, sometimes by a successful book. But this situation, too, was a stimulating one. As for academia, George the scholar – he would have been bored silly. He satisfied this side of himself – and it was a genuine side – by publishing his enormous historical series, and good, popular works of history and science by distinguished academics.

I liked George, and wasn't disturbed by traits which irritated other people. One of these was his habit of seeming to promise something – and then doing nothing. Robert Kee described George coming up to him at a party and drawing him aside. 'This is *absolutely* confidential Robert, not a word. Big opportunities are opening up in Russia – very big. They are looking to put all their literary imports and exports down one channel and it seems the channel could be Weidenfeld and Nicolson. Tens of thousands, hundreds of thousands of pounds of course. If we bring this off – how would you like to run it?' Suitably flattered and impressed, Robert said he'd think about it. Half an hour later, hidden by a pillar or potted palm or something, he heard Weidenfeld's voice, 'This is *absolutely* confidential John, not a word,' and the identical monologue ensued. This was still my honeymoon-breakfast period and it so happened that George had put this to me, in exactly those words, a few days before. But I could see people were wrong to take such proposals seriously. They were both less and more than actual proposals. They were really musings aloud. They were his way of working things out; he had to talk, to offer, in order to plan. He was, of course, showing off too, but he was also saying, I admire you, I like you, perhaps, if something like this ever did happen, I could put it your way, we could work together. People took him seriously and were then angry when nothing transpired. Soon after this my stock began its inevitable (and deserved) decline and our breakfasts came to an end.

(15)

One of my allies at W & N was Barley Allison, who'd given me the Doenitz photographs. I believe she'd put in some money and there-fore had a certain independence. She was the senior editor, in charge of fiction. Aged about forty-three then, she had clearly been very attractive and was so still in a battered way. She was thin, lively, funny and had a wide mouth with prominent buck teeth, teeth, as she explained, that were a miracle of 1950s dental surgery. The entire top row was suspended by an elaborate tangle of wires and gantries from a single obstinate molar, the only tooth still with roots. She chain-smoked through a holder, drank Mary Campbell-strength Martinis and her only defect was she sometimes talked too much. She gave you a trapped feeling at these times as though she'd sunk her teeth into your ear. She used to get attracted to her novelists and sometimes managed to seduce them. She used to discuss with me how it might be possible to prise Dan Jacobson away from his wife – an entirely fruitless fantasy since he was happily married. But she did get Saul Bellow into her bed. I remember Bellow slumped at a too-early morning meeting after one of these encounters, his head still reeling from Martinis, trying to see if it was possible, as one had read, to prop eyelids open with matchsticks (it wasn't). As things got rougher, I used to go to Barley for advice and it was she who finally advised me to resign. A few years later she removed her money and started the Allison Press, taking Bellow with her.

Another ally was the sales manager Geoffrey Ritson. Perhaps it would be more accurate to say I was his ally. Geoffrey, a lapsed Catholic in his mid-thirties, was a burly, gregarious, sensual, badger-like figure, who knew that the level of reps and buyers at which he operated – and he operated with great skill – was largely fuelled by drink. He was also a womaniser. He would stagger in at ten to four from drinking with the manager of the W. H. Smith on Waterloo Station, say, smelling of pub – of beer, whisky, cigarette smoke, reminding me of my father; or even later, smelling of Spanish Burgundy and faintly, subliminally, of sweat, scent and sex, and thank me for fending off George or Nicolas Thompson or his wife in the country looking after their five children; the wife, with her resigned, sad and rather attractive voice whom I would sometimes have to ring and explain that Geoffrey couldn't make it back home that night for this reason or that; and how sorry he was, and watch him set to in our office to cook the books.

In fact, we both spent a lot of our time covering our tracks. My incompetence was masked because George had a genius for generating publicity. Geoffrey wasn't incompetent, exactly, but faced with George's endless all-the-stops demands he regularly and wildly exaggerated how many books he could sell, thus dictating how many were printed, and then had to hide the truth when the returns poured in. And now I learnt another facet of George's character – he couldn't bear to sack people. He kept Nicolas Thompson to do this. Unfortunately, when it became clear that Geoffrey had to be replaced, Nicolas was on some extended trip. George's solution was to employ another sales manager, assuming Geoffrey would take the hint. Geoffrey ignored both hint and new sales manager, whose task he easily made impossible. George dithered about this for a while, and then employed a third sales manager. Eventually, Nicolas returned and sorted it out.

My own downfall came over Nabokov. I was vaguely aware of the negotiations to buy and publish *Lolita* – I seem to remember George had to agree, among other things, to publish everything Nabokov had ever written or ever would write – but from my carpet-level view of events at Weidenfelds only two things impinged: my excitement at seeing a writer with whom I was becoming almost too obsessed as I had been with Proust; second, horror at the publicity I knew I would be supposed to and couldn't create.

About the second, I needn't have worried. George, with his usual mixture of squeamishness and kindness, adroitness and deviousness, had engaged a professional for all the PR without telling me. I was introduced to this figure at the last second as I got into the car to go to Southampton to meet the Nabokovs off their boat from America. 'Mr Taylor's going to help you with the publicity Jonny.'

Mr Taylor, with his boxer's face and tabloid mind, had taken in the sex potential of *Lolita*, but was baffled by the literary 'angle'. What *was* this exactly? How could he (*he*, not *we*!) *sell* it? As I tried to explain the fascination, the delicacy and subtlety, of the Nabokovian sensibility and the pyrotechnics of his art, Mr Taylor fell silent.

The meeting with my hero was far too brief, another in that long line of Sassoon encounters. I was shy, and also intimidated by Nabokov's wife Vera. While the tabloid boxer sat mercifully silent, I said how I admired *Lolita* (George had given me the Olympia Press edition as a working copy), and how I'd discovered him for myself, aged sixteen, with *The Real Life of Sebastian Knight*. I remember asking him if he thought *Lolita*'s success would change his life. 'It already has,' he said. 'When we were packing just before we left the ship, I found I'd lost my muffler. I began to fuss. I fuss about such things. Then suddenly I remembered. It didn't matter! I was rich! I could just go out and buy another muffler!' I noted the use of the American 'muffler'.

In fact, neither Taylor nor myself was needed. *Lolita* raised its own firestorm of publicity, and eventually sold something like 200,000 copies, by which time I'd left Weidenfelds.

The issue that brought me down was the *Lolita* advertisements, but the first cracks in my reputation had begun six months before. Nicolas Thompson had made one of his lightning, adjutant-like tours of investigation. Squeezing for the first time into Ritson's and my remote minute office he at once spotted the last three Doenitz showcards beside my filing cabinet. 'What are those?' 'What? Oh those – three Doenitz showcards left over,' I said insouciantly. '*Three Doenitz showcards*,' barked Nicolas, his blue eyes flashing furiously. 'You ordered that much too many? *Three* too many? For goodness' sake, have you no idea how to conduct this job? No idea of economy?' and, pale with simulated anger, or perhaps real anger, he embarked on a long, sarcastic dressing down.

For the *Lolita* ads, of unprecedented size, I'd used the same strikingly erotic illustration as the Italian publishers – an insolent, sultry, sensuous nymphet pouting with half-closed eyes and half-slipped shift. I was going over the proofs with Nicolas.

'I suppose you've got clearance on the photograph?'

'No. There wasn't any need. The Italian publishers used her.'

Nicolas at once hit the roof, his habitual destination in these exchanges. Didn't I realise copyright and libel laws were *totally* different in Britain and Italy? If we used this girl's face without permission, she could take us to the cleaners. I said she was some obscure fourteen-year-old Italian actress. *Actress*, cried Nicolas – even worse. There was one ad – in *The Bookseller* – it was too late to change. 'We'll be taken to the cleaners,' said Nicolas grimly.

After I'd dealt with the fairly extensive changes Nicolas's, in my view, ludicrously exaggerated anxieties necessitated, I went to see Barley. She said she thought this incident might well lead to my being sacked. 'There have been murmurings for some time.'

I arranged to see George the following morning. He looked extremely uneasy when I came into his office. 'If it's about the *Lolita* advertisements Jonny . . . '

'No, no, George. Nicolas and I can sort that out. It's more important than that,' I said. As he knew, I was writing a novel for them. The extra day a week made a great difference, but now I needed to spend more time on it. Perhaps I could come back when it was finished. But now . . .

My resignation was received with something more than relief, almost joy. I'd done brilliant work, brilliant, but of course the book was *far* more important, they were all eagerly looking forward to it, it would be a major acquisition, all-the-stops, the first of *many* books, a *series* . . .

And so, in rows of dots and unfinished sentences, my career in publishing came to an end. I left the following week having briefed my successor who I discovered had, typically, been engaged two months before.

(16)

For the next six months, from the end of November 1959 to June 1960, I worked in a bookshop, as a tutor, did journalism and sponged.

At first, Mary Campbell let me stay at Stokke for about seven weeks, feeding and housing me in return for nothing really. I used to cut brambles. The weekends were crowded; during the week I was often alone. To earn some money, I was writing a long article on mental illness with which a now-defunct magazine called *Time and*

Tide eventually led the first two issues of its expensive revival. I concocted the article from long talks in pubs with Sonia Orwell's brother, who was a psychiatrist at the Maudsley, and also from a Penguin book on the subject. The articles, my first published work, were eventually called 'How to Go Mad'.

In the afternoons, apart from brambles, I went for long masochistic walks, blown for miles along the Wiltshire Downs, through the falling beech leaves of Savernake Forest, beside the black, sinisterly motionless water of the Kennet Canal, often feeling that I was beginning to exemplify the title of my article.

My madness felt like a return of those attacks of 'loudness' which I described at Snape much earlier, but in a different form and even more threatening. I felt that some fragile mental barrier was about to give way and that my personality would be engulfed, would break up. As the feeling mounted, I would start to run along the Downs, through the forest, to try and escape or smother the fear and panic by exhaustion. I think now it was due to Eliza. Although the pattern of indecision was still operating – with longer and longer intervals apart and shorter and shorter and more painful reconciliations – I really knew the affair was over. The phrase, he or she had become part of me, is not an idle one. To leave or be left is to destroy.

I spent the two months following Stokke working in the book-shop of my uncle Heywood Hill in Curzon Street. I helped sell the children's books in the basement, and learnt how satisfying it is to receive actual money in return for goods, especially if you know that a proportion of it, even if a minute one, will eventually come your way. But my main task was writing carefully enticing, but bibliographically exact descriptions, in a short paragraph or two each, of the 620 books they were putting in their next catalogue. As I mastered the simple but esoteric language and its thirty or so technical terms, I came to look forward to my peaceful days surrounded by books.

I also learnt that the dynamics of the shop itself were not all that peaceful. The cause of tension and dissension was Mollie Friese-Greene, the wife of Heywood's partner Handasyde Buchanan.

Heywood had started his bookshop in 1936 after serving a six-year apprenticeship with Charles Sawyer, the antiquarian-book dealer in

Grafton Steet. One of his ideas was that it should be like a drawing
room, partly to let him sell a few objects and pictures, but largely so
that people would feel at ease buying books. Apart from the class
connotations of 'drawing-room', inevitable given his background
and the shop's clientele in 1936, it was really the same idea that
motivates the bookshops today that sell coffee and have armchairs
and tables to read at.

Mollie made quite sure that no one who worked there would feel
at ease in Heywood's shop. Tall, sinuous, dark-eyed, sharp-tongued
and clever, some deep dissatisfaction and bitterness with herself and
her lot caused bile to accumulate steadily until she had to relieve
herself in sudden vicious discharges of sarcasm and criticism, like
someone pulling a lavatory plug. She would foment difficulties
between Heywood and Handy and then take Handy's side. I used to
observe Heywood's pain with distress.

So did Anne, his wife. My father's younger sister, Anne was my
favourite among his siblings. I got on best with her and she was the
only one I loved. She had the Disraelian looks of the family, an
original slightly disorganised but often brilliant mind, a wild sense of
humour sending laughter out in spouts and barks, and great generosity
and kindness. She could also, like my grandmother, be ferocious,
relentless and fairly amoral on behalf of her family – something I later
benefited from. She could not bear to see her husband suffer and for
some years worked with Machiavellian skill to get Mollie forced to
work from home and not in the shop, without at the same time
offending Handy.

Nothing much happened in the shop, aside from the tensions
generated by Mollie. It was successful* and often full, especially at
Christmas. Heywood said that at these times it was like an eight-
hour cocktail party without any drink. Customers, many famous in
their day – Sitwells, Evelyn Waugh, Anthony Powell, Diana Cooper
etc. – came and went, naturally ignoring the humble cataloguer.

---

* It still is. Heywood seemed mild and unassuming – but he had a will of
  iron. Nancy Mitford who worked there called him the Pocket Napoleon.
  When he left, the shop was taken over by John Saumarez Smith who ran
  and runs it with panache, charm and canny skill.

Even Siegfried Sassoon came and ignored me, having forgotten we'd ever met. I did have one aim of my own — I had been told that Handy had a stock of erotica, discreetly concealed. But I was too shy to ask him. Nor could I find it.

The day before I left, I was working in the basement among the children's books. Moving the Beatrix Potters, I suddenly noticed a sliding panel in the case that contained them. I slid it back — and there was the shelf of erotica! But my triumph was short-lived and unsatisfactory. I remember one slim book, privately printed in Paris, with drawings by Cocteau. I think there was a volume of Rochester's verse. Then I found quite a large quarto volume in a dark blue slip-cover. I pulled the book free and an extremely realistic, beautifully made, flesh-coloured rubber breast sprang up. I was about to open the book — and see copulating couples emerge? Lesbians? Penises? — when I heard the slow, unmistakeable sounds of Handy's heavy footsteps at the top of the stairs. Guiltily, I began to put the book back into the slip-cover, but the nipple jammed against the edge of the board. Clumsy in my haste, I couldn't force it down. Handy was coming closer. I shoved and squeezed and finally managed to ram it home, the breast now flat, get it back behind the panel and was just in time to be innocuously checking the price of *Mrs Tiggywinkle* when Handy stomped in.

Three weeks later, in March 1960, I had arrived on the edge of Dartmoor to take up my post as tutor to the four children of the wealthy Cornish businessman and his ex-ballet dancing wife Yvonne.

(17)

The somewhat anachronistic post of tutor had come about after I had answered a desperate and urgently worded advertisement. The only qualifications, aside from a modicum of education, had been to have had measles, the illness which had prevented the four children returning to their four separate smart little prep schools.

There were three boys (twelve, nine and seven) and one girl (Susan, aged thirteen). Their disparate ages meant that, in most subjects, I had to plan four separate lessons for each class. Ever since what I regarded as the ridiculous restrictions at Bryanston, I had decided that the ideal education lay on Summerhill lines. The smart little prep schools were clearly all extremely conventional – one even had beating. At my first class, they all stood up when I came into the room. They called me 'Sir'. In a single exhilarating stroke I abolished everything they had become accustomed to. I was to be called 'Jonny'. Of course I hoped they would attend lessons, but they were voluntary. We would discuss together appropriate punishments for transgressions – though I didn't suppose there would be transgressions.

A. S. Neill, in his accounts of Summerhill, describes the deliriously wild behaviour with which his young pupils reacted to their release from their restrictive, often brutal, English boarding schools in the 1930s. It often took a year before they settled down. My own regime descended immediately, once what I had said sunk in, into almost total chaos. The children ran yelling about the house, the garden and out on to Dartmoor. No one attended any lessons. To Yvonne, watching appalled, anxious and astonished, I counselled patience. But I rapidly realised my experiment had failed. Given a year perhaps . . . but Susan had her Common Entrance at the end of the summer term. On the fourth day, I was forced to reimpose rigid discipline. Once again I became 'Sir'. All lessons were compulsory. 'Lines' were the punishment, or household tasks. Bells rang and whistles blew. We had nature walks or three-a-side football (Yvonne, with her ballet skills, excellent here). We had exams and prizes and prep. My ideals had collapsed at the first push but at least there was no beating.

It was extremely hard work and I eventually became very tired, not just from teaching but from finishing my novel and, above all, from my continuing indecision than which nothing is more tiring. I knew everything was over. Of course it was. At the same time, I thought perhaps it wasn't. I would find I had arrived at my usual position – it wasn't really over, but if it wasn't, surely it should be, or perhaps surely it should not be. As so often before, I would imagine I was back for ever in Montpelier Square – and at once feel a surge of relief. But this would be swiftly followed by anxiety, doubts, the desire to escape. I would reverse the situation and leave – and at once feel a surge of relief and excitement. And this repetitive seesaw was accompanied by arguments with which I was so familiar they often hardly seemed real any more. But because they had repeated themselves endlessly endlessly, let me just repeat once again and for the last time some of the endless balancing and counterpointing and repeating that had gone on for so long, and still went on, in my head: what if I had been rich, or it had been my house and friends, or I had been forty-five? To admit such things counted seemed an admission of emotional feebleness, to demean 'love'. So, though they did weigh in the balance, I felt they had to be *dis*counted if I was to discover the kernel of my problem. Didn't they also represent, or express, her possessiveness, her desire, as I saw it, to dominate me? Against this, there was the need, psychological as well as physical, for sex; but then again – my inexperience giving the counter of sex a single value – any leaving would involve that. It wasn't particular to this leaving. And didn't the same thing apply to my fears – the fear of losing the security, the safety, the familiarity, the comfort, the delicious food and unlimited drink, the fear of having to hunt for women again, the fear I would never find anyone else I would love so much or who would love me? Surely, these fears too would accompany my leaving or being left by anyone? Much more important was the fact that from twenty-two to twenty-six, a time of huge changes, probably the equivalent of ten years at the age of forty, say, all my thoughts had been concentrated on her so that she had entwined herself into me in that peculiarly intimate way we mean when we say, when I said earlier, that someone has become part of us. 'To leave is to destroy.' To leave Eliza meant smashing all of that, all those changes that had taken place in me, or so it felt.

This was of course the same mechanism that I had recognised at work when I decided to give up writing and discovered that I couldn't; the mechanism, that is to say, that was at the root of *One Foot in the Clouds*. I was able, therefore, to transpose feelings about Eliza, disguised, straight into the book. Similarly, although my indecision about whether I should write or not had in fact lasted, at most, a day, I was able to put my indecision about Eliza, which had lasted at least a year and a half, suitably altered, into *One Foot* . . . That is, a novel of which the last third seems to be about a writer wondering whether to write or not is really about the end of an affair.

In the novel, the hero decides at the end of the book that he will write after all. I did this because I was still besotted by Proust and wanted my narrator to decide he would write a book when he had in fact already written it. One might think, therefore, that since the hero returned to writing, the resolution of my own indecision would be to return to Eliza. But in fact, when I'd finished *One Foot in the Clouds* and sent it to Barley, I found the opposite had happened.

Spring came early that year and walking between the steep, primrose-dotted banks of the narrow lanes and then out under oceans of air, exalted by the beauty and by my months of abstinence, exhausted, striding across the open moor, larks rising, I realised with delight that I was at last free of her. This, at least and at last, I could tell my mother.

(18)

I say at least because I often didn't tell my mother what happened to me because she nearly always became too upset and anxious. In fact, if I wanted, I could tell her anything. After Nell, for instance, fascinated and amazed about everything to do with sex, I said what particularly delighted me was the smell of making love. My mother agreed. She said the first dirty joke she'd been told was of the blind man who lifted his hat every time he passed a fish shop. The only thing I didn't tell her, to spare my feelings not hers, was about Madame Kitty and my fear I was impotent. But she found that out for herself anyway by reading my journal. I realised this when, some months into my affair with Eliza, my mother said, 'Well, at least you can sleep with anyone you like now, can't you?'

However, when I went to Hartington Road after Dartmoor, she wasn't particularly pleased at my news. She was too worried about what I might be suffering or would suffer. I tried to reassure her and after two days returned to London.

(19)

Carlton Mews had come to an end. But in London I managed to borrow a high-ceilinged studio room, with a balcony, off Eaton

Square. At a party of Nell's, I met a tall, slender, to me (and a good many others) unbelievably beautiful Swedish girl called Ulla and took her back to my romantic studio that same night.

Barley wrote to me about my book. She had given it to Elizabeth Jane Howard who had said it was not worth publishing for reasons which Barley was tactless enough to let me see and which showed Elizabeth Jane Howard had completely failed to spot the new Proust, as well as everything else about the book. Barley had then sent it to Francis Wyndham, who had strongly urged publication. She herself, Barley added, had some small changes she would like made, but – yes, Weidenfeld and Nicolson accepted it! An advance of £100 on signature, £100 on publication.

I wrote and asked Gerald Brenan if I could come and stay, bringing Ulla. He agreed. Ulla was an artist and therefore, by definition, penniless, but since I was about to get the equivalent of £1,250, I could overdraw and was able to buy both air tickets. Ulla took so many clothes that, despite a trunk and two cases, all her small tins of oil paint had to cram into my single suitcase. We were also burdened with rolls of canvas and unmade-up stretchers. But on 3 May 1960 we flew out to Gibraltar on the same propeller-pulled Dakota flight I'd taken alone a year and a half before.

(20)

Ulla and I were together about two and a half months, three weeks of them in Spain. She was twenty-two, with long golden hair, a huge mouth filled with perfect teeth, and a long, golden body like a sort of Scandinavian Masai. She had highly eccentric eating patterns, but she was intelligent, amoral, resilient, enterprising, funny, her lovely mouth suddenly loosing explosions of laughter, and – precursor of how many millions to come? – 'into' tarot cards, astrology, yoga, Buddhism, mad diets, getting brown, marijuana and, of course, art.

I don't really know how good Ulla's paintings were. Nearly all girls seem to have a natural talent for painting just as they do for swimming. Her palette was vivid, a fact I viewed with a rather jaundiced eye since most of her tins of oil paint, as a result of the unpressurised luggage hold in the Dakota, had exploded inside my suitcase, ruining my small wardrobe (there were also crimson and yellow splodges on the manuscript of my novel, which I'd brought out in case Barley asked for changes). But in a way it didn't matter whether her paintings were good or bad. Though she painted with concentration (focusing on Morning Glory), and talked about sales and exhibitions, I discovered that she did not depend, as I had thought, on painting for her income. Her father was a Swedish businessman with enterprises both in Sweden and England. Though she was to become even richer when he died, Ulla had been left a great deal of money by an English grandfather and her financial and other affairs were managed by Lord Goodman. Her 'millions' – or at least hundreds of thousands – escaped when plump Goody metamorphosed into plump, embezzling Baddy. Alas, Ulla's money succumbed many years later to rapacious husbands.

Gerald's house was on the edge of the little village of Churriana, about six miles from Torremolinos, itself perhaps still just describable as a *pueblo*. The big house was cut off by a fifteen-foot-high wall on three sides of its garden and by its tall, blank-seeming front facing the little, eucalyptus-lined street leading into the village. You came in through a side door, along a wide but low and rather dark passage, and then suddenly – paradise! Beyond a giant pecan tree and past an equally giant avocado with a hammock, there was blazing sun and colour – orange and lemon trees, shrubs and maize, tufted reeds and clipped vines, flowers in trim box-hedged beds, the ordered riot of an enormous southern garden, its two acres seeming like a small estate. Gerald had lost most of the ground floor of his large, airy, mid-nineteenth-century house to a sitting tenant, but he still had five or six bedrooms, a bathroom, a library and an open sitting area upstairs, and a tower or *mirador* still higher.

It was at once one of the most peaceful and most stimulating places I've ever known. The *alberco*, the small, ochre-coloured rectangular irrigating tank outside the house, slowly and musically filled all day and all night; every morning and every evening Antonio the gardener would open it and water would pour down a pipe and flow out into the innumerable dug channels running all over the garden and along one after another of which Antonio would divert the stream with his mattock. If there was a breeze the tall bamboos, some as thick as a man's thigh, clacked together as they rose past the library windows. Gerald wrote all morning. So did I (my journal). Ulla painted (Morning Glory). Gamel Brenan drifted about the garden in her melancholy way, butterflies fluttering from her path, dreaming of the past, of her reading, composing her melancholy and beautiful poetry. Sometimes she would drift into the downstairs dining room for a small wine glass of sherry.

The peace quickly became for me highly deceptive. I soon learnt that the real love of Ulla's life was her younger brother Viktor. Viktor was seventeen, almost unnaturally beautiful, I heard, gifted, even brilliant, wayward, poetic and already experimenting with the drugs that would eventually destroy him. Ulla hadn't slept with him, not so much because he was her brother – the mere fact of incest would hardly have deterred her – but because he was gay. He was having an affair with a thirty-six-year-old, bisexual American beat poet called Ned Buckley. Viktor had had to go back to Sweden. Ned was staying a little further up the coast. Ulla asked Gerald if she could invite him to stay for a few days. Gamel had just left for her annual visit to the Powyses, so Gerald said yes.

Almost the moment Ned came stooping out of the dark passage dramatically into the bright sunlight and walked lightly towards the glass-topped table where we were all having lunch, Ulla fell in love with him. I realised she had really decided to fall in love with him long before, probably in London. It was a way, quite apart from his immediate American attractiveness, of expressing her love for Viktor.

For three days I watched in an agony of jealousy while Ned – with his freckled good looks, his short, reddish hair and his dancing blue eyes and pointed nose, his impeccable credentials (friend of Ginsberg, friend of Kerouac), his dazzling frankness, openness, and sexual honesty ('When I come, like I have to laugh. Real *loud*. Sure it can be embarrassing. Some chicks don't dig it'), his poetry, his general all-over condition of total cool (already becoming a buzz word then) – fell in love too. Or at least, fell into desire. But the only complication was he also fell in love, or into desire, with me at the same time. It was a complication; it also enabled me to keep them apart for ten days.

Why don't we go off together, all three? Ned would ask. 'A

partouse'. Yes, I agreed, we might. Ned had brought a lot of dope, shit, grass, skunk or whatever marijuana was called then (drug vocabularies change faster than any others in order to keep those who are in, *in*). After supper he would roll huge joints and spliffs and jays.

Jealousy is a form of madness. In the wide, high-ceilinged, blue-tiled corridor off which the bedrooms led there was a fair-sized nineteenth-century Spanish table made of some heavy South American hardwood, with a thick velvet tablecloth under which, in winter, you could put your legs to warm them at a charcoal brazier there. As soon as Ned arrived Ulla had become irritated by me. On his second night, she suddenly got impatiently out of our bed. She was boiling. She'd sleep in the *mirador* or the hammock in the garden. I lay, the moon shining in out of the hot night, upset and hurt, and suddenly realised – *she's gone to Ned*. I slipped swiftly out of bed and up to his room at the end of the long corridor, the tiles cool under my feet. I listened. I couldn't hear them, locked in their embrace. I got a chair but the door was too high to see through the semi-circular glass panel above it. Should I try and ease open the door? Then I remembered the Spanish table at the other end of the corridor. Endowed in my madness with the strength of ten men, I staggered with this monstrous object all the way to Ned's door (I tried the table a few weeks later. I couldn't even lift it.) I placed the chair on top and climbed up. I could see Ned's hair on the pillow, like a small pile of pale sand in the moonlight. He was alone. Panting, I staggered back, the table now banging deafeningly against the walls on either side. No one seemed to hear.

The next night, after supper and several joints, Ned guided my hand under the table and between his legs, like Hussein. Did they always do this? It was as if he'd shoved one of his enormous spliffs down his tight green cotton shorts. He looked at me for several moments, then smiled and released my hand. Much later, when everyone had gone to bed, he said, 'We've got to make it, us three. When are you going to make up your mind?'

'I'm on the edge Ned. I'm havering. I guess I will; but Ned?'

'Yes.'

'While I decide, would you promise not to sleep with Ulla?'

Ned went into shocked silence at the idea of this unheard-of restraint. Then, with a deep breath, he said gently, smiling, 'For you Jonny, yes. Sure. But not for ever.'

Two mornings later, Ulla arrived in our bedroom, her eyes red. She sat on the bed. She didn't bother to dissemble but began to cry. She hadn't slept. She was desperate. 'Did you sleep with him? With Ned?'

'No.'

'Please don't Jonny. What am I to do? He doesn't even look at me now.'

'You know he wants us to go away together, all three. A *partouse*.'

'*Does* he?' Ulla looked surprised, and not very pleased. 'Well, I suppose so. We could. Are you going to?'

'I doubt it. I could almost say no. I said I'd decide in a few days. But Ulla – I won't sleep with him, but on one condition. That you don't make love to him either till I've decided.'

Ulla was pathetically grateful. She only wanted to talk about Ned. She wouldn't sleep with him, except he didn't seem to want her. How could she get him interested in her again? He'd seemed to reciprocate. Then this coldness. He had eyes only for me. She was in such pain. I counselled coldness in return. Avoid him. People always loved what they couldn't possess. Had she read Proust?

Of course, I didn't believe either of them. I followed one or other whenever both went out of my sight. I said I was going to write in the *mirador*, but that was only because I could survey most of the garden from it. I stopped having a siesta so as to remain on guard. The fragile truce seemed to be holding, except – what happened when I was asleep? I got up several times in the night and patrolled.

The climax, if that is the word, came ten days after Ned's arrival. That night he rolled bigger joints than ever, like logs. I had had marijuana before and though I was later to have one very odd experience with it in Tangier, I was beginning to hate it. It made a situation that was paranoid enough even more paranoid. Clogged and silenced, I became permeated with a sort of dulled horror. Terrified of appearing 'uncool', I sucked in noisily and held my breath and passed the logs round in the approved way. I had a furious thirst which I tried to quench with a great deal of Gerald's cheap

Spanish wine on top of a lot of equally cheap metallic Malaga gin.

I don't remember the sequence of events at all, but much later Ned was leading me to the far end of the hot, heavily scented garden. The cicadas were making my brain vibrate. Somehow I found myself kneeling between his legs. Then, after what seemed like hours, time was drugged too, I suddenly heard floating out into the night, high above the garden and the trees, on and on and on, above me as, choking, I wrenched myself away and began to be violently sick, the high, wavering, uncontrollable sound of Ned laughing.

(21)

I realised after this that I couldn't stand any more. Gerald, who after Gamel left each year, allowed a great many young people into his house partly to observe their love affairs (and often help pick up the pieces), had been roughly aware of what was going on. I now told him precisely and begged him to get rid of Ulla and Ned.

While they packed up and left, Gerald and I went to stay with the Americans, Bill and Annie Davis, in La Cónsula just up the road from Churriana. The house had been built in the mid-nineteenth century by a Neopolitan and, with its long, elegantly balustraded balcony and slender marble pillars, it had an Italian feel. There was a large garden, a small swimming pool, enormous trees and little lawns and a tennis court; there were nannies, servants and gardeners.

The Davises were an intriguing couple. Bill, nearly fifty, a big, bald, shambling man with a deep, hoarse, mechanically indistinct voice, walked with a slight slouch or list as if holed below the waterline. A New Yorker, he was an ex-alcoholic and there was an air of controlled violence about him. Capable of a kind gesture, dangerous if crossed socially (he once knocked someone out for arguing about his choice of restaurant), cunning, coarse, a snob, moderately well-read, this complex, opaque man had very little money. This, and there was a lot, was all his wife's. Though, as I got to know them better, it was clear that Bill depended on her emotionally as well as financially, Annie thought her life with him hung by a tenuous thread. Flustered, genuinely kind and gentle, she was not at all stupid, but she moved and spoke and even seemed to think very very slowly; then all at once her curious slab-like Amerindian or Mexican face would come alight and she'd say something apposite.

The Davises, too, had a flow of guests during the summer. When someone big came, which they seemed always to do completely unexpectedly – Hemingway or Ordoñez, say, or Orson Welles – Bill behaved outrageously. Guests already installed were asked to leave immediately and those about to come were cancelled. Local friends, however close, were banned. The big iron gates were locked and guarded by two barely controlled Alsatians. The only exception to these expulsions and embargoes were Gerald and Gamel. Already famous (and eventually celebrated among Spaniards for his books about their country), he and Gamel were always asked up and paraded. Gerald, deeply disapproving of Bill's behaviour, could never resist these invitations.

A little later that summer Gerald's publisher, Jamie Hamilton and his wife Yvonne, came to stay at La Cónsula. Jamie Hamilton extricated me from a very unpleasant dilemma I now found myself in. Early in June, I had received a large parcel containing a long letter from Barley, a copy of the manuscript of my novel heavily annotated in her hand, and my contract. The letter was a detailed critique of *One Foot in the Clouds*. One by one characters and incidents were examined, found wanting and removed until, in the middle of the letter, there came this sentence: 'So we are now left with something of a problem – no book. However don't despair, I think I see our way out.' Barley then proceeded to rewrite my book – new characters, new plot and sub-plots, new ending. I was horrified and soon, sitting in the *mirador*, did indeed despair. It was Gerald who saved me. He had read *One Foot* . . . and liked it, or so he said; he also used it to protect himself from Jamie Hamilton. Gerald had just finished his own novel, *A Holiday by the Sea*, and Jamie was reading it. Jamie's only tactic with authors he planned to publish was extravagant and continual flattery. No doubt usually effective enough, Gerald hated it. His defence was to say, you may think my novel is good, but you should read a new young author I've got staying with me. Soon after Barley's bombshell arrived, Gerald took my manuscript up to La Cónsula, cannily also taking my Weidenfeld contract so that Jamie could run his eye over it, since I didn't have an agent. 'Young' and 'new' would probably have been enough, but no publisher in London at that time could have resisted a chance to do down George. Jamie doubled the Weidenfeld advance on the spot and I, too, became (the much more amenable) recipient of his praise. I wrote to Barley saying I couldn't make her changes and would have to try and find another publisher. I enclosed her contract.

Soon after this, in July, I went to stay at Mijas in the mountains behind Fuengirola. David Tennant lived there with his fifteen-year-old daughter Sabrina.

(22)

Mijas, up a steep zig-zag narrow road unmetalled at the top, was still, physically at least, more or less untouched by the cancer of mass tourism starting to rage along the lymph systems of the coast. The little whitewashed houses that lined its twisting, undulating streets were lived in by locals, some of whom worked the land or kept goats, a few of whom were just beginning to find employment below. There was one *bodega*, dark and cool, sawdust-floored, with, at one end, large barrels of the *vino corriente*, and smaller ones of *manzanilla* and the heavy, sweetish Malaga wine. Children and chickens ran in the streets and laden donkeys ambled or trotted through. There was a faint smell of dung in the air, of dust, of whitewash, of frying oil.

David Tennant had retired to El Palomar, walled, comfortable, with, at nearly 2,000 feet, a magnificent view out over the coast to the sea far below and, on clear days, to North Africa. Retired, he liked to say, like an eagle to its eyrie or, as Cyril Connolly did, like a wasp that's lost its sting. Not quite lost, in my view. Very intelligent, gifted, even brilliant when young, this handsome scion of that doomed family – doomed by their many talents as much as by wealth – had once been famous for his dash and charm and wit. Piloting a tiny private plane, he used to land in the little English fields of the 1930s to read the signposts. Perhaps his had been one of the planes I'd looked up at, aged five, as it droned above Snape. And as a young man in 1925 he had created a club in Soho, the Gargoyle, which he ran with panache and success till after the war. But by the time I met him alcohol had taken too great a toll. Apart from sudden huge walks in the *sierra* above the house, his principal occupation, not a very onerous one, was recording his rain gauge. That – and drink.

In fact, though not particularly demanding, David took his rain gauge with great seriousness. He had a semi-official position as climate observer for the *Sierra Mijas*, and had had an extremely expensive, very sensitive instrument sent out by Negretti and Zambra. This consisted of two small buckets into which precipitation was directed. When bucket A was full it sank down, an oscillator clicked and recorded the amount, it tipped over, voided its contents and was then held down waiting to rise again. Meanwhile, bucket B had risen, was slowly filled in its turn, sank, the oscillator clicked, bucket B tipped over and was in its turn held in waiting. The contents of the buckets vanished into the swimming pool. Each month, David filed his graphs and reported anything unusual to the Meteorological Centre in Granada.

His daughter, treated with that typical upper-class mixture of love-when-it-suited-them and total neglect, had been there two months on her annual shuffle between her mother Virginia, married now to Henry Bath, and David. Her friend Sheila (whom David, to his family's financial consternation, later married) had left some weeks before. In her loneliness and air of a wild animal abandoned, her extraordinary sense of humour and seeming maturity, her exquisite cat-faced beauty, she moved me and fascinated me. At first our hours were regular, if late. We got up at twelve and had orange juice, coffee and eggs from Paco's hens probably laid that morning. (Paco was David's servant, who cheated him outrageously.) We would walk up into the *sierra*, or into the village (Sabrina spoke Spanish). We plunged into the tiny, icy pool, sunbathed, talked, and I read her long passages from *One Foot in the Clouds*. I wooed her with a necklace I made from the spikes of the century cactuses which dotted the landscape. ('They flower once every hundred years,' Gerald used to say, 'and then die. The perfect expression of romantic love.') After a while, Sabrina and I were sleeping together in the little *caseta* at the top of the garden. But slowly our pattern changed to fit in with David's. He would appear at six every evening. After a very light breakfast, he would go out and inspect his rain gauge. Then it was time for the first drink – wine, later Fundador. Lunch was at midnight – invariably chicken, English chicken which Paco bought in frozen batches from Gibraltar. We went to bed after supper at around 6 a.m. Night had become day.

Nothing disturbed us, except when once, rather drunk, I peed into David's rain gauge. He arrived from inspecting it that evening pink with excitement. 'There has been a *tormenta!*' he cried, his arm raised and fist clenched and shaking near his chin in a characteristic gesture. 'A *tormenta* of unprecedented force! I slept through it. I shall get Paco to wire Granada.' He opened a bottle of champagne to celebrate. Two days later there was a report of an 'unusual rainstorm in the *Sierra Mijas*'. But nothing else happened. The hot days passed slowly and peacefully into the hot nights. There seemed no reason ever to leave.

However, leave I did – and very abruptly. One late afternoon, Sabrina came to me white-faced. She'd got VD. Was she *sure*? Absolutely sure. Although I had no symptoms yet myself, I was not surprised. Wounded vanity at once connected it to Ulla. Obviously she had been sleeping with Swedish sailors or similar rough trade. Now I faced the wrath of a father. There was an outburst of Fundador-fuelled rage. I must leave at once, that very evening. Paco would take me to Gerald on the back of his motorbike. I promised Sabrina we would see each other as soon as I could manage it and then, as she watched red-eyed, Paco and I wobbled out of the gates and, as the sun began to set, away down towards the coast, the *costa del humillación*.

(23)

Almost the first thing I did after getting back was to go and have some primitive and unpleasant tests in Torremolinos. I didn't have VD and I sent the results, with a terse note to David, and a long letter to Sabrina, off to Mijas. I can't think why I ever believed I did have VD – probably, as I said, the immediate assumption, hope even, that Ulla would leave some disgusting memento of this sort.

There followed the last three days with Eliza I mentioned earlier, after which we did not see each other for three years; eventually we became close friends. Finally, about thirty years later, more than that.

But immediately after this last parting there followed what were not affairs, but two-week-long incidents, with girls whose names I can't remember, but who fell temporarily into what Gerald liked to see as the safety net of his Churriana house. I should add that if this succession sounds as if I found it all extremely easy, I didn't. Unless someone actually threw themselves at me, which very occasionally did happen, Madame Kitty, the fraught lateness of my beginning, always meant I found it terrifying and thought, initially, I was bound to be rejected. I can't remember ever managing to seduce anyone when I was sober – not then, nor since.

From time to time, news filtered down about unfortunate events up in Mijas. Some months before, David had bought a vast and extremely expensive Buick Riviera which his son-in-law Euan Graham, a tall, very amusing young man, had driven out to him from England. David, like all the rich, hated to pay anything if he could avoid it and again, like most of the rich, was arrogant enough to think he could get away with anything. To avoid the 'tax importo' he had registered the car in Spain in the name of Paco. One evening, going to get the car from the garage, he found it had gone – along with Paco and his family. Nothing he could do.

I now got to know Gerald much better. I grew very fond of him and also fascinated by him, in particular by his conversation. V. S. Pritchett (VSP) said that Gerald was the best talker in England, not excepting Cyril, at this time, and he reminded Frances Partridge of Virginia Woolf, able, like her, to 'send up brilliant, fantastic roman candles of talk'. In these moments of inspiration, Gerald even surprised himself. 'I listened to myself talking,' he wrote to Ralph once, 'and wondered where the words came from – surely not from out of my head.' But I preferred him calmer, sitting with a few people – me and Julian, say, who came out from Rome where he was working then, and stayed at La Cónsula and used to join us for supper. The style of Gerald's conversation at those times was drifting and discursive, throwing out, in perfectly formed and balanced sentences, speculations and observations, like how beautiful England seemed when he went back, yet how after Spain only half-awake; England was the most poetical of countries and of course there was a close connection between poetry and sleep. And, continuing from this, how important daydreams were and that this was the reason literature was the major art. His opinions formed while he talked and were often deliberately provocative. 'There is a fundamental, irremediable sentimentality in all Victorian novelists, it seems to me. They call into play too many of our lower feelings, just as films do. One hopes bad characters will reform, one hopes good characters may be spared, whereas in the greatest novels one watches, surely, without hoping at all.' VSP, writing about Gerald's *Thoughts in a Dry Season* in the *New York Review of Books*, remarked on the extraordinary variety of his talk – moving from 'the habits of birds, the problems of abstract art, T. S. Eliot's deficiency in an historical sense, the nature of pretty girls, the ups and downs of sexual life, the moral and social influences of architecture . . . And this ends with an odd aside that gives sparkle to the learned phrases of his talk. The bishop who completed Salisbury Cathedral had been Queen Philippa's chaplain, a dwarf who was notoriously impotent. He built the finest spire in England.' And if you had suddenly had enough, as you could, of one of the long narratives of the coast,* say, then you had only to say, 'Yes, how amazing Gerald, but what exactly did you mean last night when you said Italo Svevo was more intelligent than Proust?' and at once the wind of talk would change, the sails swing and fill, and Gerald would be off on another tack, his small black eyes glittering. He was, that is to say, the most accommodating of talkers, quite without aggression (rather rare in noted conversationalists) and (also rare) as happy to

---

* Gerald loved gossip and sexual anecdote and these narratives were, in fact, seldom boring. I recorded one in my journal. Gerald had become fascinated by a Swede called Sven who had a room above the Bar Central in Torre-molinos. Sven's only aim was to have girls – hundreds, even thousands. 'He used to go to the beach,' said Gerald, 'find an unattached girl, sit not far from her and stare at her. He would stare and stare with unwavering blue eyes from his brown face. Then he'd suddenly get up, go over and say, "Come." Mesmerised, she usually followed. When he'd fucked her he wrote her name in an enormous book. I occasionally called on him. Sometimes Sven would be lying absolutely exhausted on his bed. He filled several books. Suddenly, quite recently, he gave the whole thing up. He became homosexual and now lives with a boyfriend. He has become gentle, calm and happy.'

listen as to hold forth himself, so that you exerted yourself, raised your game, and some of my happiest times in Spain were spent in those long warm nights, the heat of the day at last dispersing, the conversation lasting two or three hours, perhaps with Julian or someone else who had dropped in, with Gerald every now and again taking wing and, when the nightingales sang to interrupt him, clapping two books together to shut them up.

Those five months established my friendship with him. Thereafter, I tried to come and see him every year; I saw him on his once-or-twice-a-year visits to England, and we corresponded – rather hopelessly on my side. You usually have to live abroad to become a dedicated correspondent. At the end of September I reluctantly packed my few belongings, plucked up courage, and set off back to London.

But before I left, there was one last affair, which continued for a while after I had returned.

(24)

Josie was eighteen and had landed in Gerald's net – as far as I was concerned, now more like a web – at the beginning of September. The odd thing about the erotomania which had been ignited by, or at least fanned by the general madness of the coast and which had raged throughout my stay – and still did – was that, although I preferred it if whoever I slept with enjoyed sex, it hardly seemed to matter if they didn't. Josie, unlike her sister Anna whom I met years later and who loved sex, wasn't particularly sexy. She didn't dislike sex quite but she didn't need it. I asked her once what it had felt like for her. Josie thought, then said – 'Thud thud thud,' and giggled. I didn't mind. She was hour-glass, dumb-bell beautiful and I only had to see her and I wanted to make love to her. She had perfect golden skin, perfect, even, very white teeth and often smelt sweetly of white wine.

Dumb-bell beautiful – but not in the least dumb. In fact she was academically extremely clever, having, unusually, an extraordinary gift for numbers. She was mischievous, humorous and teasing, liking to conceal her cleverness and then suddenly let it flash out, taking people unawares and making them seem foolish. My physical passion for her continued when I got back and one weekend I took her down to stay at Glyndebourne. George and Mary Christie had been friends of mine at Cambridge. It was quite a crowded weekend and I was aware of politely and silently raised eyebrows. John Christie, a formidable man, was still alive and active and at about one-thirty in the morning, hurrying naked down the corridor to Josie's bedroom, I came upon him shuffling along in his dressing gown. There didn't seem to be anything to do but smile, say 'Goodnight sir,' and hurry on. Mary told me later that her father-in-law had been outraged and it was only with the greatest difficulty she had dissuaded him from having me thrown out the following morning. That evening we played racing demon and the raised eyebrows were startled to find that Josie beat them effortlessly – and then at poker which we also played.

In fact, all the liaisons begun in Spain continued in London, and I somehow picked up a fifth. At one point I was sleeping with all five. Two things brought this period to an end. The first was when, if I can use the expression, all the balls I'd been desperately struggling to keep in the air crashed to the ground. I'd written to them all and also to Julian in Rome. I remember one of the embarrassing (and boastful) phrases in the letter to Julian: 'My life is a tangle of girlish limbs.' Unfortunately I put Julian's letter into the envelope for Josie and hers into his. (Julian was delighted: 'I'd no idea you'd even *noticed* my breasts.') I similarly muddled up all the other letters. The second thing was that I realised I was in love with Sabrina and wanted to try and be only with her.

Frances Partridge in *A Pacifist's War* wrote: 'People are laughed at when they have too many shots at marriage, failing and trying again. But they shouldn't be, for they are after the best thing.' I didn't fully understand or appreciate the truth and depth of that 'best thing' Frances was writing about until I was over fifty, but the amazing thing is that Sabrina and I stayed together for ten years and six or seven of them were very happy.

(25)

It was amazing because, just sixteen, Sabrina was really too young, not just to set up house with someone, but for anyone to expect anything like that to last. I was fully aware of all this but found myself impelled by, I eventually worked out, three profound effects Eliza had had on me. The first proper love affair is meant to set the pattern for all those that follow, and for many years so it seemed. That sadness that had hovered at the edges of my affair with Eliza followed me for ever after. I invariably had to choose young women whom people either disapproved of my being with or who would clearly not stay with me, or me with them, or both. Sabrina's age was therefore ideal. Then, from now on I was never long with whomever it was than I began having fantasies I should be with someone else. I don't mean anything simple by this – like just fancying other women. Of course, I did this the whole time. What I mean is that I would suddenly be certain that *I really should be with that someone else*. I would feel again deep echoes of that long and painful oscillation. In fact, I never went with whomever I'd picked for the role. In any case, I was determined Sabrina and I should stay together. Finally she was entirely dependent on me for everything – even, or especially, money. She seemed to have no money at all. Since I had felt I was being smothered by Eliza's houses, money and friends this suited me perfectly. Once she felt safe with me Sabrina was able to abandon the hollow confidence which had enabled her to survive the intense anxieties and insecurities, the confusion and conflicts engendered by her non-family family and an alcoholic father she also loved. It took most of the time we were together to rebuild herself and when she was at last strong enough she took off to lead a life of her own. I realised she had used me to accomplish this, but I also saw I had used her in the same sort of way. Most young people who love each other and live together are imposing or working out things of this sort.

(26)

The first thing we had to do was find somewhere to live. Initially, I was in 3 Rathbone Place in what the landlord, a small-time Rachman, called a 'Unit'. This was a room about twenty feet by fifteen feet painted garish hospital yellow and divided by plasterboard partitions which ended a foot below the high ceiling. In one half was a minute kitchen, itself divided by another plasterboard partition behind which was a very small bath with a gas geyser. The other half, the bedsitter, held the narrow bed and a hard wooden armchair. It was heated by a tiny, noisy gas fire, with fragile white crenellated elements like fairy castles and a coin-fed meter fixed so that the gas cost about ten times what it should have. There was a toilet on the landing shared by the ten other inhabitants of our tall building opposite the Marquis of Granby pub.

Sabrina had a room in a flat in Percy Street, about two hundred yards along from Rathbone Place. It belonged to, or was rented by, Poppet Pol, one of Augustus John's daughters and the mother of Talitha Pol, who also used the Percy Street flat as a base. It was much preferable to the hideously uncomfortable Unit and Sabrina and I slept there as often as we could, me leaving only if Augustus, Talitha or Poppet turned up.

Augustus was eighty-one and came up every fortnight or so, arriving rather late with carrier bags full of bottles of red wine. If we were having supper he would open some and join us. I never got to know him well, but it was slightly more than a Sassoon acquaintance-ship. We went with him one morning on a demonstration against the Bomb in Trafalgar Square. After it Sabrina and I, Augustus and Mavis Wheeler, an officious, rather silly woman who used to appoint herself his minder, all went to the Royal Court Hotel bar in Sloane Square where he liked to drink. While we sat at a table, Augustus's primitive hearing aid, controlled from a box, suddenly began to emit piercing electronic squeaks, causing him distress. Mavis fiddled with it ineptly and I saw she was turning the volume knob the wrong way. I turned it back and the squeaks stopped. In his relief, Augustus threw his still burning cigarette high into the air over his shoulder. It described an arc and fell by chance down inside the shirt of the only other person there, a man with his back to us drinking at the bar. There was a brief pause while the cigarette, as it were, took root, and then a tremendous bellow of pain and frantic slappings and pullings, after which the man came furiously over to our table. But when he saw Augustus and recognised him, he became immediately mollified, indeed actually pleased. 'It is an honour,' he said, 'to be set on fire by someone as talented and distinguished as you sir.'

When he'd gone back, Augustus muttered, 'Oscar used to say "The great thing about being a gentleman is you don't have to behave like one."' Reminded by this, he described how he'd met Wilde a few times. His death had been terrible and after it fluids exploded from his mouth, his ears, his nose and all his other orifices. 'The mess was appalling,' said Augustus. 'They even had to clean the ceiling.'*

The old roué was still not beyond seduction – or attempted seduction. Sabrina turned up in the Unit at 6.30 one morning with a coat over her nightdress and said Augustus had suddenly appeared in her room and clambered into her bed. 'You can be the last person I make love to,' he said – rather a neat line. Sabrina had said she'd love to be that but she'd get them some coffee first. Bemused, Augustus had watched her leave. When they met in the Percy Street flat again he said to her, 'Do you know what happened to that beautiful mermaid who used to live here? She was going to get me some coffee last week and then suddenly vanished.'

For a while during this period we lived on the final part of the Hamish Hamilton advance which I got when *One Foot in the Clouds* was finally published in 1961. By chance, I met Cyril at a party soon after it came out. He came up, beaming benevolently, 'Five or six pages of your book gave me great pleasure. I have always thought that readers should pay an author, over and above the price of the book, when they give pleasure. How much do you think a page is worth?' This was a serious belief of Cyril's and in some ways admirable. It was also meant kindly. But I was rather wary of him by now and couldn't help noticing a patronising element. Besides, what about the other 282 pages? However, I was becoming very anxious about money. 'A pound do you think, Cyril?' He duly handed over six pounds.

I dare say Cyril was, in fact, not far out. But the book was widely and very well reviewed, though how much this was due to the generous custom then of indulgence towards first novels I don't know. Julian, now reviewing for *Time and Tide*, wrote, 'An enormously enjoyable read, very readable, very funny, very intelligent

---

* Richard Ellmann, in his marvellous biography, gives a similar account, but says it came from Wilde's friend Reggie Turner who presumably also told it to Augustus.

and very well written . . . He is wonderfully articulate and assured and may well develop into a major novelist.'

The advance and Cyril's generous contribution came to an end and I got another job as a copywriter at Ogilvy and Mather – O & M. After a few months, we found a third-floor flat at 18 Warrington Crescent, close to Warwick Avenue underground. Julian took the flat above us. We were so close and saw each other so frequently that I think Sabrina sometimes felt we were all in the same flat – and was not entirely pleased. Yet she too became very fond of him.

(27)

' . . . may well develop into a major novelist'. I have said that there was an element of flattery in Julian's approach to his friends, but I think on reflection that that is both unsubtle and inaccurate. Flattery is to pay people exaggerated compliments, which you don't believe, for your own ends. But he didn't do this. Julian genuinely saw the qualities in people which he extolled; indeed he often saw qualities which weren't there; he *created* qualities around them, and all this, while usually very pleasant for them, gave him in an unobtrusive way a feeling of control over them, a feeling, too, that they and he together were in some sense special.

I also noticed early on in our friendship how much he enjoyed, almost needed, things to be in the past – a past far enough away to require recalling. 'Do you remember how we put that ridiculous boat on the Mere at Thorpness?' he'd say, though it had only happened the month before when he'd come to stay at Snape, but this gave a feeling of longevity and stability to his friendships which increased their intimacy and which he found reassuring. It was a trait that may have derived from his childhood, brought up in the bulky shadow of his grandfather Hilaire Belloc. To small, quiet-voiced, sharp-tongued Eleanor Jebb and to a lesser extent to her gentle husband Reginald Jebb, Belloc was a Great Man. There was no point living in the present when the past had been so glorious and at Shipley Mill, near Horsham, where they lived, nothing had been altered since Belloc's day, nothing had even been *dusted* since Belloc's day. When I slept in Belloc's room I had the feeling I was sleeping in his still unwashed sheets. I actually found a set of his false teeth in the cupboard behind the bed. Julian grew up in a house where Past was Best. He also grew up the adored, very late youngest son – so his past was best too. And this cast of mind, not unlike Proust's perhaps, may have enabled him both to observe his friends as accurately as he did – and also add to them, create them. Alain de Botton, in his interesting little book about Proust, suggests we can only 'see' something properly if we re-create it in our mind's eye – and putting something into the past allows the distancing, the time as it were, to do this.

He was like Proust in other ways. He, too, used to give colossal tips in restaurants and to taxi drivers. As George de Lauris said about the French writer, Julian too 'took an interest in you, instead of trying to make you interested in him'. I wondered much later, however, if another of de Botton's observations didn't apply to Julian. Did Proust, wondered de Botton, keep 'buried in his heart, where they turn[ed] sour, other quite different opinions'? which outraged the French writer's friends when they recognised their portraits in his book. If Julian could have written the novels of which he was certainly capable, could have managed to express and expel those quite different opinions, he might have felt a great relief. He started at least ten novels, and sometimes got quite far – four or five chapters. Then something, some irresolution, some lack of stamina or confidence, perhaps a distaste for delving or perhaps just because he'd chosen a length not suited to him, caused him to give up. Yet several of those beginnings were very good indeed.* There were extremely painful things obvious on the surface of his life at its end, but there was also, I felt, a sense of buried anger.

---

* Julian was also great fun and very funny, to be with – but of course I've forgotten most examples of this. I remember driving down to Shipley and passing so many suburban houses with the often curious names people choose, we began to invent names ourselves. One of Julian's contributions was 'The Thighs'. A regular reviewer of novels for many years, he would send me phrases that caught his eye. 'Her wry, taunting breasts' was one such. He also enjoyed the quotes publishers chose from other reviewers. 'I may borrow this comment,' he wrote to me. 'What do you make of "A novel with a curious tang to it"?'

At the same time, I certainly didn't feel this for many years. It may simply have been that he saw (and added to) qualities in others because he was not confident they existed in himself – and that in the end this lack of confidence, crudely tormented by people at the BBC, overwhelmed him.

But there was no sense of buried anger or buried anything else at Warrington Crescent, though there was a great deal of *un*buried rubbish. Julian had a single large studio bedroom-sitting room, a bathroom and a fair-sized kitchen which rapidly filled with the unemptied dustbin and empty wine bottles and mould-filled milk bottles of bachelorhood. When you could hardly get into the kitchen and the bottles had started down the stairs he'd have a clear-out. The world, or at least the Church Commissioners who were our land-lords, hadn't heard of roof insulation then and his top-floor flat was very cold in winter. Julian kept it warm by leaving his gas oven on full day and night with the door open.

Sabrina and I had a more palatial apartment a short flight below him. Our bedroom looked down into Warrington Crescent, there was a sitting room where I installed a Pither stove, where we ate and which looked out over one of those spacious, leafy London gardens; then two steps up, giving an illusion of a second floor, to a small bathroom and the bath in which I heard that President Kennedy had been assassinated; finally, the minute kitchen. Next to our bedroom was an even smaller bedroom. At first this was occupied by Richard King, a Downside friend of Julian's and Cambridge friend of mine, and a dark beauty Vivian Walker, his girlfriend. They had nowhere to live and very little money, and kept all their clothes in a suitcase, though in fact Richard didn't need many clothes since he preferred, in our Pither warmth, just his voluminous grey vest and pants. Witty, very clever, very kind, and later to reveal an iron entrepreneurial nerve, he would say in a soothing voice – 'There is no need to worry. I am going to be very *very* rich. Just hang on.' In fact, they were tactfully often out, but after three months Sabrina became under-standably rather restless. 'Vivian *does* help with washing up but not *enough*.' I liked them being there. Living together, a process of continual learning, often benefits from dilution, especially at first. Besides, I went out to work every day.

(28)

I think I got my job at Ogilvy and Mather largely because of my grandmother. When I was about seven she had impressed on me the importance of shoe trees. The first thing Stanhope Shelton, the creative director, did when I walked into his office was look at my feet.

'I see you use shoe trees.'

'Yes.'

'Good.'

Shelton, or Shelly, was one of those short, bulging-eyed, testosterone-packed men whose presence you can feel the moment they enter the room. You can feel them coming down the corridor before they enter the room. He spread a maverick, creative fear about the department, drank a good deal, made passes at some of the mature women – and had the odd, instinctive genius necessary to lead in advertising or tabloid journalism.

I thought I'd lost the advantage gained by my shoes when Shelly opened *One Foot in the Clouds* which I'd brought along to buttress my rather meagre Benson specimens. Robert, the hero, had worked briefly as a copywriter. Shelly read out the passage in front of me. 'Robert hated every minute of it. He swore that never, ever, however desperate, however poor, would he ever have anything to do with advertising again.'

I was muttering embarrassedly about it being a novel, when Shelly interrupted: 'This just shows you how the eye of someone reading an advertisement immediately picks out the one thing that might interest them.'

The arrangement I made with Shelly was that I would work full time for two years. Then they would consider letting me work part time.

Perhaps the Parnassian element I mentioned earlier exaggerated the quality of my peers – but not much. About a quarter of the copy-writers wrote: Fay Weldon, ex-policeman poet Edwin Brock, the novelist Nicholas Salaman and David Wevill; a year after me Salman Rushdie appeared and when O & M took over Bensons (becoming Ogilvy, Benson and Mather) Gavin Ewart and Yeatman reappeared.

Nor was it just writers. Ernest Lough was there. The cherub-faced, angel-voiced boy, who had sung 'Oh for the Wings of a Dove', had matured into a small, tough, hard-bitten, briskly efficient account executive. We worked together on an improved imitation of Brylcreem called Trugel; a thickish, semi-translucent, colourless goo, it was like rubbing come into your hair – but effective.

Julian Orde, with her man's name and clay pipe, was my group head and also had writing ambitions. While I was there she had a radio play accepted about a dentist. Now about forty-seven, when young she had had Bohemian leanings and once had a brief affair with Dylan Thomas. She said that one morning she'd got up to buy them breakfast and asked him if he wanted anything. 'Yes,' said Dylan, 'leave your breasts on the bed.' Her breasts were still very impressive. Her marriage to an Abercrombie was rocky and she had intense, platonic, affair-like relationships with her young male copy-writers. OBM was in Brettenham House, on the right just before you cross Waterloo Bridge for the station, and she would take us (usually singly) to the Wig and Pen Club in Fleet Street and we'd get drunk.

She had had years of psychoanalysis and was in some ways difficult, but I grew fond of her. She was also complicated. She liked to dominate and could take offence. Sometimes she irritated me. She knew I wanted to go on writing, she also knew I had no money. 'You'll just have to write your way out of here by your boot straps,' she said, in a tone which showed clearly I wasn't capable of that – if it was that easy she'd have done it herself. I was reminded of my father when we rolled drunkenly outside the Arch. Although her Wig and Pen Club companions were almost invariably male and despite, she said, her long almost sexless marriage, she never made passes at them. Yet she did at Anne Semple, so that pretty Canadian copywriter told me. Perhaps Julian really preferred women. Her attitude to advertising seemed ambivalent. As we drank we would giggle at its absurdity. Consultants would be engaged, for grotesque fees, to give us lectures. I remember one who reminded us and reinforced the age-old importance of 'Now' and 'New', something we hardly needed reminding of. In the Wig and Pen afterwards Julian said, 'I once saw an advertisement with the headline '*New! Now at last! Owl wall-clock with revolving eyes!!*' Yet she was in fact passionate about her job, fanatical, and when, about fifteen years after I'd arrived, she was sacked in the most brutal manner, she soon got cancer and died.

Once again, forgotten figures wobble up from the bottomless reservoir of memory, becoming clearer and clearer until they are bobbing about on the surface: Geoff Thompson, a big, kind, lugubrious man who got electric shocks from the carpets and suffered an acute and chronic allergic reaction eventually, it turned out, to Mrs Thompson, whom he loved; Douglas Haines who boarded up his house, laid in two months' supply of tins and bought a shotgun to repel strikers in 1974; large Bea Dugdale, who had the electricity account (one of her headlines: 'My Hot Plates Satisfy My Needs!') and who, as evidence mounted, refused to believe smoking caused cancer (it was charred meat); cancer again with Mr Balham, under whom I worked on the Players account (the 'love' campaign – 'People love Players'). Jewish, apparently grim but kind, with an ironic, contained sense of humour, he died while I was there of lung cancer. We suspend disbelief, even laugh at the energy of the dying in operas – at Mimi's last aria in *La Bohème* or Maria singing her heart out, her heart which has just been pierced through by a dagger, in *Rigoletto*, yet the dying do sometimes display an extraordinary last burst of strength. Mr Balham got up from his bed in his last moments, and walked to the open window, flung his arms wide as if about to take flight, and dropped dead. Something similar happened, much closer to me, at Snape. So, Mr Balham rises through the water of the reservoir, eyes closed, face white, arms outstretched; still more follow him: Mary Gowing, Spencer, Leonard Blunden, John Armstrong, Clive Aldred, Peggy . . . wobble up – and then sink back into the depths, probably for the last time.

Actually, for some reason, Mary Gowing has bobbed up more than once. She had learnt her craft in the Ministry of Food during the war. Small, tough, kind, a lesbian, she did much work for charity and later ran an organic farm with her partner. She was probably the most gifted copywriter among us, running the egg and milk accounts. She invented the 'Add an Egg' campaign – 'Add four eggs to custard and it cuts like a cake.' She, like Julian, was fanatical. The egg account was in jeopardy and we were all asked to contribute ideas. Though, with her brilliance, Mary ran her accounts, they were nominally in Alec Worster's group at that time. One morning, during this period, Mary strode into Alec's office, her eyes gleaming triumphantly, 'Listen to this Alec. I think we've got it.' She paused for effect, then, glancing down at a sheet of paper, read out dramatically, 'When a hen lays an egg it crows! And why not?' – another pause – 'An egg is something to crow about!' Alec nodded appreciatively. 'Very good Mary, very good indeed. Except . . . ' he began to look doubtful, 'except, is it a *hen* that crows? I think it may only be the cock.' Mary screwed up her piece of paper and threw it into the waste-paper basket. 'You've just destroyed a whole weekend's work Alec.'

Mary died, and Fay Weldon took over her accounts. Nearly all advertising campaigns and slogans and headlines are joint efforts, but Fay's successes were less joint than most. She was as skilled at writing copy as she is – and this is rare – at writing novels. 'Go to work on an egg' was largely hers, as were 'Unzip a banana' and 'Drinka pinta milka day'. Fay became, and has remained, a friend.

I was never brilliant, or even very good – but I did become competent. After a year I was made a group head myself and put over three other copywriters. Salman Rushdie was one of them. He had been made aggressive by ill treatment at Rugby and confidence in his gifts made him arrogant, but he was clever, amusing and a congenial, generous supper host (though I wouldn't have liked to have been his girlfriend). He was useless to have as a copywriter because he was no good at it, though he was quite sure he knew all about it, as he did about everything else. So bad was he that I'm ashamed to say I decided he was incapable of writing good English – forgetting, in my exasperation, that advertising copy isn't English. I was astonished, years later, to discover that *Midnight's Children* was extremely well written.

I did win one prize – a Silver Quill for three advertisements I did for *The Queen* magazine, which had been bought by, or for, Jocelyn Stevens. P. L. Stobo, who had arrived with Bensons, was the director on the account. He was quite certain we should centre any campaign on Stevens – 'It's a natural Jonny. Headline – "The Queen and I".' But when I went to see Stevens he said that what struck him was how often men he talked to said their wives made them buy the magazine.

I dutifully did Stobo's 'natural' (read obvious) campaign, but also did one of my own which ran the headline, 'Caroline *makes* me buy *The Queen*'. Not unnaturally, seeing his own idea so exactly embodied, Stevens chose my campaign, to Stobo's chagrin.

Copywriters usually supplied the ideas then, even though TV meant advertising became increasingly visual. This continued through the 1960s into the 1970s. Research also became more detailed, thorough and voluminous. Huge briefs would thump on to one's desk. Yet no one really knew what would constitute a successful advertisement – nor do they now. This meant you could get your campaigns through only by persuasiveness, force of will or by becoming creative director. I was too impatient to be persuasive or to engage in the necessary manoeuvring, not tough enough for the real in-fighting, and would never, by design as well as lack of advertising talent, become any sort of director.

After a year as a copy head, OBM agreed I could work part time, at first four days a week, then three. This was to continue for another twelve years, but my position was always precarious.

For some extraordinary reason, while staying with Peta Lambe, my mother was taken to an Advertising Convention party in Edinburgh. I think it was probably through Bobby Bevan, ex-chairman of Bensons and now important at OBM. She was put next to Shelly. At some point, she mentioned she had a son at OBM. Oh, asked Shelly, who? My mother told him. 'Oh yes, I know,' said Shelly. 'Nice chap. Such a pity we had to sack him.' '*Sack* him,' cried my mother, aghast. 'Did you say you had to sack him?' 'I'm afraid so,' said Shelly. 'Have some more wine.'

My mother rang me up in a state of acute agitation early next day. She always expected this would happen – whatever job I was in. 'You never told me you'd been sacked.'

'I haven't been. Here I am.'

'I sat next to your Mr Shelton last night and he said he'd had to sack you.'

Now I too became agitated. I hurried round to Peter O'Neil, whose ill-defined position seemed to include being personnel officer. He said, 'Oh yes, I've been meaning to get hold of you. It will probably be OK, but I was going to say you should lie low for a while.'

Lie low – what did that mean? For several months I crept about Brettenham House like a soldier dropped behind enemy lines, peering round corners, diving into cupboards or toilets if anyone of rank appeared. Eventually, Peter said – 'You can relax now. It's passed.'

I never knew why I had been sacked. It may have been my shoes. Fay said she met me once coming to work from Charing Cross tube and one sole was flapping. Apparently I said I knew that but I hoped Shelly would see it and realise how under-paid I was. No doubt he did see it and decided at once I must go.

In fact, through broke all the time, I wasn't all that under-paid because on a three-day week I could support us and soon start to bring up a family.

(29)

Before this, I met Tim Behrens. He was having an affair with my cousin Harriet and she was pregnant. Anne rang me up.

'She's got to have an abortion. She won't unless Tim agrees. You've got to persuade him.'

'But I don't know him. I've never even *met* him. Anyway, it's not my business. *Anyway*, why should she?'

Anne and I wrangled for some time, but Anne was not – *is* not – easy to stop in such circumstances. So a week or two later, deeply embarrassed, extremely reluctant, I arrived at Tim's squalid room/studio near King's Cross. I had brought a bottle of red wine to facilitate my impossible task.

I have never met anyone so instantly and instinctively sympathetic nor someone with whom I got on so well so quickly. We finished the wine, then went out to get some lunch and drank another bottle. After some of the third, I had to go – and suddenly remembered the purpose of my visit. 'Oh, Tim – Anne told me to tell you Harriet *must* have an abortion.' We roared with laughter and I hurried off. Fan Behrens was born about seven months later in July 1963.

Tim, at this time, had just finished his affair with Raffaela, the beautiful Italian girl in the boiler room. 'You must meet her.' Raffaela had been taking a brief break from her entanglement with the Italian film director, Luigi, who, like her then, divided his time between

London and Rome. As a result Tim became a great friend of Luigi's too. I found later this was a pattern of his. Often he became closer and for longer with husbands and lovers, or ex-husbands and ex-lovers, than he did with the women themselves. 'Her thing with Luigi won't last,' said Tim. 'He's a notorious womaniser. Actually, I think he probably prefers horses. He told me that when he first had sex it was with a pony when he was fourteen on his father's estate in Tuscany. The pony enjoyed it so much Luigi was sometimes frightened he'd be squashed against the wall of the stable. Ever since, his usual fantasy when he's fucking is of riding a racehorse and winning – which means orgasm.'

Tim's charm extracted such confidences effortlessly, often immediately. But it wasn't, isn't, charm, quite. 'Charm' suggests a spell, some magic that entrances you, and blinds you – charming people are not *really* what they seem. Tim was more like my mother in the way he completely absorbed, and became absorbed in, his friends. As a result, like her, quite often several people at once think they are closest to him, his 'best friend'. He is the only male friend who has made me jealous.

But I found his gift – the extraordinary way he could captivate both men and women – unsettling in another way, since it reminded me of an aspect I suspected in myself.

(30)

I, too, made friends easily, but it seemed to me easily because superficially, even hypocritically. It was an extension of the 'squash friends' anxiety that had plagued me for a while at Bryanston. On the one hand I enjoyed these 'friendships', a particular form of energy was exchanged. On the other – who was this 'I' who could have such a wide and disparate range of acquaintance? I became obsessed with the idea that this 'I' didn't exist; it was a fabrication, false, assumed. The 'charm' that I exerted was precisely what I've just said it wasn't with Tim – that is, a spell to convince other people (and me) that my friendliness was real, that *I* was real.

Susan Blackmore and John Gray, among others, would say what I felt was a genuine insight. In her book, *The Meme Machine*, she argues

24 With Gerald (hatted) in 1957. Also Marion
Harewood (later Thorpe) and Ronald Duncan.

25 Party at Richard and Vivian King's.
Right: The host – Richard King. *Below, left to right*:
Julian Jebb, Vivian, J.G-H, Diana Crawfurd, friend
and literary agent (later Diana Baring), Candida and
Rupert Lycett Green. Candida looking very like her
father John Betjeman.

26   For many Christmases we and the Cranbrooks had a group photograph taken by our neighbour Donald MacLennan. *Left to right, back*: Gathorne, Sophie, me, Juliet, Hughie; *front*: Fidelity, Jock, my mother, Rose, Tina. Sammy was in the army; my father in the Far East.

27   Rock garden at Snape during an Aldeburgh festival in the early '70s. My father is next to John Nash. Frances Partridge is taking a photograph.

28   Marrying Sabrina Tennant at Hampstead in October 1963.

29 Nicky in 1965, eighteen years before I met her again.

30 A very blurred Uncle Bob looking at one of the even more blurred old master drawings (Mantegna? Michelangelo?) Their unexpected and dramatic sale in 1976 transformed our financial lives.

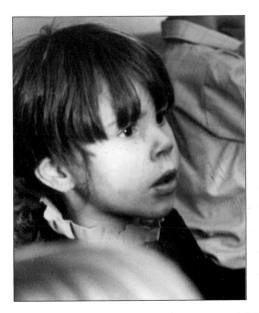

31 Every year Olwen Vaughan gave a children's party at the French Club, to which Jenny (born in 1965) and Ben (born in 1967) always went.

32　Tim Behrens and my cousin Harriet in 1967, four years after the birth of their daughter Fan, which I was supposed to have stopped.

33　My grandmother and me at Snape, practising the ancient craft that was once to precipitate my descent, briefly, into the criminal working classes.

34　Splitting logs at Snape. The wood my grandmother and I worked in together can be glimpsed in the background.

35 Cyril Connolly. Late 1950s. A time when he was apt to cause me difficulties, as he did later disappointments.

36 1978. Me with Eddie, who is leaving Snape for the last time on his way back to Athens and death. Anne behind us.

37 My mother and Rose outside the side door at 18 Hartington Road about 1954. The vine has started its mad growth,

38 My mother in the kitchen at Number 18 Hartington Road. The meter whose terrifying ticking she several times tried to stifle with a cushion can be seen to the right.

39 My father's marriage to Mary Smartt in 1974. Her brother Bernard behind with Anne.

41 Julian in 1984 at a party given by Rose, Nicky's sister. Eight days later he killed himself.

40 In Malaya. Sammy in the middle, his wife Grace sitting, daughter Penny behind. To the fore is Bernard Fergusson, the cousin who was so extravagantly and extraordinarily outraged by my book about nannies.

42 My father with Bert Allen, landlord of the White Hart in Aldeburgh and the man he asked to come and see him, with Mrs Allen, as he lay dying.

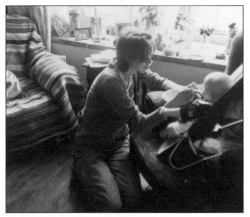

43 Jenny feeding her son, my first grandson, Rudy Mellen at Blacksmith's Yard . . . and Ben, with his daughter Moffy, my first granddaughter.

44   1999 – and my stepsons Joseph, Noa and Becalalis getting flowers for Noa's wedding later that day.

45   Part of the wood at Snape flattened by the freak hurricane of October 1987.

46   Ben and Fan Behrens watching Algy Behrens blow out his candles; Algy who, quite unwittingly, was eventually to prise Snape from my grasp.

47   Nicky and me showered with confetti after our marriage at Brixton Town Hall in 1985. Her sons Noa and Joseph behind us.

48   Nicky, just back from painting in her studio, outside the side door of our house in Binham, North Norfolk.

49   Working on the biography of Gerald Brenan while in Spain.

that the 'self' doesn't really exist; it is an illusion, a construct, perhaps necessary, perhaps harmful, but in no proper sense 'real'. Her ideas are interesting but complex – and by definition not entirely sympathetic to an autobiographer. Nor, in fact, was I really convinced by her central arguments. She said, for example, that you can't find any central 'place' in the brain conforming, with decisions, judgements, feelings and so on, to a 'self'. There is only a general and massive seething of activity, of processing and interacting. But to suppose there should be an actual isolated place for the self, as it were a cellular homunculus, seems odd, almost naïve. You cannot, for instance, find any central 'place' where memories are stored – yet no one questions the existence of memory. Then, she makes much of the discovery that if 'I' decide, say, to move my foot, this decision can be detected a split second *earlier* in the brain than the equally measurable activity of the conscious 'I' doing its deciding. But all that this seems to show is that a good deal of our self exists and operates below the level of consciousness, something Blackmore, who admires Freud, elsewhere acknowledges.

At any rate, none of these speculations was there to upset me in the London of the 1950s and '60s, when these feelings were periodically strong and unpleasant. I decided then that they were the last destructive ripple of leaving Eliza. In my mind, they echoed the attacks of 'loudness' I'd had at Snape and for this reason, as I explain later, there is a possibility that they may have been fundamental to my becoming a writer. But out of them came the idea of a novel in which the first-person hero, I would call him Chamil Descartes (French extraction, 'I think and therefore am not'), would find one day that he could physically and mentally actually 'become' other people. Chamil, obviously, would be me, but with *universal* resonance – do we not all feel we are composed of different people? (To this extent Susan Blackmore is certainly right.) Very early on I knew the final sentence of the book. Chamil, in hospital, thinks he is cured. But to his astonishment he once again becomes someone else – one of the female nurses, say. To his astonishment – and his delight: 'I was myself again.'

In August 1962, Sabrina and I went to Cefalu in Sicily with Julian and Tristram and Virginia Powell. While there I began *Chameleon*.

(31)

By 1964 my wages at OBM went up to £3 an hour. With a certain amount of fiddling and with great care I felt we could live on two and sometimes three OBM days a week. I set practically everything against income tax and paid almost none.

We also got married. David Tennant gave us £1,000, a good deal of which went to buttress the OBM days a week but also meant we could afford a honeymoon in Greece.

Eddie, when I asked his advice, said, 'You should definitely go to Samos my dear. Pythagoria is particularly delightful.'

The only delightful thing about Pythagoria was the tunnel a few miles from it which Pythagoras had had bored through a mountain to demonstrate the practical use of his geometrical theorem about right-angled triangles. (They bored from either end at angles specified by Pythagoras and to their amazement met in the middle.) There were no tourists, no signs, nothing except a track leading to the ruins of a small temple among some olives behind which, in the hot sun and the sound of cicadas, we eventually found, following Eddie's vague directions, the tunnel entrance. It was cool at once inside and you could still see the incisions in the rockface cut two and a half thousand years before, but after a few yards became too dark and frightening to continue without a torch.

Pythagoria itself was appalling. Very hot, almost deserted, a few dilapidated houses, one taverna serving inedible food – nothing but an inappropriately large and empty harbour. This was the clue. Eddie had been going through difficult times recently, which he had faced with stoicism, on the whole, but also a good deal of the selfishness adversity brings out. The reason he'd recommended Pythagoria had been because the Greek navy used the dock there every year during manoeuvres. At which point Eddie, a tall, now familiar if odd figure to the thousands of ratings, would arrive as well. He had been thinking, that is, of himself.

(32)

When Eddie had been axed by the Foreign Office, a first-class family row began to blow up, initiated by Anne. She at once wrote to Jock. Eddie had nowhere to live, almost no money, it was a clear case for help from the eldest brother. This was not how Jock saw it. He had been helping Eddie in small ways for years: paying debts, advancing loans which were never repaid, writing letters to support overdrafts. These last stopped when Eddie's debts became so huge he went bankrupt and overdrafts were forbidden. Now Jock was to be forced into supporting this improvident ne'er-do-well for the rest of his, Eddie's, life. He could live to be ninety. Jock refused to do anything. So what do you suppose Eddie will do, wrote Anne, starve? Eddie should get a job, Jock wrote back tersely. The letters from Anne became longer. Jock's terser still, and angrier. Eventually, Anne said Eddie, who was staying at Snape, would have to go to Glemham and plead his case himself, something he dreaded. He came back shaking with repressed rage, humiliation and misery about his future.

'How was he?' asked Anne.

'Awful,' said Eddie. 'We argued and then he shoved across an advertisement he'd cut from the *East Anglian* for a job as porter on Ipswich Station.'

Now Anne bombarded Jock with furious letters almost daily, several about twenty pages. Fidelity came to dread the arrival of these thick, instantly recognisable missives landing like missiles on the breakfast table, and then the subsequent explosions. Even Granny, who hated these family dissensions, was dragooned by Anne into writing on Eddie's behalf.

At last Jock relented, as he'd probably always realised he'd have to. He wouldn't give Eddie money directly, but would invest a sum on his behalf, the capital eventually returning to Jock. He would also buy and give him a small flat in Athens. Both things, and they were generous considering how provoked Jock had been, he did.

Eventually, the tiny Foreign Office pension and Jock's tiny investment allowance were augmented by the state pension. A lot of his old friends liked having Eddie to stay. He managed, though, as I said, it meant more and longer stays at Snape.

The trouble was Snape quite quickly got on his nerves. All her life, my grandmother on the whole relied on her family for companionship and intimacy, but she had a few local friends and those, as well as the clergyman and the schoolmaster and other humble figures, used to call. Eddie would sit impatiently uninterested. It wasn't their humbleness that mattered. Eddie was certainly extremely conscious of class – as were all his and previous generations (and as a great many people still are). It is difficult to say if he was a snob – or at least to what degree he was. Certainly, in some respects, he was and it is likely, if you'd met him casually, that he would have seemed so. Waving impatiently and imperiously at waiters and porters with his rather feminine flipper-like hands, a disdainful expression on his eagle face, he probably felt, though he would have denied it, superior to most people, a common result of an Eton education then, indeed an education at most public schools. But if by snob is meant someone who pays excessive or even any deference to what is seen as elevated social positions or who is frightened of being thought in too low a social position, then he was completely indifferent to such things. The only thing that concerned him was whether people bored him or not – and he was easily bored.

Which is not to say he didn't prefer as friends what he saw as his own class – who doesn't? Anne's second daughter Lucy fell in love with, and eventually married, Geordie from the lowlands of Scotland, a very good-looking young man on Sean Connery lines. It caused a stir in the family because Lucy, a beauty who also liked sex (a much rarer combination than people suppose) had hitherto ranged – except for a brief foray into the Beatles – more or less exclusively in *Debrett's*. Eddie said to Anne, 'He's a nice man, I think, a pleasant kind man. Yes, my dear, one has to admit he's working-class. I do rather wish he'd gone to Eton and Oxford – but I like him.'

The people who called on Granny at Snape had also failed to go to Eton and Oxford. And Eddie's range was narrow. They very quickly bored him. The mentally challenged and eccentric figures who cooked and sometimes cleaned also bored him, and irritated him too

– especially when my grandmother told him he couldn't expect them to empty his brimming chamber pot.

Furthermore, he felt he couldn't or shouldn't forage for sex in Suffolk in his usual way, though this didn't stop him fancying the locals. There was a surly, beefy sixteen-year-old who used to serve petrol at the garage just before Saxmundham. Eddie would go and put a gallon of petrol, or even half a gallon, into my grandmother's car. Paralysed by attraction, Eddie couldn't even ask his name. Then, one day, he dared. To his astonishment and delight the youth seemed to say Beauty. '*Beauty*,' said Eddie. 'Did you say *Beauty,* my dear?' 'Booty, Booty,' repeated the boy gruffly and eventually Eddie got it. 'Ah, Bertie, of course. Bertie. Well Bertie, my dear, I think we'll have *two* gallons today.'

But all these trials were made more difficult by his collapsing health. He developed diabetes and this, together with the reappearance of the venereal disease contracted long ago on the shores of Lake Galilee, meant various toes had to be lopped off. But far worse was his liver. The 1st Earl, a fervent evangelical, had chosen as his motto '*Armé de foi Hardi*' ('Armed with Hardy faith'). Faith had all but vanished in the family, but Eddie was armed with an extraordinarily hardy liver. He never had a hangover and could therefore drink as much as he liked with impunity. In the mid-1960s, after years of appalling abuse, his liver finally rebelled. Eddie was told if he drank more than a pint of beer a day he would get cirrhosis and die.

He was miserable. No money, no sex – and now no drink. I remember coming upon him, head in hands, staring into the fire at Snape, tears rolling down his cheeks. '*Je suis foutou,*' he said. '*Foutou.*' He tried substitutes. In his vast reading, he remembered an account of some towns in South America. The drunken mayhem had been so excessive on saints' days that they had banned alcohol. Instead, trays of little scent sprays filled with ether had been sold at street corners. A few puffs had induced a swift and pleasant euphoria. Eddie bought a scent spray and ether and would leave the room when people arrived, returning, no doubt to the surprise of the schoolmaster and clergy-man, like a blast from an operating theatre. My grandmother eventually told him he must take it in his bedroom. He also asked me to get him marijuana, which he'd had in the Middle East. I eventually succeeded (it was quite difficult then), but neither pot nor ether was really any substitute for drink.

It was during these years that I got to know him better and, despite frequent exasperation at his selfishness, grew fond of him. Among his friends and acquaintances, he was famous for his wit, but as usual nearly all this has vanished. It is not wit I remember so much as a general feeling of indulgence and humorousness, his idiosyncratic observations and the original, often funny way he put things, the depth and range of his knowledge and his intelligence when he could be bothered to use either, and his quickness. Leaning forward for my grandmother to fill his teacup (they always sat one each side of the fire), Eddie suddenly let out a deafening series of farts. 'Help!' he said, 'I'm disintegrating.' Another, similar time, his hand shook so that the cup rattled in the saucer. 'It sounds like two turtles copulating,' said Eddie. At a third teatime − I suppose all these teas because drink had been dethroned − Anne and Heywood, who came down more and more often, took him out to the Wentworth Hotel in Aldeburgh, which at that time had delicious scones. Eddie, who was greedy, soon finished the meagre supply of butter pats. 'More butter please, waiter.' Two more pats were brought − and finished. 'More butter please, waiter.' Two more pats. At this, Eddie beckoned with the characteristic rather languid flapping of his hand, like Hitler saluting, camp I suppose though Eddie wasn't very camp, and said very slowly and with emphasis, 'Waiter, when I say I want more butter, waiter, I want you to bring me *so much* butter, waiter, that I say "Waiter, *goodness*! Waiter! What a lot of butter, waiter" waiter.'

I see from my journal that I was staying briefly at Snape one winter with Anne and Heywood and Eddie when Rosamond Lehmann bought a cottage at nearby Peasenhall. I suddenly remembered a story someone had told me about Eddie when he was young.

'Eddie, is it true you once peed into Rosamond Lehmann's handbag when you went to the cinema together?'

'Perfectly true my dear,' said Eddie; 'but you must understand it was at the end of one of those very extreme early surrealist films, by Buñuel I think, with donkeys pouring with blood on grand pianos and streams of ants coming out of people's eyes, that sort of thing my dear.' I asked him if she'd minded. 'I think she was rather pleased,' said Eddie, 'but I'm not going to take it up with her.'

Later in the visit they were discussing John Hill. His fragile health had taken another blow – progressive softening of the bones. This apparently causes considerable pain and is irreversible. In fact, John, like many people of fragile health, lived, as I've said, into his eighties – but certainly in increasing discomfort and pain. 'It's too cruel,' said Anne. 'Poor John – deep depression, his lungs, and now this.'

Eddie had been listening in silence, champing his nearly toothless jaws (he rarely put in his false teeth). Suddenly he said, 'This isn't really relevant my dear, but I remember Simon Edwards, in the army, had a story that one of his soldiers was talking to him and said that his uncle had had softening of the bones and "they 'ad got softer and softer sir, softer and softer, and softer and softer until in the end, sir, 'e was nothing more than a jelly, no more than a *jelly* sir".' Eddie heaved and laughed and said the words with great relish.

In fact, Anne and Heywood came more and more often, soon to live there, because that slow glide down to death which was my grandmother's old age (she was eighty-six in 1965) now began to accelerate. Up till then, she'd been more or less as usual. She'd driven her car into the rock garden one afternoon and Anne had forbidden her to drive any more, but she still gardened, still dealt with 'the servants', still wrote her long not very interesting letters, still followed our lives, still read *The Times*'s births column every day, muttering irritably if more girls were born than boys. But then her memory began to go. She went out less. Now, when I stayed, I cut the trees down alone and told her what I'd done. And, just as she had with me twenty-five years before, when we played cribbage in the evening I used to let her win.

As her memory went, this once confident woman became anxious and repetitive. With her not driving, Eddie had to do the shopping when he was there. Try as he would – and he did try – not to be impatient at her querulousness, he did get impatient. Once again, he took to calling at 18 Hartington Road for relief – but here, too, collapse had begun.

(33)

My father had been a good doctor when young, and remained an intuitive and gifted diagnostician till the end, but with age and drink his skills declined. I remember him being one of the last doctors alive to use and advise Dover's Powders, a remedy, I now read, first prescribed by Dr Thomas Dover in 1705, when it was a compound of opium – which was probably what appealed to my father. Also, at sea then, out of reach of hospitals, especially in war, doctoring could be demanding. I still have the enormous and pioneering five-foot Anglepoise-type lamp he designed and had built for operations in his surgery, with its round, two-foot wooden base through which it was bolted to the deck. But on the whole service medicine is less demanding than general practice in a shore population, principally because there are no old. All your patients are fit young men. My father grew rusty; he continued to read the *BMJ* and *The Lancet*, but he went on no refresher courses.

As his naval career drew to a close, his postings became bizarre. He did a year on Nelson's *Victory*; this was followed by two years – 1961 and '62 – on the *Discovery*, the sailing ship which had taken Scott to the Antarctic. My father's task on these ancient vessels was to vet recruits. The *Discovery* was moored in the Thames not far from OBM. Sometimes I would go and have a sandwich lunch with him on board, bending my head as I went down the hatchway and again under the low door of the bulkhead into his cabin-office. We would sit chatting, drinking whisky and ginger, while the *Discovery* rocked gently, the river slapping at its sides.

My father had a room in Malden during this period which had a curious roll-top gas stove on wheels for self-catering. He cooked me and Sabrina a lobster thermidor one evening. But he was only ten minutes' walk from Mary and spent much of his time with her. He still thought no one knew about his exciting double life, though in fact my mother had long since found out about it, and to continue the concealment he cleverly created a Maldon couple, 'great friends', called Harris, who often asked him to stay at weekends. My mother was, on the whole, happy to go along with this.

In 1963 the navy decided to retire him with a reduced pension, but he managed to get a job with the army at Colchester, which meant he now spent most weekends at 18 Hartington Road – unless the Harrises asked him to Maldon, which they did at judicious intervals. Then in 1964 the huge volumes of toxic black smoke which had belched in and out of his lungs for the past twenty-five years finally got to him and, having diagnosed it himself first, he was found to have cancer of the jaw. The treatment, for which he had to go up to Millbank, near the Tate in London, as well as destroying the cancer, also destroyed his salivary glands.

It also left him very weak, which necessitated continual absences from Colchester, a weakness compounded because eating with his dry mouth seemed to become almost impossible. Food was tasteless. My father, for long a small eater, became a smaller one; each tiny meal, as slippery as my mother could make it, took an hour to wash down with whisky. Then one day my mother rang me, distraught; would I come down and help get my father into hospital?

He was shrunken and unshaven in bed and unable to walk. I found I could lift him quite easily. This man, whose pendulum I had once glimpsed out of the corner of my eye level with my head, this man towards whom I had had strong feelings, anger that he had left me in the war, admiration in his uniform, on his ships, love when we got drunk together at night, talking and talking, when I was sixteen – this man now so light.

He was suffering from severe vitamin deficiency, with especially bad neuritis. Amazingly, his liver seemed all right – the *foi Hardi* again I suppose – but he had to spend several weeks in hospital. When he came out, in mid-1965, it was to learn that he'd lost his job at Colchester.

This was a blow as bad as any. In particular, my father felt humiliated. Though he looked at least ten years older, he was only fifty-eight. He had expected to work till he was sixty-five. My mother described him tense over the table in the room next to the kitchen, smoking heavily, vitamin pills and whisky beside him, applying for jobs. Over four or five months, he wrote more than seventy letters – to prisons, to schools and mental hospitals, to businesses – answering any advertisement that seemed remotely possible. He didn't get a single interview; often he didn't even get a reply.

Once again, their finances became the central anxiety. My father now lived permanently at 18 Hartington Road and there was therefore a rise in some household bills – particularly in drink bills. They were still paying off Jock's loan and Rose was at Felixstowe College, a fee-paying girls' school; after which, in 1967, she was to go to Oxford and would need an allowance. There was almost nothing left to sell, except the Picasso, and that my mother still refused to sell. Eventually, it was decided that my parents needed an allowance themselves. I can't remember exactly who contributed – certainly me and Sammy a little, the bulk from Anne and Heywood, John and Sheila, and Bob; Fidelity said she wouldn't contribute since my father's troubles were entirely due to drink. (None the less, when Rose reached her sixth form, Jock gave her an allowance, and generously increased it to £60 a year when she went to Oxford. The fees were paid by her grant.)

These events, as can be imagined, did not exactly help my mother's struggles to drink less – nor did they help anything else. Her psoriasis and blood pressure both got worse. The electricity meter, an ugly grey cast-iron lump above the back door in the kitchen, made an extraordinary loud ticking, as if the house was about to blow up from lack of money. I remember my mother furiously stuffing a cushion over it to silence its menacing calculations. She also comforted herself by a pathetic fantasy. Although her dividend statements must have shown how small her capital was, she used to say to me, 'Well, at least you'll all get something quite substantial when I die.'

But it would be a mistake to give the impression that these disasters made Hartington Road a gloomy place to be or visit. It wasn't. My father recovered, after a fashion. He traded in the Morris at Carter's garage for a red Mini and later traded that for a nearly-new Robin, one of those unstable-looking three-wheelers now discontinued. He made Mr Carter soup it up with two carburettors, a large exhaust and regular fine-tuning. In this, the car equivalent of a wheelchair, he would suddenly pass unsuspecting BMWs or Mercedes with a devastating roar. He still saw Bert Allen every day in the White Hart, just as my mother still had her regular telephone sessions each morning and now, busy in London, one of the callers would sometimes be me. Her sense of humour remained, particularly with the Harrises, who gave her regular rests from my father when they asked him to stay.

However, she didn't let my father off entirely scot-free here. He would become very uneasy, almost panic, if asked questions about the Harrises. 'What is Mr Harris *like*?' my mother asked one day. 'You often see them but you never tell me about them. Why don't we have them to stay?' My father stared at her, horrified. 'Anyway, what does he look like?' My father, in fact, had quite a developed sense of fantasy, but now he looked round the room, his mind clearly blank. 'For goodness' sake,' said my mother, 'has he *no* distinguishing features? Bald? One leg?' My father, in a nightmare, searched the room again. Suddenly he blurted out, 'He has a moustache,' and with that, she told me, my mother had to be content. She tried again on another occasion. 'I asked him what Mr Harris did.' Again, apparently, my father, his face haunted, became paralysed. He stared at the floor in silence. 'You must *know* what he does. Or does he do nothing? Let's have them to stay.' At this, galvanised by terror, my father said desperately, 'He's in light engineering.' This was all my mother ever learnt about the Harrises.

I still had weekends there but much less often. Coming up to bed after my parents, there would be a light on in each room, their doors open, and each radio would be on a different channel. Without disturbing the Nembutal slumbers, I would go in and turn everything off. Sometimes Sabrina would come down with me. Later still, we would bring the children.

(34)

Jenny was born on 16 August 1965 and just before, as couples often seem to do, we moved. We bought 54 Northumberland Place and were in by July. Bought! I was now told something which had been kept from me. Sabrina had a 'small' trust. It seemed large enough to me – £20,000. It was called the 'A Trust'. Jock had given me £2,000 when we married for precisely this purpose and I contributed it to the £12,000 the house cost.

Ben was born eighteen months later, on 22 February 1967. This was by design. We thought they would be closer companions like that and so relieve their parents. I now think it was a mistake. They are very close today, but it took about fourteen years of warfare before they settled. Also, two young children are four or five times more work than one.

Instincts woken early are stronger later on. My sister Rose had made me long for a little child of my own when I was sixteen. I found I was seized by a devouring *appetite* of paternal/maternal love when Jenny, and then Ben, appeared. I thought I knew all about babies. Of course, I didn't; we relied on Spock, the guru then; but I retained a confidence. If I had been less confident Sabrina, who was only twenty-one when Jenny was born, would have had more.

At the same time, there were advantages. I was quite clear we shouldn't have a nanny or *au pair*, which in any case we couldn't possibly afford (the wonderful 'A Trust' apparently didn't stoop to anything as vulgar as *income*). But the pre-awakened appetite meant I enjoyed sharing the labour of babies. We went on a holiday to a farm in the Dordogne, belonging to a Madame Lambotte, when Ben was eighteen months old. We seemed to live virtually with Mme Lambotte's animals. The evolution of nappies at that point had reached Napisan. You still had towelling nappies but you just slapped them roughly clean in water, soaked them for a few hours in Napisan, rinsed them, wrung them out and hung them out to dry. That was all. I remember hanging out the nappies in the sun at Mme Lambotte's feeling overwhelmingly happy and singing a meaningless two-line ditty again and again.

> 'Old mother slipper-slapper slopped out of bed;
> Slip-slop-slipper-slapper slopped out of bed.'

A curious thing happened on the holiday. Ben's gums suddenly became swollen and tender and he began to dribble a great deal. We took him to the doctor in the village who recognised the symptoms immediately. '*Mais oui – bien sûr. C'est les vaches.*' Foot and mouth was endemic in France in 1968 and Ben had caught it. The doctor said it was fairly rare, but he always had a few cases each year. He gave us pills and Ben recovered.

By 1966 I had had a job, or part-time job, for several years, I had published a novel, and I had accumulated a solicitor, a house, a wife, a daughter, I even had an accountant – all the paraphernalia of adulthood which even now can seem unreal to me – but perhaps it was all this that ended my uneasiness about identity. Or perhaps it was the writing of *Chameleon*, which I finished that year. I finished it writing seven or eight hours a day over five days in a monastery near Maidstone. I had started going to write in monasteries before the children were born but they were now sometimes essential.

I had wanted not just to demonstrate the inherent instability and haphazardness of the 'self' in *Chameleon* but also use it as a particularly penetrating way of exploring character – the reader 'becoming' each person in turn. But in the end I funked it, funked 'universal resonance', and just used the device in pursuit of comedy. However, the book was edited by a tall young man called Christopher Sinclair-Stevenson, later to become an extremely successful publisher, coincidentally saving my (financial) life. Partly thanks to him, *Chameleon* did moderately well when Hamish Hamilton brought it out in 1967. The reviews were good. 'Cool' was continuing its way up and I remember Lorna Sage's review contained the phrase, ' . . . told with first-rate verve and impeccable cool'. Another important factor was that, adding to my paraphernalia, I now had an agent, Diana Crawfurd who, as well as being beautiful, had the ability to wring noughts out of publishers as easily and joyfully as I wrung Napisan out of nappies. As well as the paperback, she sold *Chameleon* in America, Italy and Albania.

But the growing gravity of adulthood was accreting matter round me at such a rate I was growing like a planet. I had already attracted a club; I now attracted a car, and a weekend cottage.

(35)

Richard King had finally, as he always said, become rich. He had a friend, Colin Forsyth, whose father had died and left him a few thousand pounds. Forsyth had been to Australia to see if he could invest it profitably. He had found a company called Hampton Gold Mining which had the mineral rights to thousands of acres of flyblown empty desert. Although the company valued the acres at a farthing each, Forsyth felt that in an expanse as large as Wales there

must be *something* worth mining. He therefore bought as many shares
as he could. Returning to England, he and Richard decided to set up
an Australian Unit Trust, including in it the mineral rights to those
thousands of acres. Shortly afterwards, nickel was found in their
desert.

The Australian nickel boom of the 1960s is now legendary.
Richard rang me up one day and said I should buy shares in Western
Mining, one of the companies involved. A week later he rang again
to see if I had done so. I said I hadn't. I was too frightened. Richard
said, 'Buy. If you lose anything, I'll pay you back.' I overdrew and
bought £100 worth of Western Mining shares.

There followed some weeks of frenzied financial greed and
excitement which I experienced only once again, eight years later
sitting at the back of an auction room at Sotheby's. Each day my
shares were more and more valuable. They doubled, then trebled,
then quadrupled, then quintupled in value. Finally, when they were
worth £2,000, I could stand it no more. I sold £1,500 worth, paid
off the overdraft, some debts and bought our first car – a second-
hand convertible Singer Gazelle. Not long afterwards, the nickel
bubble burst and the shares collapsed. I still have the remnants of
that extraordinary supernova and they bring me in £8 a year.
Richard, of course, had got out long before.

The cottage was another act of generosity on the part of one of my
rich friends. Brought up in the country, I found I couldn't stand
London unless I got out at least one weekend in two. Hartington
Road and Snape were now quite often not possible (Eddie rapidly
became irritated by children). But Jennifer Ross, the wife of Alan
Ross, had a house near Hassocks in Sussex. We had got on well ever
since, then Jennifer Fry and aged twenty, she had been taken to see
me in Milner Street by her lover at the time, Eliza's half-brother,
Mark Culme-Seymour, a friend of my father's. Jennifer was a beauty,
with huge eyes in her sweet round face, and a light rippling laugh.
She gazed at me asleep in my little bed and then, pointing at me, said
to Mark, 'I want one of *those*, Mark.'

She now said to Sabrina and me, why didn't we borrow the
cottage in the garden at Hassocks? The cottage had two little bedrooms, a bathroom, a sitting room and a kitchen. It was immaculate

(everything about Jennifer was immaculate). Outside, there was a heated swimming pool in the large, immaculate garden, with immaculate trees and immaculate lawns, and on autumn evenings wisps of steam would drift off the chlorinated waters and vanish through the clipped box and yew hedges. We borrowed the cottage most weekends (for nothing) for ten years.

My club wasn't free – but owing to the kindness of someone not at all rich, there were months at a time when it felt like it.

(36)

Olwen Vaughan's French Club was at 4 St James's Place in the compact eighteenth-century house where George Sand and Chopin had once briefly lived. There was a basement room, seldom used, next to the kitchen, a bar on the ground floor with a few battered armchairs, and the dining room on the first floor. On the right as you came in, with three bay windows to the floor and the original walnut panelling, there was an elegant room with ten or so chintz-covered tables which could hold when full, which it often was, about thirty people. To the left, there was a small area with glasses and bottles, then an alcove pantry and a lift in which food came rumbling up from below. Olwen lived in the small flat at the top. This once charming building now houses Morant Wright Management Ltd.

Olwen had been an early cinéaste, involved with the documentary film-makers of the 1930s and the Film Society, precursor of the British Film Institute, and figures from the past sometimes tottered into the club. I once saw Basil Wright having lunch. She'd started the club itself during the war for the Free French, and de Gaulle and his minions used to eat there.

On the whole, the food was good. The menu was unvarying and it is engraved on my stomach. First, a choice of potted shrimps, *oeuf dur mayonnaise* (with an anchovy laid across it), soup of some sort, pâté, tomato salad; second – a mess of chicken with ratatouille, *saucisse de Toulouse* with mashed potato, *quiche Lorraine*, *cervelle au beurre noir*, *boeuf bourguignon*, ham and salad and sometimes *boudin*. (I remember my first meal there. I ordered *boudin* and Barry, the gentle part-time waiter, whispered in my ear, 'I should tell you – *boudin* can be *shattering.*' I ordered *saucisse de Toulouse* instead.) Lastly – *crème au chocolat*, caramel, stewed or plain fruit, various cheeses. From time to time Olwen would go to Paris and then there would be a very good cheese and *escargots*. The coffee was good and the carafe wine, in brown snail-like pottery, was OK, at least the red was. Once, pouring it out, a thick raft of mould flowed into my glass, though such things were rare. There were better wines in bottles which I couldn't often afford. But the prices were reasonable and the subscription two pounds a year.

I loved the French Club. I started going in the late '50s for lunch, two or three times a week, and invariably ate there for dinner when we went out, and continued doing this till Olwen dropped dead on Spetsai Airport (she loved Greece) and the club closed a little later in 1972. After a while, Olwen let me run up bills and sometimes I didn't pay for several months, or paid in instalments. It is the only club I've ever had and the only place of that sort I've felt at ease in and been welcomed. Anne, the pretty, lively young woman who ran it under Olwen, would give me Olwen's table just opposite the door if I'd forgotten to book. Once the children were born, Sabrina and I ate there alone or with Julian or Tristram and Virginia Powell or anyone; Olwen let us use her flat and we'd carry up Jenny and Ben, and they would sink almost out of sight into the great powdery bosom of her soft frowsty double bed.

The clientele was too wide to generalise, but a few politicians ate there, thinking no one knew about it. I remember just after Peter Shore joined Wilson's government he had lunch there with Marcia Williams (later Lady Falkender). I was alone at the next table and, though the dining room was full, they spoke in low, conspiratorial tones. Suddenly I heard her say, 'Another person you must look out for, who'll stab you in the back if they get half a chance, is . . . ' I shoved my napkin to the floor and leant almost horizontal in my effort to hear but the name and sex of this evil figure were lost.

Olwen let me use the downstairs room for my fortieth birthday. I was with Anna then, and Julian, Richard and Vivian King, Nic and his wife Caroline and my sister Rose came. I remember I was suddenly overwhelmed by despair and age. I was forty and had achieved nothing, nothing. I was a failure. I was forty. Soon I'd be fifty. I sobbed uncontrollably. The only person who could, finally, comfort me was Rose.

I was allowed to go on eating and drinking, alone or with friends, as long as I liked. I could help myself to more wine, provided I made a note of it. Sometimes, going out at twelve or later, Olwen would be slumped asleep at her table opposite the door. If she wanted to go to bed before we left, she'd give me the key and tell me to lock up and push the key through the letterbox. Once, I'm ashamed to say, I abused this kindness. One night Tim Behrens and I had been drinking and talking until nearly three. I was rather drunk and as we went out noticed rows of wine glasses set out for a do the next day. Perhaps Lady Falkender and Peter Shore were celebrating some coup. On an impulse, I peed into as many glasses as I could. No one said anything afterwards, perhaps because the carafe white was, in fact, rather nasty.

(37)

By 1966 it was clear my grandmother, now aged eighty-seven, couldn't manage alone any longer, not even with Eddie – who in any case, since he came to stay only when he was broke, was not there often enough. Her cancer operation and radiation had weakened her, strong as she was, and it seems a peculiarity of our family that at about eighty-six the marbles start to roll. Heywood sold his bookshop and he and Anne came to live at Snape.

Granny's short-term memory had now become highly erratic, though this had, she explained, one unexpected advantage. She had always reread books she liked. She must, for instance, have read Darwin's account of his voyage in the *Beagle* at least ten times. But now she found she needed only one book. This was a light comedy called *The Nutmeg Tree*. 'By the time I reach the end I've forgotten the whole thing so I start again at the beginning.'

There was another symptom, no doubt very common. Like Hal in *2001: A Space Odyssey*, her memory cells seemed to die deeper and deeper until only the very earliest were still active. All the old stories – 'At your *age* and your *weight* Dorothy . . . ', 'The Strong Man of Tilwilly' – vanished, to be replaced by much earlier ones I'd never heard before. I remember her crying, aged three, because she was locked in a first-floor lavatory, I suppose at Kelburn, and the gardener putting a ladder up and climbing in through the window to rescue her. 'It was a big bumble bee that frightened me and made me cry.'

But she could sometimes be jolted out of even the more disturbing aspects of this decline. Eddie, the least patient of us despite his efforts, was to take her into Saxmundham to see the optician at twelve o'clock. My grandmother at once became agitated. '*When* are we going, Eddie?' she asked three minutes later. 'Twelve o'clock, Ma,' said Eddie, deep in his crossword. Three minutes later, she asked again. 'Twelve o'clock, Ma.' Three minutes later . . . three minutes later . . . three minutes later . . . When she'd asked twenty-three times (Eddie was counting) he put down his paper and said, 'Twelve o'clock – AND SHUT THE FUCK UP.' My grandmother stared at him in astonishment, then picked up the poker and said, loudly, 'Shut the fuck up yourself,' and threw the poker into the fireplace.

She grew steadily weaker. Eventually, Anne moved her down into the dining room because she couldn't manage the stairs, even helped. After her eighty-ninth birthday in March, she could no longer get out of bed. Yet the momentum of past strength carried her on. The doctor came every other day: it could be two months, it could be two weeks, it could be tomorrow. Finally, when I rang up as usual, Anne said she was unconscious and they were taking it in turns to sit with her, while a nurse, paid for by BUPA, was now sleeping in her room.

It was the following morning that there occurred the extraordinary moment in my grandmother's dying which, describing it later, made Anne shiver with fear again. The nurse had come out to get Anne for her turn to sit. When Anne came in her mother, who hadn't moved for a week, who was clearly long past movement or anything else, was sitting upright on the edge of the bed, with her feet on the floor, looking out of the window. As Anne watched, she raised both arms and cried out strongly – 'My life! My life! My life!' She died that evening.

The funeral was oddly jolly, as funerals often are. There were few people, nearly all friends having already died. Bob, like my mother believing over-attachment to the mother produced homosexuals, said he had been very worried before about the effect on his psychological stability but was pleasantly surprised. He felt fine. I remember, as we tramped behind the coffin up through the garden at Glemham to the plot of ground where she was to be buried beside her husband Gathorne, Bob stepping to one side, vaguely behind a small bush, and peeing. I too felt much less than I'd imagined, indeed almost nothing. I supposed that really the grandmother I'd known and loved had died three years before.

A few weeks after she died, Anne gave me back two presents I'd given her when I was fourteen – the horse I'd modelled in clay and the fish I'd carved in alabaster when I first went to Bryanston. It was as though I'd only lent them to her.

Then early that autumn, I imagine about six months later, Sabrina and I went to stay with Nic and Caroline in a mill house belonging to Caroline's brother Paul in La Monstierre in France. One afternoon, I went for a walk alone in the forest nearby. Suddenly, I found that tears were streaming down my cheeks. I looked around and saw that I was walking through thick pine trees. I had returned once more to the wood at Snape which my grandmother had planted and where she and I had worked together so often and for so long.

PART FOUR

Bob's Your Uncle – If You're Lucky

(1)

I'm sure Bob was saddened by his mother dying, but I doubt if he cried – though he cried easily. A sensitive, gentle man, he was tougher than he looked, both mentally and physically.

The last could be a drawback when staying with him, which I did about twice a year. It was all right when Kyrle Leng was still alive. Taciturn, still good-looking in a craggy way, often irritated by Bob, Kyrle was ingenious, practical, effective – the water was always hot, meals prompt, the glass-sided beehive, which stood buzzing beside the bath, firmly sealed. From this, and from his other hives, Kyrle made mead. They had lived together since Bob had left Oxford and when Kyrle suddenly died in his mid-forties of a brain haemorrhage, it was an appalling blow.

Bob recovered eventually but the Mill House, in Stanford Dingley about twenty miles from Reading, gradually became less and less comfortable. Unfortunately, Bob was impervious to discomfort. In its beautiful setting beside the Pang, the big house was damp and chilly, but he was very proud that he was somehow able to subdue but just keep alive the old coke boiler so that the heavy cast-iron radiators gave off almost no heat at all. He washed his towels only every three or four months and a growing, sodden heap composted in the corner of a bathroom increasingly populated by bees. He developed other shortcuts and savings; for instance, the dishes were always licked after meals by the big, friendly, smelly dogs. Perfectly hygienic, no doubt, since they were afterwards washed up in the sink – but you always felt that, rather unsteady after the pub, Bob probably missed some.

The pub was invariable. Bob loved pubs. We'd go, often with his Italian friend, almost son, Carmine, the same age as me, very occasionally with Carmine's wife Shirley, either to the Bull or the Boot, depending on current feuds. They were crowded and noisy but Bob, in a way Eddie wouldn't have dreamt of doing, wasn't capable of doing, had made genuine friends in the village. His rapid, staccato upper-class voice and rather odd appearance – he dressed like a spiv in the 1940s, his crinkly hair oiled flat, and used a pervasive musky scent which augmented his other smells of snuff and Imperial Leather soap – had long been totally accepted. Easily a match for them in repartee, he was teased, admired, consulted, deferred to. We'd arrive at six or seven and, pints of beer and pints of pee later, stagger back, deafened, choking from cigarette smoke, when the Bull or Boot closed. Bob was a good if slapdash cook, mostly Italian, and he'd slap up some pasta, the dogs would lick the plates and he and I would go and talk beside the log fire smouldering in the drawing room, drinking cheap red wine or else Strega, a very strong Italian liqueur which he made from a kit in a way I've never seen since.

Talk I say – in fact, on my side mostly listen. Bob could be an exhausting reminder that to forget and omit are as important as to remember and include, in conversation as in art; but none the less with his talk began the pleasures of staying with him that offset the occasional pain. He was extraordinarily well-read and fascinating about books (both my bugger uncles were far cleverer, far more knowledgeable and much more cultivated than I was or am). He knew a great deal about painting, music, churches, architecture, botany, Italy . . . The garden, about which he wrote some of his best books, wound beside the little, trout-filled river (Kyrle had caught them, Bob wrote poems about them). Not only the garden, but the countryside around was beautiful. I particularly loved the Blue Pool about a mile from the village in whose perfectly clear and considerable depths you could see where a spring stirred and gently moved the clean white sand at the bottom as it endlessly bubbled up and the water seemed to be creating itself.

The house, apart from about 8,000 books, some very valuable from his days at Elkin Matthews, and dozens of odd or beautiful objects, was full of paintings, prints, drawings, etchings etc., skilfully bought on his small private income – water colours by John Piper, drawings by Stanley and Gilbert Spencer (all these artists friends of his), small engravings by Dürer and van Leiden, a lot of Samuel Palmers, a Gainsborough, a Cotman, a lot of Churchyards – a nineteenth-century Suffolk painter he collected – and many more.

In fact, Bob had a strong feeling for art and an intuitive eye. Jules, a Cockney friend he'd made when he'd worked as a labourer for nine months in London at the end of the war, had a junk shop in Reading – old toilets and cookers, fireguards, broken lawnmowers, paperbacks, anything he could pick up. One day Bob saw a strip of rolled-up canvas, an old painting. He unrolled it. 'How much do you want for this, Jules?' 'Five bob, Mr Bob.' Bob looked at the painting. 'I think it's worth more than that, Jules.' 'All right – ten bob to you Mr Bob.' 'Jules,' said Bob, forcibly restraining himself, 'it could be worth a lot more. Think about it. I'll be back tomorrow.' He was there the moment the shop opened. 'Have you sold it?' 'Sold what, Mr Bob?' 'That painting I saw yesterday.' 'It's where you left it.' Once again, Bob unrolled the canvas. Once more he insisted Jules ask more. Finally, he said, 'Look Jules, I'll give you five pounds for it.' 'All right, Mr Bob.' Two days later Bob was on his way to Bernard Berenson, a great friend of his, the painting concealed in his suitcase. Berenson agreed with Bob that it was a Watteau. It was later added, as 'Head of Mezzetin', to what became known as the 'Gathorne-Hardy Collection'. But Bob, on Berenson's advice, immediately insured it for £3,000 without, as far as I know, a twinge about Jules.

He once took me to see the Gathorne-Hardy Collection. It had been accumulated by a famous Victorian art collector called John Malcolm. The paintings he bought are now in the National Collection but, at the time he was collecting, drawings by painters were apparently not much valued; also, to get something he really wanted Malcolm often had to buy whole bundles of drawings he wasn't interested in. During the 1860s he gave a lot of those to his son-in-law, Alfred Gathorne-Hardy, and they were eventually left to his son, Geoffrey Gathorne-Hardy, Bob's uncle, whose house was not far from Stanford Dingley. When I saw them, it was clear, first that they were now extremely valuable, and second, from what Bob said, that they would soon come to him. My Great Uncle Geoffrey was then in his nineties.*

We had to step over a large pool deposited by Geoffrey's Alsatian bitch just inside the door of the unlocked, leaking, billiard room where the 'Collection' was kept. The 120 or so drawings, mostly framed now, some tiny but some quite large, were hung, piled or leant against the walls – one Da Vinci, three Michelangelos, Lippi, Rubens, three Rembrandts, one Holbein, three (or was it four?) Mantegnas, Bruegel . . . I followed Bob round as he lectured me. 'But Bob, what will you do when they're yours?' 'I'll try and add to them. Eventually, they'll all go to the Ashmolean – I couldn't possibly break the Collection up or sell it of course.' Of course, but I remember a moment of disappointment.

Bob's life had been transformed when he had met Logan Pearsall Smith in 1928. Bob was twenty-six and working with Eddie in Elkin Matthews; Logan was sixty-two – an extremely wealthy expatriate American writer, a mini-Henry James on the literary and social scene then. He thought Bob had talent and, in return for one or two days' help with his own books, gave him the equivalent of £12,000 a year in order to write. With his own small private income and Kyrle's very considerable one, Bob now had no need to work; he wrote five novels, a good deal of poetry, a travel book about Amalfi and five books about flowers and gardening. He was, he finally realised, not a novelist nor, really, a poet; his flower books were excellent and three of them were illustrated by John Nash – but Bob's best book was the one stung from him by Logan himself.

The roots of this were money, madness and wounded feelings. Logan had not only promised to give Bob his income for life, but also kept trying to press on him substantial sums to make this certain. Bob always refused. Unfortunately, Logan suffered from

---

* He was a modest, quiet, unassuming and extraordinary man. A war hero – Military Cross and Croix de Guerre – he lost a foot in the First World War. He was one of the founders of the Royal Institute of International Affairs, and wrote a definitive history of the subject. He was a poet and a lover of Norway, wrote an account of the Norse discoveries of America and translated Ibsen when he was eighty-seven. He died aged ninety-four.

manic-depressive cycles which, after a short but violent episode of madness on a trip they made to Iceland in 1938, eventually became so extreme that at the end of his life in 1946 he should probably have been certified. He cut Bob's allowance by two-thirds and then turned furiously against him, ranting and raving and accusing him of stealing, lying and injuring him in innumerable petty ways. Finally, just before he died, he stopped the allowance and cut Bob out of his will altogether. The book which resulted – *Recollections of Logan Pearsall Smith* – described in detail their eighteen-year friendship and its terrible destruction.

In some ways, it is a curious book. The *Trivias*, Pearsall Smith's main works which both he and Bob felt certain would survive, are collections of aphorisms and epigrams which they both polished and rewrote and repolished until they were as sharp and as brilliant and as sterile as diamonds. The books have long gone out of fashion. Bob's over-valuation of Logan now seems exaggerated. His account of their life working, travelling and corresponding is often hilarious, since Logan, when manic, was indeed hilarious. But it is the retelling of the madness and of the insults and calumnies which grips; and under this one can detect the sad, outraged, querulous, self-justifying figure of little Bob, the third son aged seven, once again being bullied and teased unfairly by his elder brothers.

The one element I am uncertain about is the one about which Bob would have been most certain – the way it is written. Bob wrote beautifully, but to me sometimes too beautifully. There can be something mannered in the mandarin elegance of his prose, in the mellifluous Scott Moncrieffian skill with which it flows, which I may be uneasy about because I have often been tempted by it myself. This, too, is out of fashion. Bob never had to write for money. He always had an income from the same money my father had put himself through medical school with and with which he had bought the London practice. Kyrle supported Bob after Logan and when Kyrle died Kyrle's money supported him. At the end of *Recollections* he says he now felt 'free' to write for money (he was perfectly free to do so before) but he had been so long under Logan's influence, who strongly disapproved of anything so vulgar, that he couldn't. I think it might have been good for him and for his books if he had had to.

By 1969, I had been working as a part-time copywriter for about eleven years and in offices for twelve. I *longed* to escape and do precisely that – live by writing books. I now began a novel which I was sure would set me free and incidentally destroy the entire office system in which I was trapped. The first, in a roundabout way, it eventually succeeded in doing – though it took another five years.

(2)

Although none of my books has been financially hugely successful, I always begin each new one confident it will be a best-seller. This is how I keep anxiety at bay. It was quite clear, therefore, how *The Office* would rescue me from its subject. But, as I said, it had a second, more ambitious aim. I still thought it extraordinary that no one but me seemed to find the office intolerable – as an institution, as a way of working, as a way of life. It was, in its way, as iniquitous as slavery in the eighteenth century or the factory in the nineteenth century. Or rather, if people had felt this before, were feeling it now, why had no one written about it in those terms? Of course, it had been used as locale or background in thousands of films and books – but never, *as itself*, been the focus, the villain.

I wrote the book as a film script. This allowed me to write a prose almost without adjectives, metaphors or similes, something which, after all the massive doses of Proust/Scott Moncrieff and Nabokov, I felt it needed. I wrote nearly all of it with great rapidity. Ritson from Weidenfeld (not George – I'd used him in *Chameleon*), Shelly, Bea Dugdale whose Hot Plates Had Satisfied Her Needs, Leonard Blunden . . . I found I was bursting with characters, condensed and distilled over twelve years. I finished the dialogue film/novel part of *The Office* in two months, an office *Under Milk Wood* in an expanding, contracting, surreally ramifying prison. But the first twenty pages, a prose introduction, partly autobiographical, partly descriptive, partly analytical, I found almost impossible. In the end (I wrote it last) it took me a further four months.

This was made harder because I realised Sabrina was gradually discovering she wanted to leave me.

(3)

The most agonising aspect about separating from Sabrina – among a number of painful things – was leaving my children. No matter how difficult things had been I had always decided we must stay together because, quite apart from loving them, I was determined I would never do to them what had been done to me – having my father suddenly taken from me.

It now seemed to me that his abrupt departure, which I couldn't even remember, had set the pattern for the three most significant events of my whole life – a pattern of separation and loss: boarding school with that moment in Anne's kitchen where I knew I would never be so unhappy again, Eliza, and now Sabrina and Jenny and Ben. Each one reinforced the others. I couldn't help boarding school, but I had chosen Eliza and Sabrina – or allowed myself to be chosen.

During the months which followed, I decided that these choices may have been, subconsciously, deliberate and for a particular reason. I had needed to leave as I had been left. That is, I had needed to repeat that first experience and the analogy I picked on was shell-shock. One explanation of shell-shock is that the mind has received a terrifying blow *unexpectedly* – it hasn't a moment, not an instant, to brace itself. As a result the blow goes far deeper and does far more damage. The endlessly repeated nightmares of shell-shocked soldiers in the First World War, for instance, again and again reliving the explosions or scenes that had horrified them, were attempts at healing – gradually the mind, by re-creating the moment itself, was eventually able to create a moment of bracing itself. At last, as it were retrospectively braced and defended, the explosion or whatever it was, could be withstood or repulsed.

It also occurred to me that perhaps this was behind Pirandello's *Six Characters in Search of an Author* – and why the play had, in a minor way, haunted me and for so long. One of the events in the play, and one fraught with consequences, took place long before when the father picked up his stepdaughter, whom he had not seen for twenty years and did not recognise, and tried to seduce her. Neither she (nor her mother) can forget or escape from this fateful and, at the time the play was written, truly terrible moment. Instead of avoiding it, they actively seek out a director and group of actors in order to play the whole thing over again. In the end they, and the three other characters, have to re-enact it themselves. But what is noticeable in the play is the *eagerness* with which they seek to do something they all vehemently protest was so frightful, which they long to escape and which they so hate being trapped by.

The play, that is, at this level, is about how terrible events in our lives have to be played, lived, again and again in order to be resolved, just as shell-shocked soldiers dream and redream the nightmare things which damaged them.

However, my own immediate way of coping with the pain of having my children taken from me, and of protecting them from the consequences which I now felt had destructively affected my life, was more mundane. I behaved as if nothing had happened. I left the house, but I insisted, much to Sabrina's exasperation, on bathing them, reading to them and putting them to bed, for a year. Exasperating Sabrina, but being allowed by her – just as she let me have them at weekends (usually in Jennifer's cottage or at Hartington Road) and during the holidays as often and for as long as I liked.

(4)

Richard King had recently rented a large terrace house in Lansdowne Road, Notting Hill Gate. He kindly said I could borrow it while I looked for somewhere to live until he needed it. He didn't, in fact, need it at all and I lived there, in great comfort, free, for eighteen months.

I remember two, out of perhaps four encounters at the beginning of this period, after which they ended. One was with Raffaela, who Tim introduced me to. Although now married to an Italian journalist working in London, she was still continuing her affair with the film director, Luigi. Tim was amazed. It had been going on for nine years. This was not just unprecedented, everyone in Italy who knew Luigi said it was impossible. Yet it was happening – in fact it continued until Luigi's death thirty years later. Raffaela had one of the most beautiful faces I've ever seen. The only face which approached hers, and indeed the one she most resembled, was that of the pagan spirit of sexual love and laughter, decked in wild flowers, which is the central figure in Botticelli's 'Primavera', the painting which had once made me cry. Raffaela and I got on well and I slept with her two or three times. The first time, as we lay back in each other's arms in the darkness in the huge bed at Lansdowne Road, I was fascinated to find rising round us the fragrant, hay-like, animal smell of hot young horse which I remembered from riding at White House Farm and at Wuppertal. The explanation of her and Luigi was perfectly simple, if unusual.

The second incident was a curious one between me and my sister Rose which, though brief, had profound consequences for us both.

One of the difficulties in my relationship with Rose was that psychologically I still felt, and acted, as if I was her father. Naturally, at twenty-two, she sometimes resented this – yet at crucial moments neither of us could help ourselves taking on our roles. She was an extremely dutiful daughter to my parents, and at an important crisis I had helped her break free from them but, thereby, confirming my position as *able* to give permission in this way. A sibling relationship of this sort could have continued all our lives and we'd no doubt have both been perfectly happy with it – until something happened that transformed our pattern.

It was after an evening wedding party in the Garrison Club at Hyde Park Corner. The tables had been made to look like enormous scarlet drums and there was a great deal of champagne. I remember, in a dark corner of the club, sprawling across one of the scarlet drums and for half an hour passionately kissing the bride who had been momentarily carried away by the orgiastic fertility rites lurking beneath all weddings. I had always loved Rose, but when we left at two in the morning I realised, after finding myself kissing her passionately too, that I also desired her – and that she desired me. We went back to Lansdowne Road, kissed, hesitated, undressed and got into bed. Years later, when I told Ambrose, he said without much interest (he often, irritatingly, showed far less interest than I considered the fascination of what I was telling him deserved) – 'Yes, you faced the taboo head-on.' We did, and the taboo won – just. But it brought about a complete revolution between me and Rose. We were equals. She became my closest friend, and has remained so ever since.

(5)

I finished *The Office* and Jamie Hamilton said it would destroy my reputation and his if he published it. Diana tried Robin Denniston at Hodder and Stoughton and he accepted it. Tiny advance.

It didn't come out till the end of 1970, but I was already writing novels for children. I eventually wrote three about a little girl called Jane, which began as stories I told Rose as a little girl. Jane was an amalgam of her, my daughter Jenny and James Bond.* However, I was increasingly struck by how suitable Cyril Connolly might be in this respect. I still used to take the children to Jennifer Ross's cottage and, because she was a great friend of Cyril's, I had news of him from time to time. I used to meet her wandering in her beautiful garden. 'I've just had Cyril on the phone,' she would say, in her voice which was both drifting and precise and often humorous. 'How is he?' '*Not* too good. Deirdre's walked out again. He rang up to ask how to make tea. I asked him what he'd done and he said (and she gave her silvery rippling laugh and imitated Cyril's clipped, flat, irritable tones): "I put some tea leaves in a saucepan and boiled them for twenty minutes and it tastes *disgusting*." ' He also had trouble boiling eggs, apparently.

I, too, was having trouble cooking. I was desperate Jenny and Ben should enjoy my food and at first took enormous trouble with complicated dishes, mostly from Elizabeth David. The children hated them. After a while, I realised that all that was required were sausages, fish fingers, Ambrosia creamed rice and cereals, and mealtimes calmed down. But before this, my defence had been: 'You think I can't cook. You should see Jennifer's friend Cyril – he can't even cook *eggs*!' Thereafter, if I was unable to see them for two or three weeks, I would send them adventure stories about 'Cyril – The Man Who Couldn't Cook Anything Not Even Eggs'. Cyril Bonhamy was

---

* Years later I sat next to Princess Diana's sister. At my name she cried out, 'Not *the* Jonathan Gathorne-Hardy who wrote the books about Jane?' This almost never happens to me. I said, 'Yes.' It seems she and her sister had been brought up on the Jane books.

hopeless at everything except writing books, at which he was very good. He had a series of bizarre adventures with various villains – bank robbers, Arab kidnappers, terrorists – where he always came out on top by luck and bad temper. Each adventure ended with Cyril getting a huge cash reward.

Finally, *The Office* was about to be published. Robin Denniston gave me lunch. I was mistakenly under the impression he had eight children and, casting about for something to talk about related to this state, I said it had always struck me as wrong the way biographers and historians wrote about the influence of parents in the childhoods of our great men and women of the last 150 years. They should really write about the influence of their *nannies* – the parents played little part till the children were much older. Robin, with the gifted publisher's quantum leap, said, 'But it wasn't just the great. We *all* had nannies. You should write a much wider book.' So it was set up. Robin offered £1,500; Diana drove him up to £3,000. My hourly rate at OBM was now £4 an hour and they agreed I could work one day a week.

I remember going into the London Library the first day I began my research and looking up 'Nanny' – nothing; 'Nurse' – nothing, and how my heart sank. But at least I had become one of the most highly paid copywriters in the history of advertising. Sometimes I would come in and find I had only one five-word headline to write – being paid, therefore, at a rate of, today, £280 a word. Sometimes I had nothing to do but correct a proof. The invention needed to fill in my invoice, on which I had to detail what I'd done, became a considerable strain and I still sometimes dream about it. (Fay Weldon, having manoeuvred herself into the same position, also found it difficult, though in a slightly different way. Eventually, OBM found she said she was working thirty-six hours a day and sacked her.)

One thing cheered me in my anxiety about the apparent total lack of anything on nurses and nannies and that was Cyril Connolly, hearing about my subject, promising he would review the book in *The Sunday Times*.

The release from advertising came just in time for a second reason. A month before it took place, I met Anna.

(6)

'As for Albertine, I no longer had any doubt, I was sure that it might well not have been her that I loved, that it might have been someone else. It would have been enough that Mlle de Stermarie, on the evening I was due to dine with her at the island in the Bois, had not cancelled the arrangement. There was still time then, and it would have been upon Mlle de Stermarie that I would have directed that activity of the imagination which makes us extract from a woman so special a notion of individuality that she appears to us unique in herself and predestined and necessary to us.'

Marcel Proust, *Remembrance of Time Past*

Why do we fall in love when we do? Ambrose's view was not unlike Proust's. He said he'd noticed that his patients fell in love only when they'd reached a certain *love-readiness*, a state, often unconscious, of wanting to be in love. He had a patient, a man, who'd fallen in love with a shadow.

It was July and Sabrina, who wanted to go on holiday and who by then knew me very well, chose Anna, a friend of hers from Spain, to help me with Jenny and Ben for two weeks. Perhaps Sabrina felt guilty – except people rarely feel guilt about leaving their partners, though they may pretend to. But I think the real reason was that she thought she could get me off her back if I was distracted by someone else.

Anna was twenty-seven, small, perfectly shaped but not the exaggerated dumb-bell of her sister Josie. Once again my mother surfaced in her full lips, her high cheekbones, her sense of humour – and in her drinking. She smelt deliciously of scent and cigarettes. When she was fifteen she had run off to Gretna Green with Fernando, a Spanish taxi driver, and had lived for twelve years, poor, very lonely and increasingly unhappy, in the slums of Malaga. She had taken their five-year-old son Pablo and run away about a month before coming to help me in Northumberland Place.

For two weeks we lived a fantasy family life. Pablo, the same age as Ben, was lively and friendly. Anna had an extraordinary power to soothe. Fifteen months later, on one of my many visits to her in

Spain, I woke, as I thought very late, with a hangover. I was in a frenzy about getting on with the nanny book. 'It's all right, it's all right,' said Anna in her soft, husky voice. 'It's only nine o'clock.' And so it was. I got up, had breakfast, did three hours' work. It wasn't until I went out into the town that I found she had changed all the clocks in the flat, including my wristwatch beside the bed. I was always being cajoled in this way. As was Pablo. I had never known such an easy, confident, secure little boy.

At the end of July, Anna and I decided to go to Tangier for five days. She told me to meet her at Sloane Square tube station, near her mother and father's flat. She turned up carrying a plastic bag.

'Is that your luggage? Did your mother mind?'

'I didn't tell her. I just said I'd be back in ten minutes.'

She didn't even ring her mother, whom I discovered was as easy-going as Anna, when we got to Tangier.

We took a small hot room in a crowded hostel/boarding house in the *kasbah*. Everyone slept and in fact lived on the roof, and I remember two American girls who spent a great deal of time naked, lovingly tending and displaying their large breasts and intimately washing by a tap in the sun and then slapping and massaging palmfuls of dark orange-scented oil all over themselves till their bodies glistened and we could smell them, Anna becoming increasingly irritated, from under our awning fifty feet away.

I had hardly touched marijuana since Ned Buckley had tried, well I suppose succeeded, in seducing me with it at Gerald's house ten years before. It made me feel mad. But I found Moroccan kif was, at first, different. It slowed time almost to a stop, and I remembered my sessions with matron's ether at Port Regis.

One afternoon we took a taxi eight miles along the coast from Tangier. There was no sand, just huge flat rocks rising from the cold blue Atlantic. We lay on top of one and sunbathed, swam and smoked kif. Suddenly, as we lay, I heard an orchestra on the cliffs above us. It was Handel, 'The Messiah'. I lay and listened. How sensible of the Tangier Philharmonic to come and practise out here, away from the traffic, the stink of exhaust, the stink of the tourists gleaming in their orange suntans. I listened entranced, half-aware of Anna diving off the rock. All at once it struck me – wasn't it actually rather odd that the Tangier Philharmonic should choose this distant barren cliff top, in the blazing summer sun, to rehearse? As I thought this, I found the sound receding and growing faint. I concentrated – and it returned. I could make it louder or softer or stop altogether at will. It was a hallucination.

The only time I had heard 'The Messiah' had been when I was fourteen and had sung in it at Bryanston. It seemed that the entire work, every note, every chord, every solo, every chorus had sunk entire and perfect into the cells of my memory and remained there for over twenty-five years. Suddenly, it had sprung out, been played in my head, but projected up on to the cliff for a quarter of an hour and then, as I decided to end it, sunk back, never to reappear. How had this been achieved?

We returned to our rooftop in the city and two days later flew back to London. Soon afterwards, Fernando arrived for a week and, as they had agreed, Anna let him have his son as often as he wanted. On his last afternoon, he'd taken Pablo to a film.

I was working on the nanny book at Lansdowne Road when Anna telephoned me that evening with terrible news. Fernando had not brought Pablo home. He'd flown back to Malaga and taken the little boy with him.

(7)

We now embarked on a struggle to get Pablo back. It took nearly two years and the end of this, for me, ultimately tragic saga was terrifying. Yet at first it seemed so simple. There was no reason why Fernando shouldn't have Pablo with him for a week or two if he wished and he could then return him to England. A telephone call soon disabused us of this. Fernando said Pablo was his son and would live with him and his family. It was Anna who would do any visiting.

I decided we would have to kidnap him back ourselves. Fernando didn't know what I looked like; Pablo, of course, did. We would go out, hire a car, I would hang around his school and their apartment and, at an apposite moment, pick Pablo up, tell him Anna was waiting in the car, we'd drive to the airport – and so home.

But first we made an appointment to discuss the whole thing with a Dr Pascales, a lawyer recommended by the Spanish Embassy. How peaceful lawyers' offices are, how far removed from the sordid, often violent worlds which are their business. Dr Pascales, in his hushed Lincoln's Inn chambers, with long, sensitive, ivory-coloured fingers, delicately flipped through an enormous leather-bound tome of Spanish law, quoting to show how, unfortunately, it was heavily weighted in these cases in favour of the Spanish national. Our only recourse, none the less, *was* the law and he knew an excellent man, Señor Oretaga Casals, in Malaga. It would take time. Patience. One thing we might be tempted to do, said Dr Pascales, and he looked at us severely, which we must on no account attempt, and that was kidnap him ourselves. On *no* account. Once more the ivory fingers flipped and then he slowly read out the penalties: 'For Mr Gathorne-Hardy, a *mandatory* sentence of twelve years and a day. And for you, Señora, a *mandatory* sentence of six years and a day. There is no remission in such sentences, no extenuating circumstances.' And, he reminded us, Spain was still, effectively, a police state.

Enveloped already by the deep chill of prison, standing miserably on the pavement, Anna said I couldn't risk it for her. Jenny and Ben. My book. I would be fifty years and a day old when I was finally released. With huge relief, feeling guilty, I agreed.

Through my OBM friend Joan's unsatisfactory lover on the *Mirror*, Derek, we found a private detective called, nostalgically, Mullins – Jeff Mullins, or 'Big Jeff Mullins' as he liked to be known. Meanwhile, Anna flew to Malaga to start the case. And I now learnt something that shouldn't have surprised me but always did. Once more, there was one of those mysterious trusts which could, if absolutely necessary, produce money. It clearly was absolutely necessary and the trust was to pay out thousands.

I should really have gone to Malaga too, but it was not till much later that Anna began to break down. Also, I was in a panic about nannies. I had books to read and slowly more and more ancient figures came creeping and wobbling like tortoises from the under-growth of nurseries deep in the past and had to be interviewed. One of these was aged 105. Their ancient charges came wobbling out too. To understand what was going on in the nursery I read Freud and a massive textbook on child psychology – *Child Development and*

Personality by Mussen, Conger and Kegan; I also read the studies of child upbringing by John Bowlby and D. W. Winnicott, which were fashionable then. A feature of these books was the importance of the mother (for me, read nanny.) But also how, though *all* the years of childhood are important, the years up to five are particularly so.

Anna returned. The case had begun on two fronts: first for custody, second to get access. Señor Casals apparently seemed competent. 'He has enormous ears,' said Anna. We also engaged Big Jeff Mullins. He was indeed big – bald, with a huge moon face pasty as a puffball, and vast hips and stomach and bottom. He was amiable and totally confident. 'A piece of cake,' he said. 'I've had several cases – a boy of six last year in Portugal. I'll go in, mosey around a bit, see what's up – and do the snatch. Piece of cake.'

He flew out for the first time four days later, with Pablo's photograph, a favourite, battered toy monkey and a map drawn by Anna of the housing estate and the school area in Malaga. He'd ring when he'd done the snatch. Anna, who'd moved into Lansdowne Road, didn't leave it until he rang from Heathrow, empty-handed.

So it was to continue for the next year. There was always something to raise our hopes and therefore, as whatever it was failed, always something to destroy them. The case was postponed for a month but Big Jeff had a new wheeze – he'd plant a lump of hash in Fernando's taxi and get him busted and he'd lose the case. Cost about ten quid. It was vital to keep up morale and we decided dinners in restaurants and drink should count as kidnapping costs. I quoted Winnicott on how Pablo's first five secure years would protect him.

Sometimes we went to Jennifer's cottage with the two children. Once, while we were there, Sabrina suddenly appeared and said could she talk to me alone. We walked up on to the Downs above Hassocks and sat on the cropped grass. She said that although she had asked me to leave, would I now come back to her? She'd been walking behind Ben in Northumberland Place – he was then about five and a half – and he'd looked so exactly like me that she realised she couldn't separate us. But it was too late. I was now in love. I said no. But from then on I felt, I feel today, that any damage done to my children – and damage was done – I was equally responsible for.

We went to Hartington Road once or twice, and Anna introduced me to her great aunt, aged about eighty-five, and here I had a curious adventure into class attitudes circa 1920.

The great aunt lived in a service flat in one of those giant, genteel, apartment blocks off Sloane Avenue. If my father had still been a London doctor she could easily have been his patient. A small armchair in her bedroom needed respringing. I said I'd do it, still confident in the skills developed at Snape with my grandmother. I bought webbing, twine, staples, horsehair, some material to secure the top and hessian for the bottom and we went with hammer and pliers to the great aunt's flat.

The old lady had clearly been running on automatic pilot for years, but she bustled about with gratitude and graciousness. Would I like a glass of sherry? A second glass? After a while, she took me through to her bedroom. But as I laid out the newspaper she had given me, a curious change came over her. Now, like some insect or slug, she began to respond automatically to a quite different set of stimuli. My voice, that I was the friend of her great niece, vanished, to be replaced by hammer and pliers, by lengths of webbing and ball of twine. Looking perplexed at this transformation, she suddenly left to return a moment later with a large bag. 'I expect you'll have to make a lot of dust,' she said. 'Not your fault, of course, but I'd better tidy away some things . . . in case . . . the dust . . . ' Meanwhile, she filled the bag with her silver-backed hand mirror, her silver-backed brushes, various little boxes, her jewellery case, and carried it all out. I eventually finished the chair and returned to the drawing room – returning at the same time from working-class armchair mender who, like all the lower classes, would certainly rob her if he got a chance, to my previous sherry-sipping, posh-voiced position of her great niece's friend.

(8)

Soon after this, Big Jeff flew out again. This was his fifth flight in seven and a half weeks, and it was to be the big one. 'There's been enough pussy-footing. This time I'll just barge in, kick the door down if necessary, grab the boy and get out. Piece of cake.'

It was surprising, therefore, when Derek rang just after Jeff had left and apologised for recommending him. What, hadn't we seen Derek's piece in the *Mirror*? Mullins had been arrested for house-breaking. To our horror, by comparing dates with Derek's notes, we discovered that each time except the first that Mullins had said he was in Malaga he was in fact engaged in burglaries across Kent and Sussex. He eventually got three years.

We engaged Dave Hart, a very different figure. This neurotic, clever, wiry and tough young man rode a deafening super-new Yamaha whose two gross, gleaming exhausts bulged out from between his legs like colossal extra genitals. 'I bet his private life's a mess,' said Anna. But he was honest. He found that Pablo was being moved about from apartment to apartment, and the school had clearly been alerted; also the other taxi drivers seemed to be involved. 'They're a Mafia,' said Anna.

The case was postponed again. In April, Richard at last either decided he needed Lansdowne Road or that he'd never need it. At any rate, I borrowed half a barge which Rose was renting on the river at Chiswick (the other half was lived in by the landlady, a highly neurotic crabbed creature of ninety-two). Then the case was postponed yet again, but there also came the first concession. Fernando, no doubt prompted by his lawyer, said that Anna could speak to Pablo on the telephone once a week. I could hear her below the deck talking and sometimes only whispering to him for half an hour – the soft rise and fall of her Spanish flowing out along the line, cajoling and soothing and sustaining, coiling itself around her little boy, an aria of mother love. Tears were streaming down her cheeks when she came up. 'He said he wanted me, he wanted to see me,' she said. We sat for a long time while the barge rocked. No more could I comfort my mother when my father had gone back to sea. At last she said, 'I can't stand it. I must go out and be near him.' She hadn't seen or spoken to Pablo for nearly nine months.

(9)

Anna took a cheap apartment in Marbella. Later, we rented a small but pretty one-floor home on the edge of Benahavis some miles west of Marbella and up in the hills.

The next stage of our attempt to get Pablo back took place in Spain. As often as I could, I would put my advertising day at the end of one week and the start of the following week, and fly out, laden with nanny notes, my fare paid by the trust, for a week or ten days. Sometimes Anna would fly back to recuperate.

Hart made a number of fruitless sorties, roaring out and arriving exhausted at Benahavis on his gleaming false genitals. But we paid him off in June when everything suddenly changed. We had engaged a new lawyer, a dynamic thirty-year-old from Madrid called Jaime Milà, whose main incentive, I realised, was that he fancied Anna. But he was effective. He at once had the case removed to Madrid, where local patriotism wouldn't operate in Fernando's favour. He also got Anna access, at first one day a month, soon afterwards once a fortnight, and after Christmas it was once a week. He said he would probably need money ('to facilitate things'). It was on his advice we stopped Hart, who was very disappointed, having planned a massive raid with four 'picked colleagues' (other debt collectors, which was how he usually made his money).

Benahavis was still a very small, untouristed *pueblo* in 1971 and 1972. Our little house, an old worker's cottage which we rented for almost nothing from Eliza, who now lived in Spain, looked down on to the village washhouse, a row of joined stone and concrete sinks each with a sloping ribbed side against which the women rubbed their clothes clean in the rush of a diverted tributary of the river in the valley below. I used to sit working on our little terrace under the tangled shade of vine and bougainvillaea as they chattered below me like Spanish sparrows.

As usual, I felt I was playing house with Anna – watering the flowers in their old coffee or Heinz tins, fetching new bombolas of gas for the cooker or hot water, shopping. We thought I should never be there on Pablo's visiting days and I would either go out or remain in London, now living a rather peripatetic life. The old crone had complained we made too much noise on Anna's recuperative visits and had asked us, and most unfairly Rose who only occasionally used it now, to leave. I lived in the spare rooms of friends.

The heat of Spanish summer died slowly away into an autumn that was nearly as hot. The flowers I had bought died in their tins. Winter, and too little rain for Andalusia. At last I finished *Nannies* and gave it to Diana, in whose spare room I was temporarily sleeping. Milà now told Anna that the case was going very well. We would win — but it would take another four months, six or seven if Fernando appealed.

But at the end of February Anna rang me up on the only telephone in Benahavis, the one in the tiny post office on the small, dusty square. She said Pablo seeing her once a week seemed worse for him than never seeing her at all. When it was time for him to go he clung to her desperately, crying and sometimes screaming. On his last two visits he'd shat in his pants. He was cracking up. I tried to explain, from Winnicott, pointlessly, in masculine fashion, that these were essentially good signs. Or, at least, indifference would have been worse. But by now Anna was crying. 'I can't take any more, Jonny. Pablo can't. We can't wait four more months. We can't take it any more.'

With a sudden sharp pain in my stomach, with sinking heart, I realised I should have to try and do it myself. Twelve years and a day. Twelve years and a day.

(10)

We prepared with care. Anna flew back and, pretending I'd lost my passport, I put her and Pablo on my new one. A Cambridge friend who was now a doctor authorised the photographs. We drew £500 from the trust. I booked a car to be picked up at Malaga. I also arranged for us to stay with Gerald. Churriana had become overwhelmed by the airport, smelling of aviation fuel, the nightingales driven away by the monstrous engines of the jets, and he had moved twenty kilometres inland to Alhaurín el Grande, with Lynda, the beautiful young woman who had come to live with him after his wife Gamel died (live with him happily, but to Gerald's great disappointment, absolutely chastely). We thought the quickest and therefore the safest plan was to do what Mullins had called the snatch from there. Benahavis was about two hours from Malaga Airport, while Alhaurín was only three-quarters of an hour, or less. We would drive there as fast as we could, catch the first plane back – and so escape. Flights were not full in March.

The day before we flew out, 31 March, Rose rang me. There was an emergency. My father had been taken to hospital with something or other and had developed violent and so far undiagnosed symptoms. It was thought his life was in danger. This was appalling – tickets, car, Gerald, in fact the climax of twenty months' effort at risk, but I felt I couldn't vanish if my father was actually dying. I could conceivably postpone everything. I asked Rose what the symptoms were. As she told me, it seemed to me she was describing *delirium tremens*. 'Is he drinking?' 'Of course not. He's far too ill.' I decided to risk it.

But once we were with Gerald and Lynda, Gerald extremely stimulated, our plan didn't seem so good. If Fernando suspected anything, Malaga Airport would be the first place he'd go to. Anna thought he wouldn't suspect. At first when she'd had Pablo, he had come too and sat balefully watching a hundred yards from the house. Gradually, he'd stopped doing this. In fact, recently he had sent Pablo with a taxi driver friend on the first and third Sundays of each month (Anna had Pablo on Sundays). 'He's probably having sex with an air hostess,' Anna said. Usually Fernando dropped Pablo off at Benahavis himself, but on these days she'd get a message late on Saturday night to meet Pablo at eight in the morning at the police station near their old apartment and the taxi driver friend would drive her and her son back to Benahavis, and return to pick Pablo up at six in the evening. Anna's day would start at 5.30 for these visits.

If everything was as usual this first Sunday in April, Anna would ask the taxi driver to take them to Gerald's house in Alhaurín. If it was Fernando, she would stay at Benahavis and we would try next week. We would go on trying till we succeeded. In the end it might be necessary to go to Malaga Airport from Benahavis after all. How could Fernando suspect? On the other hand, if he did . . .

We decided to change our plans. We would do the opposite of what would be expected. Excitedly, Gerald produced maps and spread them over the table. We would drive away from the airport north to Ronda, then north again until near Seville, turn north-west and across to the frontier with Portugal halfway up the border, and so on to Lisbon and a flight home. Once across the border we were safe. We would have till six o'clock, when Pablo had to be back with Fernando or his substitute. After that, whoever it was would no doubt contact the police.

But now there came a serious setback. Gerald and Lynda were about to set off on a long-planned trip with their car to Greece and then back via Italy. Gerald had suddenly realised that after we had kidnapped Pablo there would be an enquiry. The substitute taxi driver would refer the police to him. He would deny all knowledge but their departure would be delayed; months, in fact a year's planning would be jeopardised.

We realised we couldn't impose this on them. Gerald was now seventy-eight. Luckily, Lynda suggested we try an American friend of theirs and Anna's called Freddie Wildman. He had rented Buena Vista outside Churriana but was away in his house in the Alpujarra. Buena Vista was empty. Anna rang him and he agreed.

On Saturday afternoon I drove Anna to Benahavis and then returned to Alhaurín. I would go to Buena Vista at eight o'clock. If the usual substitute routine took place, she would come there too; if Fernando turned up – not.

I had terrible diarrhoea when I got back to Gerald's and had to swallow a quarter of a bottle of kaolin and morphine, another of my possibly dying father's favourite nineteenth-century remedies. I drifted into a Mogadon sleep and woke from it far too early with a now familiar refrain as usual running through my head – twelve years and a day, twelve years and a day . . .

(11)

I had to take more kaolin and morphine when I got up. Lynda had prepared a picnic. Gerald, guilty that he was not playing the role he'd promised, hovered awkwardly. He said they'd stand at the bottom of their track and wave us past.

I tried to drive slowly to Churriana, aware of the brilliant sun, aware of the sparkling Spanish spring, aware I couldn't take it in. I arrived too early. Seven forty-five a.m.

I parked the hired car out of sight at the back of the house. Ralph and Frances had taken Buena Vista several times and I knew it quite well. I wandered aimlessly, looking at my watch. At eight o'clock I finished the kaolin and morphine. At eight-fifteen, I went and hid in the small downstairs shower. I tried to read a paperback of Camus's *The Plague* that I'd found on a table. Cicadas already. At eight-thirty-one I imagined the whole thing was off. I felt huge relief.

Three minutes later I heard a car. There was the sound of Spanish voices. The car drove off. I waited; then, with beating heart, walked out to the front.

Anna and Pablo were standing in the drive. Pablo was taller, with tousled black hair. He was sucking from his bottle which Anna kept at Benahavis. I went and picked him up, this little boy who had been the centre of everything we'd done for nearly two years. As I held him tightly, I suddenly found I was choking back tears, swept by a rush of intense, unexpected emotion. I put him down and ran to get the car.

I drove so fast past Gerald and Lynda I didn't see them (but Anna did – she said they waved), wriggled through Alhaurín, all these southern *pueblos* were like mazes, and so out on to the Coin–Ronda road, the map over Anna's knees, the route highlighted, while Pablo, who could speak only Spanish now, chattered questions behind us – 'What's he saying?' 'He asked where we're going, I said to a lovely place to picnic' – until all at once he lay down along the back seat and fell asleep, so that Anna said, 'He knows something's up but doesn't want to be part of it', a sentiment I shared rather strongly just after we'd woven our intricate way through Ronda (two hours' driving feeling like five minutes) and I suddenly saw in my rear-view mirror two distant motorbikes which seemed to be catching us up fast and wished we hadn't had this absurd idea which allowed hours of potential pursuit, though in fact many months later we learnt that the substitute taxi driver had gone at once to Fernando who had raced to Buena Vista and then raced to Malaga Airport and at that very moment when I wished we were there ourselves the airport police were, albeit not very enthusiastically, despite Fernando's furious urgings, checking departures, and then the motorbikes were now definitely and rapidly gaining since they were far faster on these twisting roads, far faster than our dangerous eighty kilometres an hour, or rather not dangerous since I habitually drove too fast, was used to it, good at it, even going 140–180 kph on the straight, when they suddenly roared past at over 160, I guessed, not police or *Guardia* at all but harmless Spanish delinquent youths and I could slow down amazed (it was now coming up to twelve) that Pablo still slept, but we hardly spoke, not to wake him, but because of the fierceness of concentration – 'I think go right here and then on till a bigger road where you go left which should say Seville to the right', which it did, so we were now within the orbit of that great city, still 405 kilometres away but exerting its gravitational pull already, soon after which point, having turned off again on to a little road, now 1.30, a brief pull-in and I peed beside an olive tree, no one anywhere, and *still* Pablo didn't wake, even with the bumps of the pitted road where I slowed for Anna to pass me hot black coffee from Lynda's thermos ('you can keep it'), sips of amphetamine, twelve years and a day, twelve years and a day, another stop, this time for petrol, and *still* Pablo slept, it was more like a coma, but at last, as Anna unwrapped the hard-boiled eggs, rolls, olives, *serano* ham and little cakes, the *aqua mineral sin gas*, at last, then, Pablo woke up and ate too as we sped through dusty flatness, driving, driving, flatness in this country the most mountainous in Europe outside Switzerland, but it was 3.30, then 4.30, then five o'clock, looking at my watch had become compulsive, 5.30, 5.43, brief pee for everyone, and now, suddenly, intense anxiety since at six Fernando could, in fact, legitimately alert the police and all Spanish frontiers and this was the one thing that Spain, inefficient Spain, did very efficiently indeed (Pascales of the ivory fingers – 'It is, I need not remind you, effectively still a police state'), and this realisation, at 6.30, when we had to stop at the border (only the third stop) came very sharply indeed when my illegal passport was taken politely from the rolled-down window of the Seat and vanished into the squat, prison-like blockhouse – and then not returned, and not returned, and when it was returned, at long last, after ten minutes, *two Guardia Civil* accompanied the passport official, but only, thank Christ, to smile and wave us on, and as we did drive on – 'We've done it!' I cried, and Anna had turned to Pablo and told him we were taking him home to England, when a jet roared low above us and Pablo started to kick and scream at the back of the car, and was hauled screaming over the seat on to Anna's knee and would stop only when Anna offered him money: a hundred? No; two hundred? No; 3-4-5-6-700? No no no no no, but, at a thousand, Pablo stopped, still gulping with sobs and brokenly told Anna, holding his 1,000-peseta note, that Fernando had said to him that if ever his mother took him he, Fernando, would get the whole of the Spanish army and the whole of the Spanish air force to chase after him and bring him back and he would beat him and here now was the air force already after him, and it took a second 1,000-peseta note and his bottle to calm him as we drove through the gentle darkness, the terrifying weight of twelve years and a day at last lifting, stopping once more for petrol, the lights of Lisbon not so far away, the river Vejo, traffic, and so, at 10.36, we arrived at the Avenida Palace, which Gerald had said was the most expensive hotel in the city, almost the last expense for the trust, and I stepped lightly from the Seat having driven more or less non-stop for nearly fourteen hours feeling as fresh as a daisy and perfectly able to do the whole drive again. Such is the power of adrenaline.

We had a second bed for Pablo put into our huge bedroom, with its crimson curtains, its ornate mirrors, its chandeliers and tassels every-where. He said he didn't want to eat so Anna tucked him in and we went down to have champagne at the bar, and then, when our omelettes were ready, a second bottle of champagne. Meanwhile, Pablo had begun to smash the mirrors, rip off the tassels, and generally demolish our bedroom upstairs, grim presage of things to come.

(12)

The nanny book – *The Rise and Fall of the British Nanny* – came out soon after Anna and I got back from our kidnapping. It was a moderate success. Although Cyril had said earlier that he would review it he must, as before in our brief dealings, have changed his mind. But the reviews were good and Auden took Cyril's place.

It was serialised in the *Observer* and I appeared on various television and radio chat shows, which had never happened before, and was interviewed by newspapers. I signed books in bookshops and attended literary lunches including one in Birmingham with, I felt rather inappropriately, a predominantly nautical theme. I sat in the middle of a long table with Chay Blyth at one end and Clare Francis at the other, both fresh from fantastic feats of single-handed navigation. One point of the lunches is to sell copies and Blyth and Francis's teetering piles sank with satisfying speed. Hodder and Stoughton had, by mistake, sent fifty copies of *The Office* – a momentary embarrassment rapidly forgotten in the exhilaration of further interviews and lunches. This state of affairs lasted a month. Then the telephone, which had rung continually, went silent. I remember the last call came at four in the morning. It was from Canada wanting an interview there and then. In fact, there was another short, faint burst a few years later when the book inspired a TV series called *Nanny* with Wendy Craig, for which I was in the powerless position of consultant.

The nanny book brought this brief flare of transient fame but no money. Diana, my agent, was on the train to Bath just after the heady period and found herself opposite Frances Partridge and Mary Campbell, whom she recognised but didn't know. Frances said, 'I wonder how much Jonny's made from his book.' Mary said, 'I know *precisely* – £20,000 *so far*.' 'But Diana,' I said aghast, 'didn't you tell them that was rubbish? You know how vital it is to appear poor.' 'I couldn't,' said Diana. 'I was too tired.'

When I say 'no money', I don't mean no money at all; I mean not enough at the time or later, not even nearly enough, to set me free from advertising. It has remained in print in various editions for the last thirty years and during that time has probably made me about £5,000 over the advance. But to remain in print at all has pleased me. So did the use of the book by the Manchester Social Services to teach trainees the mechanisms and importance of early upbringing in a palatable way. But the thing that pleased me most of all was that it came out while my mother was still alive. Another year and it would have been too late.

(13)

Number 18 Hartington Road, in fact sliding slowly downhill, seemed on the surface fairly stable. My father had established a routine. His base was his chair in the sitting room (called the drawing room). Here, I realise now, he showed the same skill at building his world in a tiny space which he'd developed in his cabins during the war, but now the inhabitants, the buildings of his little world, were the *Shorter Oxford Dictionary*, some volumes of the 1910/1926 *Encyclopaedia Britannica*, tobacco, Rizla rolling papers, drink, his huge glass pee jar which held a litre and a half, telescope, the daily papers (they took the *Mirror* and the *Telegraph*), string and jigger for belt work,* current reading. He remained extremely curious and interested almost till he died. During the day he read whatever engaged him at the moment – Churchill on the Second World War, say, or the history of the Far East, whatever he could find out about Shackleton (the encyclopaedias were for this), and he particularly enjoyed his *Hakluyt's Voyages* in eight volumes; at night, before being doused by drink and Nembutal, he'd read Hornblower and John Buchan.

There were occasional visits to the Harrises and regular excursions to Snape and Glemham in his souped-up Robin. Every morning he'd go down to the White Hart for a drink with Bert Allen. Bert now became his closest friend and was given, a considerable honour, a cutting of the vine, which he planted against the outside toilets of his pub. Given its head, never pruned, this triffid-like plant rampaged

---

* My father, incidentally, was not an amateur in this work. Not much remains – some belts and purses, a bell-pull, a tiller from one of HMS *Carinthia*'s lifeboats which he was covering and rescued when they were sunk. Sammy recently took some of this to Des Pawson in Ipswich at the Museum of Knots and Sailor's Ropework, the only museum of its kind in the world. Pawson had many examples of ropework going back many years and said my father's was among the finest he'd seen. What I had taken rather disparagingly to be 'string' was, he said, almost certainly Strutt's Macramé twine, or possibly cobbler's twine, that is, linen thread. The tiller was covered in heavier cotton seine twine – fishing line material. My father's work is now on display there.

about to such an extent that customers eventually had almost to hack their way through to get inside.

Abroad in Aldeburgh, walking slowly, my father would raise his hat to people he recognised – a figure of note, the respected surgeon commander enjoying his well-earned retirement. When this, not fantasy quite, perhaps assumed role is the word, was strong on him he would go to the more genteel East Suffolk for his morning drinks. Anna and I went there with him once. Suddenly in the saloon bar/ lounge my father downed his large whisky at a gulp, banged his stick on the table, and said loudly, 'What you don't understand Jonny – *bang* – is I'd like to – *bang* – fuck – *bang* – your – *bang* – wife – *bang, bang, bang, bang.*' The saloon bar/lounge, already quiet, went deathly silent. I said I did realise that. When we left, once more the respected retired surgeon commander, he doffed his hat with old-world charm left and right.

The endless battles between him and my mother, as she tried to get him to eat, were long, silent and, for her, exhausting. These were not only due to his lack of saliva or because fighting her was the last way he could assert his manhood. I also had a strong feeling that ancient nursery conflicts with his strict nanny had returned as he sat staring obstinately at his glass of Complan, or refused to have a bath or ignored or frustrated my mother's efforts to tidy round his chair.

I had the same feeling as I watched him sucking up to Jock and Eddie and trying to impress them. I would watch Eddie humiliate him, and all this made me ashamed of him – and ashamed that I was ashamed – and angry with them. I think his drinking was partly the result of those younger brother family dynamics, compounded by his brutal prep school, which had damaged his confidence when young – and thereafter.

Drink, now providing him with most of his calories, was more vital than ever. I remember finding him at 9.30 in the morning once (after an apparently sleepless night), in his grey vest and pants, his thinning grey hair on end, filling a tumbler from the barrel of disgusting sherry. Rose used to say whenever she saw a tramp with Special Brew she was reminded of our father.

His drinking no doubt contributed to, and certainly made more turbulent, the collapse of his health. I forget all the diagnoses – one was another abscess on the lung — but every four or five months his temperature would soar and he would be rushed into hospital with something dangerous. These emergencies would always be chaotically accompanied by DTs (my supposition about this while I was kidnapping had been quite right). For a while my father's life would be despaired of. Then he would return to 18 Hartington Road and slowly recover.

These episodes were a strain on everyone; especially, of course, on my mother.

(14)

My mother was proud of the success of *Nannies*, but what pleased her most was that she didn't have to worry about my offending anyone. All my novels made her very anxious — because they contained portraits of real people; sometimes of people actually in Aldeburgh.

Not all my family felt this. Three or four years after the book had come out I met Bernard Fergusson at a party in London. A distinguished establishment figure who had been, among other things, Governor General of New Zealand and who, in a book *Beyond the Chindwin*, had written well about the Chindits and Orde Wingate under whom he'd served. He was a second cousin of my father's. 'Ah yes,' he said, peering at me through his monacle, 'now you are — you're — let me see, Jock's boy.' 'Antony's boy,' I said. We chatted aimlessly for a moment, then Bernard's face suddenly pinkened. 'Wait a minute, wait a minute — didn't you — aren't you the author of that book about nannies?' I said I was. Bernard now turned bright red. 'An absolute outrage,' he said. 'Washing the family's dirty linen in public. Outrageous, monstrous.' Extremely surprised, I asked him what he meant. It turned out to be my great grandmother sitting naked on the knee of her naked, eighteen-year-old cousin. 'But Bernard,' I said, 'that was a hundred years ago.' 'That doesn't make the slightest difference,' said Bernard furiously, and stalked away from me.

Worry over money (despite the substantial sum she still imagined she would leave), anxiety about my father and exasperation with him, exacerbated my mother's psoriasis and blood pressure. And, just as my father had his collapses into hospital, the continuing strain on her manifested itself in periodic and sometimes extraordinary physical symptoms. At one time a series of painful boils appeared in her armpits. Then one week in 1972 her forehead suddenly swelled alarmingly. Rose, who was there, said by several inches, as if her head was about to burst. Later, her chin did the same. Rose was terrified by these events and begged, then shouted at my father to *do* something, but he ignored her and buried his head in his paper, impotent.

The swellings went down. My mother recovered. And during it all, in the mornings, she was as usual – as amusing and as much sought after, with her long telephone conversations and Mrs Gooding coming in with Aldeburgh gossip and, refusing to let my father bomb along as he wanted, out to Snape in the unstable Robin.

My reading had led me largely to accept, like most people I suppose, what can loosely be described as the psychoanalytic view of how we develop and operate. It seemed to me that some if not all of my mother's ills were to an extent psychosomatic, their origin therefore partly in her childhood and later life (it eventually became clear that this was true of her psoriasis). She would listen patiently while I explained this and when I begged her to see someone, a therapist, would agree, Yes, perhaps it would help – and do nothing. One of the Aldeburgh doctors clearly felt the same, and tried himself. But though anything from fifty per cent to eighty per cent of the illnesses GPs deal with are the result of mental distress, they have no training at dealing with it and he achieved nothing.

All the burdens on her were obvious, but I wonder now the extent to which she felt wasted. She never said so. Her class and generation did not expect to be of use, to work or have careers. But certainly my mother *was* wasted. Her extraordinary gift of empathy, for drawing people out, has passed to Rose, who has become a brilliant and successful therapist. I wish something similar could have happened to my mother.

She battled with drink, and at one time Rose and I thought we had found the solution – champagne. The bubbles in champagne, we discovered, meant that my mother couldn't drink as much of it as she could wine. The champagne cure was expensive, but everyone was happier (in fact, as it progressed, we had to buy cheaper but equally bubbly substitutes). Then the distant training of her grandfather and his courtesan wife Go-Go reasserted itself. We began to find empty champagne bottles concealed in the linen basket and realised we'd failed.

Financial anxiety was temporarily allayed when they finally sold the Picasso – for £1,600. Two months later it went for £5,500 at Sotheby's. Nothing else looked like changing. We kept on expecting the main and most obvious of the obvious burdens – my father – to die; but he kept on not dying. I didn't want this, exactly. I loved him. But it would have made a huge difference to my mother. In May 1973, Rose and I decided* we would have to confront them and insist it would be better for both of them if my father lived with the Harrises, that is, Mary. After all, the ancient and most effective cement in their marriage had always been absence.

Shortly after this, on 28 June, and before we had done it, I got a call at OBM from Rose. My mother had been taken into Ipswich Hospital with what Dr Pauley, her GP, thought was a minor intestinal 'blockage' (her perennial trouble). But the surgeon in Ipswich thought it could be cancer and had sent specimens to be tested. I should come at once. Rose was in tears.

(15)

The events that followed were so painful that I was unable to record them in my journal until 28 July, but they took place during the eight days between Sunday, 2 July and Sunday 8 July. I see that I saw her that first Sunday.

'Luckily, I sensed the seriousness of it before they found the cancer,' I wrote. 'I saw her the day before the operation for a colostomy. She was extraordinarily radiant. A curious quick, sweet smile, very open; she was so loving I felt I was going straight to her heart, that she was open from the heart. Her skin, those terrible raw,

---

*   I say Rose and I decided as if Sammy didn't exist. He very much did exist, but he was still in Malaya, from where he returned briefly only every two years. Not until he came back for ever with his beautiful Malayan wife could he play a full part, but by then both our parents were dead.

scaly patches, sore and ugly, which had tormented her for years, were already healing – her psoriasis was vanishing.'

I was now supporting two families and was once again working three days a week at OBM. When I left her that Sunday I felt sure she would die during the operation. When she didn't I felt a surge of hope. Perhaps at last she would be well.

But the result of the operation was devastating. She was so 'riddled with cancer', in the surgeon's words, that he decided it was impossible to operate and had sewn her up again. Ever since she had, at eighteen, seen her mother die of bowel cancer, her greatest fear was that she would get it herself. We felt it was better not to tell her that this was what had happened.

I drove down to 18 Hartington Road again. Rose and I went in at different times each day; my father, unwell, less often. My mother was fairly dopey and I would sit with her for an hour or two, stroking her hand and whispering to her.

On Thursday we were told that she was unlikely to live more than forty-eight hours. She was just sixty-four. I had earlier sent a telegram to Sammy, who rang that evening, very upset. His son Dee had just been born and was dangerously ill in intensive care. He didn't feel he could leave, and I agreed.

'I said goodbye to her on Friday,' I wrote in my journal. 'Not openly, but inside. She was dozing, under morphine. We spoke – except for once – very little, but I felt completely with her, linked very close, and her with me, more than for years, when I was a boy, a child. I felt so strong with love and able to help her. She made little puzzled expressions, then little frowns, raising and lowering her eyebrows, eyes closed. When I spoke to her, she smiled that quick sweet smile. She said, "Are the doctors pleased with me?" I said they were very pleased, she would soon be well. She meant with her behaviour, her bravery as well as her progress (she hadn't been told about the cancer). She was sweating and turning, the fan not cooling her, obviously in pain. I asked if it hurt. She said, "Yes, it does. And they don't know why." I felt cold anger. I said, "I'll make them give you more morphine." I went and told the nurse she should be given more morphine at once. An argument, almost a row. I sent her to ask the doctor and if he refused, to get me, then went and stroked my mother's hand. After a while, the nurse came in and gave her another injection, and she relaxed. When the nurse had gone she said, "Did you do that?" with that expression of pride in me, confidence in me, that I know so well. I said, "Yes, and I'll see they don't let you have any more pain. I shall speak to Dr Pauley tonight." Mummy opened her eyes and said, "Dr Pauley requires a great deal of tact." "But I *am* tactful Mummy." She dozed, I sat and stroked her hand. It was strong and firm, rounded like Rose's. She stirred and said, "I feel so guilty." For some reason, I knew at once what she meant. "You mean us in different houses in the war?" "Yes. I've always felt guilty about it." I had wanted to tell her what I owed her, what she had done, to tell her how I loved her, every day, but I hadn't been able to. I wasn't sure before that she would die. I said – "How do you think I have been able to do the things I have done, with my books, withstand the leaving from Sabrina and Eliza, if it wasn't for you? How do you think Sammy has been able to build his whole life, his family, his plantation, but for you? Why do you think Rose is so strong and happy, but for you? Your love has made us so strong. You have made us able to be happy. You need never feel guilty. You have done the most wonderful thing in the world." Tears poured down my cheeks, but I pressed it into her, pressed in the truth and my love and she relaxed and whispered, "You make me so happy." I sat some more and left.

'On Saturday she didn't really know I was there, but when she felt my hand she gave that quick, sweet smile. Then she was unconscious, her mouth slack, breathing heavily but still those fleeting expressions of puzzlement and frowning.'

As I drove away from hospital an odd thing happened. All at once I heard, from the seat behind me, a sudden loud howl as if some animal, or dog, or wolf, was in great pain. Frightened, I stopped the car and looked quickly back – but there was nothing there. It had been me howling.

That night I drank a good deal of red wine, about two bottles, and fell into a drunken sleep around eleven. I was shaken awake about two and a half hours later and at once had an extraordinary sensation of release. I knew my mother had died and had come to tell me that. I was aware of her winging away, herself released, higher and higher, far far away. It was so strong and definite that I reached muzzily for the bedside light and looked at my watch. Twenty-five past one.

I was woken again by Rose at nine-thirty, her face red with crying. My mother had died at ten past one that morning. I could see it would have taken at least fifteen minutes to get me awake.

(16)

Not until years later did I learn about the dying. They rise and fall in the sea of unconsciousness and even under deep anaesthesia people have taken in words said, and even actions – pressures of the hand, their forehead stroked. 'The solitude of the dying is the worst thing and I see how they feel it,' Gerald Brenan wrote as he sat by the side of his dying mother. 'One must accompany them, holding their hand, to the very edge of the river.' I did not do that because I did not know and I now bitterly regret it. I would have sat beside my mother all day and all night for as long as she needed it, for as long as she was still alive.

(17)

The busy aftermath of death for a while delays its sting: there are discussions about whom should be rung up and then the ringing up, soon letters have to be answered, wills have to be read, the funeral arranged, drink and food bought and the house made neat for after the funeral – for a short while a pleasant feeling of importance fills those at the centre. The will was brief. My mother, as I had long suspected, had enough capital left to give me, Sammy and Rose one thousand pounds each. There was nothing else. Any furniture was left to my father until he died. All her letters had been burnt by Gathorne, at her request.

Aldeburgh Church was packed for the funeral. The only slightly discordant note was struck by my father, who asked the clergyman if it was possible for the grave to be dug deep enough to hold three people.

I think this more or less summed up what he had been feeling, consciously or unconsciously. My mother's affection had always revived when he was once again carted off to hospital. She would call him Ant, as she must have done when they were in love. No doubt her heart sank when once again he arrived back, but affection remained even then. I don't think my father really minded my mother's death at all — or not much. Although the alacrity with which he had conceived of a grave for three showed it hadn't been far from his mind, he had in fact never expected to marry Mary. For one thing, he had decided he shouldn't leave my mother and, like all of us, he thought he'd die before her. Then, he didn't at all want to leave his home, his vine, his cabin, his *things*. And he was still enjoying the cunning secrecy of the Harrises. Suddenly — it all changed. He was free! He could do what he liked — in everything. I remember being infuriated by him, a few nights after my mother died, when he practised, rather drunk, hurling his throwing knife into the sitting-room door, something he would never have dared do before.

He was astonished to find we all knew who the Harrises really were, but rapidly adjusted. He wouldn't live with Mary — yet. I think he had in mind the concept of 'the decent interval' (it turned out to be two months). The pattern would be — a week in London with Mary; then a week at 18 Hartington Road. The burden of this last — and it was considerable — was shared by me, Rose and Mrs Gooding.

I now began to learn just to what extent drink had become the major element in his life. He would get up very slowly between eleven and one, sitting on the edge of his bed smoking and creeping into his clothes, the huge pee jar on the floor beside him, the pee sometimes a rich dark whisky-brown but more usually an electric yellow from the vitamin B forte. When he was vaguely half-clothed he would slowly haul himself downstairs as if descending from rigging, and have two tumblers of the disgusting sherry. Drinking would then go on gently till he went to bed. His need for this continual drip-feed became particularly noticeable when I drove him up to London. After an hour in the car he would begin to point out pubs — that's a very nice little pub; I've had a lot of drink there; that used to be a bloody good pub. As we got further and further from Aldeburgh, among pubs he had never visited in his life, he would recognise more and more. But soon there weren't enough. He would start to create pubs. He'd point to a bank or a shop on a corner – that used to be a very good pub, can't think why they turned it into a bank. Then he'd site them anywhere – that would be an excellent place for a pub; so would that; bloody silly place for a post office. By the time we reached London he'd worked himself into a rage that every building, every house, every street didn't consist entirely of pubs: why the fuck's sake don't they have a pub there, or there – or *there* come to that? That's a perfect place for a pub.

This desperation was partly induced by the fact that I always refused to stop at any of the pubs, real or imaginary. I said there wasn't time, and so it always seemed. But, though looking after, and driving him about was exasperating and very time-consuming and though I longed for him to marry Mary, I see now that I didn't like the speed with which it had all happened. I felt, that is, a Hamlet-like anger and wanted to punish him.

I quite often took Jenny and Ben on these trips to Hartington Road. My father was good with them and enjoyed this. Sometimes I took Anna and Pablo; but my life with Anna was beginning to get very difficult indeed.

(18)

At first, the momentum of kidnapping Pablo, which for eighteen months had made our life so absorbing and purposeful, our inter-mittent if frequent times together so intense, continued in the two-roomed basement flat my children's book agent, Laura Cecil, had found for us in Primrose Hill.

For several months it seemed likely, indeed certain, a tearful Pablo told us, that his father would try and kidnap him back. Every time we went out we scanned Rothwell Street for possible snatchers, Spanish Dave Harts or even Fernando himself. We warned the local primary school. Even when Anna eventually won her case in Madrid, we could still not relax. Fernando was given nine months' leave to appeal and pending that she was denied legal custody – he, meanwhile, was given more time to re-kidnap.

But the most tragic aspect was what had happened to Pablo himself. The strong, confident, exuberant little boy I'd met first had become frightened, clinging, terrified of going to sleep, terrified if Anna left him for a moment. At the same time as weeks and then months passed and there came no sign from Fernando, who had in fact abandoned his case as hopeless, Pablo (and Anna) increasingly looked to me to be his father. I had rented a small cottage near Watton in Norfolk so that I could take Jenny and Ben there, with Anna and Pablo of course, at weekends and during school holidays. But Pablo now began to be very jealous of Ben and, stronger than him, used to bully him. More and more, I went to the cottage with Jenny and Ben on my own.

Anna, not surprisingly, resented this and I realised even then that I should have taken quite different and more decisive steps. I should have married her, become Pablo's legal guardian and dealt with what, after all, was a common sibling problem. That I didn't was partly due to a second element – my terror, growing into a certainty, that Anna would one day leave me.

There was, in fact, considerable outside pressure on her to do this. It slowly emerged, as the war-time excitement of the kidnapping died away, that since she was twenty (she was now nearly thirty) Anna had suffered from depressions. To my dismay, I realised that, as with Eliza, I would have to be, among much else, amuser and cheerer up (the role my mother had played with everyone except herself). But the depression that now gripped Anna in Rothwell Street became so overwhelming and went on so long that she began to see a psychotherapist, an American Dr Paul Sabbag.

There is a temptation among therapists with new patients (or clients, as they like to call them) to get rid of any current partner. This gives a satisfying sense of clearing the decks for a new start. The neurotic problems they are investigating are almost certainly behind the choice of partner who is therefore by definition a mistake. In the case of Sabbag, this temptation was much increased because, I discovered several months later, he had fallen in love with Anna, or rather, more precisely, he wanted to sleep with her himself. The upshot was that she said he wanted me to go and talk to him. The interview was not easy. He questioned me closely about my parents, and about Sabrina, Jenny and Ben. I had asked Anna why he wanted to see me. 'He wants to hear about Sabrina.' I therefore talked about

Sabrina at some length. 'I sense something, a faint figure within you, which doesn't get its own way,' he said when I'd finished. Nettled, I said I'd be interested to know on what he based this 'something'; I thought that on the whole I did get what I wanted. 'All right, all right,' said Sabbag briskly, 'I did say "faint".' He didn't reassure me, either, by explaining, I thought glibly, that the reason Anna had hitherto always left her men was because as a little girl she had wanted to escape her family. But, most importantly, he said that if I wished to remain with her, I must go into therapy myself. 'There is imbalance in a partnership where only one is engaged in self-exploration.' He could recommend a good therapist – Dr Gordon Ambrose.

Ever since my article, 'How to Go Mad' in *Time and Tide*, but especially since *Nannies*, I had been urging other people as well as my mother that they should see a therapist. As for me, years of intense introspection in my journal had resulted in thorough and profound self-knowledge. It was totally unnecessary for me to see anyone. But, since Anna said unless I did she would leave me, I reluctantly agreed to give it a try.

And there was of course, as with all new lovers, the last lover – in this case the Wife; but even here the real trouble was, too, my concern for Jenny and Ben. Their happiness and security, it seemed to me, depended to a large extent on Sabrina's happiness and security, since they were with her more than with me. I therefore worried a good deal over this – an anxiety encouraged by Sabrina. Because I couldn't properly discuss it with Anna I wrote about it in my journal. I also, stupidly and provocatively, bought an enormous cast-iron Edwardian safe in which to keep my journal. Two men could hardly lift this very heavy, rather beautiful object. Every night, when I got back from OBM, and had my bath, Anna would take the key of the huge safe from my pocket, open it and read my journal. To her, it seemed entirely full of entries about Sabrina. Soon, she became furiously jealous. If I tried to explain that it wasn't Sabrina as Sabrina I was concerned about but Jenny and Ben, she became even angrier. Why wasn't I equally or more concerned about Pablo? I clearly wanted to be back with Sabrina, with my *family*, why the hell didn't I fuck off and *go* back?

Did she really think this? I *didn't* want to go back. Couldn't she see

that, couldn't she *feel* it? The trouble is men and women are rational
beings. That doesn't mean quite what it seems to. On the contrary. It
usually means that having decided we want to do something we seem
to find it necessary to have a reason, something at least superficially
rational, to explain and justify it. The 'reason' for leaving me,
something she had already decided on, was to be that I was still really
in love with Sabrina and wanted to go back to her. But Sabbag had to
endorse this. I see now that her telling me that he wanted to hear
about Sabrina, in whom he had no interest at all, was in fact, as far as
Anna was concerned, a move of considerable cunning.

All these things were compounded by what we drank. In order to
save money, I had taken to making wine in enormous glass carboys
from cheap kits I bought in Woolworths. It was not so much the
quantity we drank, though the quantity was considerable, as that the
various additives and residues made my wine poisonous. Our hangovers became terrible. Sammy, coming to England for his two-yearly
leave, collapsed into bed for twenty-four hours after an evening with
us and I had to ring up and postpone his meeting with Head Office,
always the most important engagement during these returns.

Partly as a result of my wine, any difficulty was exacerbated until it
became an argument and then a row. And the most terrible rows
were the jealous rows. But curiously enough the most intractable of
our difficulties, the one underlying all the others, even the jealous
rows, and from which they derived their ferocity, we never mentioned at all. Through no fault of his own – if it was anyone's fault it
was mine – it was really Pablo, who had brought us so close together,
who finally drove us apart.

Two weeks after I had started going to Gordon Ambrose in his
Devonshire Street consulting rooms, Anna left me.

(19)

I didn't find out definitely that she'd gone until about three weeks
later. I had driven Jenny and Ben to Tim and Harriet's house La
Bertinga in Lecchi, Tuscany. I was to stay there two weeks and then
Sabrina would come out and take over, while I went back to go to
Tangier with Anna. Patch-up time.

I rang Rothwell Street several times from the village telephone but there was never any answer. Finally, I rang Anna's mother, Patricia. This large, kindly woman, who liked me, was so evasive I guessed at once what had probably happened. 'But if she isn't with you, where is she?' 'I don't know.' 'Is she in England?' 'I don't know.' 'But you must know *something*.' 'Oh dear,' said Patricia in a trapped, unhappy voice.

It was while driving furiously back in the Singer Gazelle that I had the odd experience in the cheap Rheims hotel I described earlier – if I couldn't possess Anna I could at least turn into her. Another curious thing took place in that hotel. During the night I woke, or thought I woke, to find the room was brightly lit. My mother came towards me and took me in her arms. As she held me close, I gradually felt the pain drawn off me. So powerful was this dream that I thought it had actually happened and even searched the room to see if I could find her. I still felt soothed and strengthened when I set off again. In fact it took eight years before I really recovered.

In London, after searching Rothwell Street for clues and trying in vain to pin down Patricia, I became convinced Anna had taken Pablo to Spain. She had at last got full legal custody and the great weight of the Spanish law and Spanish police were now on her side and not Fernando's – who, in any case, Jaime Milà had said, had given up. Since I had failed as a substitute father, she might well have thought she must try, for Pablo's sake, to re-establish relations with the real one. Besides, Anna loved Spain.

I had two weeks left of my holiday to find her. I told Patricia where I'd be and flew out on an open ticket to stay with Gerald. Enquiries at our favourite bars and restaurants and among the one or two friends of hers I'd met in Malaga uncovered nothing. Perhaps, I now thought, she wasn't trying to see Fernando but just felt she needed a holiday. Like many women, Anna was at least half fish and one of the things she loved most about Spain was swimming. She would certainly go to the beach we'd used so often below Benahavis. I decided to stay with Eliza, whose house was close. She listened to me, with great patience and kindness, for hours; and as I described again and again to her what had happened, what I felt, it was strange to realise I must once have had the same feelings about her – and that now they had completely vanished.

Break-ups always take place when the weather can make them worse – in England during the dull cold and icy frosts of February; in Spain in August, when the sun is murderous. I tramped the grey, packed, Mediterranean sands past the Guadalmina Hotel below Benahavis and as far as the San Pedro Playa, battered by the murderous sun, for four days. Dozens of times I thought I saw Anna in the back of a head, the way of diving, even just in a pair of neat brown bare feet. It was like being in love and searching the crowd at a station. Everyone for a moment is the person you love.

'*Like*' being in love! I had never stopped being in love, I was more in love than ever. I had, towards the end, repeatedly asked her to marry me but by then – perhaps after all glib, lecherous Dr Sabbag was right about her – the desire to leave me was galloping. Anna had once told me, laughing, that for the last nine months of her marriage to Fernando, whenever she saw him, even when they were apart, one refrain repeated itself insistently, endlessly, in her head: 'I must leave him, I must leave him, I must leave him, I must leave him . . .'

On my fourth evening, I stopped in Benahavis to ring Gerald, as usual on the only telephone there, in the hot little post office on the hot dusty little square. You gave the number, then waited while the old woman slowly connected you, then the telephone would ring in its little cubicle. On the fourth evening, Gerald said Anna had rung him and left a message for me.

'What is it?'

'Why not come back and I'll give it to you here? It may be painful, Jonny.'

'Tell me now.'

'She said,' began Gerald, and his voice was trembling, 'what she said was, "Tell Jonny I've fallen passionately in love and I never want to see him again."'

I flew back next day – work is the only antidote to such things, and I had at last nearly decided to accept a commission to do another book.

(20)

After *Nannies* came out I was asked to write about other British institutions; in fact, I don't think there was a British institution I wasn't asked to write about: GPs, nurses, consultants, hospitals, barristers, solicitors, judges, police, prisons, the navy, the air force, the army, Parliament, the House of Lords, universities . . . I should of course have done this. One route to success in writing, as in most things, is to stick with success, or at least to go in one direction, one area. But the idea of doing this bored me. I wanted to write fiction – or if non-fiction as well, then not just one sort of non-fiction. Lack of money twice forced me to give in, but I resisted as long as I could, and when I did give in did so for personal as well as professional reasons.

I now wrote the third and last of the Jane books, and the first Cyril book. In this, Cyril is kidnapped by three Arab terrorists – Massif, Assif and Yassif – who mistake him for the notorious IRA bomb-maker, Flan O'Noonagan, whose skills they wish to use. Cyril, who is actually me not Cyril Connolly, is however like his namesake in two respects: he is both a gourmet and extremely greedy. He is flown to a remote oasis, locked up and forced to subsist entirely on sheep's eyes.

But Cyril and Jane were not going to help me escape from my endless part-time copywriting. Nor was I going to be given large sums to write a novel, since none of my other novels had made anyone very much, if any, money. When Hodder and Stoughton, after half a dozen other establishment set-ups, suggested I write about public schools – they already had an American publisher – I realised I could make this the second volume of a general study of middle-class upbringing from birth to eighteen, something which didn't exist – at least not in the way I saw it.

But now I found that, having longed to get out of advertising and offices for about seventeen years, I was too frightened to take the jump. Hodders and Viking in New York offered enough to live on till 1977. But what then? I would be forty-four. What about the next thirty or forty years?

This was the only time that Ambrose directly intervened in my life or even gave me any specific advice. I had continued to see him after

Anna left, partly because I had become fascinated, largely because I realised I didn't know myself nearly as well as I thought I did.

Ambrose said, 'You have always thought of yourself as a writer, haven't you?'

'Yes.'

Ambrose: 'Well then.'

So I jumped. Terrified, I resigned from OBM. Several months later my courage, if that's what it was, was fortuitously rewarded, or rather underpinned, by something completely unexpected. My Uncle Bob, only just seventy, suddenly died.

(21)

Late in 1973, Bob went into a London hospital under BUPA for a minor operation to straighten a finger which had constricted itself so that it was permanently clenched into his left hand. By a terrible mischance (one in a million, we were told) his liver — the *foi Hardi* again — probably, it seemed, weakened by litres of home-made strega and thousands of barrels of Stanford Dingley beer, succumbed to the anaesthetic. Three days after the operation I was told he was dying. By the time I saw him, he was yellow and unconscious and seemed beyond response.

But I now learnt something that had been kept from me. Unlike my vague and very temporary gloom, when Anne had learnt that Bob proposed to leave his collection of Old Master drawings to the Ashmolean, of all places, she was outraged. Didn't Bob realise whose side he was on? The Glemhams had inherited money, we hadn't. How could he just throw away this chance, the only one we'd ever have, to inherit some too?

Anne, in defence of her children, and here this perforce included, thank God, me and Sammy and Rose, was as ferocious as her mother had been when in 1926 she'd gone storming down to Kent on behalf of Jock and reduced Rupert D'Oyly Carte to tears. Anne had been working on Bob for a year. At first he was not very receptive. He had been much looking forward to leaving the Gathorne-Hardy Collection to the Ashmolean. There had been flattering meetings — as flattering as only such august cultural institutions can be. Perhaps a special room or rooms could be set aside for a permanent display. Perhaps the *Robert* Gathorne-Hardy Collection, since he planned to revamp and improve it by judicious sales and purchases; he'd throw in the Watteau he'd found in Jules's junk shop; he'd work with Julien Stock at Sotheby's.

But Anne was wily. She pointed out that Geoffrey Gathorne-Hardy could equally have left it all to the Ashmolean. But he hadn't. He'd kept it in the family. He'd left it to Bob. Then she played on Bob's kind heart, on his brotherly fondness for Eddie and my father, both ageing, in poor health, poor; she played on Bob's feelings about literature, the high calling of his art. And here a card of particular force was me. Bob was sympathetic to my writing; Anne made him sympathetic to the fact I had no money. He himself had been helped, indeed for many years supported, by Logan; did he not think he should in his turn support his nephew?

Gradually, rather reluctantly, Bob came round. Dreams of the Ashmolean rooms in permanent exhibition, the Robert Gathorne-Hardy Collection, were abandoned. He had finally said, Yes – he'd leave the Collection equally to Anne, my father and Eddie. But Anne soon realised this wasn't going to help anyone. When Bob died, and if the Collection was sold – and it *would* be sold – it would, as the tax was then, mean eighty per cent death duty. When she and her brothers died, each of their shares would incur eighty per cent death duties. There'd be, essentially, nothing left. Once more she went to work, and at last, a month before, Bob had caved in – the Collection was to be left, divided equally, to the nephews and nieces: me, Sammy, Rose, Harriet and Lucy.

Draft clauses had been drawn up by our solicitor, Christopher Parrish; Bob had approved them – but hadn't yet signed the final codicil to his will. Now he was in hospital, dying.

The law has made provision for such situations. Provided it is certain the contents of the will have been agreed beforehand, a person dying or too ill to write their signature can make 'a sign of assent' in front of two witnesses who do not stand to benefit. Anne now rushed up from Suffolk with Jock, who had agreed to be one of the witnesses. Christopher, a family friend as well as a solicitor, hurried in from his office. Together they all stood round the bed.

Christopher bent over and asked Bob gently to make a sign that he agreed to what he had already agreed. The yellow figure did not stir. Now Jock asked him, but this time loudly. But before long, Anne had thrust them aside and was shaking Bob and yelling at him – 'BOB, MAKE A SIGN.' A nurse, hearing all this shouting, put her head in, took one horrified look at this shocking scene, and hurriedly withdrew. 'MAKE A SIGN BOB.'

And then, at last, the eye of the earl, honed in the woods and out on the beet fields of his great Suffolk estates to catch the rapid zig-zag of the woodcock, the sudden spring and whirr of the partridge making its dash for life, this bright, aristocratic, eagle-eye caught the last feeble flicker of his brother's consciousness. 'I saw his little finger move,' said Jock. 'So did I,' said our solicitor. Thank goodness two such sharp-eyed witnesses, both of high reputation, both beyond reproach, were present during the final moments of my now potentially very wealthy gay uncle's life.

(22)

So great were the complexities of probate, of arranging the sale, the tax, the setting up of trusts and trustees and so on, that it was to be nearly three years before any of us saw any money. But two things did happen at once. Tim's father, Michael Behrens, had his own merchant bank. Loans against the future sale of the drawings were raised and my father and Eddie were each given £500 a year.

The second thing was that I discovered that my rich and generous friends had often, out of tact, behaved differently with me than they did among themselves. Jennifer Ross, for example, suddenly asked me if my 'advisers' had talked about a new tax haven somewhere or other, or if I thought she should just stick to Geneva. Richard said it could be worth my while putting some venture capital into a scheme he was joining to raise sixteenth- and seventeenth-century galleons from the sea bed in the West Indies. I said I'd certainly consider it. Have to ask the 'advisers'.

In the end all this, this feeling of joining a new, hitherto invisible club, died away when it eventually got round that I wasn't really, in terms of what I could spend, very much richer than I'd been before.

But for a while I, too, even without any actual cash, felt buoyed up
by the knowledge that some, at some time, must be going to arrive.

'The rich,' Gerald wrote, 'think love is the most important thing.
The poor know that it is money.' In this respect I had always been
among the rich and remained so, only in my case it was now the lack
of love that had become the most important thing.

(23)

As Ambrose and I got to know each other better, he would very
occasionally, when his guard was down, let slip observations at a
tangent to the process I was, with his help, engaged on. Although I
still thought about Anna most of the time, I hardly spoke about her
with him. But one day, after I'd mentioned, for some reason, the
cruel message passed on by Gerald which had so devastated me in
Benahavis, he said, 'I don't think that is very likely, as a matter of
fact. I know she was still seeing Paul Sabbag when you started
coming here and I remember Paul saying that he had had to put her
into a nursing home for three weeks at the time you were in Spain.'
(This was true. Several years later she told me that after her
breakdown she had lived with her mother. She had had no lover.
She also said she had no idea why she had left me. But I knew the
main reasons.)

I digested what Ambrose had just told me and then said, 'What did
Dr Sabbag say to make you agree to take me on?' I knew Ambrose
had far too many patients, like all good therapists.

'He said – most unprofessional and not like him – "Get Gathorne-
Hardy off my back will you, Gordon?" '

I suddenly realised what this could mean. 'Do you think he fancied
her himself?'

'Oh, *goodness* yes,' said Ambrose.

Death is the best form of divorce. If Anna had died, I would have
got over her far quicker. As it was, for a long time after she left I was
beset by feelings of menace. I had, which I hadn't had since I was a
child, attacks of loudness. Walking in Battersea Park that autumn,
from the squalid basement flat I'd taken in Stockwell, the leaves
sounding like claws on the tarmac pathways as they blew towards me,

I would suddenly see her ahead of me, as I had when searching the beaches in hot Spain, which it now seemed she'd never gone to.

I met up with Raffaela again. She was still beautiful, still with her husband, still with Luigi and once again, for a night, with me. But I found I couldn't make love to her. I was not infrequently impotent with women during this period – about a year – but instead of minding as I would have done fifteen years before, it seemed entirely appropriate. I don't think sex, if it works, can ever be totally joyless – for men at least; but those brief liaisons, of which there were about four or five, were certainly not particularly joyful.

Then I met Sarah. She was thirty-four, divorced and living with her three children in a pleasant terrace house, wore spectacles (I've always found spectacles attractive) and drove a Citroën 2CV, which gave her an exciting left-bank, left-wing air. In fact she'd just ended a two-year affair with a Parisian journalist who was a communist. She was earnest, gentle, liked making love, a wonderful dancer, a very good cook, rather timid but, to complete this four-line partner-wanted ad, she had astonishing outbreaks of boldness.

I said earlier very few people feel guilty about leaving – at least about the person they've left. They may feel guilt about the children or vaguely uneasy because they took all the furniture. But the partner, whatever other people think, had it coming. Besides, their *feelings* dictated what they did. Everyone knows *feeling* is what counts.

I do feel guilty about the way I behaved with Sarah. We were together eight years (with a break of ten months in the middle). I knew from the beginning she would have liked me to marry her and finally expected it, and I knew from the beginning I never would. But I couldn't stand being alone any longer.

While I was with her I had my only two authentic experiences of God – or of the gods – the first early on, the second, last thing.

(24)

We had gone to Crete for a holiday. To Xania, where a friend, the painter Johnny Craxton lived, though he was away then. Our hotel, its main feature, was on the half-ring of the harbour and our room looked on to it. Another feature was the Down's syndrome son of the house, an enigmatic loutish adolescent figure who used to lurk near the terrace staring at the women guests or suddenly appear in the corridors. He would squat outside the rooms of couples, his ear pressed to the door, hoping to hear them make love. I twice found him crouched outside our door.

I read in one of the guide books that Zeus had been born in a cave in the mountains directly across from us on the other side of the island. It seemed to me from the map that it should be possible to reach it by a small road behind Xania. The map, more a rough, brightly coloured tourist indication than a reliable guide, directed us to Osimosis.

We made up a picnic and hired a small motorbike. Not one of the supercharged genitals that Hart had roared about on, but more than a scooter. I had last mounted this sort of thing at Lydford and the Poplars when I was sixteen, but after a wobbly start we set off at twelve noon, directed, or redirected, decisively by the garage owner up a road signposted Cherison.

It was July. As we bounced along in the sun the sound of our engine joined the cicadas, Sarah's arms were light round my waist, the little road coiled up and up into the mountains. At first metalled, it soon became a rough, much steeper, dust- and stone-filled track, the engine roared, the sun now beat down ferociously, at times it was so steep we could only grind up in first with hardly enough momentum to keep our balance, kicking with our feet. After two hours I was getting tired, I had bruised my left foot, and then suddenly I over-accelerated, the motorbike skidded forward and sideways, dragging us along as it fell. We were both badly shaken.

At three, we reached Cherison. It was a dead end, high in the mountains, very quiet and clear, an eagle or perhaps it was a buzzard circling above us. Looking at the tourist map I thought I saw where we had been wrongly directed. We went back a little way and had our picnic in a grove of twisted olives. It was hot and peaceful, the air full of the sound of bees. The olive trunks were enormous, twisted clockwise as if with the immense force needed to corkscrew them down into the mountain rock. We set off again at 3.30.

By 4.15 we were back at the garage. We drove back along the road and there was the sign – Osimosis 37 kilometres.

But what kilometres! Another narrow road coiling up and up into the mountains – metalled, thank the gods – steeper and steeper, the bike sometimes only going at 14 kilometres an hour, up and up and up, great ravines and mountains succeeding each other with greater and greater grandeur until it was as though we were approaching the place of absolute beauty. It began to grow cold with the height. At five o'clock, already numb from four and a half hours of continuous riding, we reached a saddle at the top and could see down on either side to the sea, hazy in the distance far below. A sign pointed up one of the nightmare tracks into the mountain, or rather up and round the precipitous side of the mountain – Osimosis 13.7 kilometres. We agreed we would go on till 6.30.

It was so high and still and clear, so empty; it had the menacing quality I've felt before on mountains, but more powerful now. The track was very rough indeed, really just loose mountainside, with terrifying drops to the right where the sides had started to slip away. Tired, longing to get there and start back, going too fast, Sarah's arms now holding me tightly, I suddenly over-accelerated again, the bike reared up like a horse and crashed forward and sideways.

I had torn out the nail of my left big toe and gashed my leg; the spinning back wheel had burned off a strip of skin down Sarah's calf about six inches long. We were trembling. I wanted to turn back but felt I shouldn't give up.

No wonder the gods were born on Greek mountains; or that Zeus was born on Crete. In the high pure air, the only sound the roar of our engine echoing away, I sensed with complete, objective clarity a god wanting me to die. I was to die here, now, rolling over and over with Sarah down the mountainside until my head split on a rock or we fell over a cliff. I felt very frightened. Then I heard take place one of those discussions which enliven Homer's account of Odysseus's wanderings, only here I was the subject. And Pallas Athene wanted the soul of the writer, but as she was about to claim it – as her father Zeus had promised – Artemis said that she, Artemis, had taken a vow that he would write one great work before he died, and this he had not yet begun. Pallas Athene was very angry but said she would take his soul once this was done. Here I entered the dispute. I asked if the great work could be a novel and I think, but I am not actually completely sure, that Pallas Athene agreed to this.

It was not quite like this, of course. I've invented the dialogue –
but not the event. I suddenly sensed, absolutely clearly, some life-
threatening presence, or presences, close to me, and with these
presences I had the silent exchange – I conveyed to the gods that they
could have my life provided they let me write one great work, a
novel if possible, and I sensed, felt, them convey the answer – Yes.

At once I became calm, and we rode on into the evening air. At
6.30 we stopped. We were still not there, though we could see up to
the black hole of Zeus's cave birthplace far across the deep valley, and
could see the track we were on winding round to it.

We arrived back at the hotel at nine o'clock, the last hour and a
half terrifying in the dark. I felt I had been beaten up. My hands were
blistered. The blood had dried round Sarah's wound but it was now
very painful. I read several years later that it is not advisable to spend
more than three hours at a time in the saddle of these machines. We
had spent eight hours almost without stopping.

Three days after this, still not fully recovered, we ran out of money
and had to go back early. But it was, I hoped, to return home and
find I would soon be rich.

(25)

Although I knew nothing about the world of art sales and auctions
and nothing about Old Master drawings, Anne had asked me to
supervise the sale of Bob's Collection.

I now learnt a little more about it. There had been a number of
revisions since I had stepped over the large pool of Alsatian pee and
seen the drawings in Geoffrey Gathorne-Hardy's billiard room. The
Da Vincis had all become followers of, as had two Rubenses, and the
Bruegel, there were two Michelangelos and not three and so on. But,
as well as the Michelangelos, there were still three Rembrandts (not
four), a Dürer, a Carpaccio, two Mantegnas, six Claudes and, of
course, the Watteau Bob had discovered in Jules's junk shop. It was
the largest and most important collection of Old Master drawings in
private hands in the world, excluding those of the Duke of Devonshire. Looking at the catalogues now, I wish we hadn't all needed
money so badly and could have kept some of them.

The obvious choice was Julien Stock and Sotheby's. For a year before he died, Bob had been working with Julien on how they could improve the Collection (everything to do with it now was in capital letters) and, selling Bob's Picasso etching, they had together bought a minuscule Piero di Cosimo and two drawings by Giulio Romano, whoever they might be.

But I thought I must explore every avenue. This extraordinary chance, coming out of the blue, would never come again. Harriet and Lucy would inherit something from Anne and Heywood, but my father, who had, to our relief, now married Mary, had made it clear that everything – that is, 18 Hartington Road and a few chairs and clocks etc. – would go to her for her lifetime. Mary was then a fit fifty-seven. Her mother lived to be eighty-seven.

I accordingly went to David Carritt, a distinguished art dealer I knew slightly (he had discovered the Tiepolo ceiling in the Egyptian Embassy in South Audley Street and Caravaggio's 'Musicians' in a Norfolk family house, among many other things). He *of course* knew about the Collection, and he would *of course* love to dispose of it – but it was too big for him. With great politeness and generosity he directed me to Colnaghi's in Bond Street. Colnaghi's too, *of course*, knew the Collection; even better in fact, since they had held a loan exhibition in 1971 when Geoffrey was still alive, an exhibition which later moved to the Ashmolean where the drawings were still expected to go. (Anne had not yet done her work.) Once again I was amazed at the deference with which I was treated. Colnaghi's said they would love to handle the sale or sales but, with considerable honesty, felt I'd do better at auction. Try Christie's.

I think Anne and I always knew Julien Stock should sell the Collection (but what pleasure we got discussing all this!) and going to Christie's seemed like a waste of time. Yet perhaps not entirely. Julien now came to me and said, in view of the immense importance of the Collection, for an auction house just as significant from a prestige point of view as the mere money involved, Sotheby's were prepared to reduce their usual premium of fifteen per cent to one per cent up to the first million pounds and only thereafter fifteen per cent.

The first million! Might there then be a second million or even a third? In my long history of worrying about money I have often woken at two or three in the morning and gradually worked myself into a panic about what I owe or what I'm going to live off in four months' time. But not infrequently I wake with the opposite worry. One of my long shots – premium bonds, football pools, the lottery (I do all three) – has come off. I am to get anything from one to sixteen million pounds. Now I am seized with as much anxiety about having too much as I usually feel at having too little. These nightmares, coupled with wild swings of elation, intensified as the sales drew near.

One per cent had, of course, swung it. But twice we were all asked to lunch at Sotheby's, with champagne and *foie gras* and all Peter Wilson's charm, no doubt to keep us sweet (we were so sweet already Peter Wilson could have put any of us into his coffee). And yet it wasn't just commercial acumen and greed. Julien himself had a genuine feeling for art and, as regards Old Master drawings, was a scholar. But I now realised something else about being (or being thought) rich. Human beings have a limited repertoire of emotions – the anger we feel if someone strikes us is not much different from the anger we feel if they cheat us out of money. Or, to put it another way, the range of a single emotion can be almost limitless. 'Love', for example, can take many forms and have many objects – a dog, a house, a schoolteacher, the love of a woman for a homosexual man, of a homosexual man for a woman, the love of the man who fell in love with a shadow. I now saw that some of those who serve the rich, sometimes, for a while and no matter how cynical they are, feel something close to love for their clients. Of course, it is because they stand to gain – and if we had withdrawn the Collection no doubt different emotions would have stirred in Peter Wilson. But for the present, he, the whole of Sotheby's, loved us and we basked in the warmth of their emotion.

And, had circumstances been only slightly different, they might have been right to go on wooing us. Tax on sales of this sort then ran, as I said, at eighty per cent. It would be possible, I had learnt, to sell a few of the drawings privately; some, for example, to the French film actor Alain Delon. He would pay £120,000. We would declare £80,000 and pay £64,000 tax. Delon would pay £40,000 into a Swiss account and it would be a simple matter to get it to us in England. Saving – £32,000. Selling a quarter of the drawings in this way would have led us to save considerable sums. Anne and I were perfectly happy to do this. But our solicitor, Christopher, was unfortunately a man of the highest probity and would have none of it.

It took more than a year to organise the various catalogues and sales. They took place in three lots, two at Sotheby's on 29 April and 24 November 1976; one, of Dutch and other northern painters, in Amsterdam on 2 May 1976.

But, in March, just before the first sale, I had to attend a rather curious event which, in fact, might perhaps have made me, properly exploited, almost as much money as Sotheby's had (hopefully) predicted from selling the drawings.

(26)

Princess Margaret had told Angela Huth that she wanted to meet some 'new writers'. I had been asked to dinner as one of them. Out of nerves, I arrived, in my hand-me-down dinner jacket (once Jock's) too early. Only Martin Amis was there. I hardly knew him (Sassoon again) but he seemed more *au fait* with royalty than I was. 'What should I call her?' 'Ma'am,' he said. 'What, always, all the time?' 'All the time.' 'What, even "Did you come Ma'am?"' Martin thought for a moment, no doubt putting himself, with his novelist's empathy, in her place. 'Yes,' he said.

The other 'new writers' arrived. Clearly, the category was broad: Derek Marlow and his very attractive then wife, Suki, Bamber and Christina Gascoigne, Bryan Forbes and Nanette Newman. And then at last – Princess Margaret.

I can't be sure what a gust of sentimentality might do to me in a referendum, but I am, I think, in principle a republican; yet, like all of us, I was immediately engulfed by a wave, a tsunami, of syco-phancy and showing off. Derek Marlow kept on about his 'friend' Tom Stoppard. Bryan Forbes said several times, 'A writer's life is very lonely, very very lonely.' My own chance didn't come till long after dinner. Princess Margaret had somehow become stuck playing Angie's upright piano – rather well, in fact, with a large tumbler of whisky precariously balanced on it like Fats Waller – but stuck. She played for twenty minutes. At last Angie managed to prise her loose and brought her over to where I was sitting on the sofa. At once, fairly drunk by now, the adrenaline of royalty made me sober, though not royalty herself, whose tumbler had been generously replenished.

We talked of this and that, until I said I had been writing a book about public schools and had recently seen her daughter at Bedales and how beautiful she was (which she was). Princess Margaret leant rather heavily against me. 'I don't live with my husband any more you know.' 'Oh,' I said, alerted. Somehow 'Ma'am' no longer seemed appropriate. There had been a great deal of speculation about them both in the press. 'Well, I'm divorced,' I said, 'or rather divorcing. It is an extremely upsetting process.' Princess Margaret was momentarily distracted. Bryan Forbes was explaining rather loudly from across the room *exactly* how lonely a writer's life was.

'I met your husband once,' I said to bring her back. 'It was years before he met you.'

'Really?' she said.

'Yes. I was a copywriter then. We did a campaign together advertising *The Queen.*'

'Advertising my *sister?*' she said, astonished. I explained that *The Queen* was a magazine. Princess Margaret digested this and leant against me again and said very quietly, 'As a matter of fact I'm going to leave him. It's going to be announced in a few weeks.' At once, clearly appalled by what she'd said, she added quickly, 'Please tell no one.' I said, of course not Ma'am. We talked about her own writing. She said she kept a journal. I urged, perhaps unnecessarily, the virtues of indiscretion in a journal. I wonder if it still exists. Shortly afterwards, she got up to talk to other new writers.

As she left an hour or two later, she came over to me and said again, 'Don't tell anyone.' Tabloid speculation, as I say, had been particularly intense just then. Perhaps if I hadn't been aware of more legitimate sources in the offing, I might have been more strongly tempted to see what they would have paid – £20,000? £30,000? It could have been as much as £50,000.

(27)

In fact, none of us could attend the first sale at Sotheby's on 29 April, but we attended the second – on 24 November – the one, in fact, that Julien Stock hoped would be the most successful.

We – that is, Anne and Heywood, Sarah and me, Nic Hill and Julien himself (as anxious as us I read in my journal; only thirty-one, still making his way, his entire reputation on the line in these three sales) – met first in Green and Abbot, behind Sotheby's, where Nic worked. Carmine arrived a little later, stiff in his suit. We had champagne, smoked salmon and pâté from Fortnums. We were excited, slightly hysterical, like children. The talk was entirely about money. At 3 p.m. precisely we were sitting in a row at the back of the crowded, but not hugely crowded, sale room.

It felt completely unreal. Indeed, many of the drawings seemed unreal – sometimes little more than doodles and often minute. The Michelangelo, a vague male torso roughly and idly sketched while he waited, as it were, in a phone box, was 24.8 centimetres by 17.5 (say, 9½ inches by 6½); the Mantagna, an exquisite bird, 18 centimetres by 11; the smallest was the Piero di Cosimo Bob had acquired himself – 8.4 centimetres by 4.8 (3½ inches by 2). Could we really expect *money* for these tiny tattered scraps?

The sale itself, too, was unreal. Peter Wilson in total command, feminine, disdainful – no, not feminine, feline – at the same time courteous, urbane and with each bidder, each bid, a scintilla of contact.

The most extraordinary moments came with the Michelangelo. This had been estimated – the upper limit – at £60,000. At £60,000 it leapt to £70,000, then £80,000, then £90,000. Julien, whose face up till then had been knotted with anxiety, suddenly began to grin in disbelief. Two spots of colour appeared in his cheeks. I winked at him. Now, as the height became greater, the steps got shorter – £95,000, £100,000, £105,000 . . . £120,000, £125,000, £130,000. There was hardly any oxygen up here, the air was freezing, but still, step by step, they dragged themselves higher and higher, higher and higher – £142,000, £143,000, £144,000. Now they faltered. It was too high. In the long silence, Peter Wilson raised his hammer, held it raised, lifted

it higher – a knife, a whip . . . and at the sight they were off again:
£145,000, £146,000, £147,000, £148,000. There began to seem no
reason why they should ever stop – £159,000, £160,000, £161,000,
£161,500, £162,000 . . . And at last, completely exhausted, like us at
the back, they did stop. One hundred and sixty-two thousand pounds.

At the end, we stood talking to Julien, chattering, still in a state of
disbelief, still children. I saw Philip Pouncy, one of the scholar-sale
figures working at Sotheby's, whom I knew disapproved of the sale –
the Collection should *not* have been broken up – and in particular
disapproved of the unrestrained, indeed shameless way we talked
about how much it might fetch. I said to him ingratiatingly I'd never
been to a sale before. 'I had no idea it would be so gentle, so polite.
Yet also so delicate – and at the same time,' I added, hoping he would
think I was not as mercenary as all my relations, 'so *indelicate.*' Pouncy
did not answer.

All the sales together fetched £928,766.25. Bob's house in Stanford
Dingly and his library brought further sums. In all, there was about
£1.1 million. (Huge sums – had we been able to wait they would, of
course, have been huger still. Julien Stock told me that the November
sale alone would today – 2004 – have probably reached £3 million.)

However, my nightmares of excessive wealth were, happily or
unhappily, not realised. Now, like a very fat person on a ferocious
diet, this wonderful, monstrous sum melted before our eyes: £9,287
to Sotheby's, eighty per cent estate duty (partly paid by handing over
a Montagna and a Carpaccio), Christopher's enormous, though no
doubt justified, bills, paying back Michael Behrens's bank with
enormous, no doubt justified interest . . . In the end, we each
received £60,000. The trust that was formed for me, like so many
with which I had been associated, didn't produce any actual income
– but it produced the equivalent. I bought a cottage in Wiltshire for
£15,000 which, ten years later, paid for half the house Nicky and I
now live in. This has meant that I have never, except once briefly,
had to pay a mortgage. I paid, with their grandmother Virginia Bath's
help, for Jenny and Ben's education. Much later I bought a small flat
in the slummiest part of Stockwell, the rent from which now supplies
much of our income. What is left brings in about £300 a year. Bob's
your uncle – if you're lucky.

PART FIVE

Death

(1)

I actually bought my cottage in Wiltshire as soon as I could after the first sale of Bob's pictures on 29 April 1976.

West Lodge is two miles outside Compton Bassett on a lane that goes to the main road which leads to Calne. It was sturdily built in 1792 with two-foot-thick walls and mullioned windows in the mock-Jacobean style fashionable then and had been the lodge of the big house which had burnt down in the 1920s – all but the stables which were now the new big house. The cottage had two bedrooms, a sitting room, a small entrance room and someone had built on a kitchen. I discovered a ten-foot-wide fireplace bricked up in the sitting room. There was a small garden back and front, both together about the size of half a tennis court. In the back bit there was an apple tree, a shed and a single big oak – my sole part of a small wood that stretched away beside the lane towards Compton Bassett.

I loved West Lodge. It was the first dwelling I had ever owned. Before that it had been rented rooms or flats or houses that belonged to whichever woman I was living with. Though I never lived at West Lodge for longer than a month at a time, I usually went at weekends or for the school holidays, and it was the first place I had had for longer than three years. It made me feel rich and stable.

Mrs Stockwell – Gladys – played up to the rich fantasy. Then aged about seventy, originally from London, but long resident in the next village of Cherhill, she came in for two hours after each weekend. When the telephone went she would pick up the receiver and say 'Mr Hardy's residence'. 'I call you Jonny when I'm talking to any friends, Mr Hardy,' she said. 'I know you don't mind.' Tough, hard-working, funny, loyal, kind, she was also obstinate, spoke her mind and was always involved in some feud or other. I still see her whenever I can.

Although of course Sarah and her children came sometimes, and friends, it was mostly for me and Jenny and Ben. We went as often as we could. In summer, we walked up to the White Horse or had picnics and collected sloes for sloe gin, or went to the swimming pool in Chippenham. When I lost my licence for a year, we bicycled every-where. In winter, it was often very cold, cold air rolling down the slope of the low hill rising to the left of the cottage and settling round it as frost. I installed central heating – which was agreed by the trustees to be a legitimate expense, though even at that early date they were nerv-ously aware of the eventual dwindling, indeed almost vanishing, of the sum under their control. I bought huge logs for the huge fireplace – bigger even than the one at White House Farm – and we would sit in front of it and watch television or play cribbage. The wind sighed its melancholy way through the wood, the logs hissed and dribbled or blew out sudden jets of steam and I would remember Snape.

Several odd things happened while I was there. It had been discov-ered that the flat farmland to the right of West Lodge on the other side of the lane away from the hill, consisted of enormous deposits of a rare, very fine white sand laid down during the Upper Palaeozoic Age when Compton Bassett and Calne had been part of a tropical sea with immense shallow lagoons. While I was there only about four acres had been dug out leaving deep, wide pits which slowly filled with rainwa-ter. I used to go and watch the man operating the excavator. One day I asked him if he ever dug up fossils. Yes, sometimes. 'But the really strange thing is sometimes, deep down near the bottom of the seam, you seem to break into a pocket. I've smelt the sea.' He knew when the sea had been there – 230 million years before.

Two other things happened soon after I bought the cottage and were to do with what I was writing then, though their significance did not emerge for several years. In an attempt to exorcise Anna, I had been writing an erotic novel about my affair with her and the kidnapping. It was virtually straight autobiography except I set it in Italy. I found what I was writing often upset me and late one foggy autumn evening, alone and rewriting what I'd done in the morning,

I went out into the garden for respite. Standing in the darkness, once again desolated, swept by my loss, I heard the sound of heavy animal breathing coming from the field beyond the cast-iron railings. Whatever it was, was large, close, but not visible. Heavy, stertorous, menacing breathing, growing louder and louder; louder and louder until it seemed it would overwhelm me. I felt frightened and hurried back to the fire, locking the thick front door.

The second incident happened when I was again alone there writing, finishing the same novel. I was sick of it. I felt the eroticism was probably a mistake and I wanted a break. One Saturday, I found a fortune teller in the local Yellow Pages and decided to go to him.

Mr Taylor lived in a semi-detached villa in a row of semi-detached villas in a suburb of Bristol. He was short, wore a suit and seemed as ordinary as a fortune teller in an Agatha Christie. He made me press my palms on to a pad of black ink and then again on to a sheet of white paper. He held my fountain pen and studied my palm prints. After this, he spoke for about twenty minutes, with frequent pauses.

I've lost the tape he gave me and remember only three of his prophecies: I wouldn't stay for ever with the person I was then with. Even at that early point, this didn't entirely surprise me. But then Mr Taylor suddenly looked worried.

'Oh dear. We're in trouble here. Bad trouble. This woman is going to sue you. You want to fight it – but there's nothing you can do. She's got you over a barrel. You have to pay – well, I can't see the sum. But you don't like it at all. But there's nothing you can do. She's got you over a barrel.'

Of course, I realised at once he was talking about the novel. I knew Anna would hate it and probably fight it. I decided I would finish it for therapeutic reasons – which I did, and it didn't help – and then put it away. It is still put away.

Mr Taylor was clearly upset by what he'd seen. Luckily, he managed to find an antidote. 'Ah – I see money coming in your early sixties. A considerable amount. You're going to enjoy the rise in your standard of living.'

The one thing Mr Taylor couldn't foretell – or wouldn't tell me about, though I asked him – was when I'd die. But death was now for a while to dominate my life.

(2)

The reason I couldn't go to the first sale of Bob's pictures was that my father was dying. He married Mary in December 1973 and they had a year together comparatively free of illness. He still had great difficulty eating, but with her he did eat. She washed his hair. The barrel of disgusting sherry remained in Aldeburgh while they lived mostly in Mary's small flat in Twickenham, near where she was still teaching. During school holidays they went to 18 Hartington Road.

I saw quite a lot of them and, as I had always done, enjoyed talking to my father. He wasn't as humorous as my mother and didn't have her insight or gift for gossip, but he had an idiosyncratic mind and a better sense of fantasy. He was always involved in some new interest about which he was interesting.

Early in 1971 he fell and broke his thigh and two years after that the crises resumed. It was really the slow conquering of his body by cancer. First it attacked his bladder. Mary had to drive him to Millbank for his treatment, which was extremely painful and meant a tube pushed up his urethra and some lethal fluid being pumped up. He took his whisky flask with him; half before, half after. From there the cancer moved to his lymphatic system.

As before, he dealt with his illness by making himself his own patient. He was also interested by his psychological reactions. I remember him telling me how he'd finished some colour supplement or other and suddenly realised he'd passed over an article on what to do with your vine in summer – unmissable before – without reading it. 'Subconsciously I thought I would be dead by the summer.'

The spread of the cancer meant more debilitating treatments. Although now very weak, he insisted on spending the Christmas of 1976 in Aldeburgh. It was very cold that year and he caught flu. When they got back to London, he was still running a temperature. Mary told me she was having great difficulty in getting him to eat. The only thing he seemed able to get down was a preparation called Slender, with a slogan, 'Guaranteed to lose *pounds*!'

Soon after this, cancer was found in his lung. Mary and I were told by an astonishingly brisk and unfeeling young doctor, who just came into the room where we were waiting, gave us the news, and walked out. Mary said my father shouldn't be told but I think, by then, he'd diagnosed it for himself. Certainly, he was very depressed and after two more days in the hospital said he wanted to go home. Millbank supplied an ambulance and Mary and he were driven down to 18 Hartington Road.

Here, he cheered up at once, though now too weak to get out of bed. Mary asked him if there was anyone he'd like to see. 'Bert and Mrs Allen,' said my father. They came up and chatted to him in his room, Bert and he drinking their usual whisky chasers, Mrs Allen sherry. 'They might have been in the pub,' said Mary.

'I came over from spending the night at Snape,' I wrote in my journal. 'He was in bed, considerably changed even from last Wednesday. Thin and shrunken, frail, almost speechless, eyes hooded, the look of death I remember so vividly from Bob (and which Mummy never had). The room crowded with yacht pictures, the floor covered in swords, flintlocks and leaning against the bookshelf his crossbow; it looks like an amalgam of a small cabin in a ship and Royalist's arsenal in 1643. A table to one side of the bed covered in tobacco equipment, Granny's cigarette case, and a glass of whisky. He lives mostly on whisky, which has to be held to his mouth, as do cigarettes. Fluid crackling in his lungs and painfully brought up by occasional violent fits of coughing which leave loops of phlegm from his moustache and beard. His arms are like sticks, the skin yellow and very thin and smooth, the veins just threads. They are giving him heroin, but he is often sick. Next to the bed hangs an enormous bell roped to a broken towel horse, itself roped upright to the chest of drawers. A string is attached to the clapper and every now and again he yanks it. It makes a great deal of noise, like Eight Bells on a battleship. Above the chest of drawers is the only non-ship picture: "La Rêve de Nou Nou". A naked girl arched achingly in her sleep, her hand round the chair-arm by the bed which is shaped like a cock. Rose and Mary are here all the time. Anne comes in every day. I said I'd come again on Monday.'

In fact, weakened by his long battle, he died much more quickly than anyone expected. I was desperately trying to write the public school book, but I went down as often as I could. My journal describes my last visit, on 17 April. 'I arrived just too late to see him alive. Mary had dressed him in his naval uniform and he was lying in Aldeburgh mortuary, so hideously altered by death and the ravages of the disease that I could hardly bear to look at him. Rose said the most terrible of the changes happened almost at once. I stood for a while, then said silently goodbye to him and left.

'The church wasn't as crowded as it had been for my mother but there were enough people for it not to be embarrassing. Bert came up to me and said, "He never did get across anyone, did he, your father." '

We packed up all the rest of his various uniforms and such clothes as I didn't want and I took four sacks down to the nearby old people's home – stupidly failing to find out that it was for old women only. Number 18 Hartington Road was sold some months later.

I was much closer to my mother, but I had loved my father. I think he felt inferior to his three brothers, but he wasn't. He was more human than any of them, not aggressive like Jock, not a bore as Bob could be, not nearly as selfish as Eddie became, wiser than them and not a snob. Perhaps not the best husband in the world for my mother, but I've seen far worse and he stuck by his two main women. The navy often took him away from us, but when he was there he was a good if rather 'hands off' father to Sammy, Rose and me. And the only thing I blamed him for – leaving me for so long when I was six – he couldn't help. If he came back and I saw him now, with his quizzical, diffident, humorous expression, I would hug him, tears would come into my eyes, and we would go down to Bert's White Hart and have several drinks and talk and then more drinks.

(3)

In fact, Bert did not long survive my father. His doctor told him he should cut down on alcohol and he did so, drastically. 'Fatal advice,' my father would have said and so it proved. The immediate effect was an attack of *delirium tremens*. Mrs Allen first realised something was wrong when Bert sat up in bed and said to her, his wife of fifty years, 'What the fuck are you doing here?' He was dead within the year.

Both Jock and Eddie began the accelerating slide downhill, with which I was becoming familiar, that same year – 1977 – and I began to feel haunted by death. I had accompanied Eddie back to Athens at the start of that year after he had been staying at Snape with Anne and Heywood (for the last time it turned out).

As Eddie got older (he was seventy-six in 1977) more and more things went wrong: cataracts in both eyes being allowed to get worse before they would operate, diabetes moving to injection stage leading to more toes off, something wrong with his liver (cancer it later transpired) and continuing aftermath of that ancient blasphemous event on the shores of the Sea of Galilee. But the most upsetting and frightening thing was his bladder. He was either increasingly incontinent or else would be gripped by a sudden stricture and unable to pee at all. One of these seizures struck as we arrived in London on our way back to Athens and Eddie had to be rushed to hospital.

When I visited him he told me his hearing was very bad again. He could hear me, but the nurses he found almost impossible. 'You know, my dear,' he said, 'I find the thing is I can't hear *lower-class* voices.' While I was sitting talking, the sister came in on a routine visit. She checked various things then, on her way out, said, 'Do you use this?' 'This' was a contraption at the end of Eddie's bed for him to brace himself against so as not to slip too far down. Eddie shook his head to show he couldn't hear. 'Do you use *this*?' she said in a loud voice. 'What?' said Eddie. 'DO YOU USE THIS?' shouted the sister. 'Do I amuse you?' said Eddie. 'I don't know my dear.' The sister stared at him with an odd, nonplussed expression on her face, and then went out without answering.

Eddie recovered and we continued out to Athens, but after I'd seen him safely into his minute but charming flat at 53 Demacharus Street, I flew back to finish and hand in the manuscript of the public school book. Then later in 1977 there was some emergency. Anne went out and came back saying the emergency was over, but it was thought I should go out to help look after him.

(4)

Eddie's third-floor flat, where I was to spend nearly a month, had two small rooms at each end of a short corridor, and two even smaller rooms next to each other in the middle. One of the end rooms was his bedroom, with an elegant wardrobe and a little,

early-nineteenth-century Provençal walnut wood cabinet/cup-
board on four legs with a design of crossed mandolins and oak leaves
carved into it. Eddie kept his chamber pot in it and had it beside the
double bed which looked out on to a view that had once been of
the distant Acropolis but was now of a tower block acting its name.
The sitting room and its balcony at the opposite end looked straight
into Mount Lykabettos, that vertical park in the middle of Athens.
Sometimes the scent of pines was strong enough to drown the smell
of exhaust fumes. Sun streamed in through the long window on to
Eddie's often beautiful possessions – the ivory letter cutter, the
fragment of an Etruscan plate, his large Paul Nash, his five hundred
books . . . the last pieces from a lifetime of selling beautiful pieces.
Next to the sitting room was a bathroom so small the bath was a sit-
up one and on the lavatory your knees jammed up under the
cup-sized basin. Next to this was the kitchen where Maria, a rather
attractive middle-aged Greek woman, came and manoeuvred every
day to cook his meals. The only thing smaller than the kitchen and
bathroom was the rickety lift which shook its way noisily up to the
third floor.

To my surprise, the flat was empty when I arrived on the
Wednesday afternoon. Alan Ansen, who lived in the flat below, told
me Eddie was still in hospital. The shabby, shambling, sixty-year-old
American, a man of infinite kindness whom Eddie treated like a
slave, said he'd been due out two days before. There was some hitch.

I remember the shock of seeing Eddie that evening. Anne had
described the Crimea-like public ward in which she'd found him –
the beds, all full, a foot apart, the place crammed with whole families,
everyone smoking, shouting, eating. Eddie had burst into tears when
he saw her. It was quite unnecessary, since Jock paid his BUPA
subscription and she got him into a private room at once, but when I
saw him I recognised the look of death again – his face yellow from
his liver, hollow, shrunk, wrinkled black pouches under his eyes.
He'd just woken up and was tumbled about in the bed, naked. He
was fairly mad and called me 'Anne' several times. After about three
minutes he said, in what I later discovered was a formula, 'Well, my
dear, you won't think me rude but I'm going to ask you to go now.'
When would he like to see me next day? 'Two o'clock in the

morning,' said Eddie without hesitation. It seemed to me the 'hitch' was obvious. He was too ill to come out.

But the next morning (at eleven, not two) he was dramatically better. Composed, not yellow, hair a bit wild, but making complete sense. 'I'm to come out tomorrow,' he said triumphantly, as though he'd defeated some enemy.

His departure next day was both upsetting and farcical. I went in at 12 noon to find Maria sitting beside Eddie, who had expected the ambulance at 9.30. He lay, a white quivering hulk of impatience, naked, dozing and groaning. 'I'm in *purgatory*,' he murmured to me several times. I went out to get some lunch but when I got back the ambulance still hadn't arrived. It finally got there at 3.30. Maria dressed him in some torn pyjamas and he was then rolled on to a large flat tray about five inches off the ground on small metal wheels and simply rushed down the crammed corridors, speeding past the Crimea wards, weaving through thronged families, men on their haunches leaning against the walls smoking, a wife comforting a husband in a wheelchair and eventually out, past an old man on crutches, into the sunlight where there was parked a ramshackle green ambulance circa 1914. Into this three men, straining, managed to lift him. Marie climbed in and sat patting his arm comfortingly. '*Don't* do that,' said Eddie, shaking her off. At 53 Demacharus Street, he was lifted, with a great deal of difficulty, on to a small upright wooden chair; this was tilted back and dragged, its legs squealing on the tiled floor, backwards and finally, somehow, wedged into the minute lift. Eddie, his lips collapsed purse-like (he never put his teeth in now), his grey eyes huge behind the cataract glasses, watched, baleful and apprehensive, one toeless stump foot lifted up above the other foot which did have toes, toes with toenails an inch long and curved. When I finally arrived at the flat they had tipped him out of the chair on to the bed, his pyjama trousers pulled down to his ankles in the tussle. 'Fuck you fuck you fuck you fuck you,' Eddie said weakly as they rolled him about.

After that we settled into a sometimes rather bizarre routine. Occasionally, we had visitors. He had a number of friends – Robert Liddell, Peter Mayne, Jonathan Sim, Alan Ansen downstairs – who were very fond of him. But Eddie was getting beyond friendship.

The first two were in their middle seventies, not rich and indeed not long to survive Eddie. They would make the arduous journey across Athens in the heat of the August day, arriving breathless and boiling hot. After about four minutes Eddie would say, 'Well, my dear, you won't think me rude but I'm going to ask you to go now' – and off they went. Alan would be dismissed almost as soon as his head appeared round the door. 'It's all right, Alan my dear, I don't need you.' Only Jonathan Sim, a young (thirty-three), good-looking friend of Julian Jebb, would be allowed to stay longer.

But for most of the time we were alone together in the little flat. Maria made us lunch and she or I cooked supper. I slept in the small sitting room and also worked there. Eddie lay in bed, stoical, querulous, tearful in turn. He was reading the whole of Shakespeare, word by single word, with the aid of an enormous magnifying glass. He did *The Times* crossword using the same instrument. He would call out clues or need more water or shout that he'd lost his cigarettes or his matches or his spectacles. I had brought out the proofs of the public school book, and had to write its introduction and also four articles. One day, I lost patience.

'Eddie – I'm trying to write a book,' I shouted. 'What are you doing?'

'I'm dying, my dear, and it isn't very nice.'

At once I felt ashamed, but noticed as often the infinite and idiosyncratic variations he managed to extract from 'my dear' – a common enough expression in the 1920s. 'My dear' to admonish (as here), to emphasise, to punctuate, to give a remark a throwaway note, as a mild endearment . . . Dr Johnson had the same skill using 'sir', an address also very commonly used in his time.

Eddie had a few minuscule pleasures – but they attempted to take even these. He was allowed cake. 'I'd like a tiny piece of cake please my dear,' he called one afternoon. Then added with typical precision, 'By that, I mean a *small* piece of cake, my dear.' But the doctor suddenly forbade this. Eddie had diabetes. He must have *diabetic* cake. Similarly, to protect the ravaged liver, he cut the daily two small gins to one. Maria baked the diabetic cake and it was revolting. That evening, I found Eddie in tears, the plate of uneaten cake on the Provençal po cupboard beside his bed. He said he felt wretched.

'Soon I will be dead.' I suddenly realised how ridiculous it was, how typically *medical*. I said we would disobey the doctor. I'd get a proper cake and buy another bottle of gin. Eddie cheered up at once. He shouted from the bedroom – 'Bring me *two* slices my dear.'

The indignity of dying. Banning cake and gin, or attempting to, was the least of it. Twice a week a man came to give Eddie an enema. He would roll him about, Eddie's huge, gaunt, yellow body helpless, stuff his finger up his arse – Eddie yelling with surprising strength and fury – and then leave him in all senses drained. Yet he wanted to live. Or rather, he was in the grip of something stronger than, separate from, mere will. 'When I see him eating,' I wrote in my journal, 'with rapid, avid, convulsive cormorant champs of his toothless jaws, it is watching some naked, snarling life force sustaining itself.'

And he did live for several more months, but I never saw him alive again. After nearly four weeks I had to fly back, very behind with my work and frightened about money.

Peter Mayne wrote and told Anne how Eddie was getting on and Alan rang up from time to time. Eddie himself had long ceased to communicate.

(5)

He died just as the public school book was about to come out: 24 May 1978. Cancer of the liver.

Anne and I flew out together. The flat was in some disarray and smelt strongly, in the heatwave then raging, of all Eddie's disabilities and sufferings. I noticed that the Paul Nash had gone and Alan told me Eddie had worried a lot about money in his last months and had finally sold it.

Almost the first thing Anne and I had to do was go and see Dr Panagopoulos, Eddie's lawyer. He had a cool, dark, spacious office in Merlin Street near Kolonaki Square about fifteen minutes' walk from Eddie's flat. Dr Panagopoulos was about forty-five, a small, neat man, highly intelligent, with smooth, shiny black hair and black eyes in an olive face. He spoke perfect English in a low, musical voice. I at once found him hypnotically reassuring. Sitting, sheltered from the heat, in that book-lined sanctum, as I was to do often in the next fourteen years, anxieties and troubles melted away. Dr Panagopoulos would make everything all right. He could even work his magic on the telephone.

On this first occasion, however, he struck, not a false note exactly, but for the only time an inaccurate one.

'We must regret,' said Dr Panagopoulos softly, 'and feel grief, at the passing of an English gentleman of the old school.'

Anne and I glanced at each other and looked down. We sat for a moment in silence. I wanted to say, 'An English *bugger* of the old school, Dr Panagopoulos,' but of course didn't. After a suitable pause, Dr Panagopoulos reached out an olive hand and picked up a document. 'I will read out Mr Gathorne-Hardy's will,' he said.

This came as a complete surprise to me though not, I found later, to Anne. But then, and now when I repeat it, it seems to me there is something almost sublime in its simplicity, its clarity and in its generosity of feeling. Dr Panagopoulos read as follows: ' "I leave everything I possess to my nephew Jonathan Gathorne-Hardy." It is signed "Edward Gathorne-Hardy".'

I looked with new eyes on the flat and everything *it* possessed when we got back. There was a new sharpness, a freshness about the fragment of Etruscan plate, each of the five hundred books, the little nineteenth-century Provençal cupboard. I also felt considerably more regret at the absence of the Nash. It hadn't been necessary (we found there was £5,000 in Eddie's Citibank account, to which the Nash had contributed £1,000). But it is a common phenomenon among the old and dying. As their powers fail, as they totter and feel vulnerable, they feel everything is collapsing, including their bank accounts. It had led to my parents selling the Picasso.

But I now began to sign and cash cheques recklessly and excitedly. The money, coming unexpectedly, not having been earned, seemed quite unreal. There were quite a lot of bills and fees for things not covered by BUPA. The funeral had to be arranged and paid for.

About eight people came to this, including Alan, Robert Liddell, Peter Mayne, Maria, Jonathan Sim and a very old eccentric Greek figure called General Thanos. It was extremely hot as we trooped through the vast necropolis, especially for Anne who, distracted by events, had by mistake put on two skirts. We passed jumbled tombs, dying flowers and similar groups with coffins. When we passed them they stopped and crossed themselves. At one point a procession of about a hundred people stopped and crossed themselves. 'Eddie would have been very pleased,' said Anne. The grave in the Protestant section was surprisingly shallow. Only about eight inches of earth would cover my uncle. I also noticed that the clergyman, a willowy, over-histrionic young man, was naked except for skimpy pants under his long gauzy priestly garment – you could just make out his dark nipples.

I had bought a lot of pastis and wine and nuts and we had them in the flat afterwards. General Thanos became very voluble. He turned out to be an admiral as well.* I asked Eddie's closest friends to come later and choose what they liked, with the proviso that I would veto anything excessive. They did come and were not excessive, though Jonathan Sim, with a large, very pretty antique Lebanese tray, was borderline. Alan told me Maria was expecting 75,000 drachmas, so I gave her 100,000 of the unreal money.

Everything was unreal. Death, which in fact gives life its reality, can for a while take it away and seem all there is. I knew Jock was dying – all my closest relatives of his generation and before had died within a few years. Aunt Mary had died soon after my mother, before I could question her about Go-Go. Athens had become the anvil of

---

* General/Admiral Thanos had helped found the Greek air force. He was eighty-three and a man of great charm. He was a genuine hero as well as a genuine eccentric. In an earlier Greek war he had landed a small biplane in a Bulgarian city square, got out, walked through the astonished populace (they had never seen an aeroplane before), pulled down the Bulgarian flag, replaced it with the Greek one and flown off again. A stamp had been issued to celebrate the incident. Between wars he had been unofficial procurer for homosexuals in the government. He made a fortune. To the soldiers he would say, 'They'll only pay 50 drachmas,' and to the cabinet ministers, 'I'm afraid they'll only do it for 500 drachmas.' The fortune had been spent. He now lived in one small room near Syntagma Square and mostly subsisted by gatecrashing parties and filling his pockets with whatever was there to eat. He was also an inventor. He had had a long glass tube blown into the shape of a cock with two glass balls at one end. You put oil and vinegar in the balls, shook the whole thing violently, and then directed the resulting orgasm on to your salad.

the sun, and walking under its hammer blows on some Eddie business or other, I was about to step off a pavement, when a car moved abruptly away from it in front of me. I looked angrily in to see the face of the driver and saw, to my horror, a skull. The car went forward further and it was just a young woman.

Anne and I stayed a few more days. I arranged to have all Eddie's furniture and books packed up and sent to West Lodge. I asked Dr Panagopoulos to have the flat cleared, decorated, furnished and let. This was eventually done and for thirteen years it brought in about £1,000 a year which was put into an account in the Citibank and paid for holidays in Greece. The life of a *rentier* is not without hiccoughs. One tenant left without paying any rent, bills of over £1,800 and with most of the furniture. But Dr Panagopoulos solved everything. In the end, in 1992, I was overdrawn £10,000; he sold the flat for £20,000, I paid off the overdraft and lived on the rest for a year.

The overdraft was partly the result of taking five years instead of three to write a biography of Gerald Brenan. Several books have cost me money in this way, but the public school book, for the publication of which I now hurried back, didn't, though I believe the American publisher lost quite a lot.

(6)

I began the public school book in 1972, just as the oil prices began to cause hyper-inflation. It was clear that coal would be vital (a fact the miners soon exploited). It seemed to me the safest thing would be if this was what my advance was paid in, or partly paid in. I asked Diana to arrange this with Hodder and Stoughton and meanwhile readied Sarah for the avalanche. Together we cleared her cellar.

The board at Hodders apparently seriously considered this, I now see, bizarre suggestion, but in the end decided it wasn't practical. If things got bad they would consider increasing the advance. Things did get bad. Inflation rose to 17.5 per cent. They gave me another £1,000 – but I would have done better with coal.

I dread starting any book, whether non-fiction or a novel, and with every book, at some point – quarter way through, halfway – I realise it is not going to be the masterpiece I'd conceived, or even just as good as the book I'd conceived. The *next* book will be that. In this I resemble all writers.

As soon as I realise the current book is not the masterpiece, I long to finish it and get on to the Next Book. With non-fiction my desperate desire for rapidity is frustrated by an excessive, often absurd conscientiousness hammered into me at Bryanston. But usually it gets easier as the end approaches. The thousands of words stretching out behind, like the miles on a journey, testify to fewer and fewer ahead. But with the public school book, the opposite happened. The huge mountain of words (eventually 480 pages, the book was at this point 60,000 words too long) towered in front of me and, with each successive sentence, had, with a superhuman effort, to be heaved forward. At the end I was near breakdown. I arranged to stay with Tim in Italy. I wanted to be as far from public schools as possible. I didn't want to read another book about them, see another one, hear another public school voice ever again. I hated them and everything about them. The day after I had finally completed the index, working till four in the morning with Sarah, I went to Victoria Station. At the enquiry office I heard myself saying, 'Could you tell me which chapter the train to Dover goes from?'

Yet it was not all hell. For one thing, it led to some curious encounters; one, a typical Sassoon-type brush with the great, was with Harold Macmillan.

(7)

Julian Jebb said he thought Diana Cooper, with whom he was friendly, might have ideas about the book. She said, 'You must meet Macmillan. I'll ask him to lunch.'

An odd element about this was that Diana Cooper lived in the same house Anna and Heywood had had on lease from the Church Commissioners for thirty years – 10 Warwick Avenue. But it had been completely changed – walls, staircase, windows, floors, all knocked down, ripped up, rebuilt. Arriving, nervous and too early, was like walking into a strange dream. Only the intermittent earthquake rumble far below of trains passing on the Bakerloo line was the same.

We were about eight, I think; I can remember only Diana Cooper, her son, John Julius, me, Macmillan's private secretary and the ex-prime minister himself. Nor do I really remember the conversation. Macmillan talked for forty bored seconds about Eton, and then took off. Far too adrenalised, I excitedly took off too until I felt a sharp kick and Diana whispered, 'Let the old boy have his say,' which, then at the peak of his second career as a raconteur, he did for the rest of lunch with considerable eloquence. All I remember him saying was that he wished he'd had the foreign policy situation pertaining then, in 1972: '*Two* communist powers makes all the difference. You can play them off against each other!' But to my horror, when we got up from the table, he came and put his arm round my shoulder and sat us both down on a small sofa.

'Tell me – what would *you* do now?'

He was referring, I luckily realised, to the current unrest among the unions – particularly the miners. What *would* I do? Call out the army? Huge wage increases? My mind went blank. At last, not really knowing what I meant but because I had been discussing him with Dr John Rae, the headmaster of Westminster, I said, 'Wedgwood Benn?'

'*Very* interesting,' said Macmillan, getting up. '*Most* interesting. That's exactly what Maurice says.'

How useful his charm must have been. Diana Cooper had great charm too. What chiefly struck me was how much she enjoyed the company of men and how, therefore, they responded to her – me included, in the two or three times we met after that in a nearby pub.

A second Sassoon meeting like this threw light, or perhaps didn't, on another prime minister, Ted Heath. I had arranged, again thanks to Julian, to see John Betjeman to talk about Marlborough. I arrived at 10.45 in the morning. 'I thought we should have some champagne,' said Betjeman. There were two bottles standing on a tray. We quickly gravitated to love and sex at Marlborough. And then sex in general. And then Ted Heath and sex. Betjeman had seen the prime minister several times, most recently at Chequers. 'Ghastly occasions,' he said. 'No attempt to choose compatible people – a black bishop next to a famous yachtsman, me and some business tycoon. I've tried to guess Heath's percentage before – not a clue.' It was Betjeman's view that everyone, every man at least, was to a greater or lesser extent homosexual. That extent was his 'percentage'. 'But this time,' he said, 'I think I spotted it.' Heath had asked his group of incompatible guests what they wanted to drink. Then he'd stumped over to a drinks table to get them. Betjeman got up and stumped over to the tray and second bottle of champagne, imitating. 'It was when he turned round I got it,' he said. He turned himself, holding the tray, and as he did so made a wonderful, dainty, camp, flirtatious, suggestive wriggle and swing, a rumba movement, with his bottom. 'Like a Nippy,' said Betjeman. 'Gone in a flash; quite unconscious, of course. You can't control that sort of thing. I'd say eighty per cent.'

I couldn't use much of this, though Betjeman was illuminating about love and sex at Marlborough. But without John Rae, I couldn't have written the book at all.

(8)

I hadn't got far researching it before I realised I was being choked off. School after school, politely, even charmingly, told me it wasn't possible for me to come and see them. At last Dr Rae of Westminster agreed to talk to me. He was also, at this time, chairman of the Headmasters' Conference. Soon after we began talking, I became aware of expanding flakes of some white substance pouring from my cigarette. Quite soon, we were in a blizzard. We could hardly see each other. I realised that Ben had stuck a lot of his 'Make a Gigantic Snow Storm!' pellets into my cigarette. Partly as a result, John Rae and I got on very well. He saw no reason why I shouldn't pursue my task. 'I'll have a word.' Opposition vanished.

Rae also gave me many other insights into the system apart from this 'I'll have a word' demonstration. He read the manuscript of the completed book and corrected a great many mistakes. He gave me several useful introductions. The one thing he didn't tell me about was the 'Jewish Quota'. The shameful fact that many public schools set a limit to the number of Jewish pupils they would admit a year. But then, none of the schools, none of the people I talked to told me about this.

Public schools are, in fact, rather extraordinary institutions – unless you have been to them, in which case they seem perfectly normal.

But it was possible, indeed it was essential, to observe them and write about them as if I hadn't been to one. Erving Goffman's *Asylums* was a great help here. I learnt from him that public schools were in very significant ways the same as the monasteries, mental hospitals, prisons, concentration camps, warships and army barracks Goffman had studied (as he had, in fact, public schools).

I became obsessed with girls' education and progressive education, for some reason ignored by the dozens of other general histories. Their writers, all public school men (no women) had also forgotten what it was like to be taken from home at too early an age. I still remembered the pain I'd felt sitting alone, aged ten, in Anne's, now Diana Cooper's, kitchen. I therefore read anthropology. Anthropologists have looked at some sixty different cultures and societies. Some are quite small – a few hundred or a thousand members. Their relevance to populations of millions can seem remote. But they are often the same size as public schools. I found that about half the societies studied had used 'extrusion' – the technical term for removing children from their families – to stamp the lessons and customs of their culture on their young. Half didn't. And the two systems were designed to produce completely different societies. This clearly had a bearing on class divisions in Britain. The state system allows children to remain at home while being taught. On the whole, the public school system does not. It seems possible we are, in a profound anthropological sense, still, two different cultures.*

The book, *The Public School Phenomenon*, came out in 1977. On the

---

* All this – Goffman, anthropology, etc. – fascinated me. But they are complex subjects; they need the space I could give them in the book. However, the anthropological analysis, if correct, is another argument for abolition which I argued for. Public schools give unfair advantages to families with money and on these grounds alone should be closed. Yet this, too, is complex. For instance, the idea that abolishing public schools would lessen the self-replicating middle-class grip on better jobs and more money is probably wrong. For one thing, it has been tried before. In the sixteenth century Catholic public schools were banned in England. The schools simply transferred to France and Ireland. The same would happen today. Then, France has no effective public school system, but it has an equally powerful and entrenched middle and upper class who operate through the medium of state lycées in areas too expensive for anyone but the well-off whole, it was very well reviewed. Once again I experienced the brief, illusory flare of short-lived fame; then, as far as anyone knew, I vanished. It sold quite well in Britain – or at least it made its advance; but rather less well in America, despite extensive and laudatory reviews (for instance, like the nanny book, a two-page spread in *Time*).

I was also attacked. One angry man said it was unprincipled to argue for the abolition of the system and then send my children through it. There was force in this, but there was still overwhelming evidence that the education given by public schools was, however unfair, better than that obtained in the state system. I didn't see why I should disadvantage Jenny and Ben in relation to their peers. Some reviewers complained because I hadn't given enough attention to their own school. But, as I say, on the whole the book was well received.

In the next non-fiction book, commissioned by Tom Maschler at Cape, I was to experience an eerie echo from the past, or perhaps from the spirit world. I also learnt more about the mechanisms at play in the minds of publishers.

(9)

Just as Weidenfeld expressed the buried, or neglected, scholar in him by commissioning popular historical works from academia, so other publishers satisfy or express some aspect of their lives by the books they commission. In 1978 Tom Maschler's marriage to Fay was going through a difficult period (they later divorced). As an old friend of

---

and which lead later to the grandes écoles and grands corps. This does not affect the anthropological argument for abolition, nor that on the grounds of fairness. But it is a balanced argument; there are two sides – essentially, equality versus liberty. Ignoring for the moment the fact they would just go abroad, a number of people think that public schools are too valuable an educational asset to be destroyed. A suggested solution is that they should be asked, or compelled, to take a high proportion of state school pupils. But this was tried in the late '40s and '50s and very few state pupils wanted to go. Perhaps it would work today. In the hardback edition I argued for abolition within a wider educational reform, but in the Penguin edition this seemed like equivocation and I went for straight abolition. Today I am uncertain.

Fay's, Tom asked me out to dinner to discuss it. Soon after this he rang me. 'It's becoming very clear to me that marriage and divorce are the two most important single subjects today. How would you like to write a book tackling the whole field?'

I had two battles over this book, both of which I lost. I wanted to call it *The Way We Love Now*; Tom wanted *Love, Sex, Marriage and Divorce*. I got some friends at OBM to put these titles, and two others, on to a list of product names being tested. *The Way We Love Now* not only came out best but by far the best. Tom, however, insisted on his title. In America the book was called *Sex, Love, Marriage and Divorce*, which may or may not say something significant about our two cultures.

Then, about two years after the book came out, that is in 1983, Tom rang me and said someone called Brenda Maddox was suing me for plagiarism.

You may be surprised to learn it is very easy to commit plagiarism by mistake. In this instance, Brenda Maddox had written a book about stepchildren called *The Half-Parent – Living With Other People's Children*. Looking through my notes I realised with sinking heart that plagiarism was just possible. Usually, I take notes from what I read – condensing, précising, etc. But every so often a book is so succinct, so well written, it is quicker just to copy out a few relevant passages. Maddox's book on the step situation was such a book. I had read it early on. I had then read some ninety other books and papers and taken sixty interviews. If I had been careless and forgotten to add quotation marks, I could easily, three years later, have copied into my book passages which were really hers.

But that didn't seem to me to be the point. I had singled out two books in the introduction as being particularly valuable. One of these was *The Half-Parent*. In the eight pages devoted to step problems, Brenda Maddox and her book are cited on every page, often two or three times a page, as the authority and source for what I am saying. It was perfectly obvious the whole section was her views and her discoveries. I regarded plagiarism as trying surreptitiously to pass off someone else's work as your own. Nobody reading my book could possibly think the material on stepchildren, the conclusions about them, were anything but Brenda Maddox's. I even, at one point, called her 'charming'. (I'd given her lunch so we could discuss these matters.)

I therefore determined to fight. Graham C. Greene, whom I'd met at Cape once or twice and was then the chairman, went with me to the offices of Rubinstein and Nash, the libel lawyers. There Michael Rubinstein showed me that four or five paragraphs and a table were, in fact, taken from her book.

'But surely,' I said, 'that isn't the real point.' I pointed out all the Maddoxes, I pointed to the introduction. 'It's perfectly clear, I say so, that all the material is hers and comes from her book.'

'You are quite right,' said the gentle, silky, regretful Mr Rubinstein. 'You do. I quite see that. But the law is also clear. If a passage from someone else's writing is used without quotation marks and without permission or direct acknowledgement, that is plagiarism.'

We sat in silence. I still felt stubborn. I would still fight, if necessary alone. Then Graham C. Greene said, 'I'm afraid the woman has you over a barrel, Jonny. There's nothing you can do.'

At the words 'over a barrel' I felt gooseflesh running down my neck and over my body. Like the Aztecs faced by their Conquistadors foretold, the fight went out of me. It was fated.

Jenny wrote a sweet, tearful-little-daughter-of-a-penniless-author letter, which we composed together, but Brenda Maddox's heart was not even remotely touched. She briskly took, as she had every right to do, her £1,500 or £2,000 – I forget the exact sum – which I borrowed from the bank and paid back over three years. The paperback had just been printed so I wasn't even able to delete 'charming'.

However, it was not all bad news. The fortune teller Mr Taylor had also said I would be rich in my early sixties. Clearly, his timing was way out. It could, therefore, be late sixties (now) or even seventies. And this débâcle did, I realised, remove from the erotic novel about my love affair with Anna and the kidnapping the embargo placed by wrongly assigning his 'over a barrel' prophecy.

(10)

The period after *The Way We Love Now*, that is the early 1980s, was
for some reason very fraught financially. One evening, at a dinner
party, I was sitting next to Sally Beauman. She was a journalist then,
who had just written a history of the Royal Shakespeare Company,
but she told me that she had recently found an extraordinarily
lucrative source of income – Mills and Boon romances. She found
she could write them effortlessly. She felt like a romance Enid Blyton
as they poured from her fingertips along the keys of her typewriter.
Three that year. A *minimum* of £20,000 each. Plus later royalties.

Twenty thousand pounds! The following day I went out and bought
eight Mills and Boon romances. I read them all (itself something of a
feat) and made a five-page analysis – length (60,000 words), timing of
first kiss (within first seven pages), character of hero, of heroine,
whether they fucked or not . . . (They didn't then, or not until the last
page after marriage. Now I believe they do. Also now Mills and Boon
will send you their own analysis.)

I then worked out a plot – essentially, like all of them, a much
coarsened *Jane Eyre*, reduced to infinitely teased desire, almost
infinitely delayed satisfaction, wealthy, apparently cruel but in the
end softened hero, exotic location, passionate, naïve, would-be
independent but much more would-be married heroine, etc. The
books were written in an oddly breathless style which I thought
could be achieved only if they were actually written at break-neck
speed.

I therefore decided to go to West Lodge and stay there alone until
I'd finished *The Man from the Sea*. It was far harder than I'd imagined.
The books are appallingly written – but it is as difficult to write badly,
to use clichés, as it is to write well, especially if to write well and not
use clichés is what you've been trying to do for twenty-five years.
There were two good images. I started the book with the dolphins,
which had played round Ralph Partridge in the sea near La Coruña,
playing about my hero. Hence the title. The second was a simile for
a grove of eucalyptus in Spain which, as they swayed in the wind,
their tall, slender, mottled trunks occasionally touching, stood like a

herd of gentle giraffes nibbling each other's leaves. But it stuck out and had to go. I thought I should immerse myself totally in Mills and Boon, reading them at the time as well as writing one. But after five days I began to feel completely mad. I read Seutonius's *Lives of the Caesars* instead. Nor could I keep it up till I had finished. This took two ten-day stints. There remained only the name of the author – and a publisher.

Two months later, in July 1981, Sylvia Thornton tripped round, in response to their request, to the offices of Mills and Boon, at that time off Davis Street, London W1. I was seen by the extremely attractive, mid-thirties managing director who, had she been less intelligent, might have been a slightly older heroine (they were usually in their early twenties) in one of her publications. *The Man from the Sea* had very nearly made it. *Very* nearly. The only defect had been that the protagonists weren't physically close together very often. Desire at a distance wasn't enough. 'We like to keep what we call "the throb" going right through the book.' I should try again and please be sure and send them the next Sylvia Thornton romance.

She was quite right. Ordinary exchanges between Melissa (Mel) and Darien I could manage.

' "What's so awful about it?" Darien's lip was curled. "You seem able to kiss my groom easily enough."'

'Mel flushed angrily, but she bit back the retort that rose to her lips.'

But their passion when they were together defeated me. I cobbled together five passages of pastiche and these had had to do. Luckily, they were enough for Sapphire Romances, a mail order imprint just started by Hamlyn. I was paid £1,000 for all rights and no further royalties and *The Man from the Sea* came out in 1982.

The print run was the second largest of anything I've written – 30,000. (The largest was that of *Chameleon* in Romania – 60,000.) I found I was one of three men out of over 150 women. I appeared on an afternoon TV show (both the other men refused). I was with Violet Winspeare, doyenne of ordinary romances, and a writer who specialised in doctor/hospital romances. (The other category is historical.) Both women had been flown in from tax havens. All I remember about the show is their outrage when I suggested there was an element, a tiny *tiny* element, of formula about the books.

I am still proud of *The Man from the Sea*, and I enjoyed letters arriving for Ms Sylvia Thornton at West Lodge. However, though £1,000 was very useful, it didn't last long and I was soon broke again. I wrote three chapters of a second romance but I could get no further. Once again, I was at the mercy of publishers.

(11)

After three months, overdraft rising, the only book on offer was one about doctors. The idea was John Gross's, then working for George Weidenfeld. Needing for my self-respect some rationale as well as money, just as I had needed to see public schools as a completion of the nanny book, I decided a study of GPs would also be a study of my father – and in a way that is what it was.

To write *Doctors*, I had to drive all over Britain, from Cornwall to the Highlands, Norfolk to Wales, and record interviews with some seventy GPs. After the last of these trips I decided to edit the 200 or so tapes at Buckfast Abbey in Devon. I had used the peace and isolation of Buckfast before, but I had already been away from Sarah for several weeks and should have spent time in London. There was an additional reason for Buckfast.

It was winter and very cold. For ten days the monastery had no other visitors. Warm enough in my little room, I worked seven or eight hours a day at the tapes. It was a strange experience, reliving those trips through the GPs' voices. I became aware of things I hadn't noticed at the time. Throughout one long interview with an exceptionally calm and competent doctor I now heard the insistent tapping of his signet ring against the edge of his desk. I interpreted this as a sign of considerable tension – and learnt from his wife months after the work had come out that he had in fact had a nervous breakdown soon after I had left.

I was still able to go for runs then and every afternoon for an hour or so I left the monastery and ran up under the bare beeches beside the River Dart, here still quite small and noisy, its icy, peat-coloured waters rushing down off the huge expanses of the wild moor from which it got its name. And soon I was up there running across those treeless billows of heath and grass and wind, escaping myself, exercise beating into me, until, exhausted, I had to turn back, the wind behind, down past the rushing river and the beeches and so back to my hot little room and the tapes again.

Three or four times I attended compline, the last service of the day. Not from any religious motive but out of politeness. This was their work and very important to them. Also, I was moved by the echoing abbey at night – the little band of monks in their black habits, the long drifting rise and fall of the Gregorian chant, answering and re-answering, answering and re-answering, still in Latin, the sense of a past stretching back 1,300 years.

On one of these nights I had my second experience of God – or gods.

It was particularly dark and windy. I sat at the back, alone in the vast abbey except for the monks in the choir stalls at the front. The spotlight on the altar, on a banner with the white head of a stag sticking out from a pillar, the candles in the choir, all made a cavern of light far down the church; all else, the roof, the extremities, me included, were in darkness. The abbey seemed submerged deep in a lake of wind and I could hear its currents swirling round the tower.

Then, as I half-listened to the chanting, to the wind, felt it all about me, I had a sudden moment of intensity – the church itself seemed to become a huge cave, something incredibly ancient, the stag a primitive wall painting, and once again, as on Crete, I was aware of a presence, or presences, and heard, so clearly that I shivered, a voice coming from the darkness: 'I am what you think I am.'

I returned to my room considerably shaken. I remained shaken for several days; indeed I returned to what had happened intermittently for a long time. What had it meant? 'I am what you think I am.' Did it mean God existed? Would I have to recast my whole life?

I suppose Pantheism came nearest to what I believed, except that Pantheism is the belief that God is present in Pan, in nature. But I hadn't really believed in God since my fight with Gathorne. I believed the opposite. It was intense feelings about nature that had led people to infer, to believe in, a God – or gods.

And not just nature. The derelict area of a railway siding, the roofs of Aldeburgh, the sitting room at the Arch . . . moments of intensity which come haphazardly, without warning, and which much earlier had made me feel I was special, a writer, gifted, but which are in fact common to all humanity, during those moments we seem to be taken over by an outside force, to be merged with what we see. So strong is the response, so swamping of self, the feeling is – *it must be something more*. And these moments, in turn, seemed to me to have developed from, or be a recurrence of, the condition of childhood and babyhood when there is no real boundary between oneself and the outside world, between the outside world and one's imagination – immersed in my mother's eiderdown I was in a field, the little silver animals were real, my 'self' was as lost as when I ran in the winter gale across Dartmoor or, walking alone, breasted the endless currents of air flowing across the great green downland which surrounded Bryanston. 'I am what you think I am' was really, or also, 'I am what you have felt.'

When Coleridge stretched his arms to the moon his fundamental Christianity was reawakened. He recognised in himself, wrote Richard Holmes, 'a profoundly religious instinct . . . about divine power radiating through the natural universe'. If I too had been a Christian believer, then it would have been this faith that would have been confirmed. 'I am what you think I am.' A truly Delphic utterance.

I had another week to go at Buckfast. Towards the end of this, Sarah rang me. She thought it might be better if we separated. Did I agree? With guilt, but guilt overwhelmed by relief, I said yes.

The reason was I had fallen in love with Nicky.

(12)

Nicky was the eldest of Eliza's three daughters, aged twelve when I first saw her. Of course, I was aware of Eliza's children but in my obsession that was about it. I was also aware of the direction Nicky's attraction already looked likely to take. It was one I'd often followed – that of slant-eyed, full-mouthed, high-cheekboned beauty.

When I met her properly again thirty years later, I was amazed by the extent to which this had happened. I think I must have fallen in love almost the moment I saw her – though the event is a blank. It was my fiftieth birthday party and apparently I asked her to marry me but I was far too drunk to remember. All I do remember was that, like my mother when I was nine, I insisted on being undressed and put to bed by my own flesh and blood – in this case Sammy on leave from Malaya.

Too cowardly to tell Sarah, it took several months before my behaviour – or rather lack of it since I spent the entire time pursuing doctors – led her to make the telephone call that released me (somewhat to Sarah's surprise I suspect. I think she thought it would bring me to heel.)

Nicky and I began to live together more or less at once, causing a slight stir among those who knew our joint pasts, which had since diverged completely. But gossip is the lifeblood of social life and everyone must contribute their quota. A blamelessly conventional life is a theft on the community.

I won't go into my life with Nicky since it is still, thank goodness, going on. Except to say I had no idea the love of one's life could come near its end and no idea that passion and interest and humour could, like that bubbling spring in the deep clearness of Bob's Blue Pool, still continually create themselves for twenty years – and for as far ahead as I can see; nor did I know that it is possible to be almost as fond of someone else's children as of your own. I do now at last understand what Frances meant: 'People are laughed at when they have too many shots at marriage, failing and trying again. But they shouldn't be, for they are after the best thing.'

Despite our divergence, I found Nicky had sometimes been nearer me than I'd realised. She'd stayed at Snape when my grandmother had been alive. She'd also been taken over to 18 Hartington Road and, to my intense surprise, told me she'd been shocked by how shabby it was. *Shabby?* It had never struck me as remotely shabby – yet, looking back, I see now that perhaps it was. I don't think you notice your own shabbiness. Furthermore, I think a *home* should be shabby. Certainly, the two joined cottages where we live now are shabby enough – and we, or at least I, don't notice at all.

One thing we resolved to do early on was to see more of Julian Jebb. Although there had been no breach and I still considered him one of my closest friends, for some reason I had seen less of him during the eight years with Sarah than I had before. By chance, Nicky and I met him at someone's morning drinks party soon after we were together (Julian drinking the champagne he'd long ago resembled) and I told him of our determination. There was something curious about his expression in response which I couldn't, can't, define, but which I still remember; it was fond but detached, his now rather puffy eyes slightly closed as if half-listening to something in the distance, very calm, a faint smile, an expression of – Ah Jonny . . . I realised later that he must have already decided to kill himself, which he did eight days later.

(13)

In a mild way, Julian had shown what might have been interpreted as self-destructive tendencies for years. He ran through two legacies, saving nothing and buying nothing lasting, at astonishing speed – one, at Cambridge and, just after, another, each of about £16,000. He was always losing or breaking things, often presents people had given him. He deliberately forgot to pay bills and his last but one dwelling, Jennifer Ross's basement flat, he set on fire – losing all the letters over many years from the friends he valued more than anything.

More serious, in a cumulative way, were sleeping pills and drink. Sleeping pills almost every night, drink starting before lunch – vodka for preference washed down with wine. He twice did two-week stints in an extremely gloomy detox centre called, rather inappropriately, St Bernard's, at what felt like a ten hours' jolting bus ride from the middle of London. I went to see him there and he was too unhappy even to try and be amusing about his fellow patients shuffling to and fro. He would stay dry for a few months but find it unbearable. Barry Humphries, who had been saved by Alcoholics Anonymous, frequently urged him to go to them but Julian wouldn't. I imagine his reaction against Catholicism made their accent on religion repugnant. In the two longest letters he wrote in explanation of his suicide he said it was because he felt he was turning into his mother. It is true Eleanor Jebb drank a good deal towards the end of her life. Tristram Powell, staying at Kingsland and going for a pee at two in the morning, found her standing in the passage with a pint mug in her hand. 'Look how lucky I am,' she said, 'someone has just given me this lovely beaker full of delicious sherry.' But more relevant was her increasingly sharp tongue and her seeming hatred of any visitor.

A growing element of aggression surfaced in Julian during his last years. It could just have been a response to the extremely unsatisfactory nature of two major areas of his life – love affairs and work. But, as I said earlier when comparing him to Proust – to Alain de Botton's Proust – I felt that he may quite often have found in himself angry feelings, or different feelings, towards his friends which his whole way of behaving with them, of loving them, had made it difficult to express. Now, these feelings began to force their way out. I remember a violent attack he made on me without warning when I went for a drink in his flat (still Jennifer's basement, repaired). I had been discussing with Richard King the possibility of raising money to buy Julian a flat of his own. Julian now suddenly asked me furiously what right I had to interfere in his affairs. I had no right. It was monstrous of me. He went on and on. Eventually, both shaking, we had to break off as we were having supper with Jennifer upstairs. An uneasy meal.

It is seldom possible to know exactly why people kill themselves, but towards the end Julian's life became more and more difficult and chaotic. He was now addicted to Ativan. He had had almost no stable love affairs. His liaisons ran into difficulties because, terrified of appearing clinging – and unable not to be clinging – he concealed it, or expressed it, by a bossy, pernickety possessiveness. This was an increasing element in his final partnership, one of the longest in his life, with a young singer called Alan Young. For two years they lived in Julian's spacious flat on Ladbroke Grove, bought with the inter-est-free loan which Julian had finally accepted from Richard (and which, of course, he was not expected to pay back and didn't). It is also possible Julian had a frustrated heterosexual side (something not often realised about homosexuals). He had strong, even passionate, emotional involvements with women. In two cases older, with Jennifer and Eliza. But there were several much younger women, younger than he was – Sylvia Millar, Tammy Broughton, Vivian King. Vivian had concrete evidence that Julian desired her. A few months before his death Julian and Alan went on holiday to Spain and then Greece. In Spain they stayed with Eliza. Julian was drinking far more heavily than she'd ever seen and was in turn aggressive or despairing and suicidal.

But the events, in my view, which finally tipped him into suicide were what he had to undergo at the BBC. For a long time there he was protected, and allowed to flower, by Melvin Bragg. But Bragg moved on and up – and Julian's later years were a catalogue of humiliation and cruelty. Younger men were promoted over him and given work he used to do. He was moved to smaller and smaller offices. He and his suggestions were ignored, he was openly despised and disliked and his work regularly rubbished, when he was given work, which became less and less often. His last film, about the Booker Prize, was cut to pieces; unfairly, since he had correctly predicted the winner – Anita Brookner.

That the BBC were aware of what they had done is suggested by their behaviour after his suicide. Alan Yentob, not his immediate boss, and so not directly responsible, but heading the department, arranged for the BBC to pay for the party after the funeral. And Julian's Alan Young, in a surprising move – surprisingly generous and, well, just surprising – was given a small widow's pension, which he still draws.

Julian killed himself with sleeping pills while Alan was still in Greece. He left the two letters I've mentioned and about ten others which simply said, 'Thank you for loving me, Julian.'

'All deaths are sad except one's own,' Gerald wrote once. Yes, sad and upsetting, but the most upsetting are those self-inflicted – because they are unexpected, because it is painful to think of the suffering that led to them, and because you think 'If only I'd . . . ' I still miss Julian, he still comes into my dreams, I still think 'if only'.

(14)

In September 1984, a few weeks before Julian's death, I'd left London where I'd been living for thirty years and gone to live with Nicky in north Norfolk.

Years before, while exploring Pompeii and Herculaneum, I'd been surprised by how much of the last, before A.D. 79 the wealthiest of all those Cities of the Plain, still lay unexcavated in its tomb of lava and mud. The reason was that this tomb itself lay under the Naples slums of Ercolano. If you were to hire a cellar, say, in one of those slum houses, sink a shaft and then tunnel out in all directions, surely you would find treasure. This is exactly what had been done in a limited way in the eighteenth century and the most beautiful and most valuable objects, statues and jewellery of that whole disaster came from Herculaneum as a result. I thought of a thriller based on this idea and Christopher Sinclair-Stevenson, who had long been running Hamish Hamilton, commissioned it.

Nicky and I went out to Ercolano. We were able to get down to the still buried Roman theatre hollowed out in the eighteenth century and the tunnels snaking away under sixty feet of hardened lava and Italian slums. We saw Dott. Maria Cerulli Irelli, Soprintendente Archeologica di Pompeii, and saw also the young man who was the architect in charge at Herculaneum – and learnt my basic ideas were all sound. We came back and I wrote the book.

It was not a great book – no danger of my life being forfeit to Olympus – but it was a competent thriller. But it was spoilt because I seemed to have misled Christopher. He had expected something more profound, something on Graham Greene lines. In an attempt to gain some depth he suggested I kill off my beautiful twenty-four-year-old heroine, which I very reluctantly did. But the book had a marvellous title – *The City Beneath the Skin*. This was the invention of Julian Evans, a brilliant young editor of Christopher's.

It was Julian Evans who suggested I write Gerald's biography. At once I felt the usual combination of dread, of inadequacy, of shrinking from the terrible labour of writing. I said I'd have to think about it. I'd also have to ask him. Gerald, at ninety-two a year before he died, deeply depressed and fairly gaga, said gloomily, 'Anyone can write my life.' But I discovered while I was there that someone was already writing it. A young American called Sam Abrams had been writing it for *two years*! Jealousy swept away reluctance. I didn't particularly want to write Gerald's life, but I certainly wasn't going to let someone else do it.

(15)

With the Gerald book we fairly rapidly moved towards financial disaster. Nicky had no money at all except what she earned from her painting, but a kind and wealthy relation gave her £800 a month. Buoyed up by this, I once again moved for a while with all the gaiety of the at least half-kept man. When Christopher asked me how much I'd need for Gerald, I said the book would take three years. With Nicky's allowance, I thought I could do it for £25,000. Two things ruined my calculations. The book took five years, and about four months after I'd signed the contract the wealthy relative found they could no longer go on paying Nicky's £800 a month – though, in generous recompense, they would pay off the small mortgage we'd had to raise to jointly buy our house (I sold West Lodge). It wasn't mentioned, but I suspect they felt they could stop since she was now being supported – which was half true.

The trouble about publishers' advances is that you don't get all of the money in advance of writing the book, a period during which you and anyone dependent on you (Nicky had three young children) still have to live. You get, say, one-third on signature of the contract, one-third on finishing the book, and one-third on publication. Christopher was kind enough to give me more earlier, but still not all the £25,000. Nicky's painting did better and better (eventually she was to provide about a quarter of our income) but I ran out after two years. I managed to raise another £22,000 through foundations and thanks to Dolf Mootham, one of the most generous of all my generous rich friends, who gave us £10,000.* By the end, I was overdrawn about £7,000.

Gerald did well – for a biography about someone almost no one had heard of. Christopher made his advance. But the thing about biographies is you can roughly guess what the sales will be. There is no reason a lot of people should want to read, or buy, a book about someone they've never heard of or are not interested in. If you write

---

* At another such crisis Tim Behrens, suddenly rich, also gave me £10,000. It is very rare, in my experience, which is extensive, for rich friends, however generous, actually to give money.

a biography of Oscar Wilde or the current top footballer, or the Queen, you'll sell in thousands or even in hundred thousands. If you write about someone unknown, however well you write, you won't even get into double figures.

I got the last part of the advance on publication in 1992, and nothing after (US and paperback sales went to Christopher). When the overdraft reached £10,000, supported as usual by our Binham home, I realised I would have to sell Eddie's flat. For the last time, I listened to Dr Panagopoulos's soothing voice flowing softly down the line from Merlin Street in Athens and inducing a state close to bliss. He thought, as I described earlier, we would get the equivalent of £20,000, and we did. I paid off the overdraft and started another novel. When I was overdrawn again for £9,000 I submitted my usual list to Christopher of books I might write.

What I really wanted to do was a study of the history and art of conversation. Christopher, however, preferred a biography of Alfred Kinsey, the American entomologist and sex researcher and my early sexual mentor in the Nissen huts of Arbroath. An advance of £75,000 was arranged and Nicky and I went to live for seven difficult months in Bloomington, Indiana, where Kinsey had lived and worked.

I had written earlier to Bloomington to make sure no one else was doing the same thing but found when I arrived that I had been misinformed. To my horror, I discovered an academic called James Jones had been writing a biography since 1972. It was clear I couldn't possibly come out before him and that really I should go straight home again, but I had already spent £10,000 of the advance on the overdraft and Christopher didn't seem likely to pay £75,000 for a history of conversation. I decided I would just have to plough on.

Biographies are nearly always to some extent autobiographies. Gerald shared my money worries and for the same reason; Kinsey my early sexual frustrations, though while with me they ended at twenty, Kinsey was twenty-seven. Since sex and money are important in people's lives, I think these identifications led to useful insights. But Kinsey was, eventually, far more sexually adventurous than me. With considerable difficulty I eventually found out that he was for many years bisexual and eventually essentially homosexual. He had sex with both husbands and wives in his team and encouraged them and his wife to do the same. Jones, since we shared sources, found all this, but he also discovered that Kinsey had carried out some rather odd sexual experiments on himself, usually involving an extreme association of pleasure and pain. Jones's book, rushed out eighteen months in advance in a panic to forestall mine, really killed the American market upon which Christopher had predicated his advance. Nevertheless, I was relieved. My book was, I think, better than his. More accurate about Kinsey, far better on his sex research, shorter, better written. But Jones's discoveries were more detailed and extensive than mine and I would have looked foolish had I come out first. I'm afraid Christopher, or rather Chatto who'd taken on the book after a publisher's *putsch*, lost quite a lot of money.

The Kinsey book was widely, lengthily and on the whole very well reviewed. But I noticed an odd thing about the reviewers. Even nearly fifty years after his death (he died in 1956) Kinsey is still a symbolic figure for the liberal sexual attitudes he preached – and which I shared. Reviewers' reactions, therefore, to my book depended less than usual on its merits than on their attitude to sexual behaviour.

I ended *Kinsey* as usual overdrawn but, finishing the novel I'd started before, it was bought by Hutchinson for enough for us to carry on for a while. I wanted to call it *Vanishing Point* but was told that, since there had been a film of that name, I shouldn't. I still don't see what difference that makes. In desperation I turned to the genius of Julian Evans. He liked the novel and said, 'You must call it *Particle Theory.*' So I did, much against my editor Paul Sidey's wishes. The title is relevant but it doesn't get to the nub of the matter. The novel is really about loss. After twice finding it in bookshops under 'science', I realise Paul was right. You can't win on titles.

As I write about these books – about nannies, public schools, marriage, doctors, about Gerald and Kinsey, about my novels and short stories and children's books and Sylvia Thornton's romance – I feel, as you no doubt feel too, in a position I have often been in and quite often observed: someone is listening with an air of slight surprise to a writer talking about their books, books which clearly loom very large indeed for them but which as far as that someone is concerned loom nowhere and in fact they didn't even know the writer wrote books in the first place.

But I can't just ignore what has been the focus of my life since I was twenty-six, or fourteen, or nine – or even, if at a distant remove, three. At the same time, I'm not really sure what I think of myself 'as a writer' at all.

(16)

I certainly don't feel a failure. Of the novels, *The Office* might have cost me my life if I'd written it after Crete; *Particle Theory* didn't, *I* think, only because I muffed the end. I like all the children's books and nearly all the short stories and novellas; of the non-fiction books, the nanny book had an original idea not fully understood before; Gerald was a good biography. In fact, I think all the non-fiction books are competent and some perhaps more than that. I am proud of my books.

Nevertheless, I can't say that so far I've exactly been a roaring success – though of course there is always the Next Book. I am quite glad I didn't know what would happen when I started out.

I think the best I can say is that I've had a go. This is not to say nothing; indeed it is to say a good deal. Given my extreme nervousness about money, it took some courage to abandon my part-time job and rely entirely on writing books. In fact this fear goes far to eclipse disappointment at any lack of sales. I am so relieved to have been kept solvent for a year or two more by each successive advance that when the book doesn't sell as well as everyone hoped I really don't care that much. It has been a considerable achievement to have kept going for so long on books alone. Most writers have other sources – not nowadays so often private incomes, but journalism, reviewing, academia, husbands or wives who earn money for them, etc. In Sweden, only eight writers are able to support themselves solely on their books.

Then – Mr Pringle was right – it took considerable stamina, not just to write the books (all books take stamina) but, while writing, to see my children often enough, for a long time support two families psychologically as well as financially, and at one point, for two years, do all this and carry out a kidnapping. I marvel at my youthful and not so youthful energy.

I have had to write non-fiction and not the novels and stories it was my ambition to write. But I have turned down many more non-fiction commissions than I have accepted because I didn't like the subjects, and so probably turned down far more money than I've made. I used to think that if primogeniture had been abolished, as it should have been and should be, and my father had received his fair share and passed my share to me, I would have written those novels. Now I'm not so sure. For one thing, my father had a way of *not* having money and I suspect his share might have vanished. For another, I haven't done badly at all, thanks to the bugger uncles and generous friends. If I had been Joyce or D. H. Lawrence, I would have sold my house, sponged even more than I have on my rich friends, and written novels. Once the central creative germ is there, the first idea, I find invention quite easy. But I have such central ideas rather rarely. Then though, as I said, I am not clever enough to be an academic, I do have a fairly intellectual mind. I enjoy ideas if they are not too difficult. I like simple narrative history and so on. It is true my (relative) poverty has forced me to write books which have employed that side of me – but I might well have used it anyway in similar books.

Our culture automatically places prose works in a hierarchy where the novel is above everything else; more significant, more profound, more worthy of praise, more difficult to write. We do this because the Greeks believed that poets were inspired by the gods – and this divine afflatus has unnoticed passed to the novel. Certainly this is the reason why, when I first realised I wanted to write, it was as a writer of novels. Yet are we right? Not about the difficulty of writing, at any rate. The *process of construction* of any writer's work is, in my experience, identical whether it is a novel, a history, a biography or an autobiography. With all of them you collect and construct from the outside world and from your imagination. To imagine is to collect and construct, to *reconstruct*, from your memory. Then the ordering, the relating of one thing to another, is just the same. At night, books you are writing buzz in your head. Ideas and images for them arrive at any moment, day or night – the gods help biographers as often as novelists. (And books in this way are companions. Writers write partly so as not to have to think about themselves, be in their own company with all their mundane problems all the time – even if the books they are writing are *about* themselves.) But a novel is not exactly more 'difficult' to write; it is just much easier to lose it, to get it wrong.

At the same time, to follow this parabola and to an extent contradict what I've just written, those ideas and images that arrive spontaneously, and which are often the most fruitful, the way in which, while writing, the words engender themselves almost under their own volition, all this does give one a strange feeling. One could speculate about this. I think all artists, whether painters, writers, musicians or sculptors, probably often have a feeling that *someone else* is doing what they are apparently doing themselves, a feeling of *being apart* from themselves – what Beckett called 'existence by proxy'. Graham Greene regarded it as necessary, providing the 'sliver of ice' all novelists required, a separation that was necessary to create, to deal objectively both with oneself and outside reality. I would go further, remembering the attacks of 'loudness' that afflicted me at Snape as a child, those feelings that I didn't exist which gave rise to *Chameleon*, I would say that those who have such feelings and similar ones, of separateness, are driven by them to create not in order to escape themselves, as I said above, but to make themselves feel real. Perhaps this was the psychological root of Plato's cave. Like all artists, he extended his private feelings to the whole world. Because he didn't feel that he and therefore the world about him were real, there must be a 'realer real' to be found beyond it. Artists find this 'realer real', create it, in their fictions, their paintings and their music.

The Greeks explained all this by their gods. We would say the unconscious. But that brings us once again to memory, since everything in the unconscious mind comes ultimately from our memory. One could say memory and the imagination are the same.

(17)

A writer cannot, therefore, know too much about memory. And clearly this is particularly true of autobiographers since it is our subject, or at least its fruits are.

I tried to explore what you could call the physical basis of autobiography. This took a long time and was often very interesting. I found that a great deal is known about what happens where in the brain. A certain limited amount is known about what takes place chemically and electrically. There is considerable evidence that we in fact remember everything that has ever happened to us. And here I learnt facts that had a peculiar resonance for me. For instance, a neurologist in the 1930s, Wilder Penfield, was poking the exposed brains of epileptic patients with a tiny electrical probe. To his astonishment, distant memories sprang up. One patient, stimulated like this, hummed an entire orchestral score which he had heard once in a concert thirty years before. In Tangier with Anna, kif had been my probe.

But I eventually decided science could not illuminate memory in the way I needed.

Neuroscience does not know where memory resides. It hasn't the faintest idea how memories are recalled, that is, it doesn't understand the act of remembering itself. But there is a fundamental reason why science cannot explain memory for autobiographers or anyone else – and as far as I can see never will. How are all the physiological changes we know or guess at transformed into living, remembered experience? Into my remembering the wind in the wood round Snape, in the pine trees my grandmother and I had worked in, or the walk in the dark, feeling my way up the creaking staircase to Nell's little attic bedroom? The translation from the language of science into the language and feeling of memory is as impossible to make now as it was in the seventeenth century when Descartes proposed his split between mind and matter to explain it. (Many scientists say there is no split, no problem. Consciousness is simply a high-level result of brain activity. We *know* this is so because we *know* there is no other source of what goes on except the brain. But this is really just to give description the validity of explanation.)

The reason science will never succeed in this area is because it is speaking a different language. An analogy is how you cannot convey, to someone born deaf, cannot bring alive, the experience of music, the actuality, with words. Nevertheless, perhaps *writers* can help with memory, since it has been one of their most important tools and most interesting subject.

(18)

The great book whose subject is time and memory – in my view the greatest novel of the last century – is Proust's *À la recherche du temps perdu*. Proust, too, thought that the whole of our past was held in our heads, but he also implies that it cannot, as it were, be dragged consciously out on the end of a fishing line, as I am doing here, or if this *is* done the result is lifeless. It can be truly recaptured only by the actions of involuntary memory. That is, unexpected chance events, attached to the past by association, bring it springing back, recaptured; not only brilliant and fresh but now, if you are a writer, made available for literature.

In Proust there are four main moments when this happens. The first, with which the book starts, is the taste of the madeleine, the little cake, dipped in tea, which brings back Combray. The last three occur towards the end of the book, when three events, three sensations, make the narrator realise what is happening: 'Two uneven paving stones in the Guermantes' courtyard bring back a flood of memories of two similar stones in St Mark's Church in Venice' – I am quoting from and for the moment following Edmund White's marvellous little study – 'Later, the sound of the noise of a hammer on the metal wheel of a train, heard years earlier when his train has stopped in the woods. Finally, a stiff napkin makes the narrator recall the starchy towel he'd dried off with when was a boy, during his first visit to Balbec.'

The significance of these three moments is, first, they awaken the realisation in the narrator that the past is not dead; therefore, second, that he can write the book that will recapture it and, third, they revive in him the energy to do it.

But – all this happens when in fact *he has already written the book*. We are at the end, already standing so to speak in the great cathedral upon whose construction he tells us he is about to begin. Did these moments really happen to Proust? I don't mean, did he have moments of involuntary memory, but was it these moments, or ones like them, which inspired Proust, which meant that he really found that the past was still locked entire inside him and found the way to recall it – or are they literary devices which let him hold the structure of the book together, to deepen it in time, and let him demonstrate the permanence of memories which are often in his case not memories at all but inventions, or a mixture of both, a device, that is, which can make inventions seem like memory, make them 'real'? A device which also made possible that wonderful and exhilarating moment which allowed him to say that he was about to begin the book which he had in fact finished.

From the first, Proust's book was taken to be autobiography as Paris society crossly identified itself. So fascinating is the resulting detective work that all subsequent commentators have done the same. It has almost been forgotten that the book is also, and far more, a novel.

If we take the discovery and importance of involuntary memory seriously it is odd that there are only four of these moments to drive this enormous book. (This according to Edmund White, but I think there are more, though still few in a novel of over three thousand pages.) In *Jean Santeuil*, a book almost as long and concerned with a good deal of the same material, there are certainly references to *memory* leading us to the truth, but there are none of these apparently essential involuntary moments. And it is surprising that there is no record in Proust's life, in his letters or in the recollections of his friends, of the importance to him of involuntary memory. Jean-Yves Tadié, in his brilliant but maddening masterpiece, marred by the venomous spleen with which he attacks George Painter, and which Tadié devoted to discovering every last item, place, event, moment, in Proust's life which had any bearing on the novel, apparently found nothing that referred to involuntary memory, nor is there any mention of it in Céleste Albaret's fascinating, and fascinatingly detailed, memoir of her life with him.

Nor do I in fact totally agree with Proust.* To me, memories drawn out on the fishing line of autobiography, which gush up that artesian well of autobiography I've mentioned, are just as alive as those of involuntary memory. Certainly I, like him, like all of us,

---

* If it is Proust. It is certainly Edmund White's Proust, but I do not remember this from *À la recherche . . . .*, and to check, I would have to read it all again. Proust is the one literary passion I will one day revisit, but to do so while trying to write something of my own would be fatal.

have experienced those moments. Unmoved at the time, suddenly finding in the pine woods of France that I was crying about my grandmother who had died six months before. Or I peel a tangerine and suddenly see the little downstairs room at Snape, it is Christmas and Sammy and I are opening our stockings, it is cold, we throw streamers across the room, excitement has woken us at four o'clock and it is still dark outside. At the bottom of each stocking there is a tangerine. But far more often, in fact nearly always, the association is inchoate, nebulous, whatever has been woken stirs, brushes the underside of your consciousness, you have a curious feeling – nostalgia, melancholy, something in your past – *you are brushed with a feeling of the past*. Proust's very precision, to me, is literary.

But I may be wrong. Perhaps I missed something in Tadié's vast tome. Perhaps it was not, as I think, a subtle and powerful literary device, but Proust really did allow those few moments, in real life not just in his book, the importance his commentators have given them. Perhaps, indeed, he actually had numerous moments like that and it was they, not just common-or-garden memory, which I'd suppose, that led him to his book. In the end, the only person one can know and must explore is oneself.

(19)

Dr Gordon Ambrose's consulting room address was 115a Harley Street; actually it was some way down Devonshire Street. He charged me £8 an hour. Not nothing, but also nothing near what he usually charged.

He was, I found out years later, older than I thought in 1974 – about sixty then, with the face of a successful second-hand car salesman, kind, intelligent, and he endeared himself to me very early on when he said, 'But I *like* your accent.' He was extremely well qualified, being not just a psychotherapist, a psychoanalyst, a psychiatrist and, of course, an ordinary doctor. He was interested in hypnosis and had written a number of books on the subject. But the great thing about him was that we could work together.

How can you describe the process of being analysed or undergoing therapy or whatever it was I went through? It is different for everyone and quite a lot of people have described it. I don't want to repeat what has been done. There are seldom revelations. You do most of the work, though Gordon Ambrose didn't believe in total silence and would occasionally make suggestions if it seemed obvious. 'You can sit for *weeks* getting nowhere if you don't.' It is a process. Very gradually, you change. But because it takes time you often forget the details of the process.

We sat opposite each other for about an hour, at first twice a week, quite soon once a week. At the end of the session, I'd write out a cheque.

You soon begin to notice that though it can be brilliant, ingenious, cunning, and very clever, the unconscious can also be corny. For instance, I had always had what I called to myself key memories, some of which I described at the beginning of this book. By 'key' I meant important. It never occurred to me that a key was also something that could unlock. I was describing one of these, my hearing Sammy cry as our mother taught him to read at Kelburn at the beginning of the war. I thought Ambrose was asleep (they all take far too many clients/patients — out of kindness, really, though I suppose money comes into it). Suddenly he said, 'But didn't you say Sammy was born in August 1936? He would have been three then. Was your mother really trying to teach him to read at the age of three in a way that made him cry?' I felt gooseflesh running down my neck and back. Of *course*, it must have been me.

This was typical. He had an extraordinary intuitive quickness. Leaning back apparently asleep (in fact, rare), he could always detect when I was evading something. The key memories I knew by heart, but usually we worked with dreams. Each week I'd bring a dream and I'd slowly go through it. Ambrose was psychoanalytically eclectic. Freud (who suited me), Jung, Ambrose himself, would all appear; he was also keen on Stekel, who broke from Freud, I think on the same grounds as Adler – the importance of dominance and aggression.

Sammy's age, like so much else in these sessions obvious when I realised it, altered another key memory. I saw now that it must have been me burning behind the fireguard in Milner Street. Sammy was only one or two then. I was sure that Bella Wildgoose wouldn't put a little boy of one next to a gas fire. Nannies could be fiends, but

Sammy was famously 'good' as a little child. He was then at the height of his goodness. I, at four or five, was notoriously naughty. I was being punished.

I don't know about the symbolism of dreams in general, but in the context of therapy and in the particular they work. The point is, if serious in this process, there are a number of things you need to discover, you *want* to discover; at the same time, you don't want to discover them. You want to conceal them because they are painful or embarrassing or shaming or threaten you or violate some taboo. Your unconscious swiftly learns how to help you, but lets you do it slowly, obliquely. You advance on the truth *sheltering* behind your dream. I would say, 'All right Gordon, *you* would say that that means, symbolises, masturbation. I am quite sure it doesn't. I know what it means. But let us assume for the moment it *does* mean masturbation and see where we go.' So we'd creep forward. I wanted our approach to be clinical, intellectual, impersonal. When I talked to him I called him Gordon, but I thought of him as Ambrose.

Unfortunately (he would say fortunately) it was quite often impossible to avoid feelings. I remember longing to get to one session because I had happy news. (You want to please your therapist. You want him to smile.) I had fallen in love and gone to Paris for five days and it had been wonderful (and lasted about that five days). Ten minutes into my journey to Harley Street, I realised I'd forgotten my dream book. I rushed back, only to find I'd locked the keys inside the squalid Stockwell basement flat. Thinking 'This is ridiculously corny, even for the unconscious', I had to go round and break the back door window to get at the bolt. I arrived at Ambrose's thirty minutes late. 'I suppose you'll see this as classic evidence of evasion,' I said. 'Actually, I've good news.' But I was hardly into my dream when I felt myself sweating. To my horror, it was clear the dream was leading me to explore homosexuality.

This took about four sessions, all difficult. I cannot remember the process. But from then on my anxieties about being homosexual, my guilt about not being homosexual, my feeling I *should* be homosexual, all faded away. I cannot even recall what those anxieties felt like, though I know they existed because I remember the incidents associated with them. I remember locking my parents and Biddy in the larder at Lydford; I remember Hussein's over-long, over-active propelling pencil – but all feeling has gone; just so, you know you were in love with some woman (or man) – for Chrissake you *lived* with them for three years didn't you? – but now all memory of emotion, of lust, of love has vanished, you feel nothing, it seems inconceivable. So it is with my complex muddle of fears and anxieties about homosexuality. Such was the skill of Ambrose.

Things didn't always resolve themselves in this way. I was describing my never-ending and inexplicable temperature at Snape aged six and being put in the little wooden hut and how I escaped and ran wildly round the garden and had a fight with the evacuee (all key memories) when Ambrose said, 'I sense a highly active, perhaps over-active little boy.' This was true. I knew people – my family that is – were eventually exhausted and irritated by my incessant chatter, my energy. I must have minded this. If it were an illness making me like that it wasn't my fault. I therefore gave myself a temperature. I drive, as I've said, far too fast and, though not dangerous, do sometimes frighten timid passengers. The odd thing was that, while we were discussing my over-activity, the frustration of the hut, trying to rein myself in, the temperature – I suddenly found I was driving like a normal, sedate, law-abiding person. For two or three months I drove peacefully; then it was back to racing.

Some things never went. It is still Sammy crying in the bedroom at Kelburn; still Sammy writhing and burning and crying behind the fireguard in front of the gas fire in Milner Street.

But a peculiarity of psychotherapy is that, once you have uncovered it, you realise you have always known what it was you were concealing – or ignoring. Arthur Miller's desire in writing *The Death of a Salesman* was 'not for the audience to ask "What happens next and why?" so much as "Oh God, of course".'

Some things I had worked out and have described – but reworked with Ambrose. People usually laugh when I describe how I once blurted out I was the general's niece. Ambrose didn't laugh; he just looked more intent. That whole curious strand which terrified my mother and which expressed itself when, as a little boy, I said I'd wear my women's underclothes *underneath* my policeman's uniform or would only dress as a nurse or tottered about on Philip's heels at Shiplake, or when Chamil's last transformation in *Chameleon* was to become a woman (a nurse, I suddenly realise as I write) and, yes, when for an instant I was a general's niece – all this was, as I said earlier, a recognition of a feminine side in what was still a male-orientated world and an identification with, and preference for, the women – nanny, mother, grandmother – who had brought me up. Yet it went only so far. I identified with them; I didn't want to become them. I have never had fantasies of dressing as or being a woman.

But the most significant thing I discovered was something so obvious that it is extraordinary – but typical of the subconscious – that I hadn't realised it before. (And yet I must have done – nearly.) I had, when I saw Ambrose, just written the book about nannies. In it, I had concluded that as a system of upbringing it had ultimately to be condemned for a single but fundamental reason. The entire premise of a nanny's life was that when her charges were four/five/six, she would leave and get another post. It was a system of child-upbringing, that is, which at a crucial point and, as far as the child was concerned, with great brutality, removed the central figure in the child's life. Yet I had never even considered the effect on me of that distant, dim, bespectacled little figure leaving me when I was four. And about whom I remembered nothing and, even discussing with Ambrose, about whose loss I felt nothing (though as I write now I feel a wave of desolation).

But there are other methods of detection. Particle accelerators in Switzerland (CERN) and in Illinois (the Fermi Laboratory) accelerate particles together, two streams in opposite directions, so that they collide at nearly twice the speed of light. Their shattering leaves spectral tracks, and it is from the nature of the tracks that they deduce the nature of these particles. They shatter in a particular *way*.

I shattered in a particular way. I had long ago decided, as I described, that the pattern of leaving or being left (not much difference) had been set up by my father leaving me. And this pattern had been *shaped* by the affair with Eliza. 'The first love affair determines all that follow.' What I hadn't realised until Ambrose was that, *of course*, my first love affair had been with my nurse. *That* was the first great separation, the first great sadness which, sometimes muted, for long stretches silent, but always there, had gone on echoing and echoing and echoing down my life. All subsequent separations – my father's, boarding schools, Eliza, Sabrina, Anna – had carried and increased a force which derived from that primal one. This explained why one aspect of my beloved Snape, from which my nanny had vanished, had seemed so sinister and given rise to what I described as attacks of 'loudness'; it explained my bad behaviour after the age of four, it explained why it was *women* with whom I couldn't stay or chose so they wouldn't stay with me. (Anna subsequently left another husband and several lovers.) And when a closely loved figure dies or leaves someone very small the world itself becomes insecure; their own self, being partly modelled on that figure, becomes insecure. I think that odd feeling that I didn't exist, the novel *Chameleon*, both have their roots here.

I explained some of these effects earlier by an analogy with shell-shock. This was not far off the mark. Ambrose would have said that terrible events when small leave intense anxiety, intense fear, that they will happen again. The only way the fear can be allayed is by in fact doing that – making them happen again. *Fear* of something is worse than the thing itself. You meet it, overcome it, for a while the (unconscious) fear goes – then it returns and with it the pattern repeats itself. What is more, the fear and the pattern it induces become familiar, we become used to it, it is, therefore, almost comforting. The galled ox misses the yoke. This, too, the cruellest thing of all, locks us still more firmly into our painful and destructive behaviour.

Yet this view of myself – what you could call the psychoanalytic view, and in which I believe – isn't the only way of looking at such things. There is a last loop in this returning parabola.

(20)

Repetition is one of the great themes in human mythology – the cycle of the seasons, the rebirth of the god, the return of the hero. I realised after Ambrose, that that was why Pirandello's *Six Characters in Search of an Author* had haunted me and haunted me in the way it did. This is the hidden resonance of the play.

The whole point of the play is that the six characters want to *re-enact* their drama. They want an author to write, a director to direct and actors to play – or better still, play themselves – the whole thing over again. They want to *repeat* it.

That is why in my memory I had the actors hovering about at the edges of a cluttered, darkened stage – about to begin, about to repeat their pattern. Indeed, you could say this is the essence of all art – experience, transformed and locked up, in words or paint or music, in novels or symphonies or paintings, and waiting to be re-experienced by others and so live again.

When Gerald was ninety-three, Nicky and I used to visit him in Spain, in Alhaurín el Grande where he now lived alone surrounded by nurses. He told me he used to have not just the same dream but the same passage of that dream again and again. His mind had become locked. The last time I saw him, not long before he died, lying in his bed, all he could say was, 'Thank you thank you thank you thank you . . . ' until I left the room. The last of all our repetitions is death.

There are further depths, or at least perspectives. What is odd about memories is not that they are often changed or falsified – this you would expect. To be forcibly trapped near a gas fire aged four or five must have been extremely unpleasant, even in memory. I therefore changed it. What is odd is that certain memories refuse to be changed. In some extraordinary way, retained in the synapses or the DNA or however they *are* retained, these memories struggle to be revived and cause distress if they are not revived. They seem to be crucial – or the mind thinks they are crucial. Evolutionary biology explains memory as being potentially essential for survival and so potentially essential to pass on to offspring. That is, these early patterns of behaviour are repeated in order that they can be imitated and learnt by our children.

I spent formative years in other people's houses. My mother's bedroom, her, me and Sammy, became our home. I discovered during my four years with Ambrose that part of me felt that this was what a family *should* be – a tight little unit existing separate from, defensive to, another family unit in which it hid. With Anna (whom it infuriated) and Sarah I tried to repeat this – taking Jenny and Ben away at weekends. I can still sometimes feel this operating in me even now with Nicky and her children.

The other day, Ben described what a good father I had been. I was slightly appalled, from the way he put it, to see that for Ben a good father had first of all to leave the mother, his wife, live separately, and then make frantic efforts to sustain and see and be with his children – as Ben himself was now doing.

It is another example of how a primitive evolutionary mechanism, in primitive terms useful, can when operating in the mind, in the conscious and unconscious, of much more complicated animals, be very destructive. A million years ago it didn't matter if a bad pattern was repeated. It would eventually breed itself out. But we don't die of these things. We just repeat our pattern – and our children divorce or beat their children or otherwise wage war on themselves and society.

These are rather complex speculations, not sufficiently worked out in too little space. Really, all I want to indicate, as the parabola does finally return, is that deep, powerful and not fully understood forces are at work. They explain why so much literature and myth is concerned with uncovering the truth; at its simplest in the detective story; at its most profound in great works of art, in *Peer Gynt* or *Long Day's Journey into Night* or *Death of a Salesman* or Sophocles' *Oedipus Rex*. They are the same forces, ultimately, which are behind autobiography.

(21)

The glass globe of my life I wanted to break and let spread on its own, now covers the world of this book. I have managed to use my journal only some twenty or so times and talk to Sammy and Rose about three times. But in two instances the research I had resolved not to do was thrust on me by chance.

My mother had had an elder brother, Philip Thorowgood. He had died young and for some reason was hardly mentioned. Then, while talking to Sammy, he suddenly remembered our mother telling him that Philip had committed suicide. My mother had said, apropos what they were talking about, 'But you see there is instability in our family.' I was both extremely surprised and, with a twinge of sibling jealousy, wondered why she had never told me. If she had, surely I would have remembered. I had never known my unfortunate uncle, but I can imagine my reaction – I would have seen such instability as an ingredient of genius. If it were true. I searched and could find nothing, but Sammy was extremely clear. Perhaps she had told me and I had, after all, forgotten. I seemed to remember, as he spoke, talk of Uncle Philip suffering from depression. I saw now that my mother's depression may not have been caused solely by barbiturates and drink as I'd thought but only been exacerbated by them. Perhaps my attacks of 'loudness' and *Chameleon* had a similar root.

Then, just after the first draft of this book, there came another altering of perspectives. For some reason, Rose suddenly decided to open a bundle of our mother's letters Gathorne had given her twenty years before. He had found them in some of our furniture still stored at Glemham and had decided not to burn these last survivors of the holocaust. There were six telegrams and forty letters, some of them ten or fifteen pages long, written between 1 September and 1 December 1930. My father was in Edinburgh becoming a doctor and my mother usually in London or Snape.

The letters were love letters, but one in particular interested me. My father has said in his last letter that he is worried he is homosexual. It is obviously something they have talked about. This is my mother's response:

' . . . I would so love it if I could be any woman or any man or anything you wanted or loved I do love all of you, you know, the perverted part and the fussing part and all the parts I don't understand . . . it's all of you I love, Antony, not just the parts that kiss me and talk to me . . . If I found out my old man was a homo? Well it might be rather bad luck on you wouldn't it having a woman tied to you, but I should think you are slightly aren't you? I mean I wouldn't be surprised but I think you would be happier if you knew definitely which way Willie preferred! . . . '

I pursued this. When I told Anne she said she remembered something that happened when she was eleven. My father, aged fifteen, was back from Eton and they were playing, as they often did, in a small clump of trees with a sandpit in the middle just outside the house. My father said, 'There's something I want to tell you but I can't because you're too young.' Anne begged and pleaded. 'Please Antony, *please*.' 'I can't. You're too young.' But he clearly longed to tell someone. He said, 'All I can say is that something happened at school which shouldn't have happened to me until I was much older.'

I talked to Fidelity. She said there was a strong component of homosexuality in Jock. He told her that this was the main reason he never drank – more convincing than the mysterious 'clot' we'd been told as children. 'He would,' said my aunt, 'allude cryptically and gruffly to "an incident" on board ship when he was sailing out east in 1930.'

This explained a good deal. It explained my father's determination that neither Sammy nor I should go to Eton. It may have partly explained why Eddie, with his outrageously flagrant homosexuality, so maddened Jock. Above all, it explained my mother's intense anxiety that I might be homosexual myself.

Jock and my father were bisexual. I doubt Jock did anything much about it – except that time sailing out to Ceylon and India in 1930. I'm not so sure about my father. I think he probably fell in love with his batman on his last aircraft carrier during the war. He wanted to bring him back and employ him. His reply, when Fidelity asked him what on earth he thought the batman could do, reveals both how totally out of touch he was with our circumstances and also the privilege of his early background. We were about to move into the Arch, tiny, cramped, primitive, and he and my mother were about to embark on the long process of selling their possessions to survive. My father said, 'He can look after my clothes.'

On his return he also looked up Bridget D'Oyly Carte, Jock's first wife, and went to bed with her. Perhaps he felt the need to revive his much more dominant heterosexual side after the years at sea; or perhaps he'd fancied her ever since he knelt outside her and Jock's bedroom and heard them making love.

My mother's letters moved me. She was no longer my mother, but a twenty-one-year-old woman passionately in love with a young man, neither of whom I'd known. He was twenty-three, and from her response to his letters, from the way he was confiding his most vulnerable anxieties, from his eagerness for her, was clearly passionately in love too. It was sad to think how in the end it went wrong.

They both died young – my mother sixty-four, my father sixty-nine. Genes are the dictator here and I don't expect to live a long time. I am aware that Pallas Athene and Artemis now seriously